The Myth of Religious Violence

The Myth of
Religious Violence

Secular Ideology and the Roots
of Modern Conflict

WILLIAM T. CAVANAUGH

OXFORD
UNIVERSITY PRESS

2009

OXFORD
UNIVERSITY PRESS

Oxford University Press, Inc., publishes works that further
Oxford University's objective of excellence
in research, scholarship, and education.

Oxford   New York
Auckland   Cape Town   Dar es Salaam   Hong Kong   Karachi
Kuala Lumpur   Madrid   Melbourne   Mexico City   Nairobi
New Delhi   Shanghai   Taipei   Toronto

With offices in
Argentina   Austria   Brazil   Chile   Czech Republic   France   Greece
Guatemala   Hungary   Italy   Japan   Poland   Portugal   Singapore
South Korea   Switzerland   Thailand   Turkey   Ukraine   Vietnam

Published by Oxford University Press, Inc.
198 Madison Avenue, New York, New York 10016
www.oup.com

Oxford is a registered trademark of Oxford University Press

Library of Congress Cataloging-in-Publication Data

Cavanaugh, William T.
The myth of religious violence: secular ideology and the roots of modern
conflict / William T. Cavanaugh.
    p. cm.
Includes bibliographical references and index.
ISBN 978-0-19-538504-5
1. Violence—Religious aspects. 2. Religion and politics—Western countries.
3. Religion—Philosophy—Political aspects—Western countries. I. Title.
BL65.V55C39 2009
201'.76332—dc22   2008053815

11 10 9

Printed in the United States of America
on acid-free paper

For Eamon

Acknowledgments

I began this book as a visiting fellow at the Kellogg Institute for International Studies at the University of Notre Dame. Special thanks to Scott Mainwaring, Chris Welna, and Tim Scully for their kind hospitality while I was in residence there.

Several colleagues and friends have read parts of the manuscript at various stages of completion and provided astute comments or made useful bibliographic suggestions. Thanks to Tom Berg, Mike Budde, David Cunningham, Tim Fitzgerald, Fred Gedicks, Brad Gregory, Stanley Hauerwas, Mike Hollerich, Russell McCutcheon, Tom Rochon, John Roth, and Scott Thomas for their generous help.

I presented parts of the argument of this book in lectures to various audiences at universities far and wide, and I have benefited enormously from their comments and critiques. Thanks are due to Michael Bartley at Oklahoma State, Michael Minch at Utah Valley University, James Sweeney at Cambridge, Michael Budde at DePaul, Peter Casarella at Catholic University, Fred Lawrence at Boston College, Ben King at Harvard, Mark O'Connor of the Dom Helder Camara lecture series in Australia, Jonas Ideström of the Church of Sweden, Arne Rasmussen at Umeå University, Chris Keller at the Film, Faith, and Justice Forum in Seattle, and Linell Cady and Matt Correa at Arizona State for inviting me to speak. I would also like to express gratitude to the many other people at these venues who gave me gracious hospitality and facilitated my visits in other ways.

Thanks to Ry Parrish-Siggelkow at St. Thomas, who provided crucial help in editing the manuscript in its final phase.

Finally, thanks to my wife, Tracy Rowan, and our sons for giving me a happy place to come home to when I got tired of religion and violence. This book is dedicated to my son Eamon, my little tiger.

Contents

The Myth of Religious Violence

Introduction

The idea that religion has a tendency to promote violence is part of the conventional wisdom of Western societies, and it underlies many of our institutions and policies, from limits on the public role of churches to efforts to promote liberal democracy in the Middle East. What I call the "myth of religious violence" is the idea that religion is a transhistorical and transcultural feature of human life, essentially distinct from "secular" features such as politics and economics, which has a peculiarly dangerous inclination to promote violence. Religion must therefore be tamed by restricting its access to public power. The secular nation-state then appears as natural, corresponding to a universal and timeless truth about the inherent dangers of religion.

In this book, I challenge this piece of conventional wisdom, not simply by arguing that ideologies and institutions labeled "secular" can be just as violent as those labeled "religious," but by examining how the twin categories of religious and secular are constructed in the first place. A growing body of scholarly work explores how the category "religion" has been invented in the modern West and in colonial contexts according to specific configurations of political power. In this book, I draw on this scholarship to examine how time-less and transcultural categories of religion and the secular are used in arguments that religion causes violence. I argue that there is no transhistorical and transcultural essence of religion and that essen-tialist attempts to separate religious violence from secular violence are incoherent. What counts as religious or secular in any given context is a function of different configurations of power. The question then becomes why such essentialist constructions are so common. I argue that, in what are called "Western" societies, the attempt to create a transhistorical and transcultural concept of religion that is essentially prone to violence is one of the foundational legitimating myths of the liberal nation-state. The myth of religious violence helps to construct and marginalize a religious Other, prone to fanaticism, to contrast with the rational, peace-making, secular subject. This myth can be and is used in domestic politics to legitimate the marginalization of certain types of practices and groups labeled religious, while underwriting the nation-state's monopoly on its citizens' willingness to sacrifice and kill. In foreign policy, the myth of religious violence serves to cast nonsecular social orders, especially Muslim societies, in the role of villain. *They* have not yet learned to remove the dangerous influence of religion from political life. *Their* violence is therefore irrational and fanatical. *Our* violence, being secular, is rational, peace making, and sometimes regrettably necessary to contain *their* violence. We find ourselves obliged to bomb them into liberal democracy.

Especially since September 11, 2001, there has been a proliferation of scholarly books by historians, sociologists, political scientists, religious studies professors, and others exploring the peculiarly violence-prone nature of religion. At the same time, there is a significant group of scholars who have been exploring the ideological uses of the construction of the term "religion" in Western modernity. On the one hand, we have a group of scholars who are convinced that religion as such has an inherent tendency to promote violence. On the other hand, we have a group of scholars who question whether there is any "religion as such," except as a constructed ideological category whose changing history must be carefully scrutinized.

There is much more at stake here than academics haggling over definitions. Once we begin to ask what the religion-and-violence arguments mean by "religion," we find that their explanatory power is hobbled by a number of indefensible assumptions about what does and does not count as religion. Certain types of practices and institutions are condemned, while others— nationalism, for example—are ignored. Why? My hypothesis is that religion-and-violence arguments serve a particular need for their consumers in the West. These arguments are part of a broader Enlightenment narrative that has invented a dichotomy between the religious and the secular and constructed the former as an irrational and dangerous impulse that must give way in public to rational, secular forms of power. In the West, revulsion toward killing and dying in the name of one's religion is one of the principal means by which we become convinced that killing and dying in the name of the nation-state is laudable and proper. The myth of religious violence also provides secular social orders with a stock character, the religious fanatic, to serve as enemy. Carl Schmitt may be right—descriptively, not normatively—to point out that the friend-enemy distinction is essential to the creation of the political in the modern state.[1] Schmitt worried that a merely procedural liberalism would deprive the political of the friend-enemy antagonism, which would break out instead in religious, cultural, and economic arenas. Contemporary liberalism has found its definitive enemy in the Muslim who refuses to distinguish between religion and politics. The danger is that, in establishing an Other who is essentially irrational, fanatical, and violent, we legitimate coercive measures against that Other.

I have no doubt that ideologies and practices of all kinds—including, for example, Islam and Christianity—can and do promote violence under certain conditions. What I challenge as incoherent is the argument that there is something called religion—a genus of which Christianity, Islam, Hinduism, and so on are species—which is necessarily more inclined toward violence than are ideologies and institutions that are identified as secular. Unlike other books on religion and violence, I do not argue that religion either does or does not promote violence, but rather I analyze the political conditions under which the very category of religion is constructed.

This book, then, is not a defense of religion against the charge of violence.[2] People who identify themselves as religious sometimes argue that the real motivation behind so-called religious violence is in fact economic and political, not religious. Others argue that people who do violence are, by definition, not religious. The Crusader is not really a Christian, for example, because he does not really understand the meaning of Christianity. I do not think that either of these arguments works. In the first place, it is impossible to separate religious from economic and political motives in such a way that religious motives are innocent of violence. How could one, for example, separate religion from politics in Islam, when most Muslims themselves make no such separation? In my second chapter, I show that the very separation of religion from politics is an invention of the modern West. In the second place, it may be the case that the Crusader has misappropriated the true message of Christ, but one cannot therefore excuse Christianity of all responsibility. Christianity is not simply a set of doctrines immune to historical circumstance, but a lived historical experience embodied and shaped by the empirically observable actions of Christians. I have no intention of excusing Christianity or Islam or any other set of ideas and practices from careful analysis. Given certain conditions, Christianity and Islam can and do contribute to violence. War in the Middle East, for example, can be justified not merely on behalf of oil and freedom, but on the basis of a millenarian reading of parts of the Christian scriptures. Christian churches are indeed complicit in legitimating wars carried out by national armies.

But what is implied in the conventional wisdom is that there is an essential difference between religions such as Christianity, Islam, Hinduism, and Judaism, on the one hand, and secular ideologies and institutions such as nationalism, Marxism, capitalism, and liberalism, on the other, and that the former are essentially more prone to violence—more absolutist, divisive, and irrational—than the latter. It is this claim that I find both unsustainable and dangerous. It is unsustainable because ideologies and institutions labeled secular can be just as absolutist, divisive, and irrational as those labeled religious. It is dangerous because it helps to marginalize, and even legitimate violence against, those forms of life that are labeled religious. What gets labeled religious and what does not is therefore of crucial importance. The myth of religious violence tries to establish as timeless, universal, and natural a very contingent set of categories—religious and secular—that are in fact constructions of the modern West. Those who do not accept these categories as timeless, universal, and natural are subject to coercion.

I use the term "myth" to describe this claim, not merely to indicate that it is false, but to give a sense of the power of the claim in Western societies. A story takes on the status of myth when it becomes unquestioned. It becomes very difficult to think outside the paradigm that the myth establishes and reflects because myth and reality become mutually reinforcing. Society is structured to conform to the apparent truths that the myth reveals, and what is taken as real increasingly takes on the color of the myth. The more that some are marginalized as Other, the more Other they become. At the same time, the myth itself becomes more unquestioned the more social reality is made to conform to it. Society is structured in such a way as to make the categories through which the myth operates seem given and inevitable.

All of this makes the refutation of a myth particularly difficult. Linda Zerilli's comments about what she calls "a mythology" apply here:

> A mythology cannot be defeated in the sense that one wins over one's opponent through the rigor of logic or the force of evidence; a mythology cannot be defeated through arguments that would *reveal* it as groundless belief.... A mythology *is* utterly groundless, hence stable. What characterizes a mythology is not so much its crude or naïve character—mythologies can be extremely complex and sophisticated—but, rather, its capacity to elude our practices of verification and refutation.[3]

Particular configurations of power in society may be groundless, but that is precisely why they are difficult to argue against, because they were not established by argument to begin with. The religious-secular distinction, for example, was not established as a rational theory about how best to describe human social life; as I show in chapters 2 and 3, it was established as the result of some contingent shifts in how power was distributed between civil and ecclesiastical authorities in early modern Europe. It was established through violence, not by argument. The only way I can hope to refute the myth is to do a genealogy of these contingent shifts and to show that the problem that the myth of religious violence claims to identify and solve—the problem of violence in society—is in fact exacerbated by the forms of power that the myth authorizes. The myth of religious violence can only be undone by showing that it lacks the resources to solve the very problem that it identifies.

The definition of "violence" that I will assume in this book is therefore the same one that theorists of the supposed link between religion and violence appear to use, although only one of the figures I examine in chapter 1 offers an explicit definition of violence. "Violence" in their writings generally means injurious or lethal harm and is almost always discussed in the context of physical violence, such as war and terrorism.[4] I will assume the same general definition when discussing violence.

When I write of the myth of religious violence as a "Western" concept and discuss how it functions in the "West," I do not mean to imply that I think that such a monolithic geographical reality exists as such. The West is a construct, a contested project, not a simple description of a monolithic entity. The West is an ideal created by those who would read the world in terms of a binary relation between the "West and the rest," in Samuel Huntington's phrase.[5] The point of my argument is, of course, to question that binary.

When I use the terms "religion," "religious," and "secular," I recognize that they should often be surrounded by scare quotes. I have nevertheless tried to keep the use of scare quotes to a minimum to avoid cluttering the text.

Because of the pervasive nature of the myth of religious violence, I have tried to be as thorough as possible in showing the structure of the myth, providing a genealogy of it, and showing for what purposes it is used. Some readers may wonder if it is really necessary to examine nine different academic versions of the myth in chapter 1, for example, or to cite more than forty different instances in chapter 3 where Protestant-Catholic opposition in the "wars of religion" did not apply. I have tried to be thorough and detailed to show how pervasive the myth is and to dispel any objections that I am picking out just a few idiosyncratic figures. I have also found it necessary to be thorough precisely because such a pervasive myth will not fall easily. The more a myth eludes our ordinary practices of verification and refutation, the more sustained must be the attempt to unmask it. It is not simply that the myth is pervasive, but that the very categories under which the discussion takes place—especially the categories of religious-secular and religion-politics—are so firmly established as to appear natural. Only a thorough genealogy can show that their construction is anything but inevitable.

This book consists of four chapters. In the first chapter, I examine arguments from nine of the most prominent academic proponents of the idea that religion is peculiarly prone to violence. The examples range widely across different scholarly disciplines and give different types of explanations for why religion is prone to violence: religion is absolutist, religion is divisive, religion is irrational. They all suffer from the same defect: the inability to find a convincing way to separate religious violence from secular violence. Each of the arguments I examine is beset by internal contradictions. Most assume a substantivist concept of religion, whereby religion can be separated from secular phenomena based on the nature of religious beliefs. I show how such distinctions break down in the course of each author's own analysis. One of the authors discussed, seeing the contradictions involved in substantivist concepts of religion, employs a functionalist concept of religion and openly expands the definition of religion to include ideologies and practices that are usually called secular, such as nationalism and consumerism. As a result, however, the term religion comes to cover virtually anything humans do that gives their lives order and meaning. In that scholar's work, the term religion is so broad that it serves no useful analytical purpose.

After thus examining nine different examples of the religion-and-violence argument, I show how such arguments immunize themselves from empirical evidence. What counts as "absolute," for example, is decided a priori and is impervious to empirical testing. It is based on theological descriptions of beliefs and not on observation of believers' behavior. In response, I propose a simple empirical test to discover which ideologies and practices are in fact prone to violence. I argue that so-called secular ideologies and institutions like nationalism and liberalism can be just as absolutist, divisive, and irrational as those called religious. People kill for all sorts of things. An adequate approach to the problem would be resolutely empirical: under what conditions do certain beliefs and practices—jihad, the "invisible hand" of the market, the sacrificial atonement of Christ, the role of the United States as worldwide liberator—turn violent? There is certainly much useful work to be done on concrete empirical cases. Where the authors discussed go wrong is in trying to construct an argument about religion as such. The point is not simply that secular violence should be given equal attention to religious violence. The point is that the very distinction between secular and religious violence is unhelpful, misleading, and mystifying.

Many of the authors I examine in the first chapter—including John Hick, Martin Marty, Mark Juergensmeyer, David Rapoport, and Scott Appleby—are eminent in their fields, and all have important insights to share on the origins of violence. The reason that their arguments fail has to do with their use of the category of religion. In the second chapter, I undertake a genealogy of the concept of religion, building on the growing body of work on how the concept has been formed in different times and places according to different configurations of power.

Claims about the violence of religion as such depend upon a concept of religion as something that retains the same essence over time, retains the same essence across space, and is at least theoretically separable from secular realities—political institutions, for example. In the second chapter, I give evidence for two conclusions. The first conclusion is that there is no such thing as a transhistorical or transcultural "religion" that is essentially separate from politics. Religion has a history, and what counts as religion and what does not in any given context depends on different configurations of power and authority. The second conclusion is that the attempt to say that there *is* a transhistorical and transcultural concept of religion that is separable from secular phenomena *is itself* part of a particular configuration of power, that of the modern, liberal nation-state as it developed in the West. In this context, religion is constructed as transhistorical, transcultural, essentially interior, and essentially distinct from public, secular rationality. To construe Christianity as a religion, therefore, helps to separate loyalty to God from one's public loyalty to the nation-state. The idea that religion has a tendency to cause violence—and is therefore to be removed from public power—is one type of this essentialist construction of religion.

This chapter has five sections. In the first two sections, I show that religion is not a transhistorical concept. The first section is a history of ancient and medieval *religio*; the second section is a history of the invention of the concept of religion in the modern West by such figures as Nicholas of Cusa, Marsilio Ficino, Herbert of Cherbury, and John Locke. In the third section, I cite work by David Chidester, S. N. Balagangadhara, Timothy Fitzgerald, Tomoko Masuzawa, and others to show that religion is not a transcultural concept, but was borrowed from or imposed by Westerners in much of the rest of the world during the process of colonization. In the fourth section, I show that, even within the modern West, the religious-secular division remains a highly contestable point. In the fifth section, I conclude by arguing that what counts as religious or secular depends on what practices are being authorized. The fact that Christianity is construed as a religion, whereas nationalism is not, helps to ensure that the Christian's public and lethal loyalty belongs to the nation-state. The idea that religion has a peculiar tendency toward violence must be investigated as part of the ideological legitimation of the Western nation-state. In the West, the religious-secular distinction has been used to marginalize certain practices as inherently nonrational and potentially violent, and thus to be privatized, in order to clear the way for the more "rational" and peace-making pursuits of the state and the market. As the following two chapters show, however, the pursuits of state and market have a violence of their own which is obscured by the myth of religious violence.

In chapter 3, I examine one of the most commonly cited historical examples of religious violence: the "wars of religion" of the sixteenth and seventeenth centuries in Europe. The story of these wars serves as a kind of creation myth for the modern state. According to this myth, Protestants and Catholics began killing each other over doctrinal differences, thus showing the intractability and inherent violence of religious disagreements. The modern state was born as a peace maker in this process, relegating religion to private life and uniting people of various religions around loyalty to the sovereign state.

In this chapter, I question the standard story by looking at the historical record. The case is not as simple as the standard story implies. Christians certainly did kill each other, marking a signal failure of Christians to resist violence. But the transfer of power from the church to the state was not simply a remedy for the violence. Indeed, the transfer of power from the church to the state predated the division of Christendom into Catholics and Protestants and in many ways was a cause of the violence of the so-called wars of religion. The shift from medieval to modern—from church power to state power—was a long, complex process with gains and losses. Whatever it was, it was not a simple progressive march from violence to peace. The gradual transfer of loyalty from international church to national state was not the end of violence in Europe, but a migration of the holy from church to state in the establishment of the ideal of dying and killing for one's country.

The first section of chapter 3 shows how the story of the wars of religion is told by early modern thinkers like Hobbes, Locke, and Rousseau and by contemporary political theorists such as Judith Shklar, John Rawls, and Francis Fukuyama. Despite variations, all these thinkers present the cause of these wars as strife between Catholics and Protestants over religious beliefs, and the solution to these wars as the rise of the modern secular state. In subsequent sections of chapter 3, I break down the myth of the wars of religion into four components and show how each is historically misleading and inaccurate.

I show how much of the wars of religion involved Catholics killing Catholics, Lutherans killing Lutherans, and Catholic-Protestant collaboration. To cite only one example: Cardinal Richelieu and Catholic France intervened in the Thirty Years' War on the side of Lutheran Sweden, and the last half of the Thirty Years' War was essentially a battle between the Habsburgs and the Bourbons, the two great Catholic dynasties of Europe. Historians generally acknowledge—as political theorists do not—that other factors besides religion were at work in the wars of religion: political, economic, and social factors. The question then becomes: what is the relative importance of the various factors? Are political, economic, and social factors important enough that we are no longer justified in calling these wars "of religion"? I show how historians are divided on this question. To decide between these two groups of scholars, one would need to be able to separate religion from politics, economics, and social factors. I argue that such attempts at separation are prone to essentialism and anachronism. In the sixteenth century, the modern invention of the twins of religion and society was in its infancy; where the Eucharist was the primary symbol of social order, there simply was no divide between religious and social or political causes. This means that there is no way to pinpoint something called religion as the cause of these wars and excise it from the exercise of public power. The standard narrative says that the modern state identified religion as the root of the problem and separated it from politics. However, there was no separation of religion and politics. What we see in reality is what John Bossy describes as a "migration of the holy" from the church to the state. Ostensibly, the holy was separated from politics for the sake of peace; in reality, the emerging state appropriated the holy to become itself a new kind of religion.

With this contention in view, I show the implausibility of the idea that the transfer of power from the church to the state was the solution to the wars of the sixteenth and seventeenth centuries. The process of state building, begun well before the Reformation, was inherently conflictual. Beginning in the late medieval period, the process involved the internal integration of previously scattered powers under the aegis of the ruler and the external demarcation of territory over against other, foreign, states. I draw on the work of a range of historians, such as Heinz Schilling, J. H. M. Salmon, R. Po-Chia Hsia, Mack Holt, and Donna Bohanan, to show that much of the violence of the fifteenth through the seventeenth centuries can be explained in terms of the resistance of local elites to the centralizing efforts of monarchs and emperors.

The point is *not* that these wars were really about politics and not really about religion. Nor is the point that the state caused the wars and the church was innocent. The point is that the transfer of power from the church to the state was not the solution to the violence of the sixteenth and seventeenth centuries, but was a cause of the wars. The church was deeply implicated in the violence, for it became increasingly identified with and absorbed into the state-building project. My conclusion in this chapter is that there is ample historical evidence to cast doubt on the idea that the rise of the modern state saved Europe from the violence of religion. The rise of the modern state did not usher in a more peaceful Europe, but the rise of the state did accompany a shift in what people were willing to kill and die for. *Dulce et decorum est / Pro patria mori* would take on normative status. I argue that the legend of the wars of religion is not simply objective history, but is itself an ideological accompaniment to shifts in Western configurations of power, especially the transfer of lethal loyalty to the emergent state.

In the fourth and final chapter of the book, I ask: what purpose does the idea that religion causes violence serve for its consumers in the contemporary West? I show how useful the myth has been in the United States in authorizing certain types of power in both domestic politics and foreign policy. In domestic politics, it has helped to marginalize certain practices such as public school prayer and aid to parochial schools. At the same time, it has helped to reinforce patriotic adherence to the nation-state as that which saves us from our other, more divisive, identities. In foreign policy, the myth of religious violence helps to reinforce and justify Western attitudes and policies toward the non-Western world, especially Muslims, whose primary point of difference with the West is said to be their stubborn refusal to tame religious passions in the public sphere. It is important to note that arguments about religion and violence are not necessarily antireligion, but are anti–public religion. Although the majority of Americans consider themselves to be religious, the overwhelming majority also regard the secularization of politics as foundational to any rational and civilized society. Muslims are commonly stereotyped as fanatical and dangerous because they have not learned, as "we" have, to separate politics from religion.

In the first section of chapter 4, I examine the use of the myth of religious violence in U.S. Supreme Court decisions since the 1940s. Previously, religion was generally seen as a unitive force, a glue that helped to bind the nation together. Beginning in the 1940s, however, the specter of religious violence was cited in case after case involving the religion clauses of the First Amendment, as the Court moved to ban school prayer, state aid for parochial schools, public religious displays on government grounds, and other practices. I note that the myth of religious violence was found useful at a moment in U.S. history in which the threat of the kind of sectarian violence against which it warned had never been more remote. I show as well how patriotism has been invoked by the Court as the cure for religious divisiveness. Patriotic public invocations of God are specifically excluded from the category of religion and are therefore not subject to the kind of restrictions put on religion. Once again, what counts as religion and what does not is not dependent on the presence or absence of belief in God, but on a political decision about the inculcation of loyalty to the nation-state.

In the next two sections of chapter 4, I analyze the way that the myth of religious violence helps to construct non-Western Others and to legitimate violence against them. I examine both academic and journalistic uses of the myth by such figures as Mark Juergensmeyer, Bernard Lewis, Andrew Sullivan, and Christopher Hitchens and show that the argument that religion is prone to violence is a significant component in the construction of an opposition between the West and the rest. If religion has a peculiar tendency to promote violence, then societies that have learned to tame religious passions in public are seen as superior and more inherently peaceable than societies which have not. Muslim societies, in particular, are seen as essentially problematic because they lack the proper distinction between religion and the secular. Indeed, Islam itself is seen as a peculiar and abnormal religion because it "mixes" politics with pure religion. Clashes between Western and Islamic governments and cultures can therefore be explained in terms of the inherently pathological nature of the latter. In attempting to understand why, for example, Iran since 1979 has seen the United States as its great enemy, U.S. support for the coup that installed the Shah's brutal, secularizing regime in 1953 can be overlooked in favor of "deeper" causes, in particular the inherently volatile nature of religion and its poisonous effects on Iranian politics. I show how the myth of religious violence is commonly used to bypass actual historical events and to find the answer to the question "Why do they hate us?" in the pathological irrationality of religiously based social orders.

In the next section, I give examples of how this kind of logic is used to justify Western military actions in the Islamic world. The logic is impeccable: if we are dealing with inherently violent and irrational social orders, there is not much hope of reasoning with them. We must be prepared to use military force. The hope is that, through both gentle and forceful means, we may spread the blessings of liberal social order to the Islamic world. Thus is the myth of religious violence used to justify violence. A strong contrast is drawn between religious and secular violence. Violence that is labeled religious is always peculiarly virulent and reprehensible. But violence that is labeled secular hardly counts as violence at all, since it is inherently peace making. Secular violence is often necessary and sometimes praiseworthy, especially when it is used to quell the inherent violence of religion.

I do not wish either to deny the virtues of liberalism nor to excuse the vices of other kinds of social orders. I think that the separation of church and state is generally a good thing. On the other side, there is no question that certain forms of Muslim beliefs and practices do promote violence. Such forms should be examined and criticized. It is unhelpful, however, to undertake that criticism through the lens of a groundless religious-secular dichotomy that causes us to turn a blind eye to secular forms of imperialism and violence. Insofar as the myth of religious violence creates the villains against which a liberal social order defines itself, the myth is little different from previous forms of Western imperialism that claimed the inferiority of non-Western Others and subjected them to Western power in the hopes of making them more like "us."

I do not have an alternative theopolitics of my own to present in this book. The purpose of this book is negative: to contribute to a dismantling of the myth of religious violence. To dismantle the myth would have multiple benefits, which I summarize in the conclusion to the final chapter. It would free empirical studies of violence from the distorting categories of religious and secular. It would help us to see that the foundational possibilities for social orders, in the Islamic world and the West, are not limited to a stark choice between theocracy and secularism. It would help us to see past the stereotype of nonsecular Others as religious fanatics, and it would question one of the justifications for war against those Others. It would help Americans to eliminate one of the main obstacles to having a serious conversation about the question "Why do they hate us?"—a conversation that would not overlook the history of U.S. dealings with the Middle East in favor of pinning the cause on religious fanaticism.

Bridging the threatening gap between *us* and *them* requires that we not only know the Other, but know ourselves. This book is intended as a contribution to that pursuit.

I

The Anatomy of the Myth

The idea that religion causes violence is one of the most prevalent myths in Western culture. From first-year university students to media commentators to federal judges, the view is widespread that religion, if it does not simply cause violence, is at least a significant contributing factor in a great many of the conflicts of human history. Academic studies of religion and violence seem to bear this out, and indeed the evidence seems incontrovertible. Blood sacrifices have been around from the earliest times. Holy wars, crusades, inquisitions, and pogroms have marked religious behavior. Religions were implicated in spreading European imperialism. Religion has legitimated the oppression of the poor and of women.[1] Oppressive political and economic structures have been seen as issuing from a divine will: "Thus religion was implicated in maintaining social structures of violence from the earliest historical records."[2] In the early twenty-first century, the readiness of the clergy to bless whatever war the United States is involved in is further evidence of religion's violent tendencies.[3] Add terrorism by Muslim fundamentalists and other religious groups, and the evidence against religion seems conclusive. In short, "the brutal facts of the history of religions impose the stark realization of the intertwining of religion and violence: violence, clothed in religious garb, has repeatedly cast a spell over religion and culture, luring countless 'decent' people—from unlettered peasants to learned priests, preachers, and professors—into its destructive dance."[4]

However, what is meant by "religion" is by no means clear. The author of the above quote, in a book entitled *Revelation, the Religions, and Violence,* gives no definition of religion or religions, despite the centrality of the concept to his argument. As in the above quote, "religion" in this text sometimes becomes "religion and culture" with no explanation of what, if anything, distinguishes the two terms from each other.[5] This type of confusion is the norm. Most scholars who write on religion and violence give no definition of religion. Others will acknowledge the now notorious difficulty of providing a definition of religion, but nonetheless will give some version of the assertion that "everybody knows what we mean when we say 'religion.'" When academics say such things, it is a sign that something is probably wrong. One should react as one would when urged by a realtor to waive an inspection.

The arguments I examine attempt to separate a category called religion, which is prone to violence because it is absolutist, divisive, and nonrational, from a secular, or nonreligious, reality that is less prone to violence, presumably because it is less absolutist, more unitive, and more rational. As we shall see, such arguments do not stand up to scrutiny, because they cannot find any coherent way to separate religious from secular violence. Once we begin to ask what the religion-and-violence arguments mean by religion, we find that their explanatory power is hobbled by a number of indefensible assumptions about what does and does not count as religion. Certain types of practices and institutions are condemned, while others are ignored.

We are presented with a range of ideologies, practices, and institutions—Islam, Marxism, capitalism, Christianity, nationalism, Confucianism, Americanism, Judaism, the nation-state, liberalism, Shinto, secularism, Hinduism, and so on—all of which have been known to support violence under certain conditions. A careful examination of the varieties of each and the empirical conditions under which each does in fact support violence is helpful and necessary. What is not helpful is the attempt to divide the above list into religious and secular phenomena and then claim that the former are more prone to violence. As we shall see, such a division is arbitrary and unsustainable on either theoretical or empirical grounds.

At first glance, this may seem like an academic exercise in quibbling over definitions, but much more is at stake. The religious-secular dichotomy in the arguments examined sanctions the condemnation of certain kinds of violence and the overlooking of other kinds of violence. Later in this book, I will argue that the myth of religious violence is so prevalent because, while it delegitimates certain kinds of violence, it is used to legitimate other kinds of violence, namely, violence done in the name of secular, Western ideals. The argument that religion causes violence sanctions a dichotomy between, on the one hand, non-Western, especially Muslim, forms of culture, which—having not yet learned to privatize matters of faith—are absolutist, divisive, and irrational, and Western culture, on the other, which is modest in its claims to truth, unitive, and rational. This dichotomy, this clash-of-civilizations world view, in turn can be used to legitimate the use of violence against those with whom it is impossible to reason on our own terms. In short, their violence is fanatical and uncontrolled; our violence is controlled, reasonable, and often regrettably necessary to contain their violence. Although the figures I examine in this chapter may reject the use of their arguments to sanction violence, the only way to ensure against this use is to abandon arguments that posit the inherent dangers of religion and thereby posit the inherent superiority of secularist societies.

In this chapter, I examine three different, overlapping types of argument for the link between religion and violence, and I show how the arguments fail. I have put the scholars being discussed into one of the three types for the sake of convenience and organization, but the organization does not affect my argument, because I am not addressing the arguments about religion on their own terms. That is, I am not assuming that there is such a thing called religion, and then arguing that religion is not absolutist, divisive, or irrational. Rather, I analyze a variety of arguments that religion causes violence and show how, in each case, the author himself cannot manage to maintain a coherent division between religious and secular violence. At the end of this chapter, I address some possible ways of trying to salvage the arguments and show that these also fail. Chapter 2 will follow with a genealogy of the distinction between religious and secular which will make clearer why the arguments in this chapter fail: they mistake a contingent power arrangement of the modern West for a universal and timeless feature of human existence.

Three Types of Argument

Over a number of years, I read every academic version of the argument that religion causes violence that I could find, across a range of disciplines. For our purposes, "religion causes violence" is simplified shorthand. No one, as far as I know, argues that the presence of religion necessarily always produces violence. Rather, the arguments see religion as especially inclined to produce violence, or as an especially significant factor among others in the production or exacerbation of violence.

The arguments I have examined can be sorted into three somewhat overlapping types: religion causes violence because it is (1) absolutist, (2) divisive, and (3) insufficiently rational. Most authors on the subject make mention of more than one type of argument, but most tend to feature one of the three.[6] In the following, each of the three types is represented by three main authors. If space and patience permitted, I could provide multiple examples.[7] For our purposes here, however, three representatives of each type will suffice. The figures chosen here are some of the most influential voices in the area of religion and violence, and they were chosen because they fairly represent the state of the argument across a variety of disciplines, including religious studies, sociology, history, political science, and theology.

I wish to make clear from the outset that I will only consider works that make transhistorical and transcultural arguments about the violence of religion *as such*. There are many other careful empirical studies that helpfully examine particular cases of violence within specific cultural contexts, such as among radical Middle Eastern Muslims or extreme right-wing American Christians.[8] Although some of these studies are less careful than others in using the term religion, their concentration on empirical description within specific contexts makes them valuable. My concern is with general arguments about religion and violence because of the way they distort empirical data and lend themselves to ideological use.

Religion Is Absolutist

JOHN HICK. In an essay entitled "The Non-Absoluteness of Christianity," pluralist theologian John Hick indicts the claims of the uniqueness and ultimacy of revelation in Jesus Christ for inciting Christians to violence against Jews in Europe and against non-Christians throughout the Third World. Claims of the unsurpassability of Christian revelation could only lead to treating non-Christians as inferior and in need of colonization to draw the unfortunate heathen up to the same level as enlightened European Christians.[9] Hick makes clear that this is not a dynamic unique to Christianity, but is endemic to religion as such: "It should be added at this point that the claims of other religions to absolute validity and to a consequent superiority have likewise, given the same human nature, sanctified violent aggression, exploitation, and intolerance. A worldwide and history-long study of the harmful effects of religious absolutism would draw material from almost every tradition."[10] The problem is one of religion as such, and not just Christianity, because Christianity is just one species of a genus of religions, each of which orbits what Hick variously calls "ultimate Reality," "the Ultimate," or "the Real." Jesus Christ, the Buddha, Mohammed, et al., all taught different ways to the same center. According to Hick, it is a constant temptation to mistake the way for the goal, the planets for the sun, to absolutize what is merely relative to the ultimate. This temptation is by its nature a temptation to violence. Hick advocates what he calls a "Copernican Revolution" in which one begins to see that one's own religion does not occupy the central place, but rather that the various religions of the world orbit around the ultimate.[11] Hick writes a great deal about recognizing the pluralism and diversity of religions. At the same time, however, he radically relativizes the particularity of each religion, for each one of them, whatever their differences, seeks to end up in the exact same place.

Hick appeals to a transhistorical and transcultural concept of religion; he is convinced that, throughout history, "religion has been a virtually universal dimension of human life."[12] But what is religion? In his 1973 book, *God and the Universe of Faiths*, Hick proposes a "definition of religion as an understanding of the universe, together with an appropriate way of living within it, which involves reference beyond the natural world to God or gods or to the Absolute or to a transcendent order or process." According to Hick, this definition includes theistic faiths such as Christianity, Islam, and theistic Hinduism, as well as nontheistic faiths such as Theravada Buddhism and nontheistic Hinduism. Hick confidently asserts that this definition excludes "naturalistic" systems of belief such as communism and humanism.[13] By his 1989 book, *An Interpretation of Religion*, however, Hick is no longer so sure that he can draw such sharp lines between what is a religion and what is not. He seems newly aware of the growing debate among scholars over whether the term religion is useful or should be scrapped altogether.[14] Hick admits the extreme difficulty of deciding whether Confucianism, Theravada Buddhism, and Marxism should be called religions; none has a deity, yet all share certain characteristics with what are normally considered to be religions.[15]

Hick tries to solve this problem by appealing to Ludwig Wittgenstein's metaphor of the "family resemblance." We call various activities "games" because each member of the group shares at least one characteristic with another member of the group, even though there is no one characteristic, or "essence," that they all share that marks them as games. Likewise, "religions" are a "complex continuum of resemblances and differences."[16] This is helpful, says Hick, but we still "need a starting point from which to begin to chart this range of phenomena." Hick suggests Tillich's concept of "ultimate concern" as such a starting point: "For religious objects, practices and beliefs have a deep importance for those to whom they count as religious; and they are important not merely in the immediate sense in which it may seem important to finish correctly a sentence that one has begun or to answer the telephone when it is ringing, but important in a more permanent and ultimate sense."[17] Hick is thus able "to locate the secular faith of Marxism as a fairly distant cousin of such movements as Christianity and Islam, sharing some of their characteristics (such as a comprehensive world-view, with scriptures, eschatology, saints, and a total moral claim) whilst lacking others (such as belief in a transcendent divine reality)."[18] Having thus "resolved—or perhaps dissolved—the problem of the definition of 'religion,'" Hick declares that scholars are free to focus their attention on whatever features of religion interest them. Hick will focus on "belief in the transcendent," though he hastens to add that this is not the essence of religion, since the family-resemblance concept does away with essences. One of the merits of the family-resemblance concept, says Hick, is that it leaves open the possibility of religions with no belief in the transcendent; it is not necessary to use belief in the transcendent as a litmus test for what is and what is not a religion.[19]

On the one hand, Hick rightly sees the flaws in trying to isolate an essence of religion, and thereby opens the door for seeing that there is no single meaningful category under which to group such widely varying phenomena as Christianity and Confucianism without including so many other institutions and ideologies—Marxism, nationalism, football fanaticism—as to render the category pointless. On the other hand, Hick continues to distinguish between cultural institutions that are religious and those that are nonreligious or secular. Marxism, for example, is repeatedly identified as a secular phenomenon, even though Hick allows it the status of "distant cousin" within the extended family of religions.[20] Marxism, Hick says, is excluded from religion when speaking of "the more central members of the religious family" but is included "when speaking more broadly."[21] However, Hick never gives any criteria for distinguishing central from peripheral. Why are Confucianism and Theravada Buddhism included in the elite central group of "world religions" while Marxism is excluded? It is impossible to make any such distinction between real religions and sort-of-religious-but-really-secular distant cousins without identifying a set of characteristics as central or essential to the concept of religion, which would be to return to the essentialism that the family-resemblances theory is meant to escape.

Is it correct in any family to identify some cousins as central and others as peripheral? I can only do so by privileging my particular point of view. My immediate family is, of course, central to me, while my cousins whom I rarely see seem peripheral. As shocking as it may seem to me, my cousins probably think of themselves as rather more central, and think of me, if at all, only when speaking more broadly of family. This type of subjective bias unavoidably creeps into Hick's analysis. His dilemma is this: if he defines religion too narrowly, it will exclude things he wants to include, like Confucianism; if he defines religion too broadly, it will include things he wants to exclude, like Marxism. His solution is to attempt to dissolve the problem of definition. If he does so consistently, however, the distinction between religious and secular dissolves too; all kinds of concerns can be ultimate concerns. Without a clear distinction between what is religious and what is not religious, any argument that religion per se does or does not cause violence becomes hopelessly arbitrary. Why focus our attention, for example, on the violence of Muslim and Christian "fundamentalisms" and not on the monumental horrors wrought by Marxism and nationalism in the twentieth century, if all belong in the extended family of ultimate concerns? One can ignore the latter only by shuffling them off to a peripheral category of secular ideologies whose tendencies to absolutism are thereby minimized. The point is not that Christian and Muslim violence do not exist, nor that they should be ignored or excused. The point is that the religious-secular dichotomy operating within the religion-causes-violence argument focuses our attention toward some kinds of violence (those labeled religious) and away from others (those labeled secular). In condemning the evils of European colonization of non-Western peoples, for example, Hick focuses on Christian missionary zeal and passes over in silence the role played by secular ideologies such as capitalism and nationalism. This is not to say that Hick has a deliberate agenda to ignore or excuse certain kinds of violence. It is rather that the argument that religion causes violence focuses attention on certain kinds of violence and, willy-nilly, diverts attention from other kinds, those designated as secular.

CHARLES KIMBALL. Charles Kimball is an academic, but his *When Religion Becomes Evil* was chosen as the top religion book of 2002 by *Publishers Weekly*, and it has reached an audience beyond the academy. It is a generous, well-intentioned, and balanced book, full of evidence of violence done in the name of faith, but also of more hopeful signs that the "major religions" have resources within them to prevent evil done in their name. Nevertheless, the book is marred by the principal problem from which the religion-and-violence genre suffers: its inability to provide any convincing way to distinguish the religious from the secular.

Kimball identifies five "warning signs" of when religion is apt to turn evil, beginning with absolutism. The middle five chapters of Kimball's book are each devoted to one of these warning signs; he also includes an introductory chapter and a concluding chapter. According to Kimball, religion is likely to turn violent when it displays any of these features: absolute truth claims, blind obedience, the establishment of an "ideal" time, the belief that the end justifies any means, and a declaration of holy war. All religions do not necessarily exhibit these features, but "the inclination toward these corruptions is strong in the major religions."[22]

At the beginning of his first chapter, Kimball describes how flustered his students become when he asks them to write a definition of religion. Kimball acknowledges the problem, but treats it as a merely semantic difficulty: "Clearly these bright students know what religion is"; they just have trouble defining it. After all, Kimball assures us, "Religion is a central feature of human life. We all see many indications of it every day, and we all know it when we see it."[23] Well, no, we don't. A survey of religious studies literature finds totems, witchcraft, the rights of man, Marxism, liberalism, Japanese tea ceremonies, nationalism, sports, free market ideology, and a host of other institutions and practices treated under the rubric of religion.[24] Kimball, on the other hand, recognizes none of these practices as religious. He deals with the problem of the definition of religion by recommending a comparative empirical analysis that begins by "gathering data and organizing the facts about a particular religion."[25] After doing so, we may make some conclusions about what all religions have in common.[26] The problem with this approach is that it begs the question about what qualifies as a religion to begin with. How do we know which phenomena qualify as religions so that we may begin our comparative analysis of them? Kimball mentions Hinduism, Buddhism, Judaism, Christianity, Islam, Shinto, Zoroastrianism, Manichaeism, Native American religions, and "indigenous tribal religions."[27] How did he arrive at this list? Why Shinto, when there is widespread scholarly doubt about its status as a religion, even among those who accept the usefulness of the category "religion"?[28] Why Native American religions, when scholars acknowledge that Native American tribes do not traditionally distinguish between religion and the rest of life?[29]

We might wish to excuse Kimball and others on the grounds that virtually every scholarly concept has some fuzzy edges. We might not be able to nail down, once and for all and in all cases, what a "culture" is, or what qualifies as "politics," for example, but nevertheless the concepts remain useful. All may not agree on the peripheries of these concepts, but enough agreement on the centers of such concepts makes them practical and functional. Most people know that religion includes Christianity, Islam, Judaism, and the major world religions. Whether or not Confucianism or Shinto fits is a boundary dispute best left to scholars who make their living splitting hairs.

This appears to be a commonsense answer, but it misses the point rather completely. The problem with Kimball's argument is not that his working definition of religion is too fuzzy. The problem is precisely the opposite. Kimball's implicit definition of religion is *unjustifiably clear* about what does and does not qualify as a religion. Kimball, for example, subjects the violence of Hinduism to close scrutiny, but passes over the violence of other kinds of nationalism in silence, despite a telling acknowledgment that "blind religious zealotry is similar to unfettered nationalism."[30] How are they different? Forms of secular nationalism do not appeal to God or gods, but neither do some of the institutions Kimball includes in his list of religions, such as Theravada Buddhism.

Kimball is typical of those who make the argument that religion is prone to violence in that he assumes a sharp distinction between the religious and the secular, without explicitly analyzing or defending such a distinction. This is not a peripheral issue; the entire force of the argument rests on this distinction. In making this assumption, Kimball and others ignore the growing body of scholarly work that calls the distinction into question. The case for nationalism as a religion, for example, has been made repeatedly, from Carlton Hayes's 1960 classic, *Nationalism: A Religion*, to more recent works by Peter van der Veer, Talal Asad, Carolyn Marvin, and others.[31] Marvin and David Ingle argue that "nationalism is the most powerful religion in the United States."[32] Kimball and others who make the religion-and-violence argument might wish to defend the religious-secular distinction against these other lines of argument, but in fact they do not. The argument that religion is prone to violence goes on as if "we all know religion when we see it," while arbitrary and undefended decisions are made as to what constitutes a religion and what does not.

What happens if we take seriously Kimball's own passing reference to the similarity between religious zealotry and nationalism, and search nationalism for the five warning signs? The first, absolute truth claims, is a regular feature of the discourse of nation-states at war. As Kimball himself states, George W. Bush, while "determined to keep the 'war on terrorism' from descending into a conflict between Christianity and Islam," invoked a "cosmic dualism" between good nations, led by the United States, and the forces of evil: "You had to align with the forces of good and help root out the forces of evil or be counted as adversaries in the 'war on terrorism.' "[33] Are not claims to the universal goodness of liberal democracy absolute truth claims? If not, what distinguishes them from being "absolute"?

The second warning sign, blind obedience, depends on the rather subjective adjective "blind." Obedience is rigidly institutionalized for those whose job is to do violence on behalf of the nation-state. In the armed forces, there is, for example, no allowance for selective conscientious objection, that is, the individual soldier deciding on the basis of conscience that any particular war is unjust. Once inducted, the soldier must fight in any war his or her superiors deem necessary, and the soldier must fight as he or she is ordered. Is this blind obedience in the service of violence?

The remaining three warning signs also seem to apply to nationalism. The third warning sign, the establishment of an ideal time, is so broadly defined that "making the world safe for democracy" or Francis Fukuyama's "end of history"[34] would seem to qualify. The history of modern warfare between nation-states is full of evidence of the fourth warning sign—the belief that the end justifies any means—from the vaporization of innocent civilians in Hiroshima to the practice of torture by over a third of the world's nation-states, including many democracies. As for the fifth sign—the declaration of holy war—what counts as "holy" is unclear, but arguably the battle of good versus evil that President Bush believed his nation was leading would fit. Secular nationalism, then, would appear to exhibit—at times—all five of the warning signs.

Perhaps at this point Kimball would want to acknowledge the difficulties with claiming that religious ideologies have a greater tendency toward violence than do secular ideologies, and simply claim that his book is only meant to be about one side of the problem. In other words, "yes, secular ideologies can be violent too, but this is a book about how to deal with religious violence. Someone else can write a book about other types of violence." This answer would be inadequate, however, for the very distinction between religious violence and secular violence is what needs to be explained and defended. Without such an explanation and defense, there is no reason to exclude putatively secular ideologies, as Kimball has done, from his analysis of absolutism, blind obedience, and the rest. If the five warning signs also apply to secular ideologies, why not frame the book as an analysis of the circumstances under which *any* institution or ideology becomes evil?

RICHARD WENTZ. One possible way of resolving the contradictions in the argument that religion causes violence is to appeal to a functionalist concept that openly expands the definition of religion to include ideologies and practices that are usually called secular. Religious studies scholar Richard E. Wentz provides an example of this approach in *Why People Do Bad Things in the Name of Religion*. Wentz emphasizes the absolutism of religion as the cause of the problem. Here, the absolute appears personified as a demon. Wentz describes being "frequently visited by a student who wants to know whether I believe in the absolute." When he looks at the student, he sees the demon of the absolute sitting on her shoulder, giggling and whispering: "Such a demon as this sits on the shoulder of people who become fanatics, crusaders, fundamentalists. He makes them nervous, so nervous they sometimes do very bad things as a testimony to the absolute."[35] People create absolutes out of fear of their own limitations. The absolute, Wentz speculates, is a projection onto a large screen of a fictional, unlimited self. We shore up a shaky self-image through the creation of bogus absolutes and react with violence when others do not accept them. Wentz, however, does not believe that this is the true nature of religion. Indeed, says Wentz, all the great religions of the world have taught that our understanding is limited; we cannot know "the Absolute," so all the absolutes that we fabricate for ourselves are relativized: "It is of the nature of the Absolute that it can condone no absolutes. It rejects them as demons."[36] Nevertheless, people fail to understand this, and so "[p]eople frequently do bad things in the name of religion because they have taken a phantom of reason and fashioned it into an absolute."[37]

Religion then appears to have a particular tendency toward absolutism and, therefore, violence. What exactly religion is, however, is hard to pin down. In his discussion of absolutism, Wentz draws on Christianity, Islam, Judaism, Buddhism, and the "great Asian traditions." Earlier in the book, however, religion designated a great deal more. African clitorectomies, Zen koans, and Sunday church services are identified as religions by their "uselessness." That is, religious behaviors relate to the aspects of human life that transcend mere biological purposes. People tell stories of order and meaning: "From this observation it is possible to conclude that most human beings are (or have been) religious."[38] On the next page, "most" becomes "all": "To be human is to be religious."[39] Religion is transhistorical, transcultural, and encompasses a very wide range of human behaviors.

Even those who explicitly reject "organized religion" act religiously. Wentz gives the example of the nonchurch-going auto mechanic who makes a ritual out of watching Monday night football. Arranging his beer and sandwiches just so, colonizing his favorite recliner, letting his belly pop open his fly—this weekly ritual is the most important thing in his life. Wentz describes it with eucharistic overtones: "He eats and drinks, his whole body giving thanks for his favorite teams, his heroes. Their bodies and blood are part of him as he eats and drinks, watches, cheers, and curses."[40] Religiousness is an inescapable universal human characteristic. Therefore, violence does not result from the fact that some people are religious and some are not, but from the fact that many misunderstand religiousness and are incapable of living with nonabsolutes and uncertainty.[41] The problem is heightened when religiousness becomes religion, that is, when this essentially interior human experience is externalized and used as a marker of identity, in such a way that it is promoted or defended against others. Wentz acknowledges, however, that the problem is not limited to what we usually think of as religions, for faith in technology, secular humanism, consumerism, and a host of other world views can be counted as religions too. Wentz is compelled to conclude,

"Perhaps all of us do bad things in the name of (or as a representative of) religion."[42]

Wentz may be right in blurring the lines between what is usually considered a religion and other types of world views. He should be commended for his consistency in not trying to erect an artificial division between religious and secular types of absolutism. The price of consistency, however, is that Wentz evacuates his own religion-and-violence argument of any explanatory force or usefulness. A more economical title for his book would have been *Why People Do Bad Things*. The word "religion" in the title ends up meaning everything that people do that gives their lives order and purpose. The term religion is therefore so broad that it serves no useful analytical function.

Religion Is Divisive

MARTIN MARTY. We have already touched briefly on the second type of argument for a link between religion and violence. Here, the indictment of religion is based on religion's tendency to form strong identities exclusive of others, and thus divide people into *us* and *them*. In a book on public religion, the famed historian of religion Martin E. Marty wants to allow a public political presence for religion, but only after it is chastened by evidence of its divisiveness. Under the heading "Religion Divides," Marty puts the argument this way:

> Those called to be religious naturally form separate groups, movements, tribes, or nations. Responding in good faith to a divine call, believers feel themselves endowed with sacred privilege, a sense of chosenness that elevates them above all others. This self-perception then leads groups to draw lines around themselves and to speak negatively of "the others." ... The elect denounce "others" for worshiping false gods and often act violently against such unbelievers.[43]

Curiously, the historical examples Marty offers to back up this claim include Ronald Reagan's designation of the Soviet Union as the "evil empire." Although it is certain that Reagan and his supporters often professed to see the United States as a nation uniquely blessed by God, it is not at all clear why such an example would count as evidence against the violent tendencies of religion as opposed to those of nationalism or patriotism. In the first sentence quoted above, Marty throws religion into a stew of ethnic, tribal, and national loyalties, while simultaneously claiming to pursue an argument about the particularly divisive nature of religion.

One might hope for some help from Marty's own attempt to state what religion is, but in his book from which this argument is drawn—*Politics,*

Religion, and the Common Good—Marty begins by offering seventeen different definitions of religion. Only after he has thus "illustrate[d] the wide range of possibilities"[44] does he offer a definition of his own. It is not exactly a definition, however, since "scholars will never agree on the definition of religion,"[45] so Marty feels compelled to "forgo a precise definition and instead point to phenomena that help describe what we're talking about."[46] Marty gives the following five "features" to help describe what he's talking about: (1) religion focuses our ultimate concern, (2) religion builds community, (3) religion appeals to myth and symbol, (4) religion is reinforced through rites and ceremonies, and (5) religion demands certain behaviors from its adherents. In describing each of these features of religion, Marty points out how each also applies to politics. For example, "ultimate concern," a term explicitly borrowed from Paul Tillich, applies not merely to belief in deities but more generally to answers to questions such as "What do you most care about? What would you be willing to die for?" According to Marty, Nazism and astrology apply under this rubric. Politics and government must also answer questions of ultimate concern, such as "How should society be ordered?" Marty proceeds similarly through the rest of the five features. Religion builds community, and so does politics. Religion appeals to myth and symbol, and politics mimics this appeal in devotion to the flag, war memorials, and so on. Religion uses rites and ceremonies, such as circumcision and baptism, and "politics also depends on rites and ceremonies," even in avowedly secular nations. Religion requires followers to behave in certain ways, and "politics and governments also demand certain behaviors."[47]

Marty is trying to show how closely intertwined are politics and religion. What he fails to do is provide any criteria for separating the two. If politics fulfills all the defining features of religion, why is politics not a species of religion, or vice versa? Of course, any definition is contestable, and scholars cannot afford to get bogged down in searching for a definition on which all can agree before intellectual inquiry can begin. Nevertheless, some definitions are more useful than others, and some serve positively to obfuscate rather than enlighten. One might argue over what qualifies as an *x*, but a definition of *x* should at least claim to provide a way to distinguish *x* from *not-x*. Marty's definition of religion claims the opposite; politics has the same features as religion. And yet, somehow, the list of five features is still meant to help us know what religion—as opposed to not-religion—is. If a thing can fulfill all the criteria of a definition of *x* and yet still be identified as *not-x*, then the definition is not very useful.

Marty tries to get around this problem by claiming that he is not giving a precise definition, but just locating some phenomena that "help describe what we're talking about." It is of course true that scholars cannot always pause to define every term they use, and for some purposes precise definitions are not necessary. There are those as well who reject essentialist definitions altogether, arguing that the meaning of every term is determined only within the historical context in which it is used. Marty, however, is pursuing an argument about religion per se. If one is trying, as is Marty, to convince the reader that "religion divides" and "religion can be violent,"[48] then one ought to be clear about what religion is. If the problem is that any definition will meet with quibbles from other scholars, the normal scholarly procedure is to give a definition that one thinks is adequate, forge ahead with the analysis, and expect to defend one's definition according to accepted standards of evidence and argument. If, on the other hand, any attempt to give a definition will be so problematic that a scholar will not even try it—if, as in this case, a leading U.S. historian of religion will not even attempt a definition of religion—then we begin to suspect that some type of mystification is afoot.

As with Kimball, the problem is not simply that Marty is vague about what religion is. The problem is that, when it comes to pursuing his argument about religion and violence, he is *unjustifiably clear* about what counts as religion and what does not. Despite demolishing the distinction between religion and politics, Marty continues to warn of the dangers of religion, while ignoring the violent tendencies of supposedly secular politics.

MARK JUERGENSMEYER. The work of sociologist Mark Juergensmeyer is perhaps the most prominent contemporary scholarship on the question of religion and violence. His most thorough work on the subject, *Terror in the Mind of God: The Global Rise of Religious Violence*, was issued in an updated edition with a new preface after the attacks of September 11, 2001. Juergensmeyer contends, "Religion seems to be connected with violence virtually everywhere."[49] This, he claims, is true across all religious traditions, and it has always been so.[50] He does not think this is an aberration: "Rather, I look for explanations in the current forces of geopolitics and in a strain of violence that may be found at the deepest levels of the religious imagination."[51] The argument, then, is built on a combination of empirical observations about some violent behaviors in the face of globalization, on the one hand, and contentions about the transhistorical and transcultural essence of religion, on the other. For the latter, Juergensmeyer employs elements of the arguments about the absolutist and nonrational nature of religion, but he concentrates on the propensity of religion to divide people into friends and enemies, good and evil, us and them. More specifically, religious images of struggle and transformation—"cosmic war"—have a tendency to foster violence when transferred to "real-world" conflicts by "satanizing" the Other and ruling out compromise or peaceful coexistence.

The first part of Juergensmeyer's book consists of case studies of what he takes to be religious violence. Abortion clinic bombers, Timothy McVeigh, Protestants and Catholics in Belfast, Zionists, Muslim fundamentalists, Sikh militants, and the Japanese Aum Shinrikyo—all come under scrutiny. This section is full of interesting interviews and empirical observations. Juergensmeyer does a good job being as fair to his subjects as possible and lets them present their own views. In the second part of the book, Juergensmeyer attempts to explain the underlying logic of religious violence. He begins by describing the acts of these groups as "performance violence." Their acts are "deliberately intense and vivid," "savage," "meant purposely to elicit anger," and "deliberately exaggerated."[52] Juergensmeyer wants to distinguish between acts of violence done for utilitarian purposes and those whose main purpose is symbolic: "I can imagine a line with 'strategic' on the one side and 'symbolic' on the other, with various acts of terrorism located in between." The takeover of the Japanese embassy in Peru in 1997 would be closer to the "strategic, political side," and the Aum Shinrikyo gas attack in 1995 would be closer to the "symbolic, religious side."[53] One thing that distinguishes religious violence from secular violence is the former's tendency to pursue symbolic targets— defined as those "intended to illustrate or refer to something beyond [the] immediate target"—rather than those with long-term strategic value. As such, acts of religious violence can be "analyzed as one would any other symbol, ritual, or sacred drama."[54]

This attempt to distinguish religious from secular political violence according to the symbolic-strategic axis begins to break down in the course of Juergensmeyer's own analysis, for he must admit the symbolic nature of politics. For example, Juergensmeyer states that symbolic acts can actually weaken a secular government's power: "Because power is largely a matter of perception, symbolic statements can lead to real results."[55] Here, Juergensmeyer wants to maintain his distinction between the symbolic/religious and the real/political, but he gives the game away by admitting that "real" power largely rests on "mere" perception. Likewise, he refers with approval to Pierre Bourdieu's work on power and symbol, from which Juergensmeyer gleans that "our public life is shaped as much by symbols as by institutions. For this reason, symbolic acts—the 'rites of institution'—help to demarcate public space and indicate what is meaningful in the social world."[56] Rather than conclude, as Bourdieu does, that the political can be just as symbolic as the religious, however, Juergensmeyer concludes, "Public ritual has traditionally been the province of religion, and this is one of the reasons that performance violence comes so naturally to activists from a religious background."[57] In the face of evidence that not just religion but politics is symbolic, Juergensmeyer seems to claim that whatever is symbolic about politics must be the purview of religion. The argument oscillates between saying explicitly "religion employs symbolism" and saying implicitly "if it's symbolic, it must be religious." Juergensmeyer's argument would be much clearer in this chapter if he simply dropped the term religion and analyzed the symbolic power of violence. Doing so would, among other gains, render explicable the appearance of the Unabomber in this chapter. The Unabomber is used to illustrate the way that symbolic violence today requires media exposure, despite the fact that the Unabomber appears to have had no affiliation with any group or ideas that Juergensmeyer would consider religious.

Once Juergensmeyer has made the symbolic-strategic distinction, he moves on to analyze the heart of the religious warrior's symbolic universe: the notion of cosmic war. "What makes religious violence particularly savage and relentless" is that it puts worldly conflicts in a "larger than life" context of "great battles of the legendary past" and struggles between good and evil.[58] Essential to religion is the larger drama of the establishment of order over chaos and evil. Worldly political conflicts—that is, "more rational" conflicts, such as those over land[59]—are of a fundamentally different character than those in which the stakes have been raised to cosmic proportions. If the stakes are thus set high, the "absolutism of cosmic war makes compromise unlikely," thus increasing the intensity of the violence.[60] According to Juergensmeyer, conflicts are likely to be characterized as cosmic war under any of the following conditions: (1) "the struggle is perceived as a defense of basic identity and dignity," (2) "losing the struggle would be unthinkable," and (3) "the struggle is blocked and cannot be won in real time or in real terms." As an example of worldly political conflict turning into cosmic war, Juergensmeyer offers the Arab-Israeli conflict, which "was not widely regarded as a sacred battle from the perspective of either side until the late 1980s."[61]

Once again, however, keeping the notion of cosmic war separate from ordinary worldly political war is difficult or impossible on Juergensmeyer's own terms. What he says about cosmic war is virtually indistinguishable from what he says about war in general:

> Looking closely at the notion of war, one is confronted with the idea
> of dichotomous opposition on an absolute scale....War suggests an
> all-or-nothing struggle against an enemy whom one assumes to be
> determined to destroy. No compromise is deemed possible. The very
> existence of the opponent is a threat, and until the enemy is either

crushed or contained, one's own existence cannot be secure. What is striking about a martial attitude is the certainty of one's position and the willingness to defend it, or impose it on others, to the end.

Such certitude on the part of one side may be regarded as noble by those whose sympathies lie with it and dangerous by those who do not. But either way it is not rational.[62]

War cuts off the possibility of compromise and in fact provides an excuse not to compromise. In other words, "War provides a reason to be violent. This is true even if the worldly issues at heart in the dispute do not seem to warrant such a ferocious position."[63] The division between mundane war and cosmic war seems to vanish as fast as it was constructed. War itself is a "world view"; indeed, the "concept of war provides cosmology, history, and eschatology and offers the reins of political control."[64] "Like the rituals provided by religious traditions, warfare is a participatory drama that exemplifies—and thus explains—the most profound aspects of life."[65] Here, we have moved from religion as a contributor to war to war itself as a kind of religious practice.

At times, Juergensmeyer admits the difficulty of separating religious violence from mere political violence: "Much of what I have said about religious terrorism in this book may be applied to other forms of political violence—especially those that are ideological and ethnic in nature."[66] In Juergensmeyer's earlier book *The New Cold War? Religious Nationalism Confronts the Secular State*, he writes, "Secular nationalism, like religion, embraces what one scholar calls 'a doctrine of destiny.' One can take this way of looking at secular nationalism a step further and state flatly, as did one author writing in 1960, that secular nationalism *is* 'a religion.' "[67] These are important concessions. If true, however, they subvert the entire basis of his argument, which is the sharp divide between religious and secular violence.

Nevertheless, Juergensmeyer attempts a summary of what distinguishes religious from secular violence. First, religious violence is "almost exclusively symbolic, performed in remarkably dramatic ways." Second, religious violence is "accompanied by strong claims of moral justification and enduring absolutism, characterized by the intensity of religious activists' commitment." Third, cosmic war is "beyond historical control." Although some secular ideas, such as class conflict, seem similar, they are thought to take place only on the social plane and within history. So in Maoism, persons can be separated from their class roles and reeducated. In cosmic war, satanic enemies cannot be transformed, but only destroyed. Fourth and finally, secular conflicts seek conclusion within their participants' lifetimes, but religious activists will wait for hundreds of years, or even for fulfillment in some transtemporal realm.

Therefore, there is no need for religious activists to compromise their goals nor to "contend with society's laws and limitations," since they are "obeying a higher authority."[68]

One can almost refute these four attempts to separate religious from secular violence using only Juergensmeyer's own words. First, Juergensmeyer himself states that all terrorism, even that of leftists and separatists motivated solely by political gain, exemplifies "performance violence."[69] There is no reason to suppose that Basque separatists killing police officers or the United States dropping nuclear weapons on civilian targets in Japan are acts that are any less symbolic or dramatic than Muslim Palestinians bombing Israeli buses or Israeli punitive raids on Palestinian neighborhoods. Second, as we have seen, Juergensmeyer himself writes of the absolutism of all war. Certainly, the wars fought by nation-states for supposedly mundane ends are couched in the strongest rhetoric of moral justification and historical duty—witness Operation Infinite Justice, the U.S. military's first name for the war on Afghanistan. Nor is there any warrant for supposing that the commitment of a U.S. Marine—*semper fidelis*—is any less "intense" than that of a Hamas militant, as if such a thing could be measured. Third, Juergensmeyer's own words quoted above indicate that war produces an all-or-nothing struggle against an enemy one is determined to destroy. In the clash of civilizations we witnessed in the early twenty-first century, the Pentagon did not seem any more interested in reeducating al-Qaeda than the latter was in reeducating the Great Satan. Fourth and finally, again in Juergensmeyer's own words, "[t]he concept of war provides cosmology, history, eschatology, and offers the reins of political control." Juergensmeyer himself says that U.S. leaders have given every indication that the "war against terror" will stretch indefinitely into the future, and Juergensmeyer comments that this war "seems so absolute and unyielding on both sides."[70] As Juergensmeyer also points out, war shuts down the possibility of compromise. He offers no empirical evidence that the presence or absence of belief in a transtemporal realm has any effect on one's willingness to flout human conventions regarding the conduct of war. Nor, by Juergensmeyer's own standards, does belief in a transtemporal realm distinguish religion from nonreligion; some of what counts as religion for Juergensmeyer—most Buddhist traditions, for example—have no such belief.

In a chapter on martyrdom, Juergensmeyer appeals to the work of René Girard to explain the connection between religion and violence. Juergensmeyer has many interesting insights about violence, symbolism, and social order, but his analysis is hobbled by the term religion. According to Juergensmeyer, martyrdom is a form of self-sacrifice and is therefore linked with sacrifice, which is the "most fundamental form of religiosity." In Girard's famous work on sacrifice, intragroup rivalries are kept from threatening the coherence of the group by focusing the group's aggression on a sacrificial victim. Juergensmeyer accepts this analysis but claims, *pace* Girard, that war is the context for sacrifice rather than the other way around. War is the basic dynamic that preserves group identity by erecting antinomies of we versus they, order versus chaos, good versus evil, truth versus falsehood. Furthermore, "[w]arfare...organizes social history into a storyline of persecution, conflict, and the hope of redemption, liberation, and conquest." In the next sentence, however, the subject changes from "warfare" in general to "cosmic war": "The enduring and seemingly ubiquitous image of cosmic war from ancient times to the present continues to give the rites of sacrifice their meaning."[71] Juergensmeyer seems to acknowledge that Girard's theory—and Juergensmeyer's own emendation of it—applies to societies in general, even supposedly secular ones.[72] Talk of sacrifice in war is endemic to modern nation-states: *Dulce et decorum est / Pro patria mori*. Nevertheless, Juergensmeyer wants to identify the social role of war in asserting order over chaos with religion.[73] Again, the argument oscillates between "religion contributes to violence understood in terms of symbolism" and "if it's violence understood in terms of symbolism, it must be religious."

Juergensmeyer could stop this oscillation by providing a definition of religion that would help to distinguish it from symbolism in general or public ritual in general, but he offers none. When he reports that Gerry Adams and the Irish Republican Army leadership emphatically considered their struggle against the British to be anticolonial, and not religious,[74] it is unclear how one would begin to decide this question by Juergensmeyer's standards. Juergensmeyer contends that those Catholics in Ireland who identified religion with the church would not think of the struggle as religious, "[b]ut those who thought of religion in the broadest sense, as part of a society's culture, saw the Republican position as a religious crusade."[75] If the conflict in Northern Ireland only becomes a religious conflict when religion is construed as some unspecified dimension of culture in general, then it seems we are left with two choices: either reconfigure the book as an exposition of the cultural or symbolic dimensions of violence, or, if something more specific is meant by religion, define religion and drop all the examples, such as that of Northern Ireland, that do not fit the more specific paradigm. Unfortunately, Juergensmeyer takes neither of these two roads to clarity.

Based on the title of the book—*Terror in the Mind of God*—one might expect that religion might specifically denote belief in God. However, of the three figures pictured beneath the title on the front cover—Aum Shinrikyo leader Shoko Asahara, Oklahoma City bomber Timothy McVeigh, and Islamic militant Osama bin Laden—only the last one professed belief in God.

Aum Shinrikyo was a nontheistic mélange of Buddhist, yogic, Daoist, and other practices, and McVeigh was a self-described agnostic. Juergensmeyer nevertheless identifies McVeigh as a "quasi-Christian" because he had some contacts with the antigovernment militia group Christian Identity.[76] Though he was an agnostic, Juergensmeyer says that McVeigh's action was "quasi-religious" because it involved a symbolic target and was set in the context of a larger historical drama of government versus the people, slavery versus liberty.[77] Similarly, the two Columbine High School students who gunned down their classmates in Colorado in 1999 were involved in the "quasi-religious 'trenchcoat' culture of gothic symbolism."[78] How this tragedy could be associated with religion is anybody's guess. Without some independent idea of what distinguishes religious symbolism from symbolism in general, the argument is always in danger of being thrown into reverse. Instead of showing how religion contributes to violence, whatever is violent and kooky gets identified as religious.

In a later book, *Global Rebellion* (2008), Juergensmeyer tries to take into account some of the historical work that has been done on the concept of religion. He cites Wilfred Cantwell Smith's work and states that religion means different things pre- and post-Enlightenment. Before the Enlightenment, religion included the public values that secularism now claims. Juergensmeyer cites Talal Asad's view that "the secular is a sort of advanced form of religion."[79] Juergensmeyer acknowledges that some nationalists have regarded secular nationalism as superior to religion because they think it is essentially different. Juergensmeyer tries to level the playing field, however, by acknowledging that the Western notion of secular nationalism is a Western construct,[80] and saying that the lines between religion and secular nationalism are blurred. He repeats a line from his earlier book *The New Cold War?* stating flatly that "secular nationalism is 'a religion.' "[81] Juergensmeyer cites Ninian Smart's contention that secular nationalism is a "tribal religion." Rather than subsuming secularism under the category religion, however, Juergensmeyer suggests that religion and secular nationalism be seen as two species of the genus "ideologies of order."[82]

Unfortunately, these attempts to historicize the concept of religion and to question the distinction between religion and the secular do not have much effect on the rest of Juergensmeyer's analysis. He continues to treat religion not as a modern construct but as a given feature of human societies in all times and places: "If the confrontation has been largely about religion, it will never disappear, since religious expression is central to culture and has endured over the millennia."[83] Although he says that "[r]eligious and political ideas have been intertwined throughout history and around the globe,"[84] he still tends to treat them as essentially different things that are subsequently combined.

Despite his comments early in the book about secular nationalism as a religion, the rest of the book treats religious and secular, and religious and political, as binary pairs that are mutually opposed. Thus, Juergensmeyer says in the conclusion of the book that the conflicts he has examined were political in origin, but then later became "religionized," which ratcheted up the potential for violence:

> Though religious ideas do not initially provoke the conflicts, as the case studies in this book make abundantly clear, they play an important role. The conditions that lead to conflict are typically matters of social and political identity—what makes individuals cohere as a community and how they are defined.... At some point in the conflict, however, usually at a time of frustration and desperation, the political and ideological contest becomes "religionized." Then what was primarily a worldly struggle takes on the aura of sacred conflict.[85]

Religion then adds a peculiarly dangerous and violent element by elevating merely mundane political conflict into a cosmic war. Religion by itself does not simply cause violence, but it has a unique capacity to exacerbate it: "Religious violence is especially savage and relentless since its perpetrators see it not merely as part of a worldly political battle but as a part of a scenario of divine conflict."[86]

Juergensmeyer's work is full of interesting empirical studies of the ideologies of violent groups and individuals. The attempt to build a general theory about religious—as opposed to nonreligious or secular—violence, however, is confused and serves to focus our attention on certain kinds of violence and away from others. Juergensmeyer's treatment of McVeigh is a good example of how this dynamic works. McVeigh spent three and a half years in the U.S. Army. After participating in the slaughter of a group of trapped Iraqi soldiers in the 1991 Gulf War, McVeigh is reported to have walked around taking snapshots of Iraqi corpses for his personal photo collection. When searching for the source of McVeigh's violence, however, Juergensmeyer does not mention his army training, but homes in instead on the fact that, although McVeigh was not affiliated with Christian Identity, he read its newsletter and made several phone calls to its compound on the Oklahoma-Arkansas border. He also once got a speeding ticket on the access road to the compound.[87] On this, and the fact that McVeigh read William Pierce's novel *The Turner Diaries*,[88] Juergensmeyer builds the case for the agnostic McVeigh as a religious warrior.

One can imagine the reaction of a Middle Eastern Muslim, who well might wonder why we need to track down small bands of Christian survivalists for evidence of divisive ideologies of total struggle against evil, when the Pentagon—with its half-trillion-dollar annual budget—is rife with such thinking. Indeed, as Juergensmeyer himself indicates, war and preparations for war require such a world view and raise the stakes to an all-or-nothing battle of us versus them. This is not, of course, to say that there is no value in studying fringe groups that do violence in the name of their beliefs, including Christian beliefs. It is rather to indicate that the theoretical divide between religious and secular violence is groundless and distracts attention from the violence of, for example, the putatively secular nation-state.

DAVID C. RAPOPORT. In his article "Some General Observations on Religion and Violence," from a symposium on René Girard's work, UCLA political theorist David C. Rapoport gives five reasons that religion and violence are related. Although it is somewhat artificial to put Rapoport's work in the second of my three types of argument—"religion is divisive"—all five of Rapoport's reasons are connected to the central issue Girard raises: identity and exclusion as the basis for social order. As a political scientist, the dividing and uniting of the body politic is the primary lens through which Rapoport views the question of religion and violence.

The first of Rapoport's five reasons concerns the capacity of religion to inspire ultimate commitment:

> Perhaps circumstances and context frame the disposition towards violence. But some relevant element seems to be inherent in the nature of religion itself. One such element is the capacity of religion to inspire total loyalties or commitments, and in this respect, it is difficult to imagine anything which surpasses the religious community. Religion has often had formidable rivals; in the modern world the nation sometimes has surpassed religion as a focus of loyalties, though significantly there is [an] increasing propensity for academics to speak of "civic religion" when discussing national symbols and rites. In any case, the ascendancy of the nation has occupied but a brief moment in history so far, and in a limited portion of the world—all of which only more underscores the durability and special significance of religion.[89]

Note the role that loyalty to the nation plays in this passage. Nationalism often acts like religion and is sometimes called a religion, but it is not a religion. We might expect Rapoport to conclude that nationalism is one of a class of world views that produce "total" loyalties—a class perhaps including Christianity, Islam, Marxism, and so on—and that such world views lend themselves to violent behavior under certain conditions. Instead, Rapoport uses the fact that nationalism inspires total commitments that produce violence as evidence that *religion* is particularly disposed toward violence. Why? Because sometimes nationalism is called "civic religion," even though it is not a religion. Why is nationalism not a religion? Presumably because nationalism is a secular phenomenon. Nowhere in the article does Rapoport try to lay out what separates religion from what is not religion. Clearly, though, Rapoport regards religion and national loyalties as two entirely different things. The nation has a history. Religion, on the other hand, seems to have an essential nature untouched by the vicissitudes of history. In Rapoport's view, the nation is a modern Western invention. Religion is timeless and universal. In this view, religion goes back to the very origin of culture and has to do with developing ways to deal with predicaments of order and disorder, domesticating violence through religious images and language.

The second of Rapoport's reasons that religion and violence are peculiarly linked is that religious language is full of violence, and therefore lends itself to bloody causes. He illustrates this point by giving several examples of explicitly secular movements that have appropriated religious language in the service of violence: the Stern Gang in Israel, Saddam Hussein's Ba'ath Socialist Party, and the Palestine Liberation Organization. Given that the Stern Gang was "secular," the Ba'ath Party "made great strides in transforming Iraq into a secular state," and the PLO "has always emphasized its secular character,"[90] how does their violence count against religion? Rapoport quotes Abraham Stern:

> Like my father who carried his bag
> With a prayer shawl to the synagogue on the Sabbath
> So I will carry holy rifles in my bag
> To the prayer service of iron with a regenerated quorum
> Like my mother who lit candles on the festival eve
> So I will light a torch for those revered in praise
> Like my father who taught me to read in Torah
> I will teach my pupils; stand to arms, kneel and shoot
> Because there is a religion of redemption—
>   a religion of the war of liberation
> Whoever accepts it—be blessed: whoever denies it—be cursed.[91]

Instead of concluding that secular liberation movements can inspire just as much passion and commitment and violence as religious movements can—or that the Stern Gang was, as Stern himself acknowledged, dedicated to a kind of religion, which throws the whole religious-secular distinction into question— Rapoport offers Stern's poem as evidence that *religion* has a disposition toward violence. As we saw above with nationalism, here secular terrorism acts like a religion and is called a religion, but is not a religion, even though it counts as evidence of religion's violent tendencies.

Rapoport's third reason to link religion and violence comes directly from his reading of Girard. In brief, the "sole purpose" of religion is to deflect intramural violence and project it, through sacrifice, onto a ritual object. Violence is contained by violence. Rapoport writes that political theorists will find this argument familiar; Girard's conclusions jibe with those of Thomas Hobbes. For Hobbes, the state contains the violence of all against all by enacting a different kind of violence, namely, the absolute coercive power of the state through its judiciary function. Whether or not one agrees with Hobbes's precise formulation, "virtually all social scientists agree that the state is distinguished by its unique relationship to violence."[92] According to Rapoport, Girard also sees the state and religion as kin, but suggests that the state arises when religion loses some of its power to control violence. Sacrificial ritual and the judiciary share the same function, but the judiciary is more effective. Rapoport agrees, but contends that the state's ability to employ violence on a scale hitherto unimaginable depends on broad social agreement on the state's legitimacy, and the state's legitimacy depends on religion:

> Indeed, in some crucial respects, the capacity of religion to generate and control violence may be greater than that of the state. The state's administrative instruments are in principle more effective, but then in the long history of the state, religion has been an essential and quite possibly the most important ingredient in the state's legitimacy.[93]

How does one explain the simultaneous secularization of the state and the exponential growth of state power in the modern era? According to Rapoport, grounding the state on wholly secular principles is a recent phenomenon dating only to the eighteenth century, and current religious revivals suggest that it may not be an adequate or lasting phenomenon. Even given secularization, "Girard's explanation of the kinship between religion and the state helps us understand better why those indifferent or hostile to religion still find its language so attractive."[94] Even the secular state, therefore, still finds the roots for its violence in religion.

Rapoport's fourth and fifth reasons for linking religion and violence follow his reading of the Girardian logic of religion and state. The fourth has to do with the tendency of religions and states to return to their origins in times of crisis, and the origins of both are in violence. Here, Rapoport claims the authority of Machiavelli, who writes, "For, as all religions, republics and monarchies must have within themselves some goodness, by means of which they obtain their first growth and reputation, and as in the process of time this goodness becomes corrupted, it will of necessity destroy the body unless something intervenes to bring it back to its normal condition."[95] The fifth reason has to do with the desperation many contemporary religious believers feel when they believe that time is running out. Messianic or millenialist expectations make believers think they must act with sudden violence. (Note that this contention is the opposite of Juergensmeyer's conclusion that religious activists are prone to violence because their time frame is unlimited and they are willing to fight with no end in sight.) Rapoport connects this final reason with his analysis of religion and the state in this manner:

> For animals and humans, as individuals or in groups, the will to fight is greatly intensified by the conviction that one is trapped and by the belief that existence is at stake. This is why states nearly always try to justify their wars as responses to aggression: as Americans we all know that the only war in which our country was united began at Pearl Harbor.[96]

How the American response to Pearl Harbor is related to religious themes like messianism or millennialism is unclear. Rapoport concludes his analysis of the reasons that religion is disposed to violence by saying, "Social scientists often stress that the state and violence are inseparable and, therefore, Girard's analysis resonates; the reasons he provides for making violence *the* core of religion are the same ones that we offer for linking violence to the state."[97]

What does the word religion pick out in this analysis? At many points, religion seems to be synonymous with something like "the ideologies, rituals, and institutions through which violence is controlled and legitimated in any given social order." If one substitutes some such locution for the word religion in Rapoport's analysis, a great deal of clarity is gained. To do so, however, threatens the distinction between the religious and the secular, and so Rapoport must persist in assuming that religion is something else. What exactly that something else is, he never says, but religion would appear to be a sui generis set of beliefs and practices, distinct from secular reality, which controls and legitimates violence in *religious* social orders but only secondarily lends itself to legitimating *nonreligious* social orders such as the modern state. All of which is tautologous.

At the heart of the problem here is an equivocation in the use of the term religion. On the one hand, religion is used to signify (1) something sui generis, theoretically distinguishable from other cultural activities in any given time and place. Religion is what modern Westerners are talking about when they talk about Buddhism, or Christianity, or Catholicism, or Lutheranism, or Sikhism. The secular is what remains when religion is separated out; the secular indicates the relative absence, or lack of public relevance, of religion. On the other hand, religion is used to signify (2) the myths and practices by which violence is legitimated and controlled in any social order. Girard employs the second of these two uses. According to Girard, "Any phenomenon associated with the acts of remembering, commemorating, and perpetuating a unanimity that springs from the murder of a surrogate victim can be termed 'religious.' "[98] "Religion" is defined in the glossary of *The Girard Reader* as "indistinguishable from culture," at least in traditional societies. Culture is defined as "[e]verything—assumptions and common ideas, roles, structures, etc.—which enables human beings to exist together without being overcome by chaos, violence, and random murder."[99]

In traditional societies, Girard is clear, religion does not pick out something distinct from culture in general. With regard to modern societies, Girard sometimes contrasts religion with "modern theory"[100] and also contrasts it with the judicial system, which would appear to put social order on a more rational basis. Religion then sometimes appears in Girard's writings as an archaism associated with myth and sacrifice; religion has been replaced by the judiciary which, as Rapoport notes, Girard believes is more effective in containing the menace of private vengeance.[101] However, Girard claims that both rudimentary sacrifice and more advanced judicial forms of containment are both "imbued with religious concepts":

> *Religion* in its broadest sense, then, must be another term for that obscurity that surrounds man's efforts to defend himself by curative or preventative means against his own violence. It is that enigmatic quality that pervades the judicial system when that system replaces sacrifice. This obscurity coincides with the transcendental effectiveness of a violence that is holy, legal, and legitimate successfully opposed to a violence that is unjust, illegal, and illegitimate.[102]

In other words, secular culture is also religious. Girard regards modern political theorists' attempts to see the origins of society in a "social contract" based on "reason" or "mutual self-interest" as based on a fundamental incapacity to understand religion, an incapacity which itself "is mythic in character, since it perpetuates the religion's own misapprehensions in regard to violence."[103] Girard argues that the belief in a divide between the religious and the secular itself has a religious purpose: "The failure of modern man to grasp the nature of religion has served to perpetuate its effects. Our lack of belief serves the same function in our society that religion serves in societies more directly exposed to essential violence."[104] What he means is that the belief in a fundamental divide between the rational, secular state and an irrational, mystifying religion itself has a mystifying function, a function that staves off the disintegration of the social order.[105] It is for this reason that Girard states, "There is no society without religion because without religion society cannot exist."[106] Even secular societies are religious. Girard does, however, hold out the hope that society can be progressively demythologized by an increased consciousness of the mechanism of victimization. This is accomplished, however, not by a progressive secularization, but by the countermythical thrust of the Christian story found in the scriptures.[107] For Girard, any moves that Western culture has made away from scapegoating are not the result of the Enlightenment and secularization, but the result of the gospel's influence.[108]

As we have seen, Girard sometimes limits religion to sacrifice and sometimes uses the term more broadly to include the supposedly more rational forms of social order like the modern judiciary. In neither case does Girard support arguments that violence is peculiarly linked to religion in the first sense of religion (1) indicated above. Indeed, Girard *counters* such arguments by denying that religion picks out any distinct cultural activity in traditional societies and by blurring the distinction between religious and secular in modern societies. Whatever one thinks of the merits of Girard's theory, the subject of his argument about religion is not some set of beliefs and practices composed of the world religions: Buddhism, Christianity, Sikhism, etc. Girard's argument is about the violent preservation of social orders, including secular ones. Girard's solution to the problem of violence, therefore, is not secularization. Girard's solution to the problem of violence is a "religious" one: he believes that Jesus Christ, the victim who ends all sacrifice, is *the* key to undoing violence. The gospel undoes myth. By no means does Girard suggest that Christians—or Buddhists, Sikhs, etc.—are absolved from deep complicity in the violent preservation of social order. What is clear, however, is that Girard's theory cannot be employed to advance the secularist argument that religion is linked to violence without equivocating on the term religion.

Rapoport's use of Girard to analyze the state's use of violence to contain violence is helpful insofar as it shows that secular social orders can be just as violent as other social orders. It is not helpful insofar as it is used to reinforce a putative dichotomy between religion and the secular and to blame the violence of the latter on the former. If Rapoport is true to his Girardian analysis, the dichotomy simply will not hold.

Religion Is Not Rational

BHIKHU PAREKH. There is a third type of argument about religion and violence, one with affinities to claims of absolutism, but more focused on the
subjective dimensions of religious belief. The claim here is that religion is
especially prone to violence because it produces a particular intensity of nonrational or irrational passion that is not subject to the firm control of reason.
"Fervor," "rage," "passion," "fanaticism," "zeal," and similar words are used to
describe the mental state of religious actors who are driven to violence. These
terms not only pervade the journalistic coverage of public religion, but are also
found in much of the scholarly literature. The following passage from Bhikhu
Parekh, a professor of political theory at Hull University, sums up much of this
line of thinking:

> Although religion can make a valuable contribution to political life, it
> can also be a pernicious influence, as liberals rightly highlight. It is
> often absolutist, self-righteous, arrogant, dogmatic, and impatient of
> compromise. It arouses powerful and sometimes irrational impulses
> and can easily destabilize society, cause political havoc, and create
> a veritable hell on earth. Since it is generally of ancient origin, it is
> sometimes deeply conservative, hidebound, insensitive to changes in
> the social climate and people's moral aspirations, and harbors a deep
> antifemale bias. It often breeds intolerance of other religions as well
> as of internal dissent, and has a propensity towards violence.[109]

Here, religion is located in the realm of nonrational, and sometimes
irrational, impulses. Precisely as such, religion threatens the rational ordering of society. Here, also, religion is identified as archaic, a throwback to
less advanced times. This story has important affinities with the dominant
Enlightenment narrative that regards religion as a primitive and dangerous
leftover opposed to reason and progress. Parekh does not, however, conclude
that religion should be extirpated or fully privatized. Parekh has been a sympathetic critic of liberalism and believes that liberalism should be more hos-
pitable to public expressions of different cultures and religions.[110] Religion
should only be domesticated and subjected in public "to the constraints and
discipline of political life."[111] Indeed, religion can make a positive contribution to public life, for "though religion has been a force for evil, it has also
been a force for good, generating a kind of energy, commitment, passion,
and willingness to suffer that sometimes have been lacking in wholly secular motivations."[112] Religion is still identified with nonrational impulses,
but these can be directed toward good as well as evil purposes. Furthermore,

these nonrational impulses seem to be more characteristic of the religious than of the secular.

Parekh would like to challenge what he thinks is a common liberal assumption that religion is concerned with the otherworldly and should be assiduously separated from worldly secular matters. He does so, however, by assuming that religion and the secular are two essentially different enterprises, but "religion represents one distinct perspective on" secular matters:

> Life and property are clearly secular matters. But they raise such
> questions as when life begins and ends, whether human life should
> enjoy absolute priority over animal life, what respect for it entails, and
> whether and when the agent or society may justifiably terminate it,
> as well as why property should be protected, within what limits, what
> is to be done when it damages human lives, and so on. Every religion
> has a view on and is actively interested in these and related questions.
> Matters of global justice, universal human rights, legitimacy of war,
> whether a country has obligations to outsiders and how they limit its
> pursuit of its national interests, and the human relation to nature are
> all secular but, again, religion has much to say about them.[113]

Given what comes after, it is hard to make sense of the opening sentence in this passage. If religion is so thoroughly entwined with "life" and "property," why are they clearly secular matters, given that secular apparently defines what is essentially not religious? What could it possibly mean to define religion in such a way that "life" falls outside its direct purview? A similar observation would apply to "global justice" and "the human relation to nature," to cite only the most obvious examples in this passage.

Some attempt to define the difference between religion and the secular would be of great help here, but none is forthcoming. In fact, Parekh spends much of his effort blurring the lines between religion and the secular. For example, "the state has traditionally claimed to monopolize morality, regarding its interests as being of the highest importance and deserving of the greatest sacrifices."[114] This despite the fact that Parekh has identified a willingness to suffer with religion and would presumably acknowledge that morality falls into religion's ambit as well. Parekh even admits that "several secular ideologies, such as some varieties of Marxism, conservatism, and even liberalism have a quasi-religious orientation and form, and conversely formally religious languages sometimes have a secular content, so that the dividing line between a secular and a religious language is sometimes difficult to draw."[115] If this is true, where does it leave his searing indictment of the dangers peculiarly inherent to religion? Powerful nonrational impulses are suddenly popping up all over, including in liberalism itself, forcing the creation of the category "quasi-religious" to try somehow to corral them all back under the heading of religion. But if liberalism—which is based on the distinction between religion and the secular—is itself a kind of religion, then the whole religious-secular distinction is in danger of crumbling into a heap of contradictions.

R. SCOTT APPLEBY. One of the most critically aware examples of the argument based on the nonrational aspect of religion comes from historian R. Scott Appleby. As director of the Kroc Institute for International Peace Studies at the University of Notre Dame, Appleby has been influential in countering the argument that religion *necessarily* tends toward violence. According to Appleby, religion has two faces, hence the title of his descriptively rich work on religion and violence, *The Ambivalence of the Sacred: Religion, Violence, and Reconciliation*. Religion is indeed "powerful medicine," but its driving passion can be and is used in the service of peace as well as in the service of violence. Both aspects of religion are traceable to the nonrational core of religion. On the one hand, religion has an "ability to sustain cycles of violence beyond the point of rational calculation and enlightened self-interest."[116] On the other hand, "religious fervor—unrestrained religious commitment"[117] does not inevitably lead to violence. There are also many examples of peaceable believers "inspired by 'sacred rage' against racial, ethnic, and religious discrimination"[118]—and a host of other social ills:

> Both the extremist and the peacemaker are militants. Both types "go to extremes" of self-sacrifice in devotion to the sacred; both claim to be "radical," or rooted in and renewing the fundamental truths of their religious traditions. In these ways they distinguish themselves from people not motivated by religious commitments—and from the vast middle ground of believers.[119]

Appleby is careful to provide a definition of religion to guide his analysis:

> Religion is the human response to a reality perceived as sacred. In the next chapter I explore the various meanings of "the sacred." At this point, suffice it to say that religion, as interpreter of the sacred, discloses and celebrates the transcendent source and significance of human existence. So ambitious an enterprise requires a formidable array of symbolic, moral, and organizational resources. In a common formula: religion embraces a creed, a cult, a code of conduct, and a confessional community. A creed defines the standard of beliefs and values concerning the ultimate origin, meaning, and purpose of life.

It develops from myths—symbol-laden narratives of sacred encounters—and finds official expression in doctrines and dogmas. Cult
encompasses the prayers, devotions, spiritual disciplines, and patterns of communal worship that give richly suggestive ritual expression to the creed. A code of conduct defines the explicit moral norms
governing the behavior of those who belong to the confessional
community. Thus religion constitutes an integral culture, capable
of forming personal and social identity and influencing subsequent
experience and behavior in profound ways.[120]

Here, questions could be raised about the absence of creeds, doctrines, and
dogmas from some things that Appleby would consider to be religions—
Hinduism and Buddhism, for example. Nevertheless, the emphasis on creed
does not seem to be central to Appleby's definition. What appears to separate
religion from other "integral cultures" that form personal and social identity
is the perceived encounter with the sacred. It is the sacred that accounts for
the ambivalent nature of religion, its capacity for extremes of violence and
peace.

For a definition of the sacred, Appleby turns to Rudolf Otto's *Das Heilige*,
published in 1917 and translated into English as *The Idea of the Holy*. Appleby
uses the terms "holy" and "sacred" interchangeably as translations of Otto's
term *das Heilige*. For Otto, the sacred is a category of interpretation peculiar to
religion. According to Appleby, Otto defines the sacred as "what remains of religion when its rational and ethical elements have been excluded."[121] The sacred
is a transhistorical and transcultural reality experienced as an undifferentiated
power beyond the moral, neither good nor evil in its immediacy. The sacred
projects a *numinous* quality that evokes extraordinary feelings in the devout.
The feeling of the numinous may be a "gentle tide" or "thrillingly vibrant," or it
may erupt suddenly into "the strangest excitements" and "intoxicated frenzy."
It has "wild," "demonic," and "barbaric" forms that can lead either to "grisly
horror" or "something beautiful."[122] The overpowering and uncontrollable
presence of the sacred is, in Otto's words, *mysterium tremendum et fascinans*; it
evokes both terrible dread and fascination. According to Appleby, this experience is translated into religion by limited human faculties, but as such it can
never be fully domesticated by human reason or language: "Religion is both
powerfully disclosive of the sacred and radically limited in its ability to understand what it discloses."[123] The two-sided power of the feeling of the numinous
and the inability to capture the sacred with human faculties of reason accounts
for the fundamental ambivalence of religion, its ability to unleash powers of
life and of death. Despite the title of the book, Appleby makes clear that the

sacred itself need not be ambivalent; only the human perception thereof—that is, religion—is fundamentally ambivalent.[124]

Appleby is keen to emphasize the nonrational and uncontrollable power of the encounter with the sacred, more keen than Otto himself, in fact. Otto does not define the sacred as that which remains when religion is stripped of its rational and ethical elements. Rather, it is the numinous that remains when *das Heilige*, the holy or sacred, is stripped of its ethical and rational elements.[125] A more serious difficulty is that Appleby defines religion in terms of the sacred, and the sacred in terms of religion; religion is a response to the sacred, and the sacred is what remains of religion when the rational and ethical elements are stripped away. Appleby's definition of religion depends on the acceptance of Otto's contention that, at the heart of the sacred, there exists a unique numinous state of mind that is essentially religious. Appleby's definition of religion would not be merely circular if Otto could provide independent verification of the existence of the numinous as he defines it. However, as Otto says, "[t]his mental state is perfectly *sui generis* and irreducible to any other; and therefore, like every absolutely primary and elementary datum, while it admits of being discussed, it cannot be strictly defined."[126] Otto contends further that *das Heilige*, in both its rational and nonrational components, is a *"purely a priori category"* of mind not subject to direct empirical verification.[127] Otto's way of investigation, therefore, is to describe the feelings of the numinous "by adducing feelings akin to them for the purpose of analogy or contrast, and by the use of metaphor and symbolic expressions, to make the states of mind we are investigating ring out, as it were, of themselves."[128] For example, Otto tries to distinguish natural feelings of dread from those associated with the sacred:

> We say: "my blood ran icy cold," and "my flesh crept." The "cold blood" feeling may be a symptom of ordinary, natural fear, but there is something non-natural or supernatural about the symptom of "creeping flesh." And any one who is capable of more precise introspection must recognize that the distinction between such a "dread" and natural fear is not simply one of degree and intensity.[129]

This capability for precise introspection is not based either on revelation or empirical investigation but appears to be an intuitive skill that some people have and some don't, like mind reading or dowsing.

For Otto, the sacred is a mysterious yet universal aspect of human experience that cannot be directly studied. Otto's analysis prioritizes an internal, intuitive, essentialist, and ahistorical category of experience that, by its nature, is secreted away in the heart of the individual and therefore unavailable to the researcher. To study institutions, bodies, symbols, political arrangements, and so forth is not to study the religious object in itself. As a historian, Appleby is aware of the pitfalls of this subjective approach. After defining religion, Appleby registers this caveat:

> It is erroneous...to imagine that some kind of transhistorical, transcultural "essence" determines the attitudes and practices of a religion's adherents apart from the concrete social and cultural circumstances in which they live. Thus I ask the reader at the outset to imagine invisible quotation marks surrounding and thereby qualifying every use of general terms like "extremist," "liberal," "militant," and even "religion."[130]

This is a salutary warning, but it directly conflicts with Appleby's definition of religion in terms of Otto's sacred. Appleby seems torn between, on the one hand, a descriptive approach to the ways in which Muslims and Christians, for example, use symbols in the pursuit of violence and, on the other hand, the need for a transhistorical and transcultural essence of religion in order to pursue a more general argument about religion and violence.

Appleby's book is full of careful descriptions of the way that symbolism drawn from Christian, Hindu, Muslim, and other traditions is used in the pursuit of both violence and peace. However, the analysis is often hampered, rather than helped, by his attempt to define religion. Such a definition makes it necessary for Appleby to say, for example, that phenomena such as "political Islam" and "Hindu nationalism" are "hybrids" of religion and politics,[131] as if one could make sense of a purely religious Islam prior to its being "mixed" with politics or a Hinduism unrelated to what it means to be Indian. Appleby acknowledges that Hinduism "lacks a strong historical sense of itself as an organized religion," but he nevertheless treats Hinduism as a religion that secondarily "lends itself" to nationalist causes.[132]

The attempt to safeguard an essentialist account of religion is especially imperiled when the term "ethnoreligious" is introduced into the study of contemporary violence. According to Appleby, three-quarters of the world's civil wars between 1960 and 1990 were driven by ethnoreligious concerns, as national identity came to be based more on ethnic and religious lines. "Like religion, ethnicity is a notoriously open-ended concept," but Appleby uses Weber's definition of ethnic groups as "those human groups that entertain *a subjective belief* in their common descent because of similarity of physical types or customs or both, or because of the memories of colonization and migration."[133] Under this definition, it is not clear why Hindus or Jews or even Muslims would not qualify as ethnic groups. Appleby acknowledges that the "distinctions between religion and ethnicity as bases for nationalism are seldom clear in practice."[134] As for the civil wars, "[m]any of these conflicts are called 'ethnoreligious' because it is virtually impossible to disaggregate the precise roles of religion and ethnicity."[135] Nevertheless, Appleby still seems, in places, to regard such disaggregation as possible and necessary. For example, in this sentence—"religious actors may identify their tradition so closely with the fate of a people or a nation that they perceive a threat to either as a threat to the sacred"[136]—the sacredness of the nation must be attributed to the identification of the nation with a religious tradition, and not to nationalism itself.

Elsewhere, Appleby acknowledges that ethnic identity *itself*—stories of birth and blood, the feeling of attraction to one's group and repulsion to outsiders—has a "normative dimension," reveals "inexhaustible depths of value and meaning," has a "transcendent dimension," and invokes "sacred warrants." In the face of this evidence that ethnicity qualifies as religion under his own definition of religion, Appleby nevertheless attributes these dimensions of ethnicity to the "role of religion" in ethnic conflicts.[137] On Appleby's own terms, it would make more sense simply to acknowledge that ethnicity and nationalism evoke attachments that are just as nonrational and transcendent as Christian or Muslim faith. To do so would threaten the singularity and peculiarity of religion as an irrational cause of violence, however, and Appleby seems compelled to pin the violence on religion. Appleby need not deny that ethnicity and nationalism can be irrational and violent too, but the more he does so, the less of an argument about religion and violence he has to make. So he must preserve something unique about religion; even if other things can be irrational and violent, religion is peculiarly so, because of the mystical, empirically unverifiable encounter with the *mysterium tremendum et fascinans*.

There is no point in trying to exonerate Yugoslav Christians and Muslims and their faith commitments from complicity in the violence that rent their nation. Appleby's analysis of the conflict in the former Yugoslavia gives a richly detailed description of Christian and Muslim participation in the violence, the use of Christian and Muslim symbols to legitimate violence, and the complicity of some churches and mosques in condoning the violence. What it does not do is provide a serious warrant for attributing violence to a sui generis interior impulse called religion. Appleby quite rightly criticizes those apologists who, in analyzing the conflict in the former Yugoslavia "downplayed the religious dimension of the war and argued that political, economic, and cultural factors were far more prominent in causing and sustaining it—as if 'culture' were a category somehow independent of religion."[138] Unfortunately, Appleby continues to treat religion as if it were a category somehow independent of culture. Responding to claims that the conflicts in the former Yugoslavia were ethnonationalist and not religious and that Yugoslavia had been extensively secularized under Tito, Appleby uses the violence itself as evidence of religion's influence: "Indeed, one might conclude that the enormity of the aggressors' acts, the demonic character of which one observer described as 'beyond evil,' indicates the presence of *intense* 'religious impulses or emotion.' "[139] If the very occurrence of intense violence can be used as evidence of the presence of religion, then we have moved from empirical evidence that religion causes violence to an a priori commitment to such a claim. As in Juergensmeyer, the argument gets thrown into reverse; if it is violent and irrational, it must be religious.

Appleby continues on to acknowledge that, under Tito, religious practice fell, indifference and ignorance of religious doctrines rose, and the influence of official church representatives declined. Appleby acknowledges that this situation of "religious illiteracy" increased the likelihood of collective violence in the post-Tito era. Far from letting religion off the hook, however, Appleby claims that, although religiously illiterate, the people remained religious. The religious sensibilities of the populace were driven underground, into the subconscious, drawing on "superstition, racial prejudice, half-forgotten bits of sacred scripture, and local custom." The manipulation of the volatility and passion of such "folk religion" for violent ends becomes, for Appleby, another element in the argument for the ambivalent nature of religion.[140] Here, the argument takes the form of identifying religion with primitive, nonrational impulses that can be used in the service of violence. Despite his best historical instincts and careful descriptive work, Appleby is poorly served by the a priori and essentialist presuppositions of Otto's definition of religion.

Much of Appleby's book is devoted to examples of the power of religious belief being harnessed for peace making. This is helpful, but less helpful than it could be, because religion is still a product of nonrational impulses secreted away in the consciousness of the individual and unavailable to empirical observation. The danger is that, despite the author's best efforts, his general theory of religion and violence will reinforce the tendency to denigrate some forms of violence as primitive and irrational, and thereby call our attention away from other supposedly more rational forms of violence. For Westerners, it is comforting, for example, to find the source of Iranian Islamic militancy in some mysterious encounter with the sacred, instead of in the not-so-mysterious encounter of Iran with U.S. and British military and economic might. In 1979, when our television screens were suddenly filled with black-robed militants in Tehran chanting and pumping fists, it was more convenient to blame the matter on a mystifying irrational religious experience than examine the empirical data, which would include the U.S.-backed overthrow of a democratically elected Iranian government in 1953 and the installation of the Shah's brutal regime.

I am not advocating the reduction of Islam to political and social causes, but rather pointing out the impossibility of reducing Islam to a core nonrational, nonempirical, personal experience of the sacred, which is only subsequently surrounded by various social and political institutions. The irony is that such a reduction as Otto recommends is not based on empirical observation and can be regarded as itself a form of mystification.

CHARLES SELENGUT. Sociologist Charles Selengut's *Sacred Fury: Understanding Religious Violence* is something of a survey of theories of religious violence. Selengut advocates a "holistic" approach to religious violence, and as such his five chapters are organized around a variety of themes, perspectives, and methodologies: scriptural obligations, psychological perspectives, apocalyptic violence, civilizational clashes, and lastly, religious suffering, martyrdom, and sexual violence. As the title of the book indicates, however, Selengut tends to focus on the essential nonrational nature of religion and its ability to whip up violent fury. Underneath all of the different explanations of religious violence, there remains an irreducible nonrational core of religion that eludes investigation. Despite his advocacy of a multidisciplinary approach to the problem, he concludes, "The nature of religious faith and commitment always remains personal, idiosyncratic, and, in the final analysis, beyond scientific understanding."[141] Religion is a transhistorical and transcultural phenomenon. As in Appleby, all sorts of mundane factors can affect religious violence, but ultimately, Selengut contends, the unique relationship of religion and violence is due to a core faith commitment that is beyond rational control and comprehension.

Why is there a unique relationship between religion and violence? In his introduction, Selengut explains:

> Religious faith is different than other commitments and the rules and directives of religion are understood by the faithful to be entirely outside ordinary social rules and interactions.... Ordinary judgment, canons of logic, and evaluation of behavior simply do not apply to religious activity. This is something that highly secularized scholars, diplomats, and ordinary people, particularly those from Europeanized Western countries with a strong enlightenment tradition, find it difficult to acknowledge: different logics and moralities govern decision making in fervently religious communities.[142]

Selengut repeatedly emphasizes the wide divide between religion and rationality. Supernatural rewards for martyrdom and religious suicide "are believed to occur in a world which is beyond scientific and rational understanding."[143]

Religious zealots feel they must resist the temptation to substitute "reasoning, compassion, and empathy" for the imperative to wage war.[144] Holy wars are examples of what Peter Berger calls "cosmization," that is, "activities that occur in the ordinary routine world of human existence but are simultaneously enacted in a supernatural realm of divine truth whose significance transcends all human understanding."[145]

Selengut tries very hard to treat the subjects of his research fairly. Some who write on religious violence are more judgmental or defensive: "We take a more neutral academic view, sometimes referred to as 'value neutrality,' in which we seek to understand the unique confluence of history, religion, politics, and group psychology that gives rise to religious violence; we will not render any particular judgments."[146] Nevertheless, Selengut's very confidence in his objectivity cannot help but establish a sharp dichotomy between secular, Western rationality and religious, non-Western irrationality:

> Faith and religious behavior are not based upon science, practical politics, or Western notions of logic or efficiency but on following the word of God regardless of the cost. Holy wars, as this perspective makes clear, may not be amenable to logical and rational solutions. Faithful holy warriors, whether in Afghanistan, Israel, Palestine, or Florida, live in a psychic and social reality entirely different from the world inhabited by secularized people. They think and feel differently about life and death, war and peace, war and killing, or dying a martyr's death.[147]

At this point in his argument, Selengut is trying to convince his Western audience that they must give up their assumptions of universal secularization and come to understand that there are people out there who think in radically different ways from them. Selengut seems to be trying to appreciate difference and Otherness. The lens through which the Otherness of religious persons is seen, however, is entirely Western. We are rational, logical, and practical. They "think and feel differently" in ways that put them "entirely outside ordinary social rules."

This lens affects the way that Selengut tells history: "Unlike Islam, Christianity has gone through an intense and protracted experience with secularization. Christians today, with some sectarian exceptions, recognize that religion in contemporary societies is primarily a private and voluntary matter over which the state and the clergy have no coercive authority."[148] By passing through the Enlightenment, Christianity has gone from the Inquisition to a greater tolerance for pluralism and a renunciation of religious violence. In Selengut's telling, these are not just contingent events, but a kind of natural progress to a higher level of understanding: "The inquisitional period illustrates the nature of a universalistic religion at a particular point in religious evolution."[149] It follows that Islam is simply at a more primitive stage of religious evolution. Modernity, which is equated with Western values, is presented as a reality with which Islam must deal. Religious violence results when Muslims refuse to either surrender to this reality or reinterpret their beliefs in its light.[150]

Selengut gives a definition of violence[151] but, as is the norm for literature on religion and violence, makes no attempt to define religion. Nevertheless, he is confident that there is a clear distinction between religious and non-religious violence. The primary difference is in the interpretation that religious people give to their acts of violence: "The violence in holy war is not conventional human violence, where individuals or groups contend with one another for secular goals such as money, power, or status; they are sacred events, being fought for God and his honor."[152] This will prove to be a very hard distinction to maintain during the course of Selengut's own analysis. For example, in describing holy war among Christians, Selengut says that "the just war doctrine has functioned effectively, as James Johnston illustrates, as holy war doctrine."[153] According to Selengut, Christianity was pacifistic for its first three centuries, but embraced the just-war/holy-war doctrine when it became identified with the Roman state: "Being in power and concerned with security and order gradually forced Christianity to articulate a holy war doctrine to justify violence in the name of religion."[154] If this is true, it directly contradicts Selengut's attempt above to distinguish holy war from "conventional human violence." Christianity only began to engage in holy war when it took on the "secular goals" of the state: power, security, and order.

In his chapter on psychological perspectives on religious violence, Selengut summarizes the argument this way:

> The psychological perspective does not focus on specific theological issues or matters of faith, but analyzes violence as a way a social collectivity deals with envy, anger, and frustration. According to psychological theorists, the accumulated aggression, envy, and conflict within any society must find an outlet or the group itself will be destroyed by internal conflict and rivalry. Religious battles against competitors or those labeled enemies, in this view, are merely ways of allowing the human collectivity to express its pent-up anger. The violence expressed by the group takes religious form and is justified by religious vocabulary, but it is primarily a way to get rid of anger and aggression that, if left uncontrolled, would jeopardize

social order and coherence. Put bluntly, religious battles are not
about religion but about psychological issues and dilemmas that take
religious form.[155]

What could it mean to say that "religious battles are not about religion" but
take religious form? As in Rapoport, the meaning of the term religion oscillates in this argument between (1) some set of ideas and institutions, which
commonly includes Christianity, Islam, Judaism, Buddhism, Hinduism, etc.,
and (2) the myths and practices by which any social order—including secular
ones—deals with conflict. Only by equivocating on the meaning of religion
could a secular society resolve its conflicts in a religious way. For example,
Selengut uses Girard to analyze the conflict between Orthodox Jews and secular Jews in modern Israel. According to Selengut, the two groups were able to
resolve their conflict by uniting behind the invasion of Palestinian territories
in the spring of 2002. This, he says, is an example of Girard's idea that "religious wars" deflect intragroup violence onto an external enemy.[156] The Israeli
example may indeed be an illustration of Girard's thesis about how societies
deal with conflict, but to say that secular Jews engage in religious wars is to
invite nonsense, given that secular means nonreligious. If every society, secular or religious, deals with internal conflict by the same psychological mechanism, then Selengut's analysis is of violence as such, not religious violence.
There is simply no basis on these grounds for trying to separate religious from
secular violence.

   In his chapter on "civilizational perspectives" on religious violence,
Selengut appropriates Samuel Huntington's thesis of the "clash of civilizations" to argue that religious violence can often be explained "as a response
to what a particular civilization understands as a threat to its religious culture, sacred places, and historical identity." Violence, from this perspective,
is a justifiable attempt to maintain the integrity of the group against real or
imagined civilizational enemies who are out to destroy the group or deny
them the possibility of fulfilling their historical and divine destiny. According
to Selengut, the clash between the West and the rest is the most significant
example of this dynamic. The United States, as leader of the West, believes it
has an obligation to promote its superior culture throughout the world: "This
proselytizing approach has always been part of the American ethos. From its
inception, the United States has had a sense of manifest destiny, a belief in the
uniqueness of America, and a religious conviction that the values, ideas, and
social organization of America should become the enduring values of countries all over the globe."[157] Despite this "religious conviction" and "proselytizing approach," Selengut identifies "secularization" as the primary attribute of

American culture that clashes with traditional religious cultures throughout the world:[158]

> The universal value of secular modernity, held by the West but championed most prominently by the United States and often made a condition for international economic and military aid from the United States or from international organizations controlled by Western interests like the World Bank, is fiercely resented by traditionally religious interests. These groups feel that the Western approach is one of religious and cultural genocide.[159]

Selengut does not say so explicitly, but "military aid" has included direct military intervention, for example, in Afghanistan and Iraq. As a result of "the West's insistence that traditional religious cultures adopt Western forms,"[160] religious groups "fight back" against the West, sometimes peacefully, but sometimes violently.[161]

Without doubt, there are non-Western groups that resist Western colonialism violently. But given that, in Selengut's own account, the West is the aggressor, why is this not framed as an account of the violence of secularism? Or, if we take Selengut's words about the proselytizing approach and religious conviction with which secularism is imposed on the rest of the world, why doesn't Western secularism count as a type of religion? Either way, there is no basis for using this account of colonial violence and anticolonial reaction as evidence that the religious is peculiarly prone to violence in ways that the secular is not. The danger of framing the account as an exploration of religious violence is that the Western reader will be tempted to ignore Western aggression and focus instead on the putatively nonrational response of non-Western Others.

Conclusion

There is plenty of important empirical and theoretical work to be done on the violence of certain groups of self-identified Christians, Hindus, Muslims, etc., and there are no grounds for exempting their beliefs and practices from the causal factors that produce violence. For example, there is no doubt that, under certain circumstances, particular construals of Islam or Christianity contribute to violence. The works discussed above—especially those of Juergensmeyer and Appleby—contain a wealth of empirical data on various ideologies and the production of violence. Where the above arguments—and others like them— fail is in trying to separate a category called religion with a peculiar tendency toward violence from a putatively secular reality that is less prone to violence.

There is no reason to suppose that so-called secular ideologies such as nationalism, patriotism, capitalism, Marxism, and liberalism are any less prone to be absolutist, divisive, and irrational than belief in, for example, the biblical God. As Marty himself implies, belief in the righteousness of the United States and its solemn duty to impose liberal democracy on the rest of the world has all of the ultimate concern, community, myth, ritual, and required behavior of any so-called religion. The debate that was revived in the late twentieth century over a ban on flag burning is replete with references to the "desecration" of the flag, as if it were a sacred object.[162] Carolyn Marvin and David Ingle's *Blood Sacrifice and the Nation* is a detailed analysis of U.S. patriotism as a civil religion—focused on the flag totem—whose regeneration depends on periodic blood sacrifice in war.[163] Secular nationalism of that kind can be just as absolutist, divisive, and irrationally fanatical as certain types of Jewish, Christian, Muslim, or Hindu militancy.

An objection can be raised that goes something like this: certainly, secular ideologies can get out of hand and produce fanaticism and violence, but religious ideologies have a much greater tendency to do so precisely because the object of their beliefs is claimed to be absolute. The capitalist knows that money is just a human creation, the liberal is avowedly modest about what can be known beyond human reason, the nationalist knows that her country is made up of land and mortal people, but the religious believer claims divine sanction from a god or gods or at least a transcendent reality that lays claim to absolute validity. It is this absolutism that makes obedience blind and causes the believer to subjugate all means to a transcendent end.

The problem with this objection is that what counts as "absolute" is decided a priori and appears immune to any empirical testing. How people actually behave is ignored in favor of theological descriptions of their beliefs. Of course, Jewish and Christian and Muslim orthodoxy would make the theological claim that God is absolute in a way that nothing else is. The problem, as the Ten Commandments make plain, is that humans are constantly tempted to idolatry, to putting what is merely relative in the place of God. It is not enough, therefore, to claim that worship of God is absolutist. The real question is, what god is actually being worshipped?

But surely, the objection might go, nobody really thinks the flag or the nation or money or sports idols are their "gods"—those are just metaphors. However, the question is not simply one of belief, but of behavior. If a person claims to believe in the Christian God but never gets off the couch on Sunday morning and spends the rest of the week in the obsessive pursuit of profits in the bond market, then what is absolute in that person's life in a functional sense is probably not the Christian God. Matthew 6:24 personifies Mammon as a rival god, not in the conviction that such a divine being really exists, but from the empirical observation that people have a tendency to treat all sorts of things as absolutes.

Suppose we apply an empirical test to the question of absolutism. Absolute is itself a vague term, but in the religion-and-violence arguments, it appears to indicate the tendency to take something so seriously that violence results. An empirically testable definition of absolute, then, might be "that for which one is willing to kill." This test has the advantage of covering behavior and not simply what one claims to believe. Now, let us ask the following two questions: what percentage of Americans who identify themselves as Christians would be willing to kill for their Christian faith? What percentage would be willing to kill for their country? Whether we attempt to answer these questions by survey or by observing American Christians' behavior in wartime, it seems clear that, at least among American Christians, the nation-state—Hobbes's "mortal god"—is subject to far more absolutist fervor than religion. For most American Christians, even public evangelization is considered to be in poor taste, and yet most would take for granted the necessity of being willing to kill for their country, should circumstances dictate.

We must conclude that there is no coherent way to isolate religious ideologies with a peculiar tendency toward violence from their tamer secular counterparts. People kill for all kinds of reasons. An adequate approach to the problem must begin with empirical investigations into the conditions under which beliefs and practices such as jihad, the invisible hand of the market, the sacrificial atonement of Christ, and the role of the United States as worldwide liberator turn violent. The point is not simply that secular violence should be given equal attention to religious violence. The point is that the distinction between secular and religious violence is unhelpful, misleading, and mystifying, and it should be avoided altogether. In the next chapter, I will investigate the modern origins of the distinction between religious and secular. For now, we may conclude that we do not need theories about religion and violence, but careful studies of violence and empirically based theories about the specific conditions under which ideologies and practices of all kinds turn lethal.

2

The Invention of Religion

In the first chapter, at the risk of trying the reader's patience,
I undertook an analysis of the varied arguments of nine major
thinkers on the question of religion and violence. I wanted to present
enough evidence that the reader would conclude that the problem
with the arguments would not be solved by coming up with novel
and better arguments for why religion has a peculiar tendency
toward violence, or by choosing a different set of authors who could
better make the argument. The scholars whose arguments I examined in chapter 1 are competent, many of them eminent in their
fields, and all have important insights to share on the genesis of violence. The problem is not simply with their scholarship, but with the
categories under which the debate takes place. The problem, specifically, is with the category "religion."

There is nothing close to agreement among scholars on what
defines religion; the inability to define religion has been described as
"almost an article of methodological dogma" in the field of religious
studies.[1] Until fairly recently, the academic debate over the definition
of religion has taken place between substantivist and functionalist
approaches. The former tend to be exclusivist, restricting the meaning of religion to beliefs and practices concerning something like
gods or "the transcendent." What separates religion from secular phenomena is therefore described in terms of the content or substance of
religious belief. Substantivist definitions of religion approximate the
common Western idea of religion as what Christians and Muslims

and Hindus and members of a few other "world religions" believe and do. Functionalist approaches, on the other hand, expand the definition of religion to include ideologies and practices—such as Marxism, nationalism, and free-market ideology—that are not commonly considered religious. They do so by looking not at content but at the way that these ideologies and practices function in various contexts to provide an overarching structure of meaning in everyday social life. Both of these tend to be essentialist approaches that regard religion as a thing out there in the world, a basic, transhistorical, and transcultural component of human social life identifiable by its content or function, if we could only reach agreement on what exact criteria separate religion from the secular.[2]

There is a significant and growing body of scholars, however, who have been exploring the ways that the very category religion has been constructed in different times and different places. According to this approach, the reason that essentialist definitions have failed to meet with agreement is not a lack of scholarly ingenuity but the fact that there is no essence of religion such that "we all know it when we see it," as Charles Kimball would have it. Religion is a constructed category, not a neutral descriptor of a reality that is simply out there in the world. Jonathan Z. Smith writes, "Religion is solely the creation of the scholar's study.... Religion has no independent existence apart from the academy."[3] I am not convinced that religion is confined to the academy; as we will see in this chapter, missionaries, politicians, bureaucrats, judges, and others have found the term useful. Smith's main point, however, is that religion is not simply found, but invented. The term religion has been used in different times and places by different people according to different interests. More specifically, the category religion as it is most commonly used is tied up with the history of Western modernity and is inseparable from the creation of what Talal Asad has called religion's "Siamese twin 'secularism.' "[4] Scholars have been exploring the ways that the construction of the category of religion has become an important piece in the ideology of the West since the rise of modernity, both within Western cultures and in the colonization of non-Western cultures. Religion is not simply an objective descriptor of certain kinds of practices that show up in every time and place. It is a term that constructs and is constructed by different kinds of political configurations.

In chapter 1, we encountered a group of scholars who are convinced that religion as such has a lamentable tendency to produce violence. In this chapter, we will encounter another group of scholars who do not think there is any religion as such, except as a constructed ideological category whose changing history must be carefully scrutinized. The scholars in the first group carry on as if they do not know that the second group exists. A few of the scholars in the first group acknowledge the problem of defining religion, but then continue on to "dissolve" the problem (Hick), ignore it (Marty), or treat it as merely semantic (Kimball). In this chapter, I will draw on the work of the second group of scholars to help explain why the arguments of the first group fail.

The point of this exercise is *not* to dissolve the problem of religion and violence by saying that religion is a fuzzy concept, so there is no such thing as religion and therefore no such problem of religion and violence. The problem is not that the implicit definitions of religion used by the first group of scholars are vague and fuzzy around the edges. With the exception of Richard Wentz, they are very clear about what counts as religion and what does not. The question is, are these distinctions arbitrary? What configurations of power authorize and are authorized by these distinctions? As I will show in this chapter, there is no transhistorical and transcultural essence of religion. What counts as religion and what does not in any given context is contestable and depends on who has the power and authority to define religion at any given time and place. As I will show in this chapter, the concept of religion as used by the theorists in chapter 1 is a development of the modern liberal state; the religious-secular distinction accompanies the invention of private-public, religion-politics, and church-state dichotomies. The religious-secular distinction also accompanies the state's monopoly over internal violence and its colonial expansion. If the religious-secular distinction develops in the context of this new configuration of power, then the distinctions made by the authors in chapter 1 should be interrogated within this history. If I can show that the very definition of religion is part of the history of Western power, then the idea that religion causes violence might not be simply a neutral, empirical observation, but might perhaps have an ideological function in legitimating certain kinds of practices and delegitimating others.

In this chapter, I will give evidence for two conclusions. The first conclusion is that there is no transhistorical or transcultural concept of religion. Religion has a history, and what counts as religion and what does not in any given context depends on different configurations of power and authority. The second conclusion is that the attempt to say that there *is* a transhistorical and transcultural concept of religion that is separable from secular phenomena *is itself* part of a particular configuration of power, that of the modern, liberal nation-state as it developed in the West. In this context, religion is constructed as transhistorical, transcultural, essentially interior, and essentially distinct from public, secular rationality. To construe Christianity as a religion, therefore, helps to separate loyalty to God from one's public loyalty to the nation-state. The idea that religion has a tendency to cause violence—and is therefore to be removed from public power—is one type of this essentialist construction of religion.

This chapter will proceed in five sections. In the first two sections, I show that religion is not a transhistorical concept. The first section is a history of ancient and medieval *religio;* the second section is a history of the invention of the concept of religion in the modern West. In the third section, I show that religion is not a transcultural concept, but was borrowed from or imposed by Westerners in much of the rest of the world during the process of colonization. In the fourth section, I show that, even within the modern West, the religious-secular division remains a widely contested point. I analyze the argument between substantivist and functionalist approaches and critique both views. In the fifth section, I conclude by arguing that what counts as religious or secular depends on what practices are being authorized. The fact that Christianity is construed as a religion, whereas nationalism is not, helps to ensure that the Christian's public and lethal loyalty belongs to the nation-state. The idea that religion has a peculiar tendency toward violence must be investigated as part of the ideological legitimation of the Western nation-state. I pursue that investigation in more detail in chapters 3 and 4.

Religio

Charles Kimball's book begins with the following claim: "It is somewhat trite, but nevertheless sadly true, to say that more wars have been waged, more people killed, and these days more evil perpetrated in the name of religion than by any other institutional force in human history."[5] Leroy Rouner's edited collection *Religion, Politics, and Peace* begins with a similar, though somewhat more hopeful claim: "Religion has probably been the single most significant cause of warfare in human history and, at the same time, the single most significant force for peace."[6] Neither author makes any attempt to support these claims with empirical evidence.

Could it be done? What would be necessary to prove the claim that religion has caused more violence than any other institutional force over the course of human history? One would first need a concept of religion that would be at least theoretically separable from other institutional forces over the course of history. Kimball does not identify those rival institutional forces, but one contender might be political institutions: tribes, empires, kingdoms, fiefs, states, and so on. The problem is that there was no category of religion separable from such political institutions until the modern era, and then it was primarily in the West. What meaning could we give to either the claim that Roman religion is to blame for the imperialist violence of ancient Rome, or the claim that it is Roman politics and not Roman religion that is to blame? Either claim would be nonsensical, because there was no neat division between religion and politics; Roman *religio* was inextricable from duty to the emperor and to the gods of Roman civic life. Similar comments apply to ancient Israel, Confucian China, Charlemagne's empire, Aztec civilization, and any other premodern culture. Is Aztec religion or Aztec politics to blame for their bloody human sacrifices? For the Aztecs, sacrifices to the gods were simply part of the proper ordering of the cosmos and society; the ordering of human society was a microcosm of the larger cosmic order. Any attempt to prove Kimball's "trite" claim about the destructive influence of religion in history would get bogged down in hopeless anachronism. The futility of this approach can be seen if we replace the word religion with the word politics in Kimball's and Rouner's claims. Is it helpful to say that politics has caused more violence in history than any other institutional force? There is a certain initial plausibility to this idea—wars have usually been instigated by kings, princes, and so on—but when we ask "Politics, as opposed to what?" we quickly see how pointless the claim is.

It is not simply that religion and politics were jumbled together until the modern West got them properly sorted out. As Wilfred Cantwell Smith showed in his landmark 1962 book, *The Meaning and End of Religion,* religion as a discrete category of human activity separable from culture, politics, and other areas of life is an invention of the modern West. In the course of a detailed historical study of the concept of religion, Smith was compelled to conclude that, outside of the modern West, there is no significant concept equivalent to what we think of as religion.[7] Similarly, politics as a category of human endeavor independent of religion is a distinctly modern concept. As Quentin Skinner says, the idea of politics as a distinct branch of moral philosophy is impossible in a medieval context dominated by Augustine's *City of God.* According to Skinner, the seeds of the modern idea of politics would not be sown until William of Morbeke's translation of Aristotle's *Politics* appeared in the thirteenth century, and even then the idea of politics as a distinct branch of inquiry and action would have to await the birth of the modern state in the sixteenth century.[8]

It is a mistake to treat religion as a constant in human culture across time and space. None of the thinkers we examined in chapter 1 would deny that religion has taken a kaleidoscopic variety of forms across the centuries of human history. But each of the theories we examined in the first chapter is about religion *as such.* This indicates a distinction between essence and form; religion is religion in any era and any place, though it may take different outward forms. Even Hick, who explicitly denies that religion has an essence, nevertheless continues to treat ancient Theravada Buddhism and contemporary Pentecostalism equally as religions. The assumption is that, in ancient

Sri Lanka or in contemporary Houston, one may identify the religion or religions of the inhabitants by looking for certain kinds of beliefs and practices.

A history of the term religion makes this assumption deeply problematic. Ancient languages have no word that approximates what modern English speakers mean by religion; Wilfred Cantwell Smith cites the scholarly consensus that neither the Greeks nor the Egyptians had any equivalent term for religion, and he adds that a similar negative conclusion is found for the Aztecs and the ancient civilizations of India, China, and Japan.[9] The word is derived from the ancient Latin word religio, but religio was only one of a constellation of terms surrounding social obligations in ancient Rome, and when used it signified something quite different from religion in the modern sense. Religio referred to a powerful requirement to perform some action. Its most probable derivation is from re-ligare, to rebind or relink, that is, to reestablish a bond that has been severed. To say religio mihi est—that something is "religio for me"—meant that it was something that carried a serious obligation for a person. This included not only cultic observances—which were themselves sometimes referred to as religiones, such that there was a different religio or set of observances at each shrine—but also civic oaths and family rituals, things that modern Westerners normally consider to be secular.[10] When religio did refer to temple sacrifices, it was possible—and common among certain intellectuals—in ancient Rome to practice religio, but not believe in the existence of gods. Although Cicero's De Natura Deorum puts forth naturalistic social and psychological theories for the origin of belief in gods,[11] Cicero himself was a priest, and retained his position on the Board of Augurs of the republic. As S. N. Balagangadhara points out, this was possible because religio was largely indifferent to theological doctrine and was primarily about the customs and traditions that provided the glue for the Roman social order.[12]

Religio was a relatively minor concept for the early Christians, in part because it does not correspond to any single concept that the biblical writers considered significant. In St. Jerome's Vulgate New Testament—the standard Latin translation for over a thousand years of Christendom—religio appears only six times, as a translation for several different Greek terms. In the King James Version of the New Testament, religion appears only five times, for three different Greek words—and not always the same ones that Jerome rendered as religio.[13] The word religio is found scattered through the Latin patristic writings, where it has a number of different meanings, including ritual practice, clerical office, worship (religio dei), and piety, or the subjective disposition of the worshipper toward God.[14]

The only treatise written entirely on religio in the patristic period was Augustine's late fourth-century work De Vera Religione. In it, Augustine distinguishes between true *religio* and false *religio,* a distinction introduced in the late third century by Lactantius.[15] Augustine's subject is not "Christianity" as a—or the—true religion alongside other religions understood as systematic sets of propositions and rites. For Augustine, *religio* means worship, the action by which we render praise. There is true worship and false worship. False worship is directed toward many gods, or toward mere created things. True worship is directed toward the one God as revealed by Jesus Christ, and so true worship is found preeminently in the church catholic.[16] There are, however, vestiges of truth everywhere and traces of the Creator in the creation. The impulse to worship is found in all human beings as the inchoate longing for their Creator, whom Augustine understood to be the Holy Trinity.[17] False worship arises when we pay homage to creation and neglect the Creator. Augustine concludes his treatise with a long exhortation against false *religiones:* "Let not our religion be the worship of human works.... Let not our religion be the worship of beasts.... Let not our religion be the worship of lands and waters."[18] For Augustine, then, *religio* is not contrasted with some sort of secular realm of activity. Any human pursuit can have its own (false) type of *religio,* its own type of idolatry: the worship of human works, lands, etc. These, not something like "paganism" or "Judaism," are contrasted to true worship: "Let our religion bind us to the one omnipotent God, because no creature comes between our minds and him whom we know to be the Father and the Truth, i.e., the inward light whereby we know him."[19]

When Augustine later addresses the term *religio* in book X of *City of God,* he finds it—along with *cultus* and *pietas*—inadequate to express the worship of God alone. Although, for lack of a better word, he will use *religio* to refer to the worship of the one true God, he finds it ambiguous because its "normal meaning" refers to devotion in human relationships, especially among family and friends:

> The word "religion" would seem, to be sure, to signify more particularly the "cult" offered to God, rather than "cult" in general; and that is why our translators have used it to render the Greek word *thrêskeia.* However, in Latin usage (and by that I do not mean in the speech of the illiterate, but even in the language of the highly educated) "religion" is something which is displayed in human relationships, in the family (in the narrower and the wider sense) and between friends; and so the use of the word does not avoid ambiguity when the worship of God is in question. We have no right to affirm with confidence that "religion" is confined to the worship of God, since it seems that this word has been detached from its normal meaning,

in which it refers to an attitude of respect in relations between a man and his neighbor.[20]

Augustine is aware that, in normal Latin usage, there is no realm of belief and practice called religion that can be separated out from merely mundane obligations like family and the oaths, cults, and obligations that bind Roman society together. Politics, culture, family obligations, devotion to God or gods, civic duties—all are bound together in one complex web of social relations. For Augustine, the right ordering of social relations must include worship of the true God; this is true *religio*. But *religio* as a general category is found in all manner of social relations, both rightly and wrongly ordered. For Augustine and the ancient world, *religio* is not a distinct realm of activity separate from a secular realm.

As we look to the medieval period, the term *religio* becomes even less frequently used in Christian discourse. As Wilfred Cantwell Smith observes, "It is nowadays customary to think of this period as the most 'religious' in the history of Christendom. Despite this or because of it, throughout the whole Middle Ages no one, so far as I have been able to ascertain, ever wrote a book specifically on 'religion.' And on the whole this concept would seem to have received little attention."[21] According to John Bossy, the ancient meaning of *religio* as duty or reverence "disappeared" in the medieval period: "With very few exceptions, the word was only used to describe different sorts of monastic or similar rule, and the way of life pursued under them."[22] This meaning holds when the word passes into English around 1200; the earliest meaning of religion cited in the *Oxford English Dictionary* is "a state of life bound by monastic vows." In time, the term came to include the condition of members of other nonmonastic orders; hence the distinction between religious clergy and secular clergy. It is still common Roman Catholic usage to speak of entering an order as entering the religious life. In the early thirteenth century, we find references to religion as indicating a particular monastic or religious order or rule, such that by 1400 we find references to religions in the plural. The religions of England were the various orders: Benedictines, Dominicans, Franciscans, etc.[23]

Thomas Aquinas wrote two addresses in which declensions of the word *religio* appear in the title, and both are defenses of religious orders.[24] However, Aquinas also used *religio* in the older sense of something approximating both "rites" and "piety." Bossy cannot be taken literally when he says that such use "disappeared" in the medieval period. Nevertheless, the ancient use was rare in the Middle Ages and did not seem to bear much weight. In Aquinas's massive *Summa Theologiae*, there is only one question on *religio*; it falls amid the seventy-six questions of the treatise on prudence and justice. Aquinas treats *religio* under the virtue of justice. *Religio* is one of the nine virtues annexed to the principal virtue justice; it is a "potential part of justice" because it renders to God what is God's due, which is reverence or worship. However, *religio* falls short of the perfection of the virtue of justice, since it is impossible for humans to give to God an equal return.[25] According to Aquinas, *religio* is a moral, not a theological, virtue because "God is related to religion not as matter or object, but as end."[26] God is the direct object of the theological virtue of faith. The object of *religio* is the rites and practices, both individual and communal, that offer worship to God.

Although *religio* primarily refers to orders of clergy in the medieval period, the ancient usage does still infrequently appear. Even when used as something approaching piety and reverence, however, *religio* is not what modern people refer to as religion. It is important to note what *religio* is *not* for Aquinas and for medieval Christendom more generally. First, *religio* is not a universal genus of which Christianity is a particular species. As does Augustine, Aquinas acknowledges that *religio* is found everywhere that worship is offered. Aquinas hesitates less than Augustine to limit the meaning of *religio* to the explicit worship of God or gods. Aquinas cites Cicero's definition of religion as consisting "in offering service and ceremonial rites to a superior nature that men call divine."[27] Aquinas would acknowledge that pagans worship their gods and use the word *religio* to describe it. He would also acknowledge, as did Augustine, that pagan worship contains within it an inchoate groping toward the one true God. But Michael Buckley overstates the case when he says that, for Aquinas, "[r]eligio looks to all of the acts by which God is served and worshipped as '*principium creationis et gubernationis rerum*,' whether Christian or not."[28] For Aquinas, pagan worship does not serve God; if pagan worship is *religio*, it is false *religio*, as in Augustine's distinction between true and false *religiones*. Aquinas says that "it belongs to religion to show reverence to one God under one aspect, namely, as the first principle of the creation and government of things."[29] He adds, "The three Divine Persons are the one principle of the creation and government of things, wherefore they are served by one religion."[30] The one true *religio* worships God the Father, Son, and Holy Spirit. Aquinas would not acknowledge a common essence of religion underlying the various manifestations of the world's religions. Talal Asad cites the case of a fifth-century bishop who, finding the yet-to-be-Christianized peasants making offerings to their gods on the edge of a marsh, said, "There can be no religion in a swamp." Asad comments, "For medieval Christians, religion was not a universal phenomenon: religion was a site on which universal truth was produced, and it was clear to them that truth was not produced universally."[31]

The second thing that *religio* was *not* is a system of propositions or beliefs. Aquinas describes the end of *religio* in specifically Christian Trinitarian language, but the main point is not about different religions holding different doctrines. In the medieval era, Christianity is not a religion to be set aside or against other religions, other systems of propositions about the nature of things and their attendant rites, e.g., Buddhism, Islam, Hinduism. Doctrine is not unimportant for cultivating true *religio,* but Christian *religio* is not a system of propositions about reality. It is a *virtue,* a disposition of the person which elevates the person's action into participation in the life of the Trinity. As a virtue, Christian *religio* is a type of *habitus,* a disposition of the person toward moral excellence produced by highly specific disciplines of body and soul.[32] *Religio* is not so much a matter of learning certain correct universal propositions about the world, but of being formed in bodily habits. As Asad comments in his study of medieval monasticism:

> The formation/transformation of moral dispositions (Christian virtues) depended on more than the capacity to imagine, to perceive, to imitate—which, after all, are abilities everyone possesses in varying degree. It required a particular program of disciplinary practices. The rites that were prescribed by that program did not simply evoke or release universal emotions, they aimed to construct and reorganize distinctive emotions—desire (*cupiditas/caritas*), humility (*humilitas*), remorse (*contritio*)—on which the central Christian virtue of obedience to God depended. This point must be stressed, because the emotions mentioned here are not universal human feelings.... They are historically specific emotions that are structured internally and related to each other in historically determined ways. And they are the product not of mere readings of symbols but of processes of power.[33]

The third thing that *religio* is *not,* in other words, is a purely interior impulse secreted away in the human soul. Christian *religio* is a set of skills that become "second nature" through habituated disciplines of body and soul. Monasticism, guided by the Rule of St. Benedict, is the most refined form of *religio,* such that Aquinas could identify monastic life as religious life proper.[34] But *religio* was not limited to monastic life. All Christian *religio* was impressed upon the body and soul by the kinds of disciplines St. Benedict prescribes. For Aquinas, *religio* incorporates both the piety of the worshipper and the external rites and disciplines of the worship. *Religio* does not differ essentially from sanctity, but differs logically, in that *religio* refers to communal and individual rites that offer worship to God: "The word religion is usually used to signify the activity by which man gives the proper reverence to God through actions which specifically pertain to divine worship, such as sacrifice, oblations, and the like."[35] Sanctity includes both these and "the works of the other virtues by which one is disposed to the worship of God."[36] Aquinas devotes one article to showing that *religio* includes an external act. Although he says that the internal acts of *religio* take precedence over the external rites, the external rites are not expendable or superfluous, for "the human mind, in order to be united to God, needs to be guided by the sensible world, since *invisible things...are clearly seen, being understood by the things that are made*, as the Apostle says [Rom. 1:20]."[37]

For Aquinas, *religio* is a virtue, and virtue is a type of habit, and habits are caused by the repetition of acts.[38] Such acts necessarily involve the body, which is not merely a container for the soul; soul and body are one psychosomatic unity, with the soul not a separate thing, but the "form" of the body.[39] This viewpoint is not peculiar to Thomas Aquinas, but is shared by medieval Christendom more generally. In the writings of Hugh of St. Victor, for example:

> [I]t is discipline imposed on the body which forms virtue. Body
> and spirit are but one: disordered movements of the former betray
> outwardly (*foris*) the disarranged interior (*intus*) of the soul. But
> inversely, "discipline" can act on the soul through the body—in ways
> of dressing (*in habitu*), in posture and movement (*in gestu*), in speech
> (*in locutione*), and in table manners (*in mensa*).[40]

What *religio* is *not* for medieval Christians, fourthly, is an "institutional force" separable from other nonreligious, or secular, forces. When Kimball says that religion has caused more violence than any other institutional force throughout history, we must ask what those institutional forces might be. In other words, to what is religion being compared in the premodern context? Is Christian religion being compared to, for example, Muslim religion? No, Kimball's claim is about religion as such, not just Christian religion. Is religion being compared to other virtues, say, fortitude or prudence? Virtues do not seem to be what Kimball has in mind by "institutional forces." Besides, in the medieval context, any attempt to isolate one virtue from another as the cause of some social effect like violence is not likely to bear much fruit. Aquinas devotes a question of the *Summa Theologiae* to showing the deep interconnection of the virtues, such that, as Saint Thomas quotes Gregory, "one virtue without the other is either of no account whatever, or very imperfect."[41] According to Aquinas, the moral virtues "qualify one another by a kind of overflow."[42]

For similar reasons, any attempt to compare religion to politics or economics or some other such institutional force in medieval Christendom is unlikely to bear fruit. This comparison seems to be what Kimball and others mean when they say that religion has caused *more* violence in human history. However, *religio* was not a separate sphere of concern and activity, but permeated all the institutions and activities of medieval Christendom. In fact, Aquinas says, "Every deed, in so far as it is done in God's honor, belongs to religion, not as eliciting, but as commanding."[43] He explains the difference between eliciting and commanding in these terms:

> Religion has two kinds of acts. Some are its proper and immediate acts, which it elicits, and by which man is directed to God alone, for instance, sacrifice, adoration and the like. But it has other acts, which it produces through the medium of the virtues which it commands, directing them to the honor of God, because the virtue which is concerned with the end, commands the virtues which are concerned with the means.[44]

For Aquinas, *religio* did not belong to a separate, "supernatural" realm of activity; not until Francisco de Suárez's work at the dawn of the seventeenth century was *religio* identified as *supernaturalis*.[45] *Religio* was not separable— even in theory—from political activity in Christendom. Medieval Christendom was a theopolitical whole. This does not mean, of course, that there was no division of labor between kings and priests, nor that that division was not constantly contested. It does mean, however, that the end of *religio* was inseparable from the end of politics. Aquinas explains that human government is directed toward the end of virtuous living.[46] For this reason, the king must possess virtue; justice easily degenerates into tyranny unless the king is "a very virtuous man."[47] More specifically, prudence and justice (the latter includes *religio*) are the virtues most proper to a king.[48] The virtuous life of the assembled people—care of which pertains to the king—is not in itself the ultimate end of human life, which is the enjoyment of God. This ultimate end is in the direct care of the priests, to whom kings should be subordinate. Nevertheless, the virtuous living to which kings direct their subjects is an intermediate end which is directed toward the ultimate end: "Since society must have the same end as the individual man, it is not the ultimate end of an assembled multitude to live virtuously, but through virtuous living to attain to the possession of God."[49] Acts of governing well, in other words, are directed toward the same end toward which *religio* is directed, and true *religio* is integral to good governing. For this reason, Aquinas rejects the idea that non-Christians should have political authority over Christians.[50]

Is religion being compared to a secular realm of activity when it is claimed that religion has caused *more* violence than any other institutional force throughout history? Certainly, the modern claim that religion causes more violence than something else depends upon the existence of a sphere of non-religion, a secular realm. As should be obvious, however, there was no such secular sphere until it was invented in modernity. The organic image of the body of Christ was fused with a hierarchical ordering of estates. There was no part of Christendom that stood outside of the holistic, sacralized order.

Nothing in the above analysis of the history of the term *religio* either disproves or proves the thesis that medieval Christendom was more violent than modern society. One may wish to argue that the invention of the religious-secular duality was, on the whole, a good thing, and that societies with such a distinction are to be preferred to societies organized like medieval Christendom. But basing such a preference on the inherent violence of religion throughout history invites anachronistic nonsense. The point is not that religion was mixed up with secular pursuits until modernity separated them. The point is that there is no transhistorical and transcultural essence of religion waiting to be separated from the secular like a precious metal from its ore. The term *religio* functioned in very different ways as part of a complex of power relations and subjectivities unique to medieval Christendom. Very different relations of power were involved in the invention of the twin categories of religion and the secular. The problem with transhistorical and transcultural definitions of religion is not just that all phenomena identified as religious are historically specific, but that the definitions themselves are historical products that are part of specific configurations of power.[51]

The Invention of Religion in the West

In the medieval application of the term, *religio* was primarily used to differentiate clergy who were members of orders from diocesan clergy. Secondarily, *religio* named one relatively minor virtue in a complex of other practices that assumed the particular context of the Christian church and the Christian social order. With the dawn of modernity, however, a new concept with a much wider and different significance came to operate under the term religion. Religion in modernity indicates a universal genus of which the various religions are species; each religion comes to be demarcated by a system of propositions; religion is identified with an essentially interior, private impulse; and religion comes to be seen as essentially distinct from secular pursuits such as politics, economics, and the like. The rise of the concept of religion thus establishes Christianity's proper sphere as the interior life, without direct access to the political. As Smith remarks, "the rise of the concept of 'religion' is in some ways correlated with a decline in the practice of religion itself."[52] What he means is that the invention of the modern concept of religion accompanies the decline of the church as the public, communal practice of the virtue of *religio*. The rise of religion is accompanied by the rise of its twin, the secular realm, a pairing which will gradually remove the practice of Christian *religio* from a central place in the social order of the West.

The creation of the modern category of religion begins in the Renaissance, with two Christian Platonist thinkers taking a central role. Nicholas of Cusa (1401–1464) uses *religio* to indicate the various ways in which God is worshipped; there are Jewish, Christian, and Arabic religions, that is Jewish, Christian, and Arabic ways of worshipping God, though there are as yet no religions called Judaism, Christianity, or Islam.[53] What is novel about Cusa's use of *religio* is that ritual practices are not essential to it; *religio* is a universal, interior impulse that stands behind the multiplicity of rites. Shaken by the violent fall of Constantinople to the Turks in 1453, Cusa wrote his treatise *De Pace Fidei* in an attempt to arrive at some principle of concord among the peoples of the earth, who worshipped in so many different ways. Burdened by the cares of the body, people were unable to come to a pure knowledge of the hidden God. God had therefore provided them with various prophets, each of whom had taught the same wisdom, but in different customs and languages: "Yet human nature has this weakness, that after a long passage of time certain customs are gradually accepted and defended as immutable truths."[54] What became obscured was that "there is, in spite of many varieties of rites, but one religion."[55] This one religion is the one wisdom toward which all beliefs and observances—some inchoately, others clearly and explicitly—point. Even the worship of many gods admits of one wisdom. A unity of rite might be the ideal, but in practice diversity of rites may be tolerated and even encouraged, "since in many cases a particular religion would actually be more vigilant in guarding what it considers to be the noblest way of manifesting its devotion to you [God] as its King"; so God is beseeched to "let there be in the same manner one religion and one cult of divine worship."[56] Religion here is clearly not identified with rites or the bodily disciplines proper to virtue, but with an interior wisdom that underlies all rites. What is needed to make this implicit concord explicit is that "man would have to walk according to his interior rather than his exterior nature."[57] The "interior man" is one who relies on supersensible reason: "all who use their reason have one religion and cult which is at the bottom of all the diversity of rites."[58]

Cusa was a Christian who believed both that Christ as the word was the source and mediator of wisdom, and that the common essence of religion was in reality faith in Christ. The one religion to which all rites point is not a kind of spiritual Esperanto. The sparks of wisdom found in each people's rites were put there by God to facilitate the eventual acceptance of faith in Christ by all nations. However, faith in Christ is not dependent upon any particular rites or particular practices, but underlies their diversity. Cusa's conception of religion, therefore, is a significant departure from the medieval use of the term as a virtue embedded in particular bodily disciplines. In Cusa, we see the beginnings of religion as an interior impulse that is universal to human beings and therefore stands behind the multiplicity of exterior rites that express it. Cusa, however, still wants to identify that universal impulse with Christianity in its revealed form. Nevertheless, Cusa's position is a precursor to the hitherto unknown idea that there is a single genus of human activity called religion, of which Christianity, Islam, Buddhism, Sikhism, etc., are the various species.

The second major Renaissance contributor to the creation of religion was Marsilio Ficino, the man responsible for the first full Latin translation of Plato's *Dialogues*. The title of Ficino's 1474 work, *De Christiana Religione*, was one of the first uses of this phrase. By it, he did not mean "the Christian religion" in the sense of a system of doctrines and practices to be set aside from the other world religions. *Religio* meant something like piety. What distinguishes his usage of the term *religio* from the ancient and medieval usages is that it is both interiorized and universalized. It is located as a natural, innate impulse of the human heart, indeed *the* fundamental human characteristic common to all. The essence of religion is thus an unchanging constant across time and space in all human societies: "all opinions of men, all their responses, all their customs, change—except *religio*."[59] *Religio* is distinguished from external actions or rites, which, as in Cusa, are multiple. Unlike Cusa, however, Ficino believes that this variety of rites is ordained by God to give beauty to the world. Each external form of worship is a more or less true approximation of the Platonic ideal. Ficino also differs from Cusa in that Ficino did not regard Christ as the true content of the universal religion. For Ficino, the "Christian" in "the Christian religion" meant "pertaining to Christ." Those who come the closest to the ideal worship of God are those who worship as Christ did; this is the practice of Christian religion, that is, Christ's way of worshipping God. There is only one universal *religio* implanted in the human heart, but there are different degrees of genuineness in living it out. The highest degree is exemplified by Christ. In Ficino's eyes, any faith can be "Christian" religion, even with no connection to the historical Christian revelation or church.[60]

The move toward religion as an interior and universal impulse would be complemented in the sixteenth and seventeenth centuries by an emphasis on belief over practice. Religion would come to mean a system of doctrines, intellectual propositions that could be either true or false. In the work of French humanist Guillaume Postel, for example, we find the idea that certain essential propositions are central to all of the world's religions. In his *De orbis terrae concordia* (1544), Postel listed sixty-seven such propositions that are common to all religions and around which the people of the world could unite, if only they would shed the superfluous externalities of rite and practice. If people could agree on these first principles, agreement on the final truths would come easily. The end result of such agreement would be that people would not be papists, Lutherans, or adherents of any particular religion, but would simply invoke the name of Jesus.[61]

In the interest of promoting universal concord, Postel uses religions in the plural to talk about "the diversity of customs, languages, opinions, and religions"[62] of the world's people, and religion in the singular to refer to the concord underlying all of the various religions. He thus comes close to introducing the idea that Christianity, Islam, etc., are species of the genus religion, but he persists in identifying true religion with Christian religion. Nevertheless, he makes an important distinction between "the narrow worship of the external church"[63] and the internal, mystical church that includes all of the world's people. Postel does not thereby dismiss the external church, with its rites and disciplines of the body, as unnecessary; he believes that the external church is the primary instrument to unite the human race. But the external church has become merely instrumental to the pursuit of agreement on the common propositions of true religion.[64]

The internal-external and belief-practice binaries were crucial to the continued formation of the religious-secular binary in the sixteenth century. This can be seen in dramatic form in sixteenth-century England, where reformers such as Thomas Becon were intent on purifying religion of dependence on the external physical world.[65] The 1552 version of the Book of Common Prayer published under Edward VI denied "any reall and essencial presence" in the Eucharist and spoke instead of feeding "in the heart by faith."[66] As Graham Ward comments, prior to this period, the *saeculum* had no autonomy from a religious realm. Stripping away the liturgical understanding of the world had a profound impact on the reconfiguration of power and subjectivity in sixteenth-century England:

> To rethink the sacraments and ceremonies as symbols or "mere outward forms" (1549 Book of Common Prayer) was to transform

the nature of materiality itself, rendering the natural world opaque, silent and inert.... A new space and a new understanding of the body were emerging, a space and a body in which God's presence was only available through the eyes of faith—and faith understood as a set of doctrinal principles to be taught, a set of interpretive keys to be passed down, passed on, for one's experience in the world.[67]

According to Peter Harrison, the transition to religion as a state of mind can be mapped especially clearly among Calvinists. For John Calvin, *religio* retained its medieval meaning as a worshipful disposition of the person, but in Calvinist circles there came to be an emphasis on religion as saving knowledge. For Calvin's followers, saving knowledge was understood in the context of election and predestination. Saving knowledge was not a grasp of doctrinal facts that guaranteed salvation, but was rather a knowledge of God's will, the assurance that one had been chosen by God to be among the saved. In time, however, saving knowledge came to indicate a body of objective truths to which the believer could assent or withhold assent. According to Harrison, the Calvinist preoccupation with knowledge and belief can in part be traced to Calvin's rejection of the Catholic doctrine of "implicit faith," that is, the idea that simpler and less educated Christians did not need to understand abstruse doctrines such as the Trinity, but merely have faith that the doctors of the church had gotten it right.[68] The Reformation's democratization of the church, in other words, meant less emphasis on mystery and more emphasis on the perspicuity of the faith.

The emphasis on religion as doctrine would receive impetus from the Arminian controversy at the end of the sixteenth century. Sensitive to the problems that Calvin's double predestinarianism created for the idea of human free will, Jacobius Arminius proposed a conditional predestination which sought to allow human agents to play a role in their salvation without giving the impression of earning it. For Arminius, human freedom came in the act of intellectual assent—a mere "I believe"—to certain central Christian doctrines. No moral acts or works were required of the human agent, thus avoiding the charge of Pelagianism that Calvin had so wanted to avoid. As a result, however, the tendency to reduce religion to assent to doctrine was magnified.[69] When Arminius's patron Hugo Grotius wrote *De Veritate Religionis Christianae* in the early seventeenth century, his purpose was to show that the Christian religion was *the* true religion, meaning that its doctrines were statements of fact. Grotius was therefore able to say that the Christian religion teaches, rather than simply is, the correct worship of God.[70]

The Reformation brought in its wake numerous attempts to encapsulate Christian faith in a set of beliefs to be confessed. The Thirty-Nine Articles, the

Lambeth Articles, and the Westminster Confession come immediately to mind. The seventeenth century in addition saw an explosion of books and pamphlets attempting to present "the Christian Religion," "the Protestant Religion," "the true Catholic Religion," or simply "Religion" in propositional form. Such efforts culminated in Nicholas Gibbon's attempt to present the Christian religion in a "scheme or diagram" that occupied one single printed page.[71] Obviously, such attempts were inspired by the context of competing Christian confessions following the Reformation. For polemical purposes, one needed to be able to state the differences between confessions clearly and succinctly.

There developed, therefore, the idea of religions in the plural. The idea of Lutheranism, Catholicism, and Calvinism as different religions was not a sixteenth-century notion. The phrase *cuius regio, eius religio,* usually associated with the Peace of Augsburg in 1555, was in fact invented by a German jurist around 1600 and could not have been used by the writers of the treaty.[72] Even Jean Bodin's *Colloquium heptaplomeres*—a discussion, written in the 1580s, among fictional representatives of Jewish, Christian, Islamic, and natural religions—used *religio* in the older sense of styles of worship, not as abstract systems of doctrines.[73] The earliest form of pluralization in the modern sense is found in the 1590s, with Richard Hooker from the Anglican side and Robert Parsons from the Catholic side writing about religions as objective and opposing sets of doctrines.[74]

After 1600, it became possible to speak of religion in general, although it was usually used to refer to "the Christian religion," which indicated that the various religions in Christendom were true or false forms of an abstract essence of Christianity.[75] As the seventeenth century progressed, it became possible to see Christianity as one species of the genus religion, there being, as Thomas Browne wrote in 1642–1643, "a Geography of Religions, as of Lands."[76] As Bossy summarizes the result:

> By 1700, the world was full of religions, objective social and moral entities characterised by system, principles and hard edges, which could be envisaged by Voltaire as cutting one another's throats. Above their multiplicity planed a shadowy abstraction, *the* Christian Religion, and somewhere above that, in an upper region of the classifying system, religion with a capital "R," planted in its new domain by people who did not usually feel or believe in it.[77]

At the same time, according to Bossy, "Christianity" was moving from meaning a body of people to meaning an "ism" or body of beliefs.[78]

The location of religion in beliefs or states of mind was the work not only of Protestant and Catholic polemicists but also of those who put forth proposals for toleration. Edward, Lord Herbert of Cherbury (1583–1648), one of the most prominent of the early modern theorists of religion, attempted to reach a concord among all the world's religions by identifying the five essential beliefs of religion as such:

> 1. That there is some supreme divinity. 2. That this divinity ought to be worshipped. 3. That virtue joined with piety is the best method of divine worship. 4. That we should return to our right selves from sins. 5. That reward or punishment is bestowed after this life is finished.[79]

Herbert thought that peace could be achieved among the world's various sects if people would only see that, underlying the various forms of life, rites, and traditions, everyone in fact acknowledged, either implicitly or explicitly, the same basic universal propositions, which he called the "common notions" concerning religion. All of the various religions were species of one universal genus, and "no period or nation is without religion."[80] Herbert was ready to submit all things to the judgment of the "truly catholic Church."[81] Herbert even went so far as to say that "it is only through this Church that salvation is possible."[82] This church, however, was not a community, institution, spiritual discipline, or integrated way of life but a set of propositions: "The only Catholic and uniform Church is the doctrine of Common Notions which comprehends all places and all men."[83] As such, salvation was immediately accessible to all, without need for the rites, scriptures, bodily disciplines, traditions, and communal guidance of any particular body of people.[84]

Herbert lays out the epistemological basis for his ideas on religion in his most important work, *De Veritate,* which appeared in 1624 and had a profound influence on Grotius, Descartes, and Locke. As Descartes would later do, Herbert tries to base his search for truth not on the perceptions of the senses but on the immediate apprehensions of the mind: "I have undertaken in this work only to rely on truths which are not open to dispute but are derived from the evidence of immediate perception and admitted by the whole world."[85] Herbert discovers in the mind a faculty which he calls "natural instinct," whose function is to provide us with an immediate apprehension of the divine. This apprehension is pure and is prior to sense perception, to experience, and even to reasoning. The five common notions issue directly from the natural instinct and are innate. It is not that the content of the common notions is given to every mind at birth, but that every mind will arrive at them if it is functioning normally without external impediment.[86] The common notions "by no means depend on some faith or tradition, but have been engraved on the human mind by God, and…have been considered and acknowledged as true throughout the world, by every age."[87] The practices of authority and tradition give way entirely to introspection. Amid the cacophony of different voices, each holding up their own particular human traditions as true and necessary and condemning the others as false, the individual is to retreat into the self and find true religion there: "since it is proper to the lofty soul, let him everywhere distinguish by the appropriate faculties internal things from external, certain from uncertain, divine from human. Nay, let him rather with serene unshaken mind despise other things, and amid the threatenings poured out over the entire world let him escape undaunted, self-possessed."[88]

Any particular doctrines and rites that arise in positive religions are a dilution of the original purity of the natural instinct as it becomes weighed down by the body and the material world. At best, such additions to pure religion are beneficial exemplifications of the underlying universal religion. Herbert seems to have regarded the particularities of Christ's incarnation, crucifixion, and resurrection in such a light, which earned him the label Father of English Deism. At worst, however, the particularities of the various religions are to be considered accretions and corruptions which distort the "perfect sphere of the religion of God."[89] Such impostures are introduced by the priestly classes for their own gain and control of the ignorant masses. Herbert is extremely critical of the priests of every religion, even as he spies evidence that the common notions are to be found underneath all the rubbish of history.[90] Herbert would not do away with all rites and priestly "externals," but would retain "the more becoming rites and ceremonies" in the hope that concentration on the common notions would lead to a "more austere, more logical worship."[91] Herbert allows that, in permitting the great diversity of religions over time and space, God must have had a good purpose in mind.[92] Nevertheless, he seems at a loss to say what that good purpose is and turns for assurance instead to the unchanging nature of true religion:

> Granted then that He has subjected all things to a series of causes acting each one upon the next, yet some things He has ordained unchangeable from the beginning of time. It is therefore clear enough, finally, that in whatever circumstance matters are altered, yet the stuff whence their existence is derived is in no way destroyed, nor the time which is their measure put aside, nor the space in which they are placed done away with, nor the plan whence comes their order changed. Vainly therefore would you seek for anything new in God. For though all things are modified by their mutual relations, yet they assume no change inconsistent with the order of nature.[93]

The idea that religion is transhistorical and transcultural is crucial for Herbert, despite the problems that it causes for him. If all people in all times and places have access to the same universal propositions, why do people not in fact agree? Herbert follows the above passage by making clear that these truths "escape the eyes of those who grope in darkness" because of free will.[94] Natural instinct does not preempt the faculty of free choice. It is to be expected, then, that due to a certain tendency to depravity, some may fall into darkness. But Herbert makes clear that universality is ultimately independent of any empirical measure of the way that people actually behave. Truth is attained by introspection, not by the mere gathering of data. Herbert repeatedly asserts that natural instinct arrives at the common notions in "normal men":[95]

> It is not what a large number of men assert, but what all men of
> normal mind believe, that I find important. Scanning the vast array
> of absurd fictions I am content to discover a tiny Common Notion.
> And this is of the utmost importance, since when the general mass
> of men have rejected a whole range of beliefs which it has found
> valueless, it proceeds to acquire new beliefs by this method, until the
> point is reached where faith can be applied.[96]

Herbert is confident, in other words, that the masses will eventually come around to the purity of his five common notions, but the truth of the common notions is independent of how people believe and behave.

The main problem with this scheme, as Peter Harrison puts it, is that it is unfalsifiable. Whenever evidence is adduced that certain people at certain times or in certain places do not in fact hold to the five notions common to all human beings, such people are simply declared abnormal.[97] In constructing an a priori religion in the minds of all people, Herbert has made his theory impervious to empirical evidence. All evidence is seen and interpreted through the lens of his religious view a priori. Herbert's scheme creates its own world, with its own boundaries between what is normal and what is not. Herbert is not discovering the timeless essence of religion, but is helping to create a new reality, a new normality, by identifying a timeless religion that is interior, universal, nonmaterial, and essentially distinct from the political. This is not only true of Herbert. Attempts to construct religion as a universal, timeless, interior, and apolitical human impulse in the early modern period are willy-nilly part of the creation of new configurations of power, especially the subordination of ecclesiastical power to that of the emergent state.

It is important to note that Herbert's interiorization and universalization of religion go hand in hand with his support of state control over the church. This may seem like a contradiction, but Herbert has no intention of privatizing worship. Herbert's scheme for toleration is part of a larger shift toward the absorption of ecclesiastical power by the rising state in the fifteenth through the seventeenth centuries. Edward, Lord Herbert of Cherbury, served the English Crown as ambassador to France and wrote a history of King Henry VIII and a short paper in English, "On the King's Supremacy in the Church."[98] In the latter document, in looking over the biblical and historical record, he finds that "noe Change of Religion, during the Reigne of their Kings did follow, which was not procured by their immediate power,"[99] an echo of the policy of *cuius regio, eius religio*. He also argues that "it is unsafe to diuide the people, betwixt temporall, and spirituall obedience, or suspend them, betwixt the Terrours of a secular death, and Eternall punishments."[100] The distinction between religion and the secular in these two passages is not yet a distinction between private and public. The private *origin* of religion in the individual's intuition of the common notions, however, allows for the state to enforce order by reducing religion to five relatively innocuous propositions and an "austere" public worship stripped of most of its formative power. As Herbert explains in *De Religione Laici,* his thesis

> procures for religion, and thence for the hierarchy and the state, an
> unquestioned authority and majesty. For since there is no clear occa-
> sion for stealing away from this undoubted doctrine, all men will
> be unanimously eager for the austere worship of God by virtue, for
> piety, and for a holy life, and putting aside hatreds along with contro-
> versies about religion they will agree on that mutual token of faith,
> they will be received into that intimate religious relationship; so that
> if insolent spirits revolt on account of some portion of it the spiritual
> or secular magistracy will have the best right to punish them.[101]

The creation of religion reduced to five inoffensive propositions thus comes with the concomitant power of the state to police the boundaries of religion and punish anyone whose more substantive version of Christianity would challenge the authority of the state and the state church.

With John Locke, we find a more recognizably liberal version of tolera-tion. For Locke, as for Herbert, religion is primarily a state of mind: "All the life and power of true religion consist in the inward and full persuasion of the mind."[102] For this reason, Locke denies to the magistrate any power to enforce religion, because the magistrate cannot penetrate the inner reaches of the per-sonal conscience where true religion resides. Locke draws a distinction between the "outward force" used by the civil magistrate and the "inward persuasion" of religion, and he argues that "such is the nature of the understanding that it cannot be compelled to the belief of anything by outward force."[103] This sharp distinction between inward and outward would be unrecognizable in medieval

Christendom, where the state of the interior soul was inseparable from the bodily disciplines and rituals that both formed and expressed the dispositions of the soul. Locke also differed from the Calvinists for whom "saving knowledge" was public and objective. For Locke, the speculative truths of religion cannot be settled by any public authority, neither that of the church nor of the magistrate. There is one true way to eternal happiness, says Locke, and religion is essentially about discovering the saving truths that reveal this way.[104] Unfortunately, controversies over this way among churches are intractable,[105] and the magistrate offers no help; "neither the care of the commonwealth nor the right enacting of laws does discover this way that leads to heaven more certainly to the magistrate than every private man's search and study discovers it unto himself."[106] True religion, therefore, is essentially a private matter of uncovering saving knowledge: "Those things that every man ought sincerely to inquire into himself, and by meditation, study, search, and his own endeavors attain the knowledge of, cannot be looked upon as the peculiar possession of any sort of men."[107]

Locke's scheme for toleration does not result in a strict privatization of Christian worship and practice. Locke continues to assume the context of a state church engaged in public acts of worship. But Locke seeks to promote civil concord by establishing a strict division of labor between the state, whose interests are public in origin, and the church, whose interests are private in origin, thereby clearing a public space for purely secular concerns:

> I esteem it above all things necessary to distinguish exactly the business of civil government from that of religion, and to settle the just bounds that lie between one and the other. If this be not done, there can be no end put to the controversies that will be always arising between those that have, or at least pretend to have, on the one side, a concernment for the interest of men's souls, and, on the other side, a care of the commonwealth.[108]

Locke defines the commonwealth in terms of the promotion of civil interests, and civil interests he defines as "life, liberty, health, and indolency of the body; and the possession of outward things, such as money, lands, houses, furniture, and the like."[109] Violence can be used by the magistrate for the securing of civil interests,[110] but violence has no place in the advancement of "true religion," especially among followers of Christ, the prince of peace.[111] The church is a "voluntary society of men,"[112] but obedience to the state is not voluntary:

> The end of a religious society...is the public worship of God and, by means thereof, the acquisition of eternal life. All discipline ought therefore to tend to that end, and all ecclesiastical laws to be

thereunto confined. Nothing ought nor can be transacted in this society relating to the possession of civil and worldly goods. No force is here to be made use of upon any occasion whatsoever. For force belongs wholly to the civil magistrate, and the possession of all outward goods is subject to his jurisdiction.[113]

Again, the contrast with the medieval Christian context is sharp. The idea that a "religious society" has no say over how civil and worldly goods are handled would be entirely foreign not only to the craft guilds whose work revolved around the liturgy,[114] but also to the monastic communities whose vows were not merely a dispossession of all concern for worldly goods, but a recognition that the religious life is intimately entwined with how one interacts with such goods.

In Locke, we find a modern version of the spatial division of the world into religious and secular pursuits.[115] In the medieval period, the *saeculum* had both a temporal and spatial dimension; it referred to this world and age, and *saecula saeculorum* was translated in English as "world without end." The *saeculum* was all of creation, written into the providential plan of God. It did not refer to some spatial area of interest autonomous from the church's concern. In the suggestive words of Edward Bailey, "It was in the secular that religion revealed its reality, as religion rather than as hobby (or fantasy, or hobby-horse)."[116] When the opposition of religious clergy to secular clergy was transferred to the new conception of religion in the early modern era, however, the secular retained its oppositional character and became that which is not religious in the modern sense. The new religious-secular dichotomy fit into the modern state's individualist anthropology, as typified by Locke. As Ezra Kopelowitz remarks:

> The distinction between the "religious" and the "secular" occurs in societies in which the individual, rather than [the] group is the primary component of social organization. The rise of the individual as the basis of social organization corresponds with the expansion of the centralized modern state, with its strong legal-rational bureaucracy that treats individuals and not groups as the primary source of social rights. Before the rise of the centralized state...."religion" was not a distinct social category that a person could choose or reject. You were born into a group, of which ceremony and symbols rooted in doctrine (religious content) were an integral part of public life.[117]

Although Kopelowitz persists in spying a "religious content" underlying medieval forms, his overall point is accurate: the religious-secular binary is a new creation that accompanies the creation of the modern state.

This brief tour is not intended to be a complete history of the development of the idea of religion in the Renaissance and early modern periods. It should be sufficient to show, nevertheless, that the idea of religion *has a history*. The first of the two conclusions for which I set out in this chapter to provide evidence is that religion is not transhistorical and transcultural. In the next section of this chapter, I will show that religion is not transcultural. For now, we can conclude that it is not transhistorical. To say, as Kimball and Rouner do, that religion has done this or that throughout history is in fact to ignore history. There was a time when religion, as modern people use the term, was not, and then it was invented. In the premodern West, there simply was no conception that Christianity was a species of the genus religion, a universal, interior human impulse, reducible to propositions or beliefs, essentially distinct from secular pursuits such as politics and economics. The point is not simply that religion has changed over time, that it used to be a particular virtue tied up with bodily disciplines in the medieval period and became a universal, interior impulse in the modern era, nor that we used not to separate religion and politics, and now we do. To say this would be to persist in maintaining that there is something lurking underneath the changes that identifies all of the various manifestations as religion. To say this, in other words, would be to say that, despite the differences between medieval *religio* and modern religion, it is still essentially the same thing that has changed. But we have seen that *religio* and religion are *not* the same thing. There is no reason to suppose that there is a one-to-one correspondence between the two. *Religio* in medieval Christendom, as we have seen, was mainly used to distinguish clergy in orders from diocesan clergy. To the limited extent that *religio* referred to piety or some such disposition, it was a specific virtue of the Christian life—a minor one, at that—one of nine subvirtues attached to the principal virtue of justice, itself one of the four cardinal (not theological) virtues. Religion in modernity, on the other hand, is said to be half of the religious-secular binary into which all human pursuits are divided. Structurally, the relative importance of the terms and the places they occupy in their respective contexts are not equivalent. There is no reason to suppose that medieval *religio* simply morphed into modern religion and that, underneath the changes, it has the same essential qualities. There are, of course, commonalities between medieval *religio* and modern religion, but *religio* as a virtue also has commonalities with modern concepts such as public allegiance, civic obligation, justice, public virtue, and a host of other concepts and practices that modernity categorizes as political.

I am not merely making a nominalist contention that every individual thing is different from everything else and no two things can share a common essence. Of course, there are commonalities and continuities among ancient, medieval, and modern ideas and practices. But the relevant commonality necessary to make Kimball's and Rouner's case—the separability of religion from politics, economics, culture, and other institutional forces in ancient and medieval times—is absent from the historical record. How could they make their case empirically? How would one go about showing, from empirical evidence, that religion has caused more violence than any other institutional force in history, when the distinction is absent from premodern cultures? How would one compare religion to politics or economics as causes of warfare in, say, the tenth-century Holy Roman Empire, when no one at the time thought or acted as if there were any such relevant distinction? One would simply have to claim the ability to spy religion lurking there, based on little more than an a priori faith that religion is found at all times in all places. Like Lord Herbert's thesis, such essentialist accounts of religion may be impervious to empirical disproof, but they are also impossible to prove without a prior commitment to finding religion in the complex historical traces left behind by people who arranged their world in a very different way than we do. It may be helpful, under certain circumstances, to use modern terms to describe premodern realities, even if the premodern actors did not think in such terms. But one would have to be clear that such terms are used as a modern way of framing the discussion and not as the discovery of modern realities lurking underneath a premodern disguise.

The problem here is not just one of misdescription or anachronism. The deeper problem is that essentialist accounts of religion occlude the way that power is involved in the shifting uses of concepts such as religion. One of the significant disadvantages of essentialist readings of religion, in other words, is that they ignore or distort changes in how the world is arranged. Major shifts in terms and practices are accompanied by shifts in the way that authority and power are distributed, and transhistorical conceptions of religion tend to obscure rather than illuminate these shifts. This is the second conclusion I have set out to show. The problem is not simply that differences are underplayed in order to identify the essential sameness of religion in all times and places. The deeper problem is that transhistorical accounts of religion are themselves implicated in shifts in the way the authority and power are distributed, while claiming to be purely descriptive.

Take, for example, John Locke's account of what he is up to when he defines religion as essentially interior. Locke does not appear to think that his attempt "to distinguish exactly the business of civil government from that of religion" is involved in the creation of something new. He describes it instead as an attempt to clarify and separate two essentially distinct types of human endeavor that have somehow gotten mixed up together. The church, whose business is religion alone, has overstepped its boundaries:

> [T]he church itself is a thing absolutely separate and distinct from the commonwealth. The boundaries on both sides are fixed and immovable. He jumbles heaven and earth together, the things most remote and opposite, who mixes these two societies, which are in their original, end, business, and in everything perfectly distinct and infinitely different from each other.[118]

Like Herbert, Locke thought he was uncovering the timeless essence of religion. Obscured by this rhetoric is the fact that both Herbert and Locke in the seventeenth century were witnessing and contributing to the rise of a new configuration of power hitherto unknown. The advent of the modern state, with its concept of sovereignty and its absorption of many of the powers of the old ecclesiastical regime, was proving that the boundaries were anything but fixed and immovable. The relationships between church and civil authorities were complex and constantly shifting throughout the centuries of Christendom. As for the contrast between religion and civil interests, we can go further and say not only that the boundaries shifted, but that there simply was no such relevant contrast before Locke and others invented it. The very claim that the boundaries between religion and nonreligion are natural, eternal, fixed, and immutable *is itself* a part of the new configuration of power that comes about with the rise of the modern state. The new state's claim to a monopoly on violence, lawmaking, and public allegiance within a given territory depends upon either the absorption of the church into the state or the relegation of the church to an essentially private realm. Key to this move is the contention that the church's business is religion. Religion must appear, therefore, not as what the church is left with once it has been stripped of earthly relevance, but as the timeless and essential human endeavor to which the church's pursuits should always have been confined.

Transhistorical accounts of religion arose in the fifteenth through the seventeenth centuries as part of a new configuration of Christian societies in which many legislative and jurisdictional powers and claims to power—as well as claims to the devotion and allegiance of the people—were passing from the church to the new sovereign state. The new conception of religion would help to "purify" the church of powers and claims that were not its proper function. The historical process of secularization and the separation of church and state were by no means uncontested or complete in these or the centuries following. In the wake of the Reformation, princes and kings tended to claim authority over the church in their realms, as in Luther's Germany and Henry VIII's

England. But this was already a significant departure from the medieval eccle-siastical order, in which, in theory at least, the civil authorities were "the police department of the Church."[119] The new conception of religion helped to facil-itate the shift to state dominance over the church by distinguishing inward religion from the bodily disciplines of the state. The new subject is thus able to do due service to both, without conflict. Those unable to so distinguish—for example, Roman Catholics whose allegiance to the pope prevented them from accepting the king's supremacy over the church—have simply misunderstood the true and unchanging nature of religion. For this reason, Locke excludes Roman Catholics from his scheme of toleration, for they have designs on civil power "upon pretense of religion."[120] True religion cannot have designs on civil power because it is essentially distinct from the political.

William Arnal draws an explicit link between modern conceptions of reli-gion and the rise of the modern liberal state forecast by Locke:

> Our definitions of religion, especially insofar as they assume a privatized and cognitive character behind religion (as in religious *belief*), simply reflect (and assume as normative) the West's distinc-tive historical feature of the secularized state. Religion, precisely, is *not* social, *not* coercive, *is* individual, *is* belief-oriented and so on, because in our day and age there are certain apparently free-standing cultural institutions, such as the Church, which are excluded from the political state.[121]

As Arnal goes on to say, our definitions of religion do not simply reflect the new reality of the modern West but help to shape it: "the very concept of reli-gion as such—as an entity with any distinction whatsoever from other human phenomena—is a function of these same processes and historical moments that generate an individualistic concept of it."[122] Specifically, the concept of reli-gion justifies the liberal state's self-presentation as an apparatus concerned with the wholly negative function of preventing the incursion of substantive, collective ends into the public sphere: "This very definition of the modern democratic state in fact creates religion as its alter-ego: religion, as such, is the space in which and by which any substantive collective goals (salvation, righteousness, etc.) are individualized and made into a question of personal commitment or morality."[123] Religion, as Arnal says elsewhere, is a special *political* category that marginalizes and domesticates whatever forms of col-lective social action happen to retain a positive or utopian orientation.[124] In the early modern era, the church was the most significant source of such social action that the state domesticated. Any attempt to break out of this segregation was condemned as dangerous and potentially violent.[125]

It is crucial to underscore that the category of religion does not simply describe a new social reality but helps to bring it into being and to enforce it. Religion is a normative concept. The normative ideal that has come to define Western modernity is, in Locke's words, "to distinguish exactly the business of civil government from that of religion." This ideal would eventually come to be marked by the separation of church and state. In practice, of course, the ideal is never fully realized and is always contested. Nevertheless, the dominant ideal is that the business of the church is religion, defined as essentially and eternally distinct from politics, which is the business of the state. Transhistorical definitions of religion enforce the normativity of this new arrangement; as in Herbert's work, the modern definition of religion helps to define the "normal mind." The normal mind is one that is able to penetrate to the true inward essence of religion. Those who will not separate religion from politics—many Muslims, for example—are often seen as less advanced and less rational than their "normal" Western counterparts.

The idea that there exists a transhistorical human impulse called religion with a singular tendency to promote fanaticism and violence when combined with public power is not an empirically demonstrable fact, but is itself an ideological accompaniment to the shifts in power and authority that mark the transition from the medieval to the modern in the West. There may be good reasons to prefer modern to medieval, or Western to Islamic, arrangements (though to pass wholesale judgment on entire eras or cultures is not the best way to proceed). But normative commitments should not be passed off as descriptions of fact. The idea that "religion has probably been the single most significant cause of warfare in human history" has a history of its own.

The Invention of Religion Outside the West

The theories of religious violence we encountered in chapter 1 are not only transhistorical, but transcultural as well. The genus religion extends over both time and space. Religion is seen as potentially problematic at all times and all places. Religion is not merely a Western phenomenon, but is something that is found worldwide, in the world religions of which varying lists are provided.

In this section, I will show how deeply problematic is the assumption of a transcultural essence of religion. In searching for the concept of religion outside the West, Wilfred Cantwell Smith wrote, "One is tempted, indeed, to ask whether there is a closely equivalent concept in any culture that has not been influenced by the modern West." Smith gives in to this temptation, and answers the question "no."[126] Since Smith, a generation of scholars has pursued his question and shown, in increasing detail, that his negative answer is correct. Furthermore, as in the case of Europe, the invention of religion in non-Western contexts was not accomplished in the absence of shifts in power and authority. The concept of religion was introduced outside the West in the context of European colonization, and the introduction of the concept often served the interests of the colonizers.

In their initial contacts with native peoples of the Americas, Africa, and the Pacific islands, European explorers reported, with remarkable consistency, that the local people had no religion at all. Amerigo Vespucci remarked on the lack of religion among the Caribbean peoples he encountered. Sixteenth-century conquistador Pedro Cieza de León found the Peruvians "observing no religion at all, as we understand it." The seventeenth-century explorer Jacques Le Maire found in the Pacific islands "not the least spark of religion," and the eighteenth-century trader William Smith reported that Africans "trouble themselves about no religion at all." Into the nineteenth century, Europeans found among the Aborigines of Australia "nothing whatever of the character of religion, or of religious observance, to distinguish them from the beasts that perish." As David Chidester remarks, these examples can be multiplied almost endlessly.[127] In their initial encounters, Europeans' denying religion to indigenous peoples was a way of denying them rights. If they lacked a basic human characteristic like religion, then native peoples could be treated as subhumans without legitimate claim to life, land, and other resources in their possession.

Once the native peoples were conquered and colonized, however, it was "discovered" that they did in fact have religions after all, which were then fitted into genus-and-species taxonomies of religion. Chidester's richly detailed work on the career of the concept of religion in southern Africa shows how the British and the Dutch denied religion to the native peoples when they were at war with them, but subsequently discovered Hottentot, Xhosa, and Zulu religions once they had been subjugated. In the Hottentot case, rebellions caused the indigenous people to oscillate between religion and no religion in the eyes of the colonizers over the course of two centuries.[128] When they were subdued, attributing religion to indigenous peoples was at once a way of depoliticizing their cultures and a way of entering their cultures into a comparative framework in which—compared to the norm of religion, Christianity—their practices would be found wanting. When religion was discovered, it was of course "primitive" religion, at the lower end of an evolutionary scale that culminated in Christianity.[129] Chidester sees the introduction of the category religion as a strategy of social control. For example, following the conquest of the Xhosa in 1857, British magistrate J. C. Warner became the first European to discover a Xhosa religion. As Warner defined it, religion was that symbol system that provided psychological security and therefore social stability. Although Warner hoped that the Xhosa would eventually embrace Christianity, a depoliticized Xhosa religion in the meantime would help to keep the Xhosa in their place.[130]

Derek Peterson and Darren Walhof's study of colonial government among the Gikuyu people of Kenya similarly shows that the term religion artificially separated out certain aspects of Gikuyu culture: "naming a certain practice or disposition religious rendered it something other than real."[131] Gikuyu life centered on *magongona*, practices that protect the living from the uncharitable dead. There was very little use of *Ngai*, a term imported from the Masai that the missionaries translated as "God." Presbyterian missionaries tried to convert the highly material, experimental nature of *magongona* into a systematic set of propositions that they identified as religion. They wanted to establish Gikuyu practices on the same footing as Christianity so that they could convince the Gikuyu of the superiority of the latter. They emphasized God as lawgiver—a concept wholly absent from *Ngai*—and tried to bring the Gikuyu into a world of abstract truths governed by God-given law. At the same time that this move helped to solidify the reality of colonial law, religion as such was identified with the dematerialized relationship of the individual soul to God. As Peterson comments:

> [R]eligion was supposed to be an otherworldly belief system, a con-
> tract agreed upon by God and believer. This disembodied, proposi-
> tional definition of religion was the template that allowed European
> intellectuals to make sense of the ideas of colonized subjects. By
> reducing difference to sameness, by disembodying subjects' ideas
> and practices, comparative religion functioned as a strategy of intel-
> lectual and political control.[132]

The history of the concept of religion in India shows how problematic and ideological is religion as a transcultural and transhistorical phenomenon. Smith finds no religion named "Hinduism" until 1829, and even the term "Hindu" was unknown in classical India.[133] Hindu was a Persian term used to refer to those on the far side of the Sindhu River. Muslim invaders used the term Hindu, but it referred to all non-Muslim natives of India, including those we presently divide into Hindus, Jains, Buddhists, Sikhs, and animists.[134] In 1941, the British census gave up the attempt to number Hindus, because—although they were able to distinguish them from Muslims and Christians—they were unable to distinguish them from animists.

In precolonial India, there was no concept equivalent to religion. Mundane human activity was classified into things one does for enjoyment (*kāma*), things one does as a means to an end (*artha*), and things one does out of duty (*dharma*). This last term has been used as the Indian equivalent of religion, but as Smith points out, dharma includes propriety, public law, temple ritual, caste obligations, and much more. Dharma does not include doctrine, such as the law of karma. Furthermore, dharma refers to mundane obligations and does not include the three ways of the *Trimārga*, which supplements mundane activity by offering paths to break away from bondage to the phenomenal world. Neither dharma nor any other term was used to indicate any peculiar institution analogous with a church: "Nor was there any term enabling an Indian to discriminate conceptually between the religious and the other aspects of his society's life."[135]

The invention of Hinduism as a religion allowed for the differentiation of Hinduism from politics, economics, and other aspects of social life, and it also allowed for the distinction of Hinduism from other religions such as Buddhism, Sikhism, and Jainism. Such differentiation was not simply an improvement on the former system of classification, however, as if new terms suddenly allowed Indians to see what they had been missing before. To the contrary, the use of the term religion has produced confusion and misdescription of the phenomena of Indian life. As Timothy Fitzgerald points out, the separation of religion from society in India is misleading in a context in which caste hierarchy, exchange of goods, ritual, and political power are densely intertwined. Dharma—the favored term for religion—includes cosmic, social, and ritual order. Louis Dumont has written that, in India, "the politico-economic domain is encompassed in an overall religious setting."[136] If this is true, Fitzgerald asks, does anything lie outside of religion? And if nothing lies outside of religion, is religion a useful term?

Similarly, differences among Hindus, Muslims, Buddhists, Sikhs, Jains, animists, and others are poorly served by the term religion. For some purposes, what Westerners consider to be other religions are included under the rubric of Hinduism. In its clause on freedom of religion, the Indian Constitution says that "reference to Hindus shall be construed as including a reference to persons professing the Sikh, Jaina or Buddhist religion."[137] The 1955 Hindu Marriage Act goes further, defining as Hindus all Buddhists, Jains, Sikhs, and anyone who is not a Christian, Muslim, Parsee, or Jew.[138] Where differences among these groups become important, it is often not purely "religious" differences that are informative. When determining the differences among the above groups, religious criteria such as beliefs about gods are usually inadequate; caste position, for example, is often far more determinative than beliefs. Muslims and Hindus in India worship at each other's shrines. As Fitzgerald comments, "This suggests that it would be difficult to separate Hindus and

Muslims simply on the basis of different religions defined by relations with superhuman beings."[139]

The above problems and more have led Frits Staal to conclude, "Hinduism does not merely fail to be a religion; it is not even a meaningful unit of discourse."[140] Other scholars acknowledge the problems, but continue to talk about a religion called Hinduism anyway. R. N. Dandekar writes, "Hinduism can hardly be called a religion in the properly understood sense of the term," though that recognition does not stop him from treating Hinduism under the rubric of religion.[141] Simon Weightman writes, "Hinduism displays few of the characteristics that are generally expected of a religion."[142] Weightman lists what Hinduism lacks: it has no founder, no prophets, no creed, no dogma, no system of theology, no single moral code, no uniquely authoritative scripture, no ecclesiastical organization, and the concept of a god is not centrally important. He adds, "It is then possible to find groups of Hindus whose respective faiths have almost nothing in common with one another, and it is also impossible to identify any universal belief or practice that is common to all Hindus."[143] Weightman continues to identify Hinduism as a religion, however, because he says that Hindus themselves affirm that it is a single religion. There are several problems here. First, the definitions of "Hindus" and "Hinduism" are circular. Hindus believe in Hinduism, and Hinduism is what Hindus believe in. Second, there is no recognition of historical factors at work. There was a time when no one in India thought he or she had a religion named Hinduism. A change occurred only after more than a century of British rule. Might there be a connection? The fact that Weightman's list of what is "generally expected of a religion" would only fully apply to Christianity should alert the reader that religion is originally a Western concept. If Indians now—after centuries of Western influence—find themselves with a religion called Hinduism, it is worth asking how that state of affairs came to pass.

When seen through the eyes of the British colonizers, the initial difficulty of fitting Hinduism into the category of religion was not due to a problem with the Western notion of religion. The problem lay in the irrational nature of Hinduism itself. Thus, James Mill in his influential *The British History of India* states:

> Whenever indeed we seek to ascertain the definite and precise ideas
> of the Hindus in religion, the subject eludes our grasp. All is loose,
> vague, wavering, obscure, and inconsistent. Their expressions point
> at one time to one meaning, and another time to another mean-
> ing; and their wild fictions, to use the language of Mr. Hume, seem
> rather the playsome whimsies of monkeys in human shape than the

serious asseverations of a being who dignifies himself with the name
of the rational.[144]

As S. N. Balagangadhara comments on this passage, "It did not occur to people then, as it does not seem to occur to people now, that this amorphous
nature of Hinduism might have little to do with its 'amazing capacities.' It is
more likely that the absence of structure has something to do with the fact
that it is an imaginary entity."[145] Though imaginary, Hinduism as a religion
was a useful concept to the colonizers. According to Mill, the pervasiveness
of religion throughout society and the failure to "properly" separate religion
from politics and economics were evidence of the irrationality of the Hindus.
James Mill—who, along with his son John Stuart Mill, was employed by the
British East India Company—argued that the despotic divine kingship and the
priestly tyranny of precolonial India were supplanted by more rational government under British rule.[146]

Two different types of European discourse about Hinduism developed in
the nineteenth century. Mill represents one type, which accused Hinduism
of being coarsely ritualistic, obsessed with endless and meaningless external
rites and ceremonies.[147] On this score, Hinduism was routinely compared with
Catholicism by European Protestants.[148] The other type of discourse about
Hinduism saw it as mystical and otherworldly. Given the pejorative implications that Catholic mysticism had for Protestants, Hindu mysticism could
also be associated with irrational and obscurantist strains of religion. On the
other hand, the mystical Orient held a certain allure for some kinds of Western
thinking. Romantics such as Friedrich Schlegel constructed a Hinduism
whose direct, unmediated absorption of consciousness into the divine became
the passionate Other to the West's overly rational identity. For this type of
Orientalism, the more apparently philosophically oriented Vedantic texts,
especially the Upanishads, became the core of Hinduism.[149] The Upanishads
lent themselves to this process because of the way that they allegorize sacrificial rituals into individual spiritual practices—for example, the fire sacrifice
agnihotra is transformed from an external ritual to an interior yogic practice of
controlling the life force (*prāna*) within.[150] What both the negative and positive
views of Hinduism have in common is the idea that a proper religion should be
essentially interior, a direct, ahistorical, and apolitical relation of the individual
soul to a larger, superhuman, cosmic reality.

The Western concept of religion may have been inadequate to the reality
of Indian culture, but it did provide certain advantages to the colonizers. The
creation of a unified religion called Hinduism established something structurally parallel to Christianity so that Christian missionaries could compare and

contrast the Christian and Hindu creeds. Of course, in such a comparison, Hinduism was seen to be woefully deficient, except perhaps in the high culture of the Vedantic texts. As Richard King comments:

> The lack of orthodoxy, of an ecclesiastical structure, or indeed of any distinctive feature that might point to the postulation of a single Hindu religion, was dismissed, and one consequence of this was the tendency to portray "Hinduism" as a contradictory religion, which required some form of organization along ecclesiastical and doctrinal lines and a purging of "superstitious" elements incompatible with the "high" culture of "Hinduism."[151]

The nonrational nature of Hinduism provided a rationale not only for the imposition of order in religious matters but for the ordering of India as a whole. As Ronald Inden writes:

> Implicit in this notion of Hinduism as exemplifying a mind that is imaginative and passionate rather than rational and willful was, of course, the idea that the Indian mind requires an externally imported world-ordering rationality. This was important for the imperial project of the British as it appeared, piecemeal, in the course of the nineteenth century.[152]

Crucial to the imperial ordering of India were the binary distinctions between rational and nonrational, modern and ancient, public and private. The Western concept of religion served these distinctions well. As a "mystical" religion, Hinduism was both nonrational and timeless, locked in an ancient, ever-repeating cycle.[153] Hinduism furthermore belonged essentially to the private realm because, as a religion, it was based in personal experiences of the individual conscience.[154] The focus on Hindu mysticism helped to separate Hinduism from the essentially distinct realms of politics and economics. If Hinduism is a religion, then it is essentially removed from the ambit of worldly power. In reality, the amorphous nature of Hinduism is due to the fact that Hinduism originally included all that it means to be Indian, including what modern Westerners divided into religion, politics, economics, and so on. But if Hinduism is what it means to be Indian, then by identifying and isolating a religion called Hinduism, the British were able to marginalize what it means to be Indian. Under British colonization, to be British was to be public; to be Indian was to be private. The very conception of religion was a tool in removing native Indian culture and Indians themselves from the exercise of public power.

Colonial hegemony in this process should not be exaggerated; colonization was not simply a one-way street on which modernity was imposed on the passive Orient. In India, nineteenth-century Brahmins themselves had a key role in establishing a certain high-culture Brahmanism based on Sanskrit texts as the norm for all of Hinduism.[155] Colonized peoples also creatively used the tools of the colonizers to forge their own identities. Sanjay Joshi, for example, has shown that early twentieth-century middle-class activists resisted British attempts to confine Hindu religion to the realm of the personal and the private by emphasizing the Hindu roots of universal values like reason, progress, freedom, and community over tradition and superstitious rites. This "republicizing" of religion eventually led to the kinds of Hindu nationalism that helped to end British rule. In the process, however, Hinduism was constructed along the model of a Western religion; it was fundamentally a generator of values. Such values, detached from superstitious rites and the traditional past, were used by Jawaharlal Nehru and others to forge India into an officially secular nation-state on the Western model.[156] In other words, even resistance to colonization often works within the parameters set by the colonizers. For this reason, as Richard Cohen points out, contemporary advocates of Hindu nationalism (Hindutva)—especially the powerful BJP—reject the confinement of Hinduism to religion: "The proponents of Hindutva refuse to call Hinduism a religion precisely because they want to emphasize that Hinduism is more than mere internalized beliefs. It is social, political, economic, and familial in nature. Only thus can India the secular state become interchangeable with India the Hindu homeland."[157]

Another religion of Indian origin—"Buddhism"—appeared on the scene in the early decades of the nineteenth century. According to Philip Almond, Buddhism was "an imaginative creation" of Western scholars: "Buddhism, by 1860, had come to exist, not in the Orient, but in the Oriental libraries and institutes of the West, in its texts and manuscripts, at the desks of the Western savants who interpreted it."[158] This does not mean, of course, that the phenomena of which Buddhism consists did not exist before the nineteenth century. The founding figure, his teachings, and the institutions dedicated to them are ancient. Until the nineteenth century, however, it was not clear that there was a separate religion called Buddhism. As Tomoko Masuzawa remarks, "Until that time, neither European observers nor, for the most part, native 'practitioners' of those various devotional, contemplative, divinatory, funereal, and other ordinary and extraordinary cults that are now roundly called Buddhist had thought of these divergent rites and widely scattered institutions as constituting a single religion."[159] Many Western scholars identified Buddhist devotions as a "branch of the vast Hindu banyan tree," paying particular attention to the Brahminical identification of the Buddha as the ninth *avatāra* of the god Vishnu.[160]

The invention of Buddhism as a distinct religion was based on the discovery of Sanskrit texts that could be used to trace the origins of disparate rites in Asia back to the figure of Gautama. Buddhism was born as a textual religion, on the model of Protestantism. Once this work was done, the actual living manifestations of these rites were understood by Western scholars as corruptions from the original spirit of the texts. The purity of the universal, interior, spiritual message of the Buddha had been debased into materialistic ritual. The Buddha was commonly presented—by Max Müller, among many others—as the "Martin Luther of the East," a reformer who had rejected the ritualism of Hinduism to found a purely spiritual religion. Where Hinduism was a particularistic national religion, Buddhism was universal, originating in the mind of Gautama and capable of being practiced anywhere. The fact that Buddhism itself had been degraded in practice from the founder's original insight did not prevent the designation of Buddhism as a world religion. It was, however, considered to be a world religion based on its original form, not on its actual corrupt forms as practiced in the Orient.[161]

Perhaps the greatest difficulty with the construction of Buddhism as a religion is that many Buddhist traditions explicitly deny belief in God or gods. This fact has caused much vexation among those who insist that Buddhism is a religion. Martin Southwold argues:

> We have shown that practical Buddhism does not manifest a central concern with godlike beings. Hence *either* the theistic definitions and conception of religion are wrong *or* Buddhism is not a religion. But the latter proposition is not a viable option. In virtually every other aspect Buddhism markedly resembles religions, and especially the religion prototypical for our conception, i.e., Christianity. If we declare that Buddhism is not a religion, we take on the daunting task of explaining how a non-religion can come so uncannily to resemble religions.[162]

The supposed fact that Buddhism "resembles religions" of course begs the question of how religions are defined. They are, presumably, things that look like Christianity, since Christianity is Southwold's admitted prototype of religion. But Buddhism lacks a god, a concept quite central to Christianity. So Southwold—determined that Buddhism must be a religion—expands the definition of religion to include any phenomenon that has *at least one* from a list of twelve attributes, a list that includes "ritual practices," "a mythology," and "association with an ethnic or similar group." Southwold goes on to say that more attributes could be added to his list in order to include other things we consider to be religions.[163] We begin, in other words, with the conviction that Buddhism must be a religion, and then we adjust the definition to include it.

Why go to such great lengths to construct a religion made up of such heterogeneous and atheistic practices? Of what use is the classification of Buddhism as a religion? For Western missionaries and scholars, it served to establish a parallel with Christianity, so that comparison could take place. In the case of Tibetan Buddhism, Donald Lopez has shown that both Catholics and Protestants were struck by the similarities of "lamaism" with Catholicism. Early Catholic missionaries to China and Tibet explained the similarities of rite and hierarchy by a process of demonic imitation of the Catholic original. Protestant scholars of Eastern religion from the mid-eighteenth century and into the twentieth century commonly saw in Tibetan Buddhism a prime example of the corruption of the spiritual purity of the original Indian Buddhism into materialistic ritualism, just as Catholicism was a degradation of the purity of the gospel. British experience in overthrowing Catholic tyranny would be helpful for the liberation of Tibet. As Lopez notes:

> It is not simply analogy that Pali Buddhism (which by the end of the nineteenth century was largely under British control) is to Tibetan Buddhism (which at the end of the nineteenth century Britain was actively seeking to control) as Protestantism is to Roman Catholicism. It is rather a strategy of debasing the distant and unsubjugated by comparing it with the near and long subjugated, subjugated both by its relegation to England's pre-Reformation past and to its present European rivals and Irish subjects.[164]

British Buddhologist L. Austine Waddell wrote of the necessity of British help in recovering the pristine state of Buddhism in Tibet from the "intolerable tyranny of the Lamas." According to Waddell, the mission of the British was "to herald the rise of a new star in the East, which may for long, perhaps for centuries, diffuse its mild radiance over this charming land and interesting people. In the University, which must ere long be established under British direction at Lhasa, a chief place will surely be assigned to studies in the origin of the religion of the country."[165] As Lopez notes, Waddell wrote this in his account of the British invasion of Tibet in 1903–1904, in which he took part.[166]

Buddhism as a world religion was not merely a European creation. Beginning in the late nineteenth century, monastic elites in Sri Lanka, China, and Japan began to posit a monolithic Buddhism as a world religion, fully equal with Christianity, with its own founder, scriptures, and established set of doctrines. This "Buddhist modernism," as it has been called, presents

Buddhism as most compatible with modern notions of reason and science, since it does not hold beliefs in supernatural deities. Buddhism is presented as essentially nonviolent and highly interior. The key practice is individual meditation, and the host of other rites practiced at the popular level is frowned upon as superstition.[167] As Lopez points out, the most important present-day advocate of Buddhist modernism is the current Dalai Lama. The Dalai Lama has presented a Buddhism shorn of the trappings of Tibetan culture, consisting instead of universal, transcultural values such as compassion. At the same time, he has moved actively to suppress the centuries-old cult of the protective deity Shugden among Tibetans in exile, considering it a less rational and less universal corruption of pure Buddhism. For the Dalai Lama, the heart of Tibet is not its material culture but its religion. By universalizing and interiorizing Tibetan Buddhism as a religion, the Dalai Lama has offered a transcultural, beatific Buddhism easily digested by Western consumers. The Dalai Lama hopes to win sympathy for the plight of Tibet under Chinese rule and win Western support for Tibetan independence. The problem, as Lopez points out, is that Tibetan religion has been made to float free of Tibet, such that it is easy for Westerners to embrace Buddhism and forget about Tibet. The reassertion of the cult of Shugden among Tibetan exiles may be understood as an attempt to take back Buddhism from the West, to make it indigestible to Western appetites.[168]

Buddhism has long been stereotyped by Western scholars as individualistic, rationalistic, interior, apolitical, and asocial. As Richard Cohen remarks, "Buddhism, thus stereotyped, is a religion that even Kant could love."[169] Cohen has shown that Buddhist traditions have not always been so detachable from such mundane concerns as culture and politics. In his study of inscriptions and other evidence of the Ajanta community, beginning in the fifth century, Cohen finds that what we now call Buddhism was about negotiating kinship and trade relations, not simply beliefs and individual salvation: "For Ajanta's Buddhists, religion was a matter of politics as much as liberation, as much a matter of instrumental power as of transcendent proof."[170] Indeed, Cohen finds the very term religion to be unhelpful, because it is commonly used to exclude material factors. He shows that the idealist assumptions that pervade scholarship on Buddhism—that Buddhism, as a religion, is about universal truth and the salvation of the individual soul—are not only a scholarly problem. Cohen shows that the same contemporary Hindu nationalists that refuse to call Hinduism a religion denigrate Buddhism as a purely religious phenomenon with no contribution to make to social and political reality in India.[171]

The creation of Shinto in Japan is one of the most fascinating examples of how—and for what purposes—the category of religion has been introduced into non-Western contexts. The term "Shinto"—which refers to worship of the kami, gods associated with natural forces such as the sun—has been known since the eighth century. Until the nineteenth century, however, worship of the kami was interwoven with rites associated with the Buddha and buddhas. Shinto and Buddhism were not two separate traditions. In the face of the forced opening of Japan to Western trade and influence in the mid-nineteenth century, however, a nativist movement clamored for the creation of a distinctly Japanese cult. The Meiji state after 1868 undertook a nationwide "separation of kami and buddhas" (*shinbutsu bunri*). The Meiji government took control of the shrines thus "purified" of Buddhism and declared that "shrines of the kami are for the worship of the state."[172]

By the mid-1870s, however, the Meiji government was under pressure both from Western powers and from educated Japanese elites who had studied in the West, such as Mori Arinori, later to be minister of education. In 1872, Arinori wrote a treatise in English declaring that the government's "attempt to impose upon our people a religion of its creation cannot receive too severe condemnation."[173] In 1875, the government officially declared freedom of religion, provided that religion did not impede the acceptance of imperial proclamations. This qualification led to an official distinction between Shinto performed at government-sponsored shrines (shrine Shinto) and that performed elsewhere (sect Shinto). Sect Shinto was conceived of as a doctrine and was therefore defined as religion (*shūkyō*, a technical term borrowed from Buddhist monastic practice meaning "group teaching" or "sect teaching"). Shrine Shinto was dedicated to the worship of the state and was not considered religion but "rites" (*jinja*). Belief in religious teachings was therefore a private matter of choice, but the performance of rituals for the state was a public duty. From the 1880s to World War II, official state rhetoric made a sharp distinction between Shinto and religion. Buddhism, Christianity, and other sects were religions, symptoms of selfishness and disunity. There was a movement, therefore, to classify all shrines of the kami as national shrines, to avoid the taint of religion.[174]

The officially endorsed national cult of Shinto had gained such power in the early twentieth century that the victorious U.S. government moved immediately to remove shrine Shinto from public power at the end of World War II. Sarah Thal explains:

> At that time all government support of Shinto shrines, teachings,
> rituals, and institutions was expressly forbidden in order "to sepa-
> rate religion from the state, to prevent misuse of religion for political
> ends, and to put all religions, faiths, and creeds upon exactly the

same legal basis." After years of denying the religiosity of Shinto, priests and apologists found themselves suddenly defined as religious, limited by the very principle of freedom of religious belief which they had once overcome by defining themselves against religion.[175]

Shinto is often identified as a religion in Western surveys of world religions. The fact that many of the prominent practitioners of Shinto explicitly have denied its status as a religion indicates how problematic the category of religion is when applied to Japan. Although Shinto and Buddhism are considered two separate religions by Western writers, Kuroda Toshio calls this idea "misleading at best" not only historically but for contemporary Japanese society as well.[176] Shinto, Buddhism, Confucianism, and so-called new religions participate in one ideological and cultural complex in Japan. Western distinctions between religion and politics, or religion and culture, fit awkwardly, if at all, in the modern Japanese context. Extricating religion from politics in such an explicitly nationalistic set of practices as Shinto is highly misleading. As Timothy Fitzgerald points out, the rituals performed in modern factories, shrines dedicated to the various kami, schools, temples, corporate headquarters, or shrines for the war dead have the same basic structure and function, which is to ensure propriety and the propitious functioning of Japanese society. Indeed, ritual actions are increasing in modern Japanese society despite the fact that fewer and fewer Japanese actually believe in gods and their ability to bring benefits. According to Fitzgerald, this fact, so strange to Western eyes, is accounted for by the fact that rites are not about belief but about social order. Religious fulfillment of obligations is not distinguishable from social fulfillment of obligations. Fitzgerald suggests dropping the word religion for the Japanese context and using "ritual" instead.[177] Peter Beyer writes, "Japanese people engage in a wide range of activities that might analytically be included as 'religious,' but which they do not usually recognize as 'religion,' " and Beyer suggests a more appropriate term than religion would be "culture."[178]

The case of China is similar to that of Japan in that modernizing elites in the late nineteenth century adopted the term religion (*zongjiao*, the corresponding Chinese word to the Japanese *shūkyō*, group or sect teaching) but refused to identify those traditions most closely identified with the national character as religion. The man most responsible for introducing the term religion to China, Liang Chichao, declared in the early twentieth century that "there is no religion among the indigenous products of China." He later made an exception to this rule for the case of Daoism, but said that this is a "humiliation" for China, because Daoism resembles such foreign products as

Buddhism and Christianity. According to Beyer, Chinese elites such as Liang Chichao rejected religion for two reasons: it was highly individualistic, and therefore inimical to national unity, and it was nonprogressive, and therefore inimical to the modernization of China. Chinese elites therefore championed "Confucianism" as indigenous, unitive, and progressive, but also as definitely *not* religious.[179]

That Confucianism would become one of the world religions in Western taxonomies is therefore a very curious phenomenon. A loose tradition of scholarly ethical precepts, lacking gods and transcendence, Confucianism is closer to what Westerners consider "philosophy." Besides having no indigenous term for religion in Chinese, there was also no word for Confucianism, Buddhism, or Daoism. Westerners consider these three to be religions, but as Wilfred Cantwell Smith points out, a single Chinese can be a Confucianist, a Buddhist, and a Daoist at the same time: "To ask a census-taker how many Chinese are Buddhist is rather like asking one how many Westerners are Aristotelian or pragmatist."[180] Since Smith wrote in 1962, however, the communist government in China has become very precise in its definition of religion, such that now the census taker might have more success in finding Buddhists. In the official 1982 document that governs religious practice in China, known as Document 19, religion is defined as an organized activity based on beliefs in supernatural beings. According to Document 19, there are five religions in China—Buddhism, Protestantism, Catholicism, Islam, and Daoism—and no others. Confucianism, Maoism, and such expressions of the national character are excluded from this list as they are superior to mere religion, which is essentially otherworldly. Also excluded from this list are "superstitious" practices such as phrenology and witchcraft, as well as new movements deemed to be "injurious to the national welfare." The official definition of religion and the list of five religions is clearly intended to establish a space for "freedom of religion," which is circumscribed and essentially nonpublic, and to proscribe new groups, such as Falun Gong, which might challenge the control of the Communist Party over public life.[181]

This brief digest of recent scholarship is not intended, of course, to be a comprehensive survey of the career of the concept of religion in non-Western contexts. It should be sufficient, however, to demonstrate the two points mentioned in the introduction to this chapter. The first is that religion is not a transcultural reality. Masuzawa puts this conclusion bluntly: "This concept of religion as a general, transcultural phenomenon, yet also as a distinct sphere in its own right...is patently groundless; it came from nowhere, and there is no credible way of demonstrating its factual and empirical substantiality."[182] Those who go looking to spy religion in all places and times—as if it were a reality that is simply there before anyone develops a concept of it—are guaranteed to produce confusion or worse. Religion is originally a Western concept, and it only becomes a worldwide concept through—and in reaction to—Western influence.

This does not mean that non-Western agents were not active in the production of the category religion. The West has never been a monolithic reality, and what defines the West has always been contested both from within and without. The West, however, is a modernizing *ideal*, a project pushed forward by certain interests both within and without countries identified as Oriental. The production of religion took place in a context established by pressures, both external and internal, to modernize and Westernize. As Charles Keyes sums up the process in Asia:

> In pursuit of "progress" free from primordial attachments the rulers of [the] modern state[s] of East and South East Asia all have instituted policies toward religious institutions. These policies have been predicated on the adoption of official definitions of "religion," definitions that (again) have tended to be derived from the West. Indeed, in most Asian cultures prior to the modern period, there was no indigenous terminology corresponding to ideas of "religion" held by Christians or Jews. Complex predispositions about the nature of religion—the primacy of texts; creeds pledging exclusive allegiance to a single deity; ethics; and a personal, privatized relation to a deity, all originating in the theologically unadorned varieties of Protestantism—were brought to Asia by missionaries in the nineteenth century. When these predispositions came to inform official discourse on religion, they were often used to devalue other aspects of religious life such as festivals, ritual and communal observances—precisely those aspects that were at the heart of popular religious life in East and South East Asia.[183]

While Keyes retains the language of "popular religious life" in Asia, Daniel Dubuisson would jettison all such language as fundamentally misleading. Religion was and remains, according to Dubuisson, a fundamentally Western concept. Indeed, Dubuisson calls religion "the West's most characteristic concept, around which it has established and developed its identity."[184] It characterizes the West because it establishes a fundamental divide between religion and nonreligion that has determined the Western view of reality and the Western organization of the world. In the West, religion is a distinct domain, separated from the rest of life. This division is found nowhere that has not been influenced by the West, but this has not prevented the West from declaring the concept to be universal. Insofar as other religions deviate from the (Western) norm, then, they may be classified as primitive, strange, unreasonable. In other words, presenting the Western concept of religion as universal declares the Western subject to be universal and the non-Western Others, therefore, as parochial. We should avoid this imposition, according to Dubuisson: "We should also avoid describing as universal values that the West alone has invented. Since their domain is always fundamentally one of conflict, these values would effectively become universal only when all the others had been destroyed and eliminated—by us."[185]

The force of this statement by Dubuisson compels us to the second crucial point to be concluded from this survey of religion in non-Western cultures: the transcultural concept of religion has been adopted because it is useful for certain purposes. In other words, religion is not a neutral scientific tool but is applied under circumstances in which configurations of power are relevant. As we have seen, this is most obviously the case in circumstances of direct colonial control, as in Africa and India, but it applies more generally to the "opening" of Asia to the West in the nineteenth and twentieth centuries. In general terms, knowledge of non-Western Others allowed for a certain measure of control of other peoples, especially since the knowledge was contained within the West's own system of classification, the West's own way of identifying what is religion and what is not. Huston Smith, one of the great twentieth-century figures in the study of world religions, once made this point with alarming candor:

> The motives that impel us toward world understanding may be several. Recently I was taxied by bomber to the Air Command and Staff College at the Maxwell Air Force Base outside Montgomery, Alabama, to lecture to a thousand selected officers on the religions of other peoples. I have never had students more eager to learn. What was their motivation? Individually I am sure it went beyond this in many cases, but as a unit they were concerned because someday they were likely to be dealing with the peoples they were studying as allies, antagonists, or subjects of military occupation. Under such circumstances it would be crucial for them to predict their behavior, conquer them if worse came to worst, and control them during the aftermath or reconstruction. This is one reason for coming to know people. It may be a necessary reason; certainly we have no right to disdain it as long as we ask the military to do the job we set before it.[186]

In more specific terms, the discourse of religion has been used to provide a tool of comparison by which non-Western practices could be shown to be deficient when compared with Christianity and Western culture more generally. Perhaps most important, the discourse of religion was also a tool of secularization, the cordoning off of significant elements of non-Western cultures into a personal, apolitical realm of belief. The irony here is that, as Russell McCutcheon says, the very conception of religion as self-caused, as directly related to individual consciousness and not directly related to material factors, and therefore utterly distinct from issues of power, is itself an instrument of colonial and neocolonial strategies of power.[187] The idea that there is a transcultural phenomenon called religion that has a dangerous tendency toward violence—and must therefore be domesticated—is not only a misdescription of reality. The idea itself should be interrogated for the kinds of power that it authorizes. The attempt to domesticate certain practices as religion, both at home and abroad, is not innocent of political use.

Defining Religion

If we concede that religion is a product of modernity and of the West, is religion at least a coherent concept in the modern West? Now that the category has been constructed in the West and in cultures affected by the West, can we use it as an objective tool of analysis to distinguish the religious from the secular and to make statements such as "religion is more prone to violence today than are secular ideologies and institutions"? In this section, I will show that, even within the modern West, religion remains a widely contested notion, and I will argue that the ability to define what counts as religion and what does not is a significant part of how public power is arranged in the West and in the rest of the world.

Wilfred Cantwell Smith was perhaps the first to recommend that the term religion be dropped entirely, concluding that the term is "confusing, unnecessary, and distorting."[188] Smith argues that the noun religion is an unhelpful reification of what does not as such exist. However, he still contends that it is possible to be religious without the concept of religion, and that the adjectival form religious escapes the danger of reification, because it refers to a personal quality of faith that is a constant in human hearts across space and time. This personal quality exists, but it is not a "thing." Faith is an inner state of heart and mind. Furthermore, faith is both transhistorical and transcultural. So Smith still wants to say, "Man is everywhere and has always been what we today call 'religious.'"[189]

Although the implications of Smith's historical work strongly hint that essentialist accounts of religion should be left behind, Smith himself is unable finally to escape essentialism. Faith for Smith is a universal inner state that only subsequently takes outward forms. Faith, however, can only be rightly understood as inextricable from outward practices located in history. Smith criticizes Aquinas for carelessness when he associates *religio* with both inner motivations and outward expressions. But for Aquinas, as we have seen, inward and outward are not two essentially different things; *religio,* as a virtue, entails the inculcating of habits through bodily disciplines, which are embedded in changing historical circumstances. For Smith, these outward forms are the mere husk surrounding the kernel of faith. As Talal Asad points out, Smith's conception of faith makes the difference between a person of faith and one who has no faith unobservable. It also happens to fit perfectly into the Western, liberal separation of private religiosity from the public realm. Despite Smith's own careful historical work, his individualized and otherworldly conception of "religious faith" floats free of concrete historical conditions and therefore diverts us from asking questions about how the religious is defined, by whom, and for what purpose.[190]

Although Smith may never have asked these questions, his work inspired new generations of scholars who do. Such scholars have critiqued substantivist definitions of religion, such as those used, explicitly and implicitly, by the scholars we examined in the first chapter (with the exception of Richard Wentz). The problem with those theories of religion and violence, as we have seen, is not that their definitions of religion are too fuzzy around the edges. The problem is that they are *unjustifiably clear* about what counts as religion and what does not: things like Christianity and Buddhism and Shinto are self-evidently religions, and things like nationalism and Marxism are secular phenomena. By showing how the concept of religion is historically and culturally relative, Wilfred Cantwell Smith opened the door to new ways of investigating religion. Rather than treat religions as self-evident entities with clear boundaries, scholars have begun to show that what does and does not count as religion is itself worthy of investigation.

Substantivist Approaches

Substantivist definitions of religion attempt to separate what Western scholars since the nineteenth century have identified as the world religions from other phenomena based on their beliefs about the nature of reality. Belief in God or gods is the usual starting place, but as a single criterion it is regarded as too restrictive, because it would exclude some belief systems that generally make lists of world religions, such as Buddhism, Confucianism, and Daoism. The category of the transcendent is sometimes offered in place of God or gods, in such a way that Buddhist talk of nirvana would qualify. Transcendence is meant to be an inclusive concept that would cover both gods and other phenomena, but its inclusiveness depends on how it is defined. Many scholars, for example, deny that Confucianism has any concept of transcendence;[191] Jan Bremmer writes that "the gods of the Greeks were not transcendent but directly involved in natural and social processes."[192] On the other hand, insofar as transcendence *is* defined inclusively, its inclusivity is difficult to control. In other words, once the definition of religion is expanded to include all the things that such scholars want to include, it becomes difficult to exclude all the things that they want to exclude. Once the transcendent becomes the focus of one's definition of religion, there is no reason to suppose that the generally recognized world religions would exhaust the category. As Timothy Fitzgerald points out, transcendent notions can include "the 'Nation,' the land, the principles of humanism, the ancestors, Communism, *ātman-brahman*, the goddess of democracy and human rights, Cold Speech, Enlightenment (in various quite different senses), the right to private property, witchcraft, destiny, the 'Immaculate Conception,' "[193] and so on.

The problem with transcendence is that, in order to be inclusive enough to embrace both Judaism and Buddhism, it must be vague. It can be given a more specific meaning by attending carefully to the contexts and ways in which it is used. But the more specific the context and usage, the more unhelpful it becomes to lump them all under the same heading. Since the study of world religions was initiated by Western Christian scholars in the nineteenth century, the meaning of terms like transcendence is almost inevitably modeled on Judeo-Christian theological definitions of transcendence based on the relationship of a Creator God to the created world. When there is no Creator God, as in Buddhism, it is difficult to see how the term transcendence can be fitted into Buddhism without doing violence to Buddhists' own self-understanding. This is not to say that the same term can never be used in describing two different traditions. It is to say that the usefulness of such terms can only be determined by highly specific analyses of particular contexts. It should not be imposed as part of a definition that determines from the start that Buddhism and Christianity are two varieties of the same thing. Transcendence can be used in the Buddhist context only by trying to ignore the Judeo-Christian theological background of the term and making it more vague and more general. In this case, the specificity that the term once had is lost, as is any reason to assume that nationalism, for example, does not belong in the same category as Judaism and Buddhism. If transcendence can refer to any perceived reality that exceeds and unifies ordinary human experience of the material world, it is hard to imagine a better candidate for transcendence than the "imagined community" of the nation. The much-used term civil religion recognizes this reality. The problem for scholars who employ substantivist definitions of religion is that they do not want to include nationalism in the definition of religion. Why not? Because it is said to be a *secular* phenomenon. But policing the boundary between the religious and the secular depends on a definition of religion that locates the religious-secular divide in just the right place. Basing a definition of religion on the concept of transcendence does not appear very promising in this regard.

Similar problems result with other definitions that attempt to separate religion from the secular by reference to a two-tiered view of reality: empirical-supraempirical, natural-supernatural, or human-superhuman. Such a two-tiered view of reality has a specific history within the West and cannot be imposed unproblematically on all cultures, many of which do not divide the world in the same way. The anthropologist Brian Morris defines religion as all phenomena seen to be supraempirical, but as Fitzgerald points out, *all* values are supraempirical, including such secular values as freedom and the rights of man.[194] The natural-supernatural divide also fails to provide the basis of a transhistorical and transcultural definition of religion, because such a divide is not self-evident. In some non-Western cultures, it is not at all clear if what Westerners call the supernatural is ontologically distinct from nature or if it is a part of nature, and some may not even have an indigenous concept of nature to begin with. Do animists, for example, divide the world into nature and super-nature? Even in the premodern West, as Nicholas Lash points out, there was no concept of nature and supernature as two ontologically distinct realms. Until the seventeenth century, supernatural was used adverbially or adjectivally to indicate someone acting above what is ordinarily expected of them, for example, a human being acting justly and truthfully through the gifts of God's grace. The term supernatural, therefore, could never be applied to God.[195] Definitions of religion in terms of perceived interactions with superhuman beings do not necessarily rely on a nature-supernature split, and thus leave open the possibility that superhuman beings are still part of nature, despite being more powerful than humans. This definition, however, still leaves the problem of determining who or what is considered superhuman in any given culture. Are bodhisatt-vas superhuman? Ancestors? Emperors? Space aliens? Saints? Sacred animals? Celebrities? As Balagangadhara points out, the category superhuman implies a hierarchy of God → humans → animals, in descending order, a hierarchy that is firmly rooted in the Judeo-Christian tradition, but absent from Indian culture, where cows are worshipped as sacred. The further problem is that the division of interactions between those with beings who are superhuman and with those who are not does not necessarily tell us anything interesting and may in fact obscure rather than illuminate certain phenomena. For example, Fitzgerald says that rituals to propitiate angry ghosts in Japan cannot be understood without reference to values such as hierarchy, deference, purity, and Japaneseness. But these values are reproduced in all major Japanese institutions; rituals directed toward the emperor, bosses of corporations, foreigners, and monkeys are just as important for understanding these values as are rituals directed at ghosts or kami. Nothing is gained by separating these into one list—labeled religion—that includes superhuman beings and another list containing the rest. In fact, much is lost by this arbitrary division. It becomes difficult, for example, to explain why people who claim not to believe in superhuman beings continue to perform rituals directed at them.[196]

The problem with substantivist definitions of religion, therefore, is twofold. First, defining religion in terms of the transcendent or the sacred or the supernatural or the supraempirical or any such terms just begs the question as to what those terms mean. If they are made vague enough to be transcultural, then they become so inclusive as to shatter the exclusivity of the category religion. Excluding systems of beliefs and practices from the list of world religions becomes arbitrary. There is no good reason for excluding all of the things that substantivists would like to exclude from the category of religion. Second, and more decisively for our purposes, even if one were able to come up with a coherent, transhistorical, and transcultural way to separate religion from the secular, there is no good reason to suppose that the distinction tells us anything important or interesting about the phenomena thus categorized. As William Arnal says, there might be a logical way of dividing the world's phenomena into things that are blue and things that are not blue, but it would not justify coming up with general theories of the nature of blueness or having Departments of Blue Studies in universities.[197] Even if one were able to come up with a coherent, transhistorical, and transcultural definition of religion which would include things like Christianity and Confucianism and Buddhism and exclude things like Marxism and nationalism and capitalism, it would not tell us anything worthwhile about the causes of violence. Indeed, to exclude Marxism, nationalism, and capitalism a priori from an investigation of violence in the service of ideology in fact *distorts* the results of any such study.

Functionalist Approaches

For these reasons, many scholars prefer functionalist definitions of religion, which tend to be more inclusive. Functionalist definitions are based not on the content or substance of a belief system but on the way that such a system functions, that is, the social, psychological, and political tasks that it performs in a given context: "Functionalists prefer to define 'religion' not in terms of *what* is believed by the religious but in terms of *how* they believe it (that is in terms of the role belief plays in people's lives). Certain individual or social needs are specified and religion is identified as any system whose beliefs, practices or symbols serve to meet those needs."[198] To repeat the example I used in chapter 1, if a nonpracticing Christian claims to believe in God, but structures his life around the pursuit of profits in the bond market and the ideological defense of the free market, then the colloquial idea that "capitalism is his religion" needs to be taken seriously. In effect, functionalist approaches are a return to the broadest meaning of the word *religio* in classical Rome: any binding obligation or devotion that structures one's social relations.

Émile Durkheim may be considered the pioneer of modern functionalist approaches to religion. According to Durkheim, "a religion is a unified system of beliefs and practices relative to sacred things, that is to say, things set apart and surrounded by prohibitions."[199] Durkheim's definition of religion thus depends on the distinction of sacred and profane. But Durkheim does not define sacred and profane based on their content. For Durkheim, *anything* can be considered sacred by a given society.[200] What matters is not content but function, how a thing works within a given society. In any society, according to Durkheim, certain things are set aside as sacred as a symbolization of communal solidarity among the members of a society. The sacred is a representation of the whole society to itself. The content of the symbol is arbitrary; what matters is the way it functions to reinforce social order. For Durkheim, it does not matter that the U.S. flag does not explicitly refer to a god. It is nevertheless a sacred—perhaps the *most* sacred—object in U.S. society and is thus an object of religious veneration.[201]

Functionalist approaches have the advantage of being based on empirical observation of people's actual behavior, and not simply on claims of what they believe in the confines of some interior and unobservable mental state. They are also less inclined to bother about restricting religion to some exclusive and arbitrary set of world religions. The disadvantage of functionalist approaches is that they expand the category of religion so broadly that the category tends to lose meaning. If nearly every ideological system or set of practices can be a religion, then calling something religious does not help to distinguish it from anything else. The danger, as we saw in chapter 1, is that we will end up with Richard Wentz, saying something like "perhaps all of us do bad things in the name of religion." Wentz has rightly seen how arbitrary substantivist definitions of religion are, but he has wrongly concluded that a greatly expanded category of religion will tell us something useful about violence.

According to Fitzgerald, the following can be found treated under the rubric of religion in the published works of religious studies scholars: totems, the principle of hierarchy, Christmas cakes, witchcraft, unconditioned reality, the rights of man, the national essence, Marxism, Freudianism, the tea ceremony, nature, and ethics.[202] Cole Durham and Elizabeth Sewell cite examples of sports, free market ideology, mathematics, belief in the possibility of cold fusion, radical psychotherapy, the use of health food, and nothingness itself being discussed under the category religion in scholarly literature.[203] One could easily add to these lists. A U.S. District Court judge, Charles Brieant, in 2001 ruled that Alcoholics Anonymous is a religion.[204] Many atheistic humanists refer to themselves as "religious humanists"; Herbert Schneider sees the humanist religion as "an effort to free religious faith and devotion from the dogmas of theistic theologies and supernaturalist psychologies."[205] Paul Carus, the founder of Open Court publishing house, promulgated a "religion of science."[206] Theologian Dorothee Sölle laments, "The new religion is consumerism."[207] Sölle's observation is confirmed by the research conducted by Russell Belk, Melanie Wallendorf, and John Sherry, who find that consumer behavior exhibits the properties of sacralization identified by Durkheim and Mircea Eliade.[208]

We might be inclined to dismiss these uses of the term religion as merely metaphorical, as if what these authors really mean is that these ideas and practices behave an awful lot like real religions, which they really are not. But this is not in fact what functionalists contend. Functionalists maintain that the only coherent way to study religion is to include everything that acts like a religion under the rubric religion, whether or not past Western taxonomies of world religions have included them. Only by refusing to make arbitrary, a priori exclusions from the category of religion can we understand what religion is and how it functions in any given society.

David Loy's "The Religion of the Market" is a good example of this approach. Loy writes:

> Religion is notoriously difficult to define. If, however, we adopt a functionalist view and understand religion as what grounds us by teaching us what the world *is,* and what our *role* in the world is, then it becomes obvious that traditional religions are fulfilling this role less and less, because that function is being supplanted—or overwhelmed—by other belief-systems and value-systems. Today the most powerful alternative explanation of the world is science, and the most attractive value-system has become consumerism. Their academic offspring is economics, probably the most influential of the

"social sciences." In response, this paper will argue that our present economic system should also be understood as our religion, because it has come to fulfill a religious function for us.[209]

According to Loy, economics is the theology of the religion that has the market as its god: "The collapse of communism—best understood as a capitalist 'heresy'—makes it more apparent that the Market is becoming the first truly world religion, binding all corners of the globe more and more tightly into a worldview and set of values whose religious view we overlook only because we insist on seeing them as 'secular.' "[210] Why do we insist on seeing them as secular? Because, Loy argues, to do so allows the regnant economic system to be seen as natural and inevitable. To enter the world of the secular is to enter the world of "facts" and to leave the religious world of "values" behind. What is gained by seeing market economics as our religion, therefore, is that we can see market economics as one particular, contingent way of seeing the world, not as an inevitable arrangement subject to the ironclad laws of nature.[211] Our refusal to see market ideology as a religion is itself an important part of the success of market ideology as a religion. The more convinced we are that our economic system is not religious but secular, the more our devotion to the market eludes critical scrutiny and appears as inescapable.

Loy stands in a long line of thinkers who have seen market economics in religious terms. Karl Marx quoted Shakespeare addressing money as "Thou *visible God!*" For Marx, "the divine power of money" lay in its ability to reduce all things to an abstract equivalence in its own image and likeness.[212] Marx thought it was not a coincidence that money was first minted in ancient temples, and he called money "the god among commodities."[213] Georg Simmel's *The Philosophy of Money* (1900) recognized that money possessed "a significant relation to the notion of God" and referred to money as a surrogate for sacrament.[214] Norman O. Brown declared in his psychoanalysis of history (*Life against Death,* 1959) that the "money complex" is the "heir to and substitute for the religious complex, an attempt to find God in things."[215] Many more examples from the twentieth century could be cited.[216] While these figures saw the religion of capitalism as a mystification of more basic economic processes, others have seen the religious qualities of market economics in a positive light. Robert H. Nelson's 2001 book, *Economics as Religion,* for example, argues that, on the whole, the replacement of Christianity and other religions by the religion of economics has ushered in an age of freedom and prosperity. Nelson shows how market economics exactly parallels the earlier role of Christianity in Western society, with its own providential god (the invisible hand of the market), sacred texts, priesthood, and plan of salvation for the recurrent problems of human history: "The Jewish and Christian bibles foretell one outcome of history. If economics foresees another, it is in effect offering a competing religious vision."[217]

Nelson sometimes refers to market economics as a secular religion. If this is not simply nonsense—like "square circle"—then it must mean one of two things: either (1) economics is one of those things usually considered secular, but it is really a religion, or (2) economics behaves like a religion, but it is really secular. If by calling economics a secular religion one understands (1), then "secular religion" is simply a nod toward the way the term secular is usually—but *mistakenly*—ascribed to economics. If one uses secular religion to mean (2), on the other hand, we must wonder what purpose the religion-secular divide serves here. Why would Nelson spend an entire book trying to convince the reader that economics behaves just like a religion, only to say that it really isn't a religion? Even if we could come up with a way, based on content of beliefs, to separate market economics from religion—e.g., religions believe in real gods, but the invisible hand is just a metaphor—it would not tell us anything relevant about the way market economics actually functions in the real world. A functionalist would say, "If it looks like a religion and acts like a religion, then it is a religion." Hence the title of Nelson's book: *Economics as Religion.*

In the wake of rolling blackouts in 2001, one of the architects of California's deregulation plan for utilities was quoted in the *New York Times* expressing his belief that competition always works better than state control. "I believe in that premise as a matter of religious faith," said Philip J. Romero, dean of the University of Oregon business school.[218] Why not take him at his word? If free market economics functions in this case as an overarching framework of belief that explains human behavior and the direction of history, nothing is gained by insisting that Professor Romero is merely speaking metaphorically. What is lost is a potentially fruitful line of inquiry into the actual functioning of economic ideas and ideologies in the real world. A functionalist need not declare that economics functions as a religion in all cases for everyone. The functionalist has the advantage, rather, of letting empirical investigation guide the determination of what functions as a religion under which circumstances, rather than ruling out entire systems of behavior and belief a priori.

Nelson's *Economics as Religion* has its counterpart in Emilio Gentile's *Politics as Religion.* The Italian political scientist says that a "religion of politics" is religious insofar as it is "a system of beliefs, myths, rituals, and symbols that interpret and define the meaning and end of human existence by subordinating the destiny of individuals and the collectivity to a supreme entity."[219] A religion of politics is not the same as a theocracy, which subordinates the state to what Gentile calls a "traditional religion." Gentile seems to use "traditional religion" loosely to mean things that are usually called religions in Western taxonomies: Christianity, Hinduism, etc. A religion of politics, on the other hand, is a secular religion because it creates "an aura of sacredness around an entity belonging to this world."[220] For Gentile, the pairing "this world/other world" seems to define the divide between secular and traditional religions. As in Durkheim, however, that divide does not make much difference; religions of politics are not just religionlike but are really religions. Whether the supreme entity to which all is subordinated is a god or a nation-state does not help to predict how a system of beliefs will function in society.[221]

Gentile distinguishes between two different types of religion of politics. The first type, "political religion," applies primarily to totalitarian regimes. Gentile defines political religion as "the sacralization of a political system founded on an unchallengeable monopoly of power, ideological monism, and the obligatory and unconditional subordination of the individual and the collectivity to its code of commandments." The second type of religion of politics is "civil religion," which applies primarily to democratic regimes: "Civil religion is the conceptual category that contains the forms of sacralization of a political system that guarantee a plurality of ideas, free competition in the exercise of power, and the ability of the governed to dismiss their governments through peaceful and constitutional methods."[222] Gentile warns that the distinction between the two types is not always a sharp one; governing regimes may be located in a position between the two types when, for example, a democratic civil religion becomes intolerant of dissent and invasive regarding citizens' rights.

The term political religion, of course, is not Gentile's creation. Indeed, most of Gentile's book consists of quoting author after author who has used the relevant terms as Gentile does. The term political religion is commonly traced to Erich Vogelin's *Die politischen Religionen,* published in Vienna just before the Anschluss,[223] but Gentile has found that Condorcet, Abraham Lincoln, Reinhold Niebuhr, and Karl Polanyi all used the term before Vogelin. Since Vogelin, there has developed an extensive scholarly literature on the subject and an English-language journal, *Totalitarian Movements and Political Religions,* dedicated to its study. Most authors who use the term political religion see religion as a basic element of any social order. For many, the rise of political religion in the West is explained as a response to the decline of Christianity as the glue that held the premodern social order together.[224]

The chief examples of political religion in the West are Marxism/communism and fascism. Marxism has been recognized as a religion since Marx's own time. The Young Hegelian Max Stirner attacked Marx's communism as just another variation on the religious theme, "only the last metamorphosis of the Christian religion." According to Stirner, communism "exalts 'Man' to the same extent as any other religion does its God or idol."[225] Ludwig Feuerbach, on whose critique of God Marx drew, would not have disagreed. Feuerbach had written in 1842, "We must start to be religious once again; politics must become our religion, but it can only do so if we, in our perceptions, have a supreme value that makes our religion of politics."[226] Marx, however, wanted science, not religion. He responded to Stirner by insisting that communism was not an ideology of any kind, but an expression of the real and material movement of history, known through the objective science of history. Many twentieth-century critics, however, would side with Stirner and see Marxism as a type of religion. The ex-communist contributors to *The God That Failed* all describe their experience with the party in religious terms: a vision for the destiny of all humanity, unwavering faith in authoritatively promulgated doctrine, communal solidarity and ritual, and so on. Arthur Koestler's contribution is typical in its recognition that "there is little difference between a revolutionary and a traditionalist faith."[227] The first chapter of Joseph Schumpeter's *Capitalism, Socialism, and Democracy*, entitled "Marx as Prophet," begins this way:

> It was not by a slip that an analogy from the world of religion was permitted to intrude into the title of this chapter. There is more than analogy. In one important sense, Marxism *is* a religion. To the believer it presents, first, a system of ultimate ends that embody the meaning of life and are absolute standards by which to judge events and actions; and, secondly, a guide to those ends which implies a plan of salvation and the indication of the evil from which mankind, or a chosen section of mankind, is to be saved. We may specify still further: Marxist socialism also belongs to that subgroup which promises paradise on this side of the grave.[228]

A. J. P. Taylor, in his 1967 introduction to the *Communist Manifesto*, wrote that communism was "the accepted creed or religion for countless millions of mankind" and that the *Communist Manifesto* should be "counted as a holy book, in the same class as the Bible or the Koran."[229] Polish philosopher Leszek Kolakowski, author of the massive and influential *Main Currents of Marxism*, also regarded Marxism as a religion, especially in its eschatology.[230] The idea of Marxism as religion is not confined to its critics. Marxist Antonio Gramsci wrote that Marxism "is precisely the religion that has to kill off Christianity. It is a religion in the sense that it is also a faith with its own mysteries and practices, and because in our consciences it has replaced the transcendental

God of Catholicism with faith in Man and his best energies as the only spiritual reality."[231]

The other prominent examples of political religions are Italian fascism and German Nazism. As early as 1912, Benito Mussolini was calling for "a *religious* concept of socialism."[232] It became commonplace among critics of the Mussolini and Hitler regimes, and among political scientists, to note the intensely ritualistic and all-absorbing nature of ideology in those regimes and to call it religion. Examples are so common that I need not belabor the point here.[233]

Of course, not everyone agrees that political systems may qualify as religions. For example, Ninian Smart recognizes that Marxism provides doctrines to explain "the whole of reality," has a plan for realizing "heaven on earth," has a well-developed public ceremonial aspect, and so on.[234] Nevertheless, Smart contends, "it is unrealistic to treat Marxism as a religion: though it possesses doctrines, symbols, a moral code, and even sometimes rituals, it denies the possibility of an experience of the invisible world. Neither relationship to a personal God nor the hope of an experience of salvation or nirvana can be significant for the Marxist."[235] What appears to define religion for Smart here is "an experience of the invisible world." There are several problems with this account, beginning with the attempt to determine what counts as the invisible world. If the divide is made on the basis of belief in an invisible world, it is not clear that, for example, Buddhism and Marxism will end up where Smart wants them. Nirvana for a Buddhist is not an invisible world, but is commonly described as the extinction of the desiring self. On the other hand, why does belief in the stateless communist utopia at the end of history not qualify as belief in an invisible world? It is hard to know how we should begin to adjudicate this question, given that Smart defines religion in terms of an interior experience that is therefore unavailable to empirical observation. On what basis could Smart dismiss Koestler's account of his own experience as a communist, which he found to be just as religious as his experience of Christianity?

The most significant problem with Smart's account for my purposes is that, even if he can find a criterion to separate godless communism—which he calls "religionlike"[236]—from "real" religions like godless Buddhism, that separation tells us nothing relevant about how Marxism and Buddhism actually function in the world. The question of violence with which this book is concerned is a question of function: do certain ideologies and practices have more of a tendency to produce violence than do others? The fact that Marxists don't believe in an experience of the invisible world, even if true, tells us exactly nothing about the tendency of Marxism to produce violence. If we are trying to determine which ideologies and practices have a greater tendency to produce violence, we are far better served by a relevant category such as absolutism, as we saw in the first chapter; absolutist ideologies do seem to have a much greater risk of producing violence. But there is no good reason to exclude Marxism from a category such as absolutist ideologies. Indeed, it would be hard to find a more absolutist ideology than Marxism, as its tens of millions of victims can attest. The point is that, if we are trying to determine which ideologies and practices have a greater tendency toward violence in the real world, then the kind of distinction between religious and secular that Smart makes is useless. We have a far better chance of success with a functionalist approach that would not exclude ideologies like Marxism on the basis of irrelevant criteria like supposed belief in the invisible world.

Advocates of liberal democracy tend to be more sympathetic with the idea of Marxism or Nazism as religions than with the idea of a civil religion of liberal democracy. Nevertheless, a wide range of scholars have argued that many liberal democracies rely on a strong civil religion to provide a common meaning and purpose for liberal nation-states. In Gentile's definition, civil religion is not a type of "politicization of religion," in which traditional religion merges with the state. Civil religion, though it may occasionally borrow elements from traditional religion, is a new creation that confers sacred status on democratic institutions and symbols.[237] Civil religion is an example of what Eric Hobsbawm and Terence Ranger call the "invention of tradition." Hobsbawm notes the general agreement that we live in an unliturgical age, and in many ways that is true. The rites and customs that structured the hours, days, and seasons of traditional societies have largely faded in the face of Western individual freedoms. Where this generalization does not apply, however, as Hobsbawm points out, is in the public life of the citizen. Here, liberal democratic societies are every bit as "liturgical" as traditional ones: "Indeed most of the occasions when people become conscious of citizenship as such remain associated with symbols and semi-ritual practices (for instance, elections), most of which are historically novel and largely invented: flags, images, ceremonies and music."[238] Rituals which many assume to be ancient are in fact the products of the late nineteenth and early twentieth centuries, when rituals were invented in Europe and the United States to stoke a nascent sense of exclusive national loyalty, supplanting previously diffuse loyalties owed to region, ethnic group, class, and church.

According to Carlton Hayes, it is this exclusivity that sets off modern nationalism from previous types of loyalties. Before modernity, people experienced conflicts among their many loyalties to locality and priest, lord and guild, and family: "But nowadays, and herein lies the fundamental difference between us and our ancient and mediaeval and early modern forebears, the individual is commonly disposed, in case of conflict, to sacrifice one loyalty after another, loyalty to persons, places and ideas, loyalty even to family, to the paramount call of nationality and the national state."[239] Nationalism qualifies as a religion because of this exclusivity. It is in its exclusivity—its jealousness—that the nation becomes not merely a substitute for the church, but a substitute for God.

Scholars have long noted the way that nationalism has supplanted Christianity as the predominant public religion of the West. Hayes's 1926 essay, "Nationalism as a Religion," puts forth this idea, which in 1960 he developed into a book entitled *Nationalism: A Religion*.[240] For Hayes, humans are naturally endowed with a "religious sense," a faith in a power higher than humanity that requires a sense of reverence, usually expressed in external ceremony. Hayes argues that the decline in public Christianity with the advent of the modern state left a vacuum for the religious sense that was filled by the sacralization of the nation, the "enthronement of the national state—*la Patrie*—as the central object of worship."[241] According to Hayes, political religion enjoyed the double advantage of being more tangible than supernatural religion and having the physical means of violence necessary to enforce mandatory worship. Benedict Anderson similarly argues that the nation has replaced the church in its role as the primary cultural institution that deals with death. According to Anderson, Christianity's decline in the West necessitated another way of dealing with the arbitrariness of death. Nations provide a new kind of salvation; my death is not in vain if it is for the nation, which lives on into a limitless future.[242]

The term civil religion was introduced by Rousseau in the eighteenth century. In the last chapter of *The Social Contract*, Rousseau proposes an explicit civil religion as a cure for the divisive influence of Christianity, which had divided people's loyalties between church and state. Rousseau does not wish to erase Christianity entirely, but to reduce it to a "religion of man" that "has to do with the purely inward worship of Almighty God and the eternal obligations of morality, and nothing more."[243] Civil religion, on the other hand, is the fully public cult of the nation-state: "the sovereign is entitled to fix the tenets of a purely civil creed, or profession of faith. These would not be, strictly speaking, dogmas of a religious character, but rather sentiments deemed indispensable for participation in society." Rousseau distinguishes here between civil religion and religion "strictly speaking"; by the latter, he seems to mean what Gentile means by traditional religion. This distinction makes little difference, however, in its practical effect. Civil religion has its dogmas, and the consequences of disobedience are severe: "As for that man who, having committed himself publicly to the state's articles of faith, acts on any occasion as if he does not believe them, let his punishment be death. He has committed the greatest of all crimes: he has lied in the presence of the laws."[244]

After the revolution in 1789, there were many in France who took Rousseau's ideas to heart and tried to create an active cult of the French nation. There developed a zealous devotion to the myth of the creation of a new humanity in the revolution. After 1791, Catholicism was actively suppressed and attempts were made to invent structures and rituals to inculcate devotion to France itself. Altars to the fatherland were erected, with copies of the French Constitution and the Declaration of the Rights of Man engraved on metal and in stone above them as objects for worship. Rites of civic baptism and civic funerals were invented. The Declaration of the Rights of Man was declared the "national catechism."[245] Most such efforts were short-lived, but France has retained a powerful civil religion, which crystallizes around reverence for its war dead and the sacralization of republican ideals.[246]

The primary example of civil religion cited by scholars is that of the United States. As early as 1749, Benjamin Franklin had argued for "the Necessity of a *Publick Religion*," by which he meant a cult of the nation and the duties of the citizen.[247] Franklin was typical of Enlightenment figures who looked to the model of republican Rome and saw how religion provided a unified sense of civic duty and loyalty. Thomas Jefferson advocated for the "reverence" of the Declaration of Independence and the "holy purpose" of adhesion to it. As Pauline Maier points out, although Jefferson's draft declaration made no reference to God, and although Jefferson was responsible for the complete separation of church and state in Virginia, Jefferson wrote in the language of medieval Christianity about the preservation of physical things associated with the creation of the declaration: "Small things may, perhaps, like the relics of saints, help to nourish our devotion to this holy bond of Union." Of the desk on which he drafted the Declaration of Independence, Jefferson expressed his hope that we might see it "carried in the procession of our nation's birthday, as the relics of the saints are in those of the Church."[248] As Maier notes, throughout the nineteenth century, virulently anti-Catholic leaders were inclined to borrow Catholic imagery to describe the nation's founding. The founders were "saints," they raised "altars" of freedom, their houses were "shrines" containing "relics," and so on.[249]

The American civil religion differs from the French in that it has tended to operate with the support of the churches. American civil religion is a curious blend of Enlightenment and Christian themes and symbols. It is especially marked by what Gentile calls a "transfer of sacredness" from traditional Christianity to the United States itself.[250] American civil religion has often, for example, mined the Puritan use of biblical images. The Puritans famously identified their colony with a new Israel chosen by God, but John Winthrop's "city on the hill" was not America but the fledgling Puritan colony. This was less difficult to justify biblically as long as the church and civil government were intertwined. With the separation of church and state after the American Revolution, however, the new Israel came to be identified not with the church, but with the United States itself. In American civil religion, the new Israel was not to bring the messiah of Israelite prophecy to the world; rather, the United States would save the world through its creation and spread of democracy, freedom, and progress. The messianic form was taken from biblical Christianity, but the content was supplied by Enlightenment themes.[251] Throughout the nineteenth century, U.S. progress was increasingly identified with the providence of a generic god, to the point of implicitly deifying the nation. Herman Melville's oft-quoted contention in *White Jacket* that "we Americans are the peculiar, chosen people—the Israel of our time" actually goes beyond the claim to God's blessings and makes the nation itself into a divine reality. Melville continues:

> Long enough have we been skeptics with regard to ourselves, and
> doubted whether, indeed, the political Messiah had come. But he has
> come in *us*, if we would but give utterance to his promptings. And let
> us always remember that with ourselves, almost for the first time in
> the history of earth, national selfishness is unbounded philanthropy;
> for we cannot do a good to America, but we give alms to the world.[252]

Christianity, Judaism, and other traditional faiths in America, which are construed as particularistic and voluntary, coexist with a public civil religion of the United States itself, which embraces the whole of the social order and is more than merely voluntary.

Robert Bellah's famous 1967 article, "Civil Religion in America," sparked significant discussion, coming as it did in the midst of the Vietnam War.[253] Bellah identifies "an elaborate and well-institutionalized civil religion in America" that "has its own seriousness and integrity and requires the same care in understanding that any other religion does."[254] Bellah argues that the civic rituals of American life revolve around a unitarian god that underwrites America's sense of purpose in the world. This god, however, is not the Christian God. References to Christ and the church are kept to a private, voluntary sphere of worship.[255] The implication of Bellah's argument is that the separation of church and state in the United States is *not* the separation of religion and state. Religion as such is not privatized; traditional religion is privatized, while the religion of politics occupies the public realm.

Although Bellah's article attracted a lot of attention, he was by no means the first scholar to identify Americanism as a religion. Will Herberg had already claimed, "By every realistic criterion, the American Way of Life is the operative religion of the American people."[256] Herberg defines *operative* religion in a functionalist way as "the system of norms, values, and allegiances actually functioning as such in the ongoing social life of the community."[257] Before Herberg, Carlton Hayes had identified the American religion's saints (the founding fathers), its shrines (Independence Hall), its relics (the Liberty Bell), its holy scriptures (the Declaration of Independence, the Constitution), its martyrs (Lincoln), its inquisition (school boards that enforce patriotism), its Christmas (the Fourth of July), and its feast of Corpus Christi (Flag Day). According to Hayes, the flag occupies the same central place in official ritual that the eucharistic host previously held:

> Nationalism's chief symbol of faith and central object of worship is the flag, and curious liturgical forms have been devised for "saluting" the flag, for "dipping" the flag, for "lowering" the flag, and for "hoisting" the flag. Men bare their heads when the flag passes by; and in praise of the flag poets write odes and children sing hymns. In America young people are ranged in serried rows and required to recite daily, with hierophantic voice and ritualistic gesture, the mystical formula: "I pledge allegiance to our flag and to the country for which it stands, one nation, indivisible, with liberty and justice for all." Everywhere, in all solemn feasts and fasts of nationalism the flag is in evidence, and with it that other sacred thing, the national anthem.[258]

If we think that Hayes is exaggerating the function of the Pledge of Allegiance, we need only consult the author of the pledge, Francis Bellamy, who said that the pledge was meant to sink into schoolchildren through ritual repetition, and added, "It is the same way with the catechism, or the Lord's Prayer."[259]

According to Carolyn Marvin and David Ingle, "nationalism is the most powerful religion in the United States, and perhaps in many other countries."[260] Marvin and Ingle have identified the flag as the totem object of American civil religion. Their fascinating book *Blood Sacrifice and the Nation* contains dozens of photographs depicting American reverence for the flag as a sacred object.[261] The flag is of crucial importance for the U.S. religion because it is that for which Americans will kill and die. For Marvin and Ingle, what makes American patriotism a religion is precisely its ability to organize killing energies. Through close analysis of rituals surrounding war and remembrance of the war dead, Marvin and Ingle argue that it is blood sacrifice on behalf of the nation that constantly renews the nation. The "ultimate sacrifice" for the nation is elaborately ceremonialized in liturgies involving the flag and other ritual objects. Blood sacrifice is an act of both creation and salvation. At the ceremonies marking the fiftieth anniversary of D-Day in 1994, for example, President Bill Clinton remarked of the soldiers that died there both that "[t]hey gave us our world" and that "[t]hey saved the world."[262]

For Marvin and Ingle, the transfer of the sacred from Christianity to the nation-state in Western society is seen most clearly in the fact that authorized killing has passed from Christendom to the nation-state. Christian denominations still thrive in the United States, but as optional, inward-looking affairs. They are not publicly true, "[f]or what is really true in any community is what its members can agree is worth killing for, or what they can be compelled to sacrifice their lives for."[263] People are not allowed to kill for "sectarian religion," which is what Gentile means by traditional religion. Only the nation-state may kill. According to Marvin and Ingle, it is this power to organize killing that makes American civil religion the true religion of the U.S. social order.

Conclusion

What can we conclude from this brief survey of some functionalist approaches to religion? The first thing to note is that, if the functionalists are right in saying that secular phenomena like capitalism and nationalism are really religions, then all of the arguments in chapter 1—except that of the functionalist Richard Wentz—fall apart. There is simply no basis for including Islam and Hinduism in the indictment of religious violence while excluding U.S. nationalism and Marxism. And we have good reasons for preferring the functionalist to the substantivist approach. The question "Does religion cause violence?" is a question of how religion functions. If secular nationalism functions in the same way as Islam to produce violence under certain circumstances, there is no reason to indict the latter and ignore the former. Even if we could come up with a substantive way to put Islam and nationalism in different categories— e.g., Islam believes in a "real" God, but the nation as god is "just a metaphor"— for our purposes, it would be as pointless as studying the violence of only ideologies that begin with the letters A through L.

Ultimately, however, functionalist approaches to the question of religion and violence are also unsatisfactory. To argue, as Wentz does, that religion has a peculiar tendency to cause violence, but to include nearly everything people take seriously under the rubric of religion, is not very helpful. At best, it is tautological: people do violence on behalf of those things they take seriously enough to do violence for. We have not learned much about the causes of violence. Not only do functionalist approaches cast the meaning of religion so widely as to render the category virtually useless, but they also suffer from the same essentialism from which substantivist approaches suffer. Functionalist approaches—like substantivist approaches—tend to assume that there really is something out there called religion that is a constant feature in all human societies across time; functionalists just argue for a more expansive definition of what religion really is, based on how it functions in all places and times. But in doing so, functionalists cling to the kind of transhistorical and transcultural idea of religion that we showed above to be groundless.

So, do we conclude that there is no such thing as religion, no coherent concept of religion, and therefore we need not bother with the question of religion and violence? No. The point is not that there is no such thing as religion. The concepts that we use do not simply refer to things out there in a one-to-one correspondence of words with things. In certain cultures, religion *does* exist, but as a product of human construction. Some scholars have cited James Leuba's *Psychological Study of Religion* (1912), which lists more than fifty different definitions of religion, to conclude that there is no way to define religion. But as Jonathan Z. Smith points out, the lesson is not that religion cannot be defined, but that it can be defined more than fifty different ways.[264] There is no transhistorical and transcultural essence of religion, but at different times and places, and for different purposes, some things have been constructed as religion and some things have not. For Western scholars in the nineteenth century, Confucianism was a religion. For Chinese nationalists, it emphatically was not.

Instead of searching—in either a substantivist or functionalist mode—for the timeless, transcultural essence of religion, therefore, let us ask why certain things are called religion under certain conditions. What configurations of power are authorized by changes in the way the concept of religion—and its counterpart, the secular—are used? What changes in practices correspond to changes in these concepts? Why deny that the natives have religion at first, then assign some of their practices to the category religion? Which practices become religion, and why? Why deny that Marxism is a religion? Why accept that Marxism is a religion but emphatically deny that U.S. nationalism is?

Supreme Court justice William Rehnquist acknowledged, in supporting a proposed amendment against "desecration" of the flag, that the flag is regarded by Americans "with an almost mystical reverence."[265] Here, the word "almost" is crucial, for American civil religion must deny that it is religion. Marvin and Ingle ask, and attempt to answer, the key question:

> If nationalism is religious, why do we deny it? Because what is obligatory for group members must be separated, as holy things are, from

what is contestable. To concede that nationalism is a religion is to expose it to challenge, to make it just the same as sectarian religion. By explicitly denying that our national symbols and duties are sacred, we shield them from competition with sectarian symbols. In so doing, we embrace the ancient command not to speak the sacred, ineffable name of god. The god is inexpressible, unsayable, unknowable, beyond language. But that god may not be refused when it calls for sacrifice.[266]

Marvin and Ingle treat nationalism as a real religion, according to their definition.[267] But for my purposes, whether or not nationalism is *really* a religion is beside the point. What is crucial are the questions they ask: why deny it is a religion? Why affirm it? What is authorized by either the denial or the affirmation? Why is it acceptable in some contexts for Abraham Lincoln to say that reverence for the Constitution is "the political religion of the nation,"[268] or for George W. Bush to say that patriotism is "a living faith" that grows stronger when the United States is threatened?[269] Why, in other contexts, is the U.S. constitutional order held as the model of secular government? With regard to the question of violence, why is violence on behalf of the Muslim *umma* religious, but violence on behalf of the American nation-state is secular? What is gained or lost by the insistence that violence on behalf of the United States is of a fundamentally different nature from violence on behalf of Islam?

To answer these types of questions, we must see how the religious-secular distinction is part of the legitimating conceptual apparatus of the modern Western nation-state. As I stated earlier, "the West," "modernity," "liberalism," and so on are not simply monolithic realities, but are *ideals* or *projects* that are always contestable. Part of the function of ideology, however, is to present these projects as based on essential realities that are simply *there,* part of the way things are. As we saw in Locke's writings, the religious-secular distinction is presented as embedded in the immutable nature of things. In fact, however, this distinction was born with a new configuration of power and authority in the West and was subsequently exported to parts of the world colonized by Europeans. Within the West, religion was invented as a transhistorical and transcultural impulse embedded in the human heart, essentially distinct from the public business of government and economic life. To mix religion with public life was said to court fanaticism, sectarianism, and violence. The religious-secular divide thus facilitated the transfer in the modern era of the public loyalty of the citizen from Christendom to the emergent nation-state. Outside the West, the creation of religion and its secular twin accompanied the attempts of colonial powers and indigenous modernizing elites to marginalize certain aspects of non-Western cultures and create public space for the smooth functioning of state and market interests.

The idea that religion has a tendency to promote violence is a variation on the idea that religion is an essentially private and nonrational human impulse, not amenable to conflict solving through public reason. In the contemporary context, therefore, the idea that there is something called religion with a tendency to promote violence continues to marginalize certain kinds of discourses and practices while authorizing others. Specifically, the idea that public religion causes violence authorizes the marginalization of those things called religion from having a divisive influence in public life, and thereby authorizes the state's monopoly on violence and on public allegiance. Loyalty to one's religion is private in origin and therefore optional; loyalty to the secular nation-state is what unifies us and is not optional.

None of this implies a grand conspiracy of intellectual and governmental elites to justify state violence. Discourse about the dangers of public religion is rather a normalizing discourse through which we explain to ourselves why things are arranged the way they are. And the dangers warned against are real. When public discourse blames terrorist attacks on religious fanaticism, common sense can see that there are dangerous pathologies linked to some of what is called religion. The problem with the myth of religious violence is not that it condemns certain kinds of violence, but that it diverts moral scrutiny from other kinds of violence. Violence labeled religious is always reprehensible; violence labeled secular is often necessary and sometimes praiseworthy.

Secularism need not be antireligion. It is rather against the undue influence of religion on public life. The first chapter of Martin Marty's *Politics, Religion, and the Common Good*—whose stated thesis is "public religion can be dangerous; it should be handled with care"—is followed by his second chapter, entitled "Worth the Risk," whose stated thesis is "public religion can and does contribute to the common good."[270] Marty tries to show how religion can participate in public life, provided it play by the rules established by the liberal nation-state. It must appeal to publicly accessible reason and avoid conflicts of loyalty between religious beliefs and the values of the nation-state.

It is possible, therefore, for many Americans to consider themselves religious and yet to maintain some version of the idea that the creation of a secular order—and the marginalization or domestication of religion in public life—is the salvation of the social order from the dangers of public religion. The divide between religious and secular must be maintained. We do so out of respect for both the secular and the religious spheres. From the secular point of view, to admit that secular nationalism is just as religious as Islam, for example, would question the whole foundation upon which the secular nation-state claims its legitimacy. From the religious point of view, it would also invite charges of idolatry. Despite the similarities between what is called religion and nationalism, then, we must deny that nationalism is really a religion. We acknowledge verbally that the nation and the flag are not *really* gods. The crucial test, however, is what people do with their bodies. It is clear that, among those who identify themselves as Christians in the United States, there are very few who would be willing to kill in the name of the Christian God, whereas the willingness, under certain circumstances, to kill and die for the nation in war is generally taken for granted. The religious-secular distinction thus helps to maintain the public and lethal loyalty of Christians to the nation-state, while avoiding direct confrontation with Christian beliefs about the supremacy of the Christian God over all other gods.

In this chapter, I have argued for two conclusions: first, that the religious-secular divide upon which the myth of religious violence depends is not a transhistorical and transcultural reality, and second, that it is part of the legitimating mythology of the modern liberal state. In the next two chapters, I will give more historical specificity to this second claim, first by examining the tale of the wars of religion and its place in legitimating the modern state in chapter 3, and then in chapter 4 by examining the contemporary uses of the myth of religious violence in marginalizing domestic religion and justifying the use of force against non-Western, especially Muslim, Others.

3

The Creation Myth of
the Wars of Religion

In this chapter, I examine one of the most commonly cited historical examples of religious violence: the "wars of religion" of the sixteenth and seventeenth centuries in Europe. The story goes that, after the Protestant Reformation divided Christendom along religious lines, Catholics and Protestants began killing each other for holding to different doctrines. The wars of religion, which encompassed over a century of chaos and bloodletting, demonstrated to the West the inherent danger of public religion. The solution to the problem lay in the rise of the modern state, in which religious loyalties were marginalized and the state secured a monopoly on the means of violence. Henceforth, religious passions would be tamed, and Protestants and Catholics could unite on the basis of loyalty to the religiously neutral sovereign state.

This story is more than just a prominent example of the myth of religious violence. It has a foundational importance for the secular West, because it explains the origin of its way of life and its system of governance. It is a creation myth for modernity. Like the ancient Hebrew Genesis or the Babylonian Enuma Elish, it tells a story of the overcoming of primordial chaos by the forces of order. The myth of the wars of religion is also a soteriology, a story of our salvation from mortal peril. In other words, the story of the wars of religion has a crucial legitimating function for the secular West. As such, this story provides important clues to the function that the larger myth of religious violence serves in the West. As I will argue in this chapter and the next, the myth of religious violence is inextricably bound up with the legitimation of the state and its use of violence.

The present chapter is an attempt to expand and deepen the argument of a brief essay I published in 1995, which has attracted some attention.[1] The essay suggested an alternative way to read the historical data from the era of the religious wars in Europe, but the article did not cover much of the data themselves. This chapter will address in greater depth some of the important historical work that has been done on this era in the development of Europe. This chapter is not intended to provide a full account of all the complex factors that produced the violence of sixteenth- and seventeenth-century Europe. The purpose of this chapter is negative; in presenting a summary and analysis of some of the most influential historiography on this era, I hope to show the implausibility of the way that the story is usually told by liberal political theorists and others who make use of it. I do not argue that these wars were not really about religion, but were really about politics or economics or culture; in my original article, I was not sufficiently clear that I wanted to distance myself from such arguments. To make such arguments is to assume that one can readily sort out what is "religion" from what is "politics" and so on in Reformation Europe. But these wars were themselves part of the process of creating those very distinctions. The creation of the modern state, in other words, was not simply the solution to the violence of the sixteenth and seventeenth centuries, but was itself implicated in the violence.

I will begin by examining how the myth of the wars of religion is used to legitimate the idea of a secular state. I will then outline the major premises of this story and proceed to analyze their plausibility.

The Myth of the Wars of Religion

Early Modern Antecedents

Elements of the myth of the wars of religion can be found in seventeenth-century political theory. Benedict de Spinoza's political writings were motivated largely by the divisions and wars that had plagued Spinoza's native Netherlands and the rest of Europe throughout his lifetime. He was born in Amsterdam in 1634, in the middle of the Thirty Years' War. The preface to his *Tractatus Theologico-Politicus* sets up religious violence as the problem to be solved by the rest of the treatise. In the preface, Spinoza writes that the cause of many wars and revolutions is the way in which the credulous masses are led to grasp onto novel and disputable religious dogmas: "Piety, great God! and religion are become a tissue of ridiculous mysteries."[2] Such prejudices defy reasoned argument and "degrade man from rational being to beast."[3] The solution to the resultant strife is Spinoza's proposal for liberty of religious thought and doctrine within a state in which the sovereign power holds "rights over everything," both temporal and spiritual.[4] Doctrine and "inward worship of God" are to be subject to no constraint—each person may think and say what he or she will—while the state is to determine all external religious rites, "outward observances of piety," and morals that pertain to duties toward others. The church is to abandon all claims to act independently of the state.[5]

Thomas Hobbes similarly indicted the English Civil War of the 1640s and 1650s as a conflict driven by religious motives and solved by the power of a centralized sovereign authority. In 1656, James Harrington published his *Commonwealth of Oceana,* which traced the causes of the war to economic and legal factors.[6] Hobbes would have none of it. In his *Behemoth,* a dialogue between two characters written in 1668 but published posthumously, Hobbes attributed the violence to ideological and psychological factors, with pride of place going to the pointless quarreling of religious actors.

For Hobbes, the basic truths necessary for salvation are plain and accepted by nearly all in a Christian commonwealth. The problem begins in the pulpit, where simple people are led astray by seditious preaching. Hobbes is sharply disparaging of the universities for introducing the baneful influence of scholasticism and the "babbling philosophy of Aristotle and other Greeks" into the churches, an influence that "serves only to breed disaffection, dissension, and finally sedition and civil war."[7] One of Hobbes's characters remarks, "It is a strange thing, that scholars, obscure men, and such as could receive no clarity but from the flame of the state, should be suffered to bring their unnecessary disputes, and together with them their quarrels, out of the universities into the commonwealth; and more strange, that the state should engage in their parties, and not rather put them both to silence."[8] Preachers have led the people astray into the labyrinthine paths of "metaphysical doctrines." How can three be one? How can the deity be made flesh? "These and the like points are the study of the curious, and the cause of all our late mischief, and the cause that makes the plainer sort of men, whom the Scripture had taught belief in Christ, love towards God, obedience to the King, and sobriety of behaviour, forget it all, and place their religion in the disputable doctrines of these your wise men."[9]

In this passage, "religion" indicates something like devotion; Hobbes's concept of religion is not yet fully modern. Religion is still the name of a virtue for Hobbes, but it is a virtue that is unthinkable apart from the state. When one character in the dialogue of *Behemoth* asks if religion should be regarded as the greatest of virtues, the other responds that "inasmuch as I told you, that all virtue is comprehended in obedience to the laws of the commonwealth, whereof religion is one, I have placed religion amongst the virtues."[10] Religion receives its authority from the laws of the nation. It has always been so among the nations of the world. It is only Christian nations, especially under the pernicious influence of the pope, that have struggled with "civil wars about religion."[11] The first twenty pages of *Behemoth* are aimed at the popes, who have always tried to usurp the kings' authority and perpetrate a disastrous division between spiritual and temporal rule.[12] The only possible solution to civil unrest is to overcome this distinction and unite both temporal and spiritual power in the monarchy. Behemoth, Hobbes's symbol of rebellion and civil war, could only be overcome by Leviathan, Hobbes's "mortal god," the state.[13]

Elements of the myth of the wars of religion can be found as well in John Locke's 1689 *Letter Concerning Toleration*. Locke does not assign blame for the wars to religion itself, nor to the diversity of religious opinion. It is rather the refusal of toleration of the different opinions "that has produced all the bustles and wars that have been in the Christian world upon account of religion."[14] The violence of the recent wars had been fomented by those intent on either "the introducing of ceremonies, or . . . the establishment of opinions, which for the most part are about nice and intricate matters that exceed the capacity of ordinary understandings."[15] If the combatants really cared about the salvation of souls, as they claim, they would direct their efforts at wiping out moral vices and behaviors.[16] Instead, they attack the religious doctrines that vary from their own "opinions," which cannot be known with certainty and cannot be compelled by outward force. Here, we see the connection between Locke's work on tolerance and his epistemology, which is based on recognizing the limits of human understanding.[17] Religion is "inward"; it is essentially about beliefs that cannot be settled publicly to the satisfaction of all by any rational method. Civil interests, on the other hand, are "outward" and pertain to the public civil authority.[18] Violence is produced when the church confuses the inward with the outward:

> The heads and leaders of the church, moved by avarice and insatiable desire of dominion, making use of the immoderate ambition of magistrates and the credulous superstition of the giddy multitude, have incensed and animated them against those that dissent from themselves, by preaching unto them, contrary to the laws of the Gospel and the precepts of charity, that schismatics and heretics are to be outed of their possessions and destroyed. And thus have they mixed together and confounded two things that are in themselves most different, the church and the commonwealth.[19]

Blame for the violence is clearly focused on the leaders of the church, who mistakenly believe that religion has to do with civil interests. That is, they seek to use the proper means of the state—coercion, meaning the deprivation of civil interests such as goods, liberty, and life—to enforce religious beliefs.

Whereas for Hobbes the violence results from an improper distinction of temporal and spiritual power, for Locke violence results from an improper confusion of religion and civil interests, two distinct realms of human activity. Locke's solution, therefore, as we saw in the previous chapter, is to "distinguish exactly the business of civil government from that of religion," without which distinction there could be no end to controversies.[20] The state is to secure a monopoly on jurisdiction over civil interests—life, liberty, health, and material possessions—and a monopoly on violence, the threat of which is necessary to protect the rights to the enjoyment of civil interests. The church is to attend to the care of souls and their attainment of eternal life.[21] For Locke, this is not a story of the rising power of the modern state nor the secularization of the state. As I noted in the previous chapter, Locke does not present this sharp distinction between religion and civil interests as a new configuration of power, but as the reestablishment of proper and natural boundaries that had become obscured. In Locke's view, if Roman Catholics are excluded from his scheme of toleration, it is not simply because Locke and the Catholics have incompatible ways of configuring the world. In Locke's view, it is rather because the Catholics have stubbornly refused to recognize that Catholicism is a *religion*, in which civil interests and temporal jurisdictions, either direct or indirect, ought to have no place. Blame for the violence, then, lies with those who continue to confuse religion with the civil order.

The European wars of religion provide the backdrop for much of the Enlightenment's critique of religion.[22] There developed a grand narrative in Enlightenment historiography—typified by Edward Gibbon and Voltaire— that saw the wars of religion as the last gasp of medieval barbarism and fanaticism before the darkness was dispelled.[23] More extreme voices, such as that of Baron d'Holbach, rejected religion *tout court*—"all religion is but a castle in the air"[24]—as inevitably productive of ignorance, and therefore of fanaticism: "We find in all the religions of the earth a God of armies, a jealous God, an avenging God, an exterminating God, a God who enjoys carnage and whose worshippers make it a duty to serve him to his taste."[25] Other Enlightenment figures, however, responded to the wars of religion by differentiating between types of religion that promoted division and those that were conducive to civic order. The majority of the examples Voltaire cites in the entry on "Fanaticism" in his *Philosophical Dictionary* are from the French wars of religion (1562– 1598); it is interesting to note that most of these and all of the biblical examples he cites pertain to the assassinations of kings.[26] Voltaire's principal concern with the wars of religion is with their disruption of civic order. In his entry on "Religion," Voltaire distinguishes between "state religion" and "theological religion." The former he defines as an official class of ministers of religion—under the watchful eye of the ministers of state—who maintain a regular public cult established by law and teach good morals to the people: "A state religion can never cause any turmoil. This is not true of theological religion; it is the source of all the follies and turmoils imaginable; it is the mother of fanaticism and civil discord; it is the enemy of mankind."[27] Though Voltaire does not directly define a "theological religion," it is presumably one that attempts to "inundate the world with blood for the sake of unintelligible sophisms."[28] As in Spinoza, Hobbes, and Locke, religious violence is essentially an epistemological problem; it is produced by wrangling over abstruse doctrinal distinctions whose definitive solution lies beyond reason's grasp. State religion may not necessarily be truer than theological religion, in Voltaire's way of thinking, but it does a better job of preserving order by emphasizing decorous public rituals and morals over doctrinal hairsplitting. For Voltaire, the solution to the wars of religion is the subjection of the church to the oversight of the state and to the service of civic order.[29] According to Voltaire, the absolutist monarchy of Louis XIV brought an end to the wars of religion and ushered in the Enlightenment.[30]

Rousseau arrives at a similar conclusion about the best answer to religious wars. In the section of *The Social Contract* on civil religion, Rousseau discusses the universal practice of theocracy in the ancient world. He asks, "Why—in view of the fact that each state had its own religion and its own gods—did the pagan world have no religious wars?"[31] His reply is, "For that very reason."[32] The gods of the ancient world were not jealous, but "each contented himself with his slice of empire."[33] People did not fight for their gods, but their gods fought for them.[34] Rousseau sees many merits in the pagan system of government, because, besides decreasing the likelihood of religious wars between nations, it lessens the likelihood of internal religious strife. Religious uniformity is enforced by the state, and religion inculcates obedience to the state as one of its foundational principles. Ultimately, however, Rousseau rejects this type of theocracy because it is based on false gods and superstition.[35]

Rousseau prefers the "religion of man," Christianity, but not that Christianity practiced by the church. The religion of man has no churches and no rites, but is to do only with "the purely inward worship of Almighty God and the eternal obligations of morality," as found in the gospels.[36] "This religion does not, however, have any assignable point of contact with political society."[37] Properly understood, true Christianity is very far from the spirit of religious war: "The Gospels preach no national religion, so that a religious war waged by true Christians is unthinkable." The problem is that true Christianity has been hijacked by the political ambitions of the church. Rousseau congratulates Hobbes for having correctly diagnosed the problem in Christianity's splitting of political authority, and he sympathizes with Hobbes's cure, the unification of church and state. Ultimately, however, Rousseau's solution differs from that of Hobbes, because he doubts that the ambition of Christian priests could be contained by Hobbes's system for long.[38] What Rousseau proposes instead is to supplement the purely inward religion of man with a civil religion intended to bind the citizen to the state. This civil religion has a few simple dogmas regarding the existence of God, the reward of the just and the punishment of the wicked, and the sanctity of the social contract and the laws of the state. All theological religions are to be tolerated, provided they do not interfere with the obligations of citizens to the state. Indeed, theological toleration must be *enforced* by the state. Theological intolerance inevitably leads to civil intolerance—"One cannot live in peace with people one regards as damned"[39]—so the state must forbid the practice of intolerant religions such as Roman Catholicism.[40] Civil tolerance, however, does not include dissent from the religion of the state: "As for that man who, having committed himself publicly to the state's articles of faith, acts on any occasion as if he does not believe them, let his punishment be death. He has committed the greatest of all crimes: he has lied in the presence of the laws."[41]

As we can see, the basic elements of the wars-of-religion narrative are already found in the seventeenth- and eighteenth-century sources of modern political theory. As the story goes, the primary cause of the wars of sixteenth- and seventeenth-century Europe was fruitless squabbling over religious doctrine: Spinoza's "tissue of ridiculous mysteries," Hobbes's "disputable doctrines of these your wise men," Locke's "nice and intricate matters that exceed the capacity of ordinary understandings," d'Holbach's "castle in the air," Voltaire's "unintelligible sophisms." These disputes would be harmless but for the way that the churches have sought to use coercive political power to enforce their doctrinal opinions. The solutions offered vary, but all center on the state's appropriation of powers hitherto claimed by the church. Hobbes would do away with doctrinal dispute by absorbing the churches into the state and making the state the undisputed arbiter of doctrinal disputes in the realm. Similarly, Spinoza's state would absorb the church, while putting greater emphasis on the individual's complete liberty to believe whatever he or she would about mere doctrine. Voltaire and Rousseau would favor a compulsory state religion of public cult and morals, while leaving the individual similarly free in matters of belief. Locke would establish clear boundaries between the proper business of the church, which is religious doctrine and rites, and the proper business of the state, which is public order and the civil interests of society. We are accustomed to drawing a sharp contrast between the liberty of Locke's church and the subservience of Hobbes's. What Hobbes and Locke have in common, however, is a significant reduction of the public power of the church and a complementary augmentation of the power of the state, justified by the need to defuse the threat of further religious wars.

Contemporary Political Theory

I think it is important and useful to show how the story of the religious wars works in some of the classic sources of modern political theory, but I will not here attempt a complete history of the myth of the wars of religion in the intervening centuries. My primary interest is in the way the story is used in contemporary political theory. It would be interesting to discover exactly when, in the development of Western political theory and historiography, the European wars of the sixteenth and seventeenth centuries came to be regarded as a consistent set, commonly identified by the capitalized moniker "Wars of Religion," and marked by a coherent cause. For now, I will simply note that they have been so marked, and I will examine their invocation in contemporary political theory.

The conclusion to Quentin Skinner's two-volume work *The Foundations of Modern Political Thought*, which appeared in 1978, notes that "the acceptance of the modern idea of the State presupposes that political society is held to exist solely for political purposes." According to Skinner, both Catholics and Protestants in the sixteenth century agreed that the government had an obligation to support through coercion the one true religion. As such:

> [T]he religious upheavals of the Reformation made a paradoxical yet vital contribution to the crystallizing of the modern, secularized concept of the State. For as soon as the protagonists of the rival religious creeds showed that they were willing to fight each other to the death, it began to seem obvious to a number of *politique* theorists that, if there were to be any prospect of achieving civic peace, the powers of the State would have to be divorced from the duty to uphold any particular faith.[42]

The basic elements of this contemporary story are recognizable from the story told by the early modern theorists: religious groups fight over doctrines or "religious creeds," and the state steps in to make peace. Nevertheless, we should note that Skinner's story gets a bit ahead of itself historically. What sounds like modern secularism and liberalism in Skinner—a state "divorced from the duty to uphold any particular faith"—is not quite what Hobbes, Spinoza, et al. had in mind, and in history such a state was not found in Europe until much later. Even Locke recognized a state-established church. It is not clear who Skinner's *politiques* are. The one he cites immediately following the passage above—Jean Bodin[43]—strongly believed that religious uniformity should be enforced by the sovereign, only excepting those circumstances in which the sovereign finds it too costly to suppress dissent.[44] As historian Mack Holt points out, most of those called *politiques* by their enemies in sixteenth-century France wanted to reunite France under the Catholic faith.[45] Holt writes, "[W]hatever else the 'politiques' were, they clearly did not favour a policy of permanent religious toleration nor any concept of putting the state above religious unity; they were deeply religious Catholics who championed the cause of 'one king, one faith, one law.' "[46]

Jeffrey Stout's analysis of the demise of authority and the rise of moral autonomy in the West makes use of Skinner's work.[47] According to Stout, with the definitive breakdown of a commonly accepted ecclesial authority following the Reformation, violence resulted, because there were no higher rational standards accepted by all parties to which to appeal. In this new situation, religious points of view were incapable of providing a reasonable basis for social peace.[48] The only possible solution to this dilemma was to secularize public discourse:

> What can be granted without hesitation is that liberal principles were the right ones to adopt when competing religious beliefs and divergent conceptions of the good embroiled Europe in the religious wars. Religious beliefs and conceptions of the good were, in that highly particular context, part of a dialectical impasse that made the attainment of rational agreement on a whole range of issues impossible.[49]

As in other versions of the myth of the wars of religion, Stout assumes that they were fought over irreconcilable religious beliefs.

Stout notes that both Immanuel Kant and John Rawls regard the original agreement reached in social contract theory to be purely hypothetical:

> My investigations suggest, however, that something very much like this agreement was in fact reached—though tacitly, to be sure—by actual historical agents in the early modern period. These agents were not, however, lifting themselves out of a state of nature, but were rather concerned to end a thoroughly social "war of all against all." Their agreement was to grant an important measure of

autonomy to the moral-political sphere—specifically, autonomy *from* religious authority.[50]

As an account of actual historical events, however, this story contains a signifi-cant gap. Like Skinner, Stout jumps from the religious wars to liberalism with no consideration of the absolutist governments with confessional states that prevailed throughout Europe from the late sixteenth to the nineteenth centu-ries.[51] Here, a distinction between the "liberal principles" of the first quote and "autonomy *from* religious authority" in the second quote would be helpful. The rising states of early modern Europe did indeed secure autonomy from reli-gious authority, often dominating the church—Catholic or Protestant—within their realms. But the idea that the wars of religion were ended by the adoption of liberal principles is hard to square with the time lapse between the end of the wars and the advent of what we would call liberalism. If "liberal principles" is taken to mean the toleration and privatization of religious practice, then lib-eral principles would have to wait—in some cases, for centuries—before being adopted by most European governments. Liberal principles were not adopted in France until after the revolution,[52] nor in Spain until the twentieth century. Roman Catholics in England were not emancipated until 1829. In Germany, the Treaty of Westphalia instituted a qualified toleration at best. The treaty reinforced the policy of *cuius regio, eius religio* in most Habsburg lands and allowed all rulers subject to the treaty to expel any dissenters with three years' notice.[53]

Political theorist Judith Shklar also locates the origins of liberalism in the wars of religion. Against those who think of liberalism as encouraging self-indulgence, Shklar sees liberalism as a heroic attempt at self-restraint, especially in its attempts to rein in violence. Shklar's concept of a "liberalism of fear" identi-fies the first political task as securing peace against cruelty. In Shklar's words:

> This is a liberalism that was born out of the cruelties of the religious
> civil wars, which forever rendered the claims of Christian charity
> a rebuke to all religious institutions and parties. If the faith was to
> survive at all, it would do so privately. The alternative then set, and
> still before us, is not one between classical virtue and liberal self-
> indulgence, but between cruel military and moral repression and
> violence, and a self-restraining tolerance that fences in the powerful
> to protect the freedom and safety of every citizen, old or young, male
> or female, black or white.[54]

The hero of this account is Michel de Montaigne, who according to Shklar rejected institutionalized Christianity for its apparently incurable cruelty and looked to the philosophers of classical antiquity for sanity amid madness.[55] Beyond Stout's dilemma of irreconcilable goods, Shklar sees religion in public life as itself tending toward fanaticism and violence.

John Rawls acknowledges the debt that his "political liberalism" owes to Shklar's liberalism of fear.[56] Like Stout and unlike Shklar, however, Rawls takes pains to emphasize that his liberalism need not make judgments on the moral status or truth claims of any religion or other kind of comprehensive doctrine. Rawls's liberalism is "political, not metaphysical"; it does not claim to be true, but claims to provide a reasonable way for incommensurable truth claims to coexist peacefully.[57] As in Shklar, the founding historical moment of liberalism for Rawls is the wars of religion. When one authoritative, salvationist, and expansionist religion gave way to three religions (Catholicism, Lutheranism, and Calvinism) that were just as dogmatic and intolerant, social conflict was the obvious result:

> During the wars of religion people were not in doubt about the nature of the highest good, or the basis of moral obligation in divine law....The problem was rather: How is society even possible between those of different faiths? What can conceivably be the basis of religious toleration? For many there was none, for it meant the acquiescence in heresy about first things and the calamity of religious disunity. Even the earlier proponents of toleration saw the division of Christendom as a disaster, though a disaster that had to be accepted in view of the alternative of unending religious civil war. Thus the historical origin of political liberalism (and of liberalism more generally) is the Reformation and its aftermath, with the long controversies over religious toleration in the sixteenth and seventeenth centuries.[58]

According to Rawls, the Reformation introduced something completely new into human history: "the clash between salvationist, creedal, and expansionist religions."[59] "What is new about this clash is that it introduces into people's conceptions of their good a transcendent element not admitting of compromise. This element forces either mortal conflict moderated only by circumstance and exhaustion, or equal liberty of conscience and freedom of thought."[60] For Rawls, there is something transcendent in religion—at least, religions like Catholicism, Lutheranism, and Calvinism—that makes conflicts over religion so much more prone to violence than conflicts over mundane matters.

In the introduction to *Political Liberalism*, from which the above is taken, Rawls lists three historical developments that "deeply influenced" the moral and political philosophy of the modern period. The first is the Reformation.

"The second is the development of the modern state with its central adminis-tration, at first ruled by monarchs with enormous if not absolute powers. Or at least by monarchs who tried to be as absolute as they could, only granting a share in power to the aristocracy and the rising middle classes when they had to, or as suited their convenience."[61] The third is the development of mod-ern science, to which Rawls devotes three sentences. Despite identifying these three factors, Rawls continues on to discuss the Reformation alone, and says not another word about the other two. The two sentences on the rise of the absolutist state are all Rawls has to say about the influence of the state. For Rawls, the problem of modernity is clearly a theological problem; the solution is political. The problem is that people believe in incommensurable theologi-cal doctrines and are willing and eager to kill each other for them. Liberalism solves the problem. How the absolutist state figures into this narrative is not clear. Is the absolutist state merely a placeholder for the liberal state to come? Somehow, despite Rawls's acknowledgment of the deeply influential rise of the absolutist state, the narrative once again skips from the Reformation to contemporary liberalism without much bother about what forces actually pro-duced the modern state. It simply appears as the solution to the problem of religious violence.

The connection between religious wars and the rise of liberalism is espe-cially tenuous when the wars-of-religion narrative is applied to the American context. An example is "Religion and Liberal Democracy" by Kathleen M. Sullivan, dean of the Stanford Law School. According to Sullivan, the Establishment Clause of the First Amendment to the U.S. Constitution not only forbade the establishment of religion by the federal government, but also positively established a secular civil order for the resolution of public moral disputes: "Agreement on such a secular mechanism was the price of ending the war of all sects against all. Establishment of a civil public order was the social contract produced by religious truce."[62] Secular grounds may be used to resolve public moral disputes. Using religious grounds, on the other hand, "would rekindle inter-denominational strife that the Establishment Clause extinguished."[63]

Sullivan seems to regard the "war of all sects against all" as a historical event that the Establishment Clause resolved. However, she also seems to regard it as a conflict that is perpetually ready to break out again if the Establishment Clause of the First Amendment is misinterpreted. In the debate with Sullivan that prompted her article, Michael McConnell argues that the government best protects religious liberty when it leaves intact religious choices that would have been made in the absence of government.[64] According to Sullivan, McConnell argues for unfettered religious liberty. Sullivan regards this as saying that "the war of all sects against all is to continue by other means after the truce."[65] McConnell believes that establishing a secular civil order to resolve moral disputes "distorts" prepolitical religious choice. Sullivan replies, "The social contract to end the war of all sects against all necessarily, by its very existence, 'distorts' the outcomes that would have obtained had that war continued."[66] After this settlement, the strong can no longer triumph over the weak in religious matters. Religion has been "banish[ed] from the public square"[67] in favor of secular public discourse as a necessary condition for peace. According to Sullivan, McConnell thinks this makes secular ideology "just another competing faith among many in the war of all sects against all."[68] Sullivan acknowledges that the culture of liberal democracy "may well function as a belief system with substantive content,"[69] but she argues, "[e]ven if the culture of liberal democracy is a belief system comparable to a religious faith in the way it structures knowledge, it simply does not follow that it is the equivalent of a religion for political and constitutional purposes."[70]

The phrase "war of all sects against all" would appear to be a conscious paraphrase of Hobbes's "war of all against all," the mythical condition of anarchy that requires the enactment of Leviathan, the state, to establish peace.[71] Sullivan uses the phrase "war of all sects against all" eight times[72] in this article without ever specifying places or dates or combatants in these wars. It is difficult to know to which wars she is referring. It might be the European wars of religion; James Madison had invoked the memory of those wars in opposing state establishment of religion. His 1785 "Memorial and Remonstrance" against government-funded religion teachers in Virginia reminds readers, "Torrents of blood have been spilt in the old world, by vain attempts of the secular arm, to extinguish Religious disscord, by proscribing all difference in Religious opinion."[73] In Sullivan's case, however, it would be odd to claim that a constitutional settlement in the United States resolved wars fought on the other side of the Atlantic Ocean. Certainly, some immigrants to the colonies in the 1640s and 1650s were refugees from the English Civil War, but that war was concluded well over a century before the founding fathers gave us the Establishment Clause. Once in the New World, Puritans and Anglicans alike built established churches which worked with colonial governments to systematically exclude dissenters. As historian Edwin Gaustad says of the American colonies, "We of today ask where the state left off and the church began; they of yesterday can only shake their heads in wonderment at so meaningless a question. It is like asking where culture starts or society stops."[74] Most colonists took the existence of a state-established church for granted. And yet there simply was no interdenominational war in America to which the Establishment Clause provided a solution. Undoubtedly, dissenters chafed under Congregationalist establishments in Massachusetts and Connecticut and under Anglican establishments in Virginia and South Carolina. Religious liberties were systematically denied in most colonies, with notable exceptions such as Roger Williams's and William Penn's experiments in toleration. Nevertheless, there was virtually no significant interdenominational violence in the American colonies. Undoubtedly, the Establishment Clause was wise policy. What is dubious is the idea that the Establishment Clause put an end to a war of all sects against all.

It may be that Sullivan intends this phrase as a mere metaphor for social conflict among religious sects short of bloodshed. For Sullivan, there is something peculiarly threatening about religious conflict.[75] But there is no reason to suppose that social conflict among members of different denominations was any more intense and threatening in the colonial period than conflicts between, for example, wealthy male white landowners and any of the subordinate groups—women, landless laborers, indentured servants, African slaves, Indians, and so on—who were denied the right to vote and excluded from participation in the public life of the colonies. Between Bacon's Rebellion in 1676 and the year 1760, there were eighteen armed uprisings aimed at overthrowing colonial governments in America, in addition to six slave rebellions, and forty significant riots mostly based on class cleavages.[76] None of these conflicts—nor any others of which I am aware—had interdenominational strife as a principal motivating factor.

Economic factors play a part in some uses of the wars-of-religion narrative, but not to emphasize class conflict. To the contrary, the rise of capitalism is presented by Francis Fukuyama—and George Will[77] and Dinesh D'Souza[78]—as the peace-making balm that put an end to religious irritations. According to Fukuyama, capitalism and the modern liberal state worked together to put an end to religious violence. In his widely debated book *The End of History and the Last Man,* Fukuyama contrasts the irrational, "thymotic" striving for recognition and superiority found in imperialism and religion with the cool rationalism of the bourgeois quest for earthly comforts. According to Fukuyama:

> [The drive for religious mastery] could displace secular motives
> altogether, as in the various religious wars of the sixteenth and sev-
> enteenth centuries.... But these manifestations of *thymos* were to
> a large extent displaced in the early modern period by increasingly
> rational forms of recognition whose ultimate expression was the
> modern liberal state. The bourgeois revolution of which Hobbes and
> Locke were the prophets sought to morally elevate the slave's fear
> of death over the aristocratic virtue of the master, and thereby to

sublimate irrational manifestations of *thymos* like princely ambition and religious fanaticism into the unlimited accumulation of property. Where once there had been civil conflict over dynastic and religious issues, there were now new zones of peace constituted by the modern liberal European nation-state. Political liberalism in England ended the religious wars between Protestant and Catholic that had nearly destroyed that country during the seventeenth century: with its advent, religion was defanged by being made tolerant.[79]

Despite acknowledging the irrational element in secular phenomena like dynastic ambition and imperialism, Fukuyama ultimately dissolves the struggle into one between the rational, peace-making, bourgeois, liberal state and the irrational, violent forces of religion:

> There was a time when religion played an all-powerful role in European politics, with Protestants and Catholics organizing themselves into political factions and squandering the wealth of Europe in sectarian wars. English liberalism, as we saw, emerged in direct reaction to the religious fanaticism of the English Civil War. Contrary to those who at the time believed that religion was a necessary and permanent feature of the political landscape, *liberalism vanquished religion in Europe.*[80]

The result of this victory was peace. In spite of the fact that bourgeois Europe—newly liberated from religion to concentrate on the "unlimited accumulation of property"—proceeded to conquer most of the rest of the world by force of arms, Fukuyama claims that imperialism is a relic of aristocracy and has nothing to do with liberal democracy. Liberalism made the West extraordinarily hesitant to go to war.[81] Twentieth-century conflicts like the Russian and Chinese revolutions and World War II are atavisms, a "return, in a magnified form, of the kind of brutality that characterized the religious wars of the sixteenth century, for what was at stake was not just territory and resources, but the value systems and ways of life of entire populations."[82] The victory of liberalism is the victory of the peaceful pursuit of material comfort over irrational ideological strife, of which the wars of religion are the prime example.

Stephen Toulmin's book *Cosmopolis* presents an interesting account of the way that the wars of religion contributed to new forms of rationality and the state in Europe. According to Toulmin, the seventeenth-century quests for certainty in philosophy and stability in politics need to be seen in the context of the chaos produced by the religious wars, specifically the Thirty Years' War of 1618–1648. While most biographies of René Descartes treat his thought in splendid isolation from the turbulence of his age, Toulmin seeks to read his and other rationalists' quest for absolute certainty against the despair for certainty produced by fruitless and violent squabbling over theological doctrines:

> Across the whole of central Europe, from the mid-1620s to 1648,
> rival militias and military forces consisting largely of mercenaries
> fought to and fro, again and again, over the same disputed territo-
> ries. The longer the bloodshed continued, the more paradoxical the
> state of Europe became. Whether for pay or from conviction, there
> were many who would kill and burn in the name of theological
> doctrines that no one could give any conclusive reasons for accept-
> ing. The intellectual debate between Protestant Reformers and their
> Counter-Reformation opponents had collapsed, and there was no
> alternative to the sword and the torch. Yet, the more brutal the war-
> fare became, the more firmly convinced the proponents of each reli-
> gious system were that their doctrines *must be* proved correct, and
> that their opponents were stupid, malicious, or both.[83]

Toulmin acknowledges that the Thirty Years' War was fought largely by mercenaries, but he declares that they fought for theological doctrines, regard-less of whether they fought from conviction or for money. War—even war by mercenaries—bred not cynicism but a heightened quest for certainty in reli-gious matters. This quest precluded a return to the tolerant sixteenth-century skepticism of Erasmus and Montaigne: "Living in a time of high theological passion, the only other thing thinking people could do was to look for a new way of establishing their central truths and ideas."[84] That new way was the rationalism of Descartes and his successors in philosophy and science. The political counterpart of the quest for certainty was the quest for stability. The Peace of Westphalia in 1648 established a stable new system of "sovereign nation-states" which took power away from the warring theological factions. The transnational authority of the medieval church was broken:

> Aside from the sheer increase in power of the nation-states, the rise
> of a literate and educated laity tilted the balance toward the secu-
> lar, and against the ecclesiastical powers. From now on, Church
> affairs were increasingly influenced by national policy. The Peace of
> Westphalia reestablished the rule agreed on in 1555, in the Treaty of
> Augsburg, by which each sovereign chose the official religion of his
> own State.[85]

Toulmin's thesis is elegant, and he persuasively argues for placing intel-lectual history firmly within its social and political context. To read Descartes' efforts to banish doubt within the chaos of his age seems to me to be a very promising way to proceed. Toulmin, however, does not extend the same courtesy to the theological disputants of the sixteenth and seventeenth centuries. Their quarrels are all cause and no effect. Theological disputes arise from the fevered minds of individual churchmen, and though they cause terrible upheavals in society and politics, theological disputes are never the effects of changes in social and political structures. As in Rawls et al., the problem is theological, and the solution is political. The rise of the "nation-state" comes on the scene as the solution, never a cause, of the Thirty Years' War.[8] The cause of the war is essentially intellectual arguments over disembodied theological beliefs.

I will give just two more examples of how the state has been presented as the solution to the wars of religion.[87] J. G. A. Pocock writes, "In continental Europe, the function of absolute monarchies and their armies was to put an end to the wars of religion, conventionally supposed to have ended with the Peace of Westphalia in 1648."[88] As in Voltaire, the Enlightenment and absolutist states are linked, as Pocock also defines the Enlightenment in terms of solving the religious wars:

> I intend to argue that [the] Enlightenment may be characterized
> in two ways: first, as the emergence of a system of states, founded
> in civil and commercial society and culture, which might enable
> Europe to escape from the wars of religion without falling under the
> hegemony of a single monarchy; second, as a series of programmes
> for reducing the power of either churches or congregations to disturb
> the peace of civil society by challenging its authority.[89]

Once again, the transfer of power from the church to the state is the solution to the violence of the religious wars. David Held seems to indicate that it was the *only possible* solution:

> However, the formation of the *idea* of the modern state itself prob-
> ably received its clearest impetus from the bitter struggles between
> religious factions which spread across Western Europe during the last
> half of the sixteenth century, and reached their most intense expres-
> sion during the Thirty Years War in Germany.... Very gradually it
> became apparent that the powers of the state would have to be differ-
> entiated from the duty of rulers to uphold any particular faith. [Here,
> Held cites the same passage from Skinner I have quoted above.] This
> conclusion alone offered a way forward through the dilemmas of rule
> created by competing religions, all seeking to secure for themselves
> the kinds of privilege claimed by the medieval church.[90]

Held italicizes the word "idea" in the first line of this passage to set it against what he has done in the previous pages of his argument, which is to explain the actual historical conditions of the rise of the modern state, as opposed to the rise of the *idea* of the modern state. Held describes the decentralized structure of Christendom from the eighth to the fourteenth centuries, in which relatively autonomous local feudal powers came to be rivaled by emergent urban elites. The "chief rival" to both of these powers was the church, which consistently sought to assert ecclesiastical power over civil authorities.[91] Beginning in the fourteenth century, the feudal system began to break down, and by the fifteenth century it was being replaced by progressively centralizing monarchies, both of the absolutist and the constitutional varieties. According to Held, the modern state emerged from absolutism, which was typified by an alliance of monarchy and nobility that absorbed lesser political powers into a unitary system of law and, eventually, territorial sovereignty:

> Absolutism and the inter-state system it initiated were the proximate sources of the modern state. In condensing and concentrating political power in its own hands, and in seeking to create a central system of rule, absolutism paved the way for a secular and national system of power. Moreover, in claiming sovereign authority exclusively for itself, it threw down a challenge to all those groups and classes which had had a stake in the old order, and to all those with a stake in the developing order based on capital and the market economy. It forced all these collectivities to rethink their relationship to the state, and to re-examine their political resources. In addition, the myriad battles and wars fought out in the inter-state system altered fundamentally the boundaries of both absolutist states and the emerging modern states—the whole map of Europe changed as territorial boundaries gradually became fixed borders.[92]

Held thus gives an unsentimental, *realpolitik* account of the rise of the state: long before the Reformation, monarchies and allied elites had begun to build the modern state through appropriation of power from the church and lesser rivals. This account is followed immediately, however, with his account of the rise of the *idea* of the state in the battle between competing religions in the wake of the Reformation. Held is doubtlessly correct that theorists of the state from the late sixteenth century onward put forth the idea of the state as the only solution to religious violence. One wonders, however, if some understanding could be gained by replacing the word "idea" with the word "ideology" in the passage cited above. It would obviously benefit state-making elites to present an increase in their power over that of the church as the salvation of Europe from doctrinal fanaticism. If the struggle between state-building elites and other powers like the church predates the Reformation by at least a century, however, it may be that the state-building process is not as innocent of the ensuing violence as the creation myth of the religious wars makes it out to be. Is it possible that the state-building process is not simply the solution but a contributing cause of the violence of the sixteenth and seventeenth centuries? This possibility will be explored later in this chapter.

At this point, let us note what the above figures, both early modern and contemporary, have in common and where they differ. They all see the transfer of power from the church to the state as the solution to the wars of religion. They differ, however, in what kind of state solves the problem. For all of the early modern figures except Locke, the savior is an absolutist type of state in which the church is absorbed into the apparatus of the state, or the state invents its own civil religion. Toulmin, Pocock, and Held similarly invoke the absolutist state as the solution to the religious wars, though they seem to regard absolutism as a necessary but temporary stage on the road to liberalism. For Locke and the rest of the contemporary figures we have examined, it is the liberal state that solves the problem. Absolutism is ignored, and the hero of the story is the liberal state that banishes religion from the public sphere.

Components of the Myth

In this section, I will lay out the basic components of the narrative of the wars of religion as used by the figures above. Subsequent sections of this chapter will examine the historical record to determine the plausibility of each component of the narrative. For the overall narrative to be true, each of the following components must be true:

A. *Combatants opposed each other based on religious difference.* The killing in the wars that are called religious took place between combatants who held to different religious doctrines and practices. We would expect to find, therefore, in the wars of religion that Catholics killed Protestants and that Catholics did not kill fellow Catholics. We would likewise expect to find that Protestants killed Catholics, but we would not necessarily expect that Protestants did not kill each other without being more specific in differentiating those who are commonly lumped together as "Protestants." Certainly, we would expect that Lutherans did not kill other Lutherans, Calvinists did not kill other Calvinists, and so on. But given that Lutherans had significant theological differences with Calvinists, Zwinglians, and Anabaptists—and those groups had great doctrinal differences among themselves—we should expect violence among different types of Protestants as well. We should expect, in Kathleen Sullivan's phrase, a "war of all sects against all."

B. *The primary cause of the wars was religion, as opposed to merely political, economic, or social causes.* Protestants and Catholics not only killed each other, but they did so for religious—not political, economic, or social—reasons.

C. *Religious causes must be at least analytically separable from political, economic, and social causes at the time of the wars.* Although the historical reality is inevitably complex, and people's motives are often mixed, we must be able, at least in theory, to separate religious causes from political, economic, and social causes.

D. *The rise of the modern state was not a cause of the wars, but rather provided a solution to the wars.* The transfer of power from the church to the state was necessary to tame the disruptive influence of religion. As we have seen, there are two versions of this narrative. In one, the liberal state tames religion by separating church and state and removing religion from the public realm. In the other, the absolutist state enforces political unity by absorbing the church. For contemporary liberal political theorists of the latter type, absolutism is a necessary but temporary stage on the way to liberalism.

We will now see how each of these components stands up to recorded history. This is important, given that the tellings of the narrative we examined above tend not to look very closely at history. Toulmin's, Skinner's, and Pocock's books contain scattered references in the notes to contemporary histories of the religious wars. None of the other figures cites, either in the main text or the footnotes, any work by any historian of the European wars of religion.

The Historical Record

(A) Combatants Opposed Each Other Based on Religious Difference

The myth of the wars of religion is an uncomplicated tale of violence between religious groups who held to different theological doctrines. Historical records of these wars, however, show many examples of members of the same church killing each other and members of different churches collaborating:

- If there truly were a war of all sects against all, one would expect that war would have broken out soon after Europe split into Catholic and Protestant factions. However, between the time that Martin Luther nailed his Ninety-Five Theses to the church door at Wittenberg in 1517 and the outbreak of the first commonly cited religious war—the Schmalkaldic War of 1546–1547—almost thirty years would pass. The Catholic prosecutor of the Schmalkaldic War, Holy Roman emperor

Charles V, spent much of the decade following Luther's excommunication in 1520 at war not against Lutherans, but against the pope.
As Richard Dunn points out, "Charles V's soldiers sacked Rome, not
Wittenberg, in 1527, and when the papacy belatedly sponsored a reform
program, both the Habsburgs and the Valois refused to endorse much
of it, rejecting especially those Trentine decrees which encroached
on their sovereign authority."[93] The wars of the 1520s were part of the
ongoing struggle between the pope and the emperor for control over
Italy and over the church in German territories.[94]

- The early decades of the Reformation saw Catholic France in frequent
  wars against the Catholic emperor. The wars began in 1521, 1527, 1536,
  1542, and 1552; most lasted two to three years.[95] Charles V was at war
  twenty-three of the forty-one years of his reign, sixteen of them against
  France.[96] Although most of these wars predate what are commonly
  called the wars of religion, they come in the wake of the Reformation
  and underscore the fact that the first decades of religious difference in
  Europe did not produce war between sects. War continued to be based
  on other factors.

- In a similar vein, starting in 1525, Catholic France made frequent alliances with the Muslim Turks against Catholic emperor Charles V.[97]

- Until the Schmalkaldic War of 1546–1547, the Protestant princes of
  the Holy Roman Empire generally supported the Catholic emperor in
  his wars against France. In 1544, Charles granted wide control to the
  Protestant princes over the churches in their realms in exchange for
  military support against France.[98]

- The first religious war of Charles V against the Schmalkaldic League
  found a number of important Protestant princes on Charles's side,
  including Duke Moritz of Saxony, the Margrave Albrecht-Alcibiades of
  Brandenburg,[99] and the Margrave Hans of Küstrin.[100] The Protestant
  Philip of Hesse had already signed a treaty to support Charles
  against the Schmalkaldic League, but he reneged in 1546.[101] Wim
  Blockmans remarks, "The fact that a number of Protestant princes
  joined Charles's army shows that the entire operation was based on
  sheer opportunism."[102]

- Catholic Bavaria refused to fight for the Habsburg emperor in the
  Schmalkaldic War, though Bavaria did provide some material assistance.[103] Already in 1531, Bavaria had allied with many Lutheran princes
  in opposing Ferdinand's election as king of the Romans, and in 1533
  Bavaria had joined Philip of Hesse in restoring Württemburg to the
  Protestant duke Ulrich.[104]

- The popes were equally unreliable. In January 1547, Pope Paul III abruptly withdrew his forces from Germany, fearing that Charles's military successes would make him too strong.[105] As Blockmans comments, "[T]he pope found a few apostates in northern Germany less awful than a supreme emperor."[106] In 1556–1557, Pope Paul IV went to war against another Habsburg monarch, the devoutly Catholic Philip II of Spain.[107]

- In alliance with Lutheran princes, the Catholic king Henry II of France attacked the emperor's forces in 1552.[108] The Catholic princes of the empire stood by, neutral, while Charles went down to defeat. As Richard Dunn observes, "The German princes, Catholic and Lutheran, had in effect ganged up against the Habsburgs."[109] As a result, the emperor had to accept the Peace of Augsburg, which granted the princes the right to determine the ecclesial affiliation of their subjects. Dunn notes that the German peasantry and urban working class "were inclined to follow orders inertly on the religious issue, and switch from Lutheran to Catholic, or vice versa, as their masters required."[110]

- Most of Charles's soldiers were mercenaries; these included many Protestants. Some of Charles's favorite troops were the High German Landsknechte, who commanded a relatively high wage but were good fighters, despite the prevalence of Lutheranism among them.[111]

- The French wars of religion, generally dated 1562–1598, are usually assumed to have pitted the Calvinist Huguenot minority against the Catholic majority. The reality is more complex. In 1573, the governor of Narbonne, Baron Raymond de Fourquevaux, reported to King Charles IX that the common people believed that the wars were rooted in a conspiracy of Protestant and Catholic nobles directed against the commoners.[112] The Huguenot and Catholic nobles "openly help each other; the one group holds the lamb while the other cuts its throat."[113] Other contemporary accounts confirm that this view was widespread.[114] Though the existence of such a grand conspiracy is doubtful, there were many examples of nobility changing church affiliation at whim[115] and many examples of collaboration between Protestant and Catholic nobles.

- Instances of Protestant-Catholic collaboration among the nobility were generally aimed at asserting the ancient rights of the nobility over against the centralizing efforts of the monarchy. In 1573, the Catholic Henri de Turenne, duke of Bouillon, led the Huguenot forces in upper Guyenne and Périgord.[116]

- In 1574, the Catholic royal governor of Languedoc, Henri de Montmorency, Sieur de Damville, who had previously fought against the

Protestants, joined forces with the Huguenot nobility to support a proposed antimonarchical constitution.[117] He led the anti-Crown military
forces in the west and south against the forces of Jacques de Crussol,
duke of Uzès, a former Huguenot destroyer of Catholic churches.[118]

- In 1575, the Catholic duke of Alençon, King Henry III's brother, joined
  the Huguenots in open rebellion against the monarchy's oppressive taxation.[119] In 1578, as duke of Anjou, he sought the hand of the
  staunchly Protestant Elizabeth I of England in marriage, in an attempt
  to secure an English-French alliance versus Spain.[120]
- A number of Protestants joined the ultra-Catholic duke of Guise's
  war of 1579–1580 against the Crown. J. H. M. Salmon comments, "So
  strong was the disaffection of the nobility, and so little was religion
  a determining factor in their alignment, that a number of Huguenot
  seigneurs in the eastern provinces showed a readiness to follow Guise's
  banners."[121]
- In 1583, the Protestant Jan Casimir of the Palatinate joined forces with
  the Catholic duke of Lorraine against Henry III.[122]
- Catholic nobles Conti and Soissons served the Protestant Condé in the
  1587 campaigns.[123]
- The Crown was not above making alliances with the Huguenots when
  it served its purposes. In 1571, Charles IX allied with the Huguenots
  for an anti-Habsburg campaign in the Low Countries.[124]
- Henry III joined forces with the Protestant Henry of Navarre in 1589.[125]
- The Catholic kings also made alliances with Protestants beyond
  France's borders. In 1580, Anjou offered the French Crown's support
  to Dutch Calvinist rebels against Spanish rule. In return, Anjou would
  become sovereign of the Netherlands, if the revolt should succeed. He
  took up his position in the Netherlands in 1582, though his reign lasted
  only a year.[126]
- The fluidity of the nobles' and the Crown's ecclesial affiliations is cap-
  tured by Salmon in the following passage:

  If the shift from feudal obligation to clientage had intensified
  the spirit of self-interest among the nobility of the sword, it was
  never more evident than in the years immediately before the
  death of Anjou in 1584. Ambition and expediency among the
  princes, magnates, and their followers made a mockery of religious ideals. Huguenot and Catholic Politiques had co-operated
  in Anjou's service in the Netherlands, just as they had at
  Navarre's petty court at Nérac. Montpensier, once a zealous

persecutor of heretics, had deserted the Guisard camp to advocate toleration. Damville had changed alliances once more and
abandoned his close association with the Valois government
to effect a *rapprochement* with Navarre. For political reasons
Navarre himself had resisted a mission undertaken by Epernon
to reconvert him to Catholicism. Not only his Huguenot coun-
selors, Duplessis-Mornay and d'Aubigné, urged him to stand
firm, but even his Catholic chancellor, Du Ferrier, argued that
more would be lost than gained by a new apostasy. More sur-
prising was a covert attempt by Philip II to secure Navarre as his
ally, coupled with a proposal that the Bourbon should repudiate
Marguerite de Valois to marry the Infanta.[127]

- Collaboration between Protestants and Catholics of the lower classes
  was also widespread in the French wars of religion, mainly in an effort
  to resist abuse by the nobility and the Crown. In Agen in 1562, the
  Catholic baron François de Fumel forbade his Huguenot peasants from
  conducting services in the Calvinist manner. They revolted and were
  joined by hundreds of Catholic peasants. Together, they seized Fumel's
  château and beheaded him in front of his wife. Holt comments, "The
  episode shows above all how difficult it is to divide sixteenth-century
  French men and women into neat communities of Protestants and
  Catholics along doctrinal or even cultural lines."[128]
- In 1578, the Protestant and Catholic inhabitants of Pont-en-Roians
  acted together to expel the Protestant captain Bouvier, who had refused
  to abide by the terms of the Treaty of Bergerac.[129]
- In 1578–1580, the widespread Chaperons-sans-cordon uprising united
  Catholics and Protestants against the Crown's attempt to impose a third
  levy of the *taille* tax in a single year. In 1579, an army of Catholic and
  Protestant artisans and peasants based in Romans destroyed the fortress
  of Châteaudouble and went on to capture Roissas. The combined forces
  moved throughout the region, occupying seigneurial manors. They were
  finally trapped and slaughtered by royal troops in March 1580.[130]
- In 1579, Catholic and Protestant parishes actively collaborated in the
  revolt in the Vivarais against the violence and corruption of the ruling
  classes. In the spring of 1580, the Protestant François Barjac led a
  combined Catholic and Huguenot force from the Vivarais against the
  troops stationed at the fortress of Crussol.[131]
- In 1586, Catholic and Protestant villages collaborated in an attack on
  Saint Bertrand de Comminges.[132] In 1591, the peasant federation of the

Campanelle, based in Comminges, joined Catholics and Protestants together to make war on the nobility.[133]

- In the Haut-Biterrois in the 1590s, a league of twenty-four villages of both Protestants and Catholics arose to protest taxes and set up a system of self-defense and self-government.[134]

- In 1593–1594, Protestant and Catholic peasants joined in dozens of uprisings in the southwest of France. Some of these consisted of a few hundred peasants, while others gathered up to 40,000.[135] The most famous of these revolts was that of the Croquants, whose articles of association required the ignoring of ecclesial differences.[136]

- If Protestants and Catholics often collaborated in the French civil wars of 1562–1598, it is also the case that the Catholics were divided into two main parties, the Catholic League and those called *politiques,* who often found themselves on opposing sides of the violence. The queen mother, Catherine de Medici, promoted Protestants like Navarre, Condé, and Coligny to positions of importance in order to counter the power of the ultra-Catholic Guises. In May 1588, the Guise-led Catholic League took Paris from the royal troops, and Henry III fled the city. In December of that year, Henry III had the duke and cardinal of Guise killed and made a pact with the Protestant Henry of Navarre to make war on the Catholic League. Henry III was assassinated in August 1589 by a Jacobin monk. With Henry of Navarre as successor to the throne, Catholics split into royalists who supported him and Leaguers who led a full-scale military rebellion against him and his supporters.[137]

- The myth of the religious wars presents the Thirty Years' War as one widespread unified conflict pitting Europe's Protestants against its Catholics. There was indeed an attempt in 1609 to expand the Protestant Union created by eight German principalities into a pan-European alliance. However, only the counts of Oettingen and the cities of Strasbourg, Ulm, and Nuremburg responded. The elector of Saxony, King Christian of Denmark, and the Reformed cities of Switzerland—in short, the majority of Protestant princes and regions—refused to participate in the Protestant Union.[138] When the Protestant estates of Bohemia rebelled against Emperor Ferdinand II in the opening act of the Thirty Years' War, they offered the crown of Bohemia to Frederick V of the Palatinate, one of the founders of the Protestant Union. The other members of the Protestant Union refused to support him, however, and the union disbanded two years later.[139]

- The Protestant Union attracted some Catholic support. The now-Catholic Henry IV of France sent troops to support the Protestant

Union's intervention in the succession crisis in Cleves-Jülich in 1610, but he demanded as a condition of support that the union sever all contact with French Huguenots.[140] The Catholic prince Carlo Emanuele I of Savoy made an alliance with the Protestant Union in 1619 because the Austrian Habsburgs had failed to solve the succession crisis in Monferrato in a way favorable to his interests. After the Bohemian Protestants were defeated at the Battle of White Mountain, Carlo Emanuele switched his support to the Habsburgs.[141]

- The Lutheran elector of Saxony, John George, helped Emperor Ferdinand II to reconquer Bohemia in exchange for the Habsburg province Lusatia.[142] In 1626, the elector of Saxony published a lengthy argument in which he tried to persuade his fellow Protestants to support the Catholic emperor. According to John George, the emperor was fighting a just war against rebels, not a crusade against Protestants; what the emperor did in Bohemia and Austria was covered by the principle of *cuius regio, eius religio*. Those who opposed the emperor were guilty of treason. The elector of Saxony even cited Luther's admonition to obey the powers that be.[143] John George would later throw in his lot with the Swedes against the emperor.[144]

- Catholic France supported Protestant princes from early in the war. France supported the Protestant Grisons in Switzerland against the Habsburgs in 1623.[145] In 1624, the minister for foreign affairs, Charles de la Vieuville, made alliances and promises of aid to the Dutch and to multiple German Protestant princes. He also opened negotiations with England to restore Frederick to the throne of Bohemia.[146]

- Cardinal Richelieu replaced Vieuville later in 1624 and demanded English and Dutch help in repressing the Huguenots. When such help was not forthcoming, Richelieu abandoned plans for an alliance with England; the Dutch, however, did send a fleet to aid in the defeat of the Huguenot stronghold La Rochelle in 1628.[147]

- While the Calvinist Dutch were helping the French Crown to defeat the Calvinists at La Rochelle, Catholic Spain was supporting the Protestant duke of Rohan in his battle against the French Crown in Languedoc.[148]

- The principal adviser of the Calvinist elector of Brandenburg, George William, was a Catholic, Count Adam of Schwarzenberg.[149]

- One of the leading commanders of the Imperial Army under Albrecht von Wallenstein, Hans Georg von Arnim, was a Lutheran. Historian R. Po-Chia Hsia remarks, "To build the largest and most powerful army in Europe, Wallenstein employed military talent regardless of confessional allegiance."[150]

- Wallenstein's foot soldiers included many Protestants, including, ironically, those fleeing because of the imposition of Catholic rule in their home territories. In April 1633, for example, Wallenstein gained a large number of Protestant recruits from Austria who left because of Emperor Ferdinand's policy of re-Catholicization there.[151]

- Private mercenary armies of flexible allegiance helped to perpetuate the Thirty Years' War. Soldiers of fortune sold the services of their armies to the highest bidder. Ernst von Mansfield worked first for the Catholic Spanish, then for the Lutheran Frederick V, and subsequently switched sides several more times.[152] Protestant Scots and English served as officers in Catholic armies, especially in France. Some, like Captain Sidnam Poyntz, switched sides several times.[153] Sir James Turner acknowledged that he "had swallowed, without chewing, in Germanie, a very dangerous maxime, which military men there too much follow, which was, that soe we serve our master honestlie, it is no matter what master we serve."[154]

- Sweden's king Gustavus Adolphus is sometimes presented as the champion of the Protestant cause upon his entry into the war in 1630. However, Gustavus found it difficult to gain Protestant allies. When Swedish troops landed in Germany, their sole ally in the empire was the city of Stralsund. Over the next few months, the Swedes gained only a few more small principalities as allies.[155] The most powerful of the Protestant imperial diets saw the Swedish invasion as a threat. They met in the Convention of Leipzig from February to April 1631 in order to form a third party independent of Swedish and imperial control.[156] After the initial Swedish victories in 1631, however, many formerly neutral territories were forced to join the Swedes. With Swedish troops approaching in October 1631, Margrave Christian of Brandenburg-Kulmbach, who had heretofore avoided any military engagement, swore his allegiance to Gustavus and agreed to quarter and subsidize his troops. The common people endured many hardships due to the presence of the Swedish troops. When the Lutheran peasants attempted to drive out the Swedes in November 1632, they were massacred.[157]

- France under Cardinal Richelieu signed a treaty with Sweden in January 1631, in which France agreed to subsidize heavily the Swedish war effort.[158] Cardinal Richelieu also made a pact with the Protestant principality of Hesse-Kassel.[159] The French began sending troops to battle imperial forces in the winter of 1634–1635, and the latter half of the Thirty Years' War was largely a battle between Catholic France, on the one hand, and the Catholic Habsburgs, on the other.[160]

- In March 1635, the troops of fervently Catholic Spain attacked Trier and kidnapped the Catholic archbishop elector. Catholic France subsequently declared war on Catholic Spain.[161]
- In May 1635, the Protestant principalities of Brandenburg and Saxony reconciled with the emperor in the Peace of Prague. Not only did hostilities between the parties cease, but the armies of the Protestant principalities were absorbed into the imperial armies. Within months, most Lutheran states made peace with the emperor on the same terms and proceeded to direct their energies against the Swedes.[162] By 1638, the Scottish Presbyterian Robert Baillie could observe, "For the Swedds, I see not what their eirand is now in Germany, bot to shed Protestant blood."[163]
- The pope, on the other hand, refused to support the Holy Roman emperor and gave his approval to the Swedish-French alliance. Pope Urban VIII's main interest lay in weakening Habsburg control over the papal states in central Italy.[164]
- In 1643, Lutheran Sweden attacked Lutheran Denmark. King Christian IV had long harassed Swedish shipping in the Baltic and given asylum to political enemies of Sweden. When word reached Stockholm that Denmark was negotiating an alliance with the emperor, Sweden decided on a preemptive strike. The conflict lasted two years. Despite the Catholic emperor's aid, Denmark was defeated and forced to sue for peace.[165]

It would be difficult to come up with a list similar to the one above for the English Civil War, in part because the major contestants—Puritans and Laudians—were factions of the same Anglican Church. However, Scottish Presbyterians entered the fray on the side of the Puritans, while Irish Catholics supported Scottish Presbyterians as a way of weakening the monarchy.[166]

If the above instances of war making—in which members of the same church fought each other and members of different churches collaborated—undermine the standard narrative of the wars of religion, the *absence* of war between Lutherans and Calvinists also undermines the standard tale. If theological difference tends toward a war of all sects against all, we should expect to find Lutheran-Calvinist wars, but in fact we find none. Although there were internal tensions in some principalities between Lutheran princes and Calvinist nobility or Calvinist princes and Lutheran nobility,[167] no Lutheran prince ever went to war against a Calvinist prince. The absence of such wars cannot be attributed to the similarity of Lutheranism and Calvinism. There were sufficient theological differences to sustain a permanent divide between the two branches of the Reformation. Such differences were serious enough to produce sporadic attempts by the civil authorities to enforce doctrinal uniformity. In the decades following Phillip Melanchthon's death in 1560, there was an effort to root out "Crypto-Calvinists" from the ranks of Lutheranism. The rector of the University of Wittenberg, Caspar Peucer, was jailed for Crypto-Calvinism from 1574 to 1586; Nikolaus Krell was executed for Crypto-Calvinism in Dresden in 1601. Many Crypto-Calvinists among the Lutherans were forced to relocate to regions friendlier to Calvinism, such as Hesse-Kassel.[168] However, the fact that Lutheran-Calvinist tensions played no part in the wars of religion indicates at minimum that significant theological differences in the public realm did not necessarily produce war in sixteenth- and seventeenth-century Europe. There simply was no war of all sects against all.

The long list above is almost certainly incomplete. It is gleaned from a reading of some standard histories of the wars of religion. Undoubtedly, a professional historian of this period could add more instances of war between members of the same church and collaboration in war among members of different churches. Undoubtedly as well, we could compile an even longer list of acts of war between Catholics and Protestants in the sixteenth and seventeenth centuries. Nevertheless, we must at least observe at this point that the first component of the myth (A) must be significantly qualified by all of the above instances in which it does not hold. As we will see, once we consider the implications of the above list, problems arise with the other components of the myth as well.

(B) The Primary Cause of the Wars Was Religion, as Opposed to Merely Political, Economic, or Social Causes

May we not simply conclude that the above list contains *exceptions* to the general rule of war between different religions in this era, but the standard narrative of the wars of religion still holds? That is, may we not claim that the majority of violence was Catholic-Protestant, and so, granting the above exceptions, the standard narrative is valid?

There are two immediate reasons that this would not be an adequate response. First, the above list contains more than just a few isolated instances. In the case of the Thirty Years' War, for example, the entire latter half of the war was primarily a struggle between the two great Catholic powers of Europe: France, on the one hand, and the two branches of the Habsburgs, on the other. Second, the above list contains more than just exceptions; if the wars in question are indeed wars of religion, then the instances above are *inexplicable* exceptions, unless other factors are given priority over religion. Why, in a war over religion, would those who share the same religious beliefs kill each other? Why, in a war over religion, would those on opposite sides of the religious divide collaborate? If the answer is that people prioritized other concerns over their religious views, then it does not make sense to call them wars of religion.

Imagine I am writing a history of World War I. I am telling the standard story of the war as a struggle between two sets of nations, fueled by complex national aspirations, when I uncover a startling fact: the English counties of Somerset, Kent, Durham, Shropshire, Norfolk, Suffolk, Cumbria, and Cornwall entered World War I on the side of the kaiser. Leaders in each of these counties declared their allegiance to the German cause, and thousands of troops were sent by ship to Hamburg to join the German forces fighting on the Western Front. I could respond to this discovery by noting these odd exceptions, but pointing out that the majority of English counties fought for the Allied powers, so the basic plotline of the war is unaltered. If I were a good historian, however, I would most likely drop everything and try to find a narrative that would take these cases into account. Perhaps nationalism was not the only force driving this war. What motivated the leaders of these counties? Did the troops from these counties go out of conviction or desperation? Were they volunteers, conscripts, or mercenaries? What grievances did these counties have against London that made them unwilling to fight for the king? What other factors besides nationalism were at work in this war?

In the actual case of the sixteenth- and seventeenth-century wars, historians generally deal with the facts from the list above by acknowledging that other factors besides religion were at work in the wars of religion—political, economic, and social factors. The question then becomes one of the relative importance of the various factors. Are political, economic, and social factors important enough that we are no longer justified in calling these wars "of religion"? The above list consists of acts of war in which religion as the most important motivating factor must *necessarily* be ruled out. But once religion is ruled out as a significant factor from these events, the remainder of the acts of war—those between Protestants and Catholics—become suspect as well. Were other factors besides religion the principal motivators in those cases too? If Catholics killed Catholics for political and economic reasons, did Catholics also kill Protestants for political and economic reasons?

Historians take different positions on this question. Opinions range from those who think that religion was an important factor among other significant factors to those who think that religion was not important, except as a cover for underlying political, economic, and social causes. Since the Enlightenment, these wars have been labeled wars "of religion." Since the wars occurred, however, there have been those who have doubted whether in fact they were actually religious wars.[169] Michel de Montaigne in the sixteenth century remarked that, "if anyone should sift out of the army, even the average loyalist army, those who march in it from the pure zeal of affection for religion...he could not make up one complete company of men-at-arms out of them."[170]

This divide is apparent if we look at twentieth-century historiography of the French wars. For much of the century, historians downplayed the role of religion in favor of supposedly more fundamental political, economic, and social causes. J.-H. Mariéjol in 1904 stressed the role of the dissident nobility of the sword who joined the Huguenot movement to avenge grievances against the monarchy and the church: "Whether it wanted to or not, [the Huguenot church] served as a rallying point for all kinds of malcontents. It ceased being uniquely a church; it became a party."[171] Lucien Romier—whose two-volume 1913 study *Les Origines politiques des guerres de religion* set the tone for much further historiography of the period—also focused on the role of dissident nobility and found their theological bona fides wanting: "In short, the nobility were thinking of their own interest and were not particularly concerned with bringing it into accord with any precise doctrine. It cannot be denied that self-ish passion and sometimes unrestrained greed persuaded many of the nobil-ity and captains to join the Protestants."[172] James Westfall Thompson's 1909 book, *The Wars of Religion in France,* which was for decades the standard text in English, took a similar approach. Thompson wrote, "Although the purposes of the Huguenots were clandestinely more political than religious, it was expe-dient to cloak them under a mantle of faith."[173] John Neale located the root of the religious wars in the weakness of the French monarchy.[174] As for the dis-sidents who opposed the monarchy, he concluded, "Generally speaking, social discontent found an outlet for itself in religious and political unrest."[175] Henri Drouot's 1937 work on the Catholic League in Burgundy saw religious factors as merely a cover for class tensions: "With the economic and monetary crisis [of the late 1580s], with civil war replacing foreign war and internal peace, social mobility ceased. Classes were more clearly defined, and above all, social tensions arose and festered, social tensions that religion could disguise in its own colors and intensify with fanaticism, but which were really the basis of local tensions at the time of the League."[176] Henri Hauser wrote of the outbreak of violence in 1562, "Elements of social and political discontent were to become much more significant than religious faith in the complex attitudes of the new Protestants, and thenceforth it became possible to speak of 'political' as well as of 'religious' Huguenots."[177] In the 1960s, George Livet's *Les Guerres de religion* identified the "economic and social crisis" of France in the sixteenth century as the principal cause of the wars.[178] Hauser's distinction between types of

Huguenots indicates that religion was not entirely forgotten as a motivating force, and some mid-twentieth-century historians, such as Robert Kingdon and N. M. Sutherland, maintained the importance of religious factors.[179] Until the 1970s, however, the dominant opinion tended to push aside religion in its search for the underlying material causes of the wars.

Natalie Zemon Davis's 1973 article, "The Rites of Violence," is considered a watershed for bringing religious factors back into the study of the French wars. Davis objects to the standard practice of reducing religious factors to, for example, class conflict, and identifies the cause of popular riots in sixteenth-century France as "ridding the community of dreaded pollution."[180] For Catholics, the rites of violence promised the "restoration of unity to the body social"; for Protestants, the goal was the creation of a new kind of unity in the body social.[181] The rites of violence were drawn from a variety of sources: the Bible, the liturgy, the action of political authority, the traditions of folk justice.[182] Their underlying function was the dehumanization of victims.[183] Such riots were religious because they drew from the fundamental values of the community.[184] Other factors, economic, social, and political, were at play in popular riots—pillaging was common, for example, indicating economic motives—but "the prevalence of pillaging in a riot should not prevent us from seeing it as essentially religious."[185]

In his 1993 review article, "Putting Religion Back into the Wars of Religion," Mack Holt identifies a number of other twentieth-century attempts to take religious factors seriously. According to Holt, the older Weberian approach is being supplanted by a more Durkheimian influence; rather than see material causes as more fundamental than religion, Durkheim identified religion with the rituals necessary to bind adherents to the social group. Holt sees this influence in the work of Natalie Davis, Carlo Ginzburg, John Bossy, Keith Thomas, and other historians who retain Durkheim's emphasis on religion as social, but give a greater role to human agency than did Durkheim. Holt then goes on to review several attempts to put religion back into the French religious wars. Denis Crouzet's massive two-volume *Les guerriers de Dieu: La violence au temps des troubles de religion*, which appeared in 1990, finds the source of the wars in the prevalence of popular apocalyptic visions of the end times.[186] The collective psychology of "eschatological anguish," rather than political, economic, or social factors, was the principal engine of the wars. The Huguenot project of desacralization was a threat to the sacral monarchy and the purity of the entire social order. The threat was interpreted in apocalyptic terms, as an attempt to create a new world. Holt also reviews Natalie Davis's student Barbara Diefendorf's 1991 book, *Beneath the Cross: Catholics and Huguenots in Sixteenth-Century Paris*. According to Holt,

Diefendorf "shows how the normal socioeconomic tensions of the period were exacerbated by confessional strife."[187] Holt notes that Diefendorf is particularly effective in showing that Catholic eucharistic imagery was used to reinforce the boundaries of the social order and identify threats to that order. Holt writes that Diefendorf's book underscores Crouzet's attempt to "restore the centrality of religion" in the French civil wars,[188] but Diefendorf herself positions her book as occupying a "middle ground" between Crouzet's book, which offers "very little room for politics," and more standard, "overly political" interpretations of the period.[189] Holt also reviews books by Denis Richet and Michael Wolfe, which do not downplay the importance of religious factors, and one that does, *Iron and Blood* by Henry Heller. Richet argues that "the 'idea of nation' was enfolded with religion during the civil wars";[190] Wolfe argues, "Although politics certainly had its place, as did questions of social interest and economic competition, these bitter conflicts were primarily religious wars."[191] Holt applauds Richet and Wolfe, but takes issue with Heller's view that the French civil wars of the sixteenth century were "from start to finish...a kind of class war from above."[192] In Heller's avowedly Marxist approach, both the Huguenot movement and the Catholic League were seen as threats to monarchy and the nobility, who put them down with force. Holt objects to the reductionism implied by Heller's blunt contention that "[r]eligion is beside the point."[193]

We have, then, one group of historians that dismisses religion as an important factor in the French civil wars of the sixteenth century, and another group that wants to reclaim religion as an important driving force among others in these conflicts. (We should note that similar conflicts of interpretation are present in the historiography of the other wars of religion beyond France.) We must at least note that historians have given us ample reason to doubt the straightforward tale of theological zealotry run amok that Voltaire, Rawls, Shklar, and others tell. *No* academic historian, with the possible exception of Crouzet, tells the story that way. With regard to component (B) of the myth of the wars of religion, then, we must conclude that the myth is at best a distorted and one-dimensional narrative; at worst, it eliminates so many of the relevant political, economic, and social factors as to be rendered false.

But is the solution simply to seek balance among the various factors? Barbara Diefendorf's question is an apt one: "Must we go from an overly political interpretation of the period to one that seems to offer very little room for politics, at least as traditionally viewed?" Should we, like Diefendorf, seek a middle ground between political and religious interpretations? Or is there a problem with the way politics and religion have been, in Diefendorf's phrase, "traditionally viewed"?

(C) Religious Causes Must Be at Least Analytically Separable from Political, Economic, and Social Causes at the Time of the Wars

In order for the myth of the religious wars to be true, religion must be at least analytically separable from politics, economics, etc. That is, even if things seem to be quite complex on the ground, and people act from a variety of motives, we must be able at least on paper to identify which motives are religious, which are political, and which are social. Though historians disagree on which factors predominated, some historians exude confidence that religious factors can be picked out from the other factors. Surely, when eucharistic doctrine is involved, the motivation can be labeled religious; when it is a matter of extending or protecting the power of the monarchy over the lesser nobility, then the motivation is clearly political. What happens, however, if, as Diefendorf says, the Eucharist creates a social body? What if, as Crouzet says, the monarchy is sacral?

An exchange between Holt and Heller in the wake of Holt's review article sheds some light on the problem. Holt had applauded the attempt to put religion back into the religious wars because he believed that it helped to restore human agency to the historical actors and explain their motivations in their own terms. Heller's response, "Putting History Back into the Religious Wars," focuses on Holt's problematic use of the term religion:

> It is undeniable that many if not most people were religiously motivated during the wars of religion. But the main thrust of Holt's discussion of contemporary historiography is to insist that such motivation is self-explanatory and should be seen as such. Yet the really historical question is to try to understand why people were so motivated. This brings us to the central problem of Holt's essay, that is, its self-contradictory use of the term religion. As we have seen, the main body of his review is devoted to praising those historians who privilege religion as the overriding motivating force while castigating those who apparently do not. But in order to fortify this view with a pedigree he begins his discussion by tracing the perspective of those who take religion seriously through Davis and Bossy back to Durkheim among others who, he admits, regarded religion not as apart from society but as an inverted representation of the force of the collective social order.[194]

Heller accuses Holt of forcing us to choose between social and religious explanations, thereby misunderstanding Durkheim: "In so far as he would assent to Durkheim's view of religion as a kind of socially generated consciousness, it is difficult to understand why Holt sees religion as a factor necessarily held apart from and superior to other explanations, such as politics, class, and economic forces, when it may in fact be their ghostly epitome."[195] This ghostly epitome seems to indicate for Heller that religion is superstructural or epiphenomenal. From Heller's Marxist point of view, religion is not an independent variable; religious acts and utterances "need to be analyzed into their social, psychological, and semiotic components."[196]

In his rejoinder to Heller, Holt contends that he has been misunderstood: "Heller and I are in fact in agreement, it would seem, that religion was not an independent variable and that by definition it had to be fully fused with society."[197] Holt states that Davis and Bossy have shown that religion in the sixteenth century is "better defined as a body of believers than a body of beliefs."[198] Holt and Heller agree, therefore, that religion is "a manifestation of the social,"[199] but Holt objects to Heller's reduction of the social to class relations. Holt wants to view the social in broader terms to include relations within other social corporations, such as parishes, guilds, and families.[200]

This exchange between Holt and Heller is helpful for its agreement in principle to eliminate religion as an independent variable in the sixteenth-century conflicts. It remains unclear, however, whether either Holt or Heller has fully escaped anachronism, the reading of a twentieth-century point of view back into sixteenth-century history. Heller clearly dismisses religion as a mere epiphenomenon of more basic social processes. There remains a sense in Holt too, following Durkheim, that the social is more basic than religion, that religion interprets phenomena as referring to a transcendent reality when they *really* refer to an immanent social process. Theistic religion, for Durkheim, remains a misunderstanding; a society thinks it is worshipping God when in fact it is worshipping itself.

The ambiguity in Holt can be detected in his book *The French Wars of Religion,* which appeared in 1995 after his review essay, but before his exchange with Heller. Holt declares on the opening page that the new approach his book will champion is that the French civil wars "were a conflict fought primarily over the issue of religion."[201] He hastens to add:

> I am not suggesting, however, that three generations of French men and women were willing to fight and die over differences of religious doctrine, whether it be over how to get to heaven or over what actually transpired during the celebration of mass. What this book will propose is that the French Wars of Religion were fought primarily over the issue of religion as defined in contemporary terms: as a body of believers rather than the more modern definition of a body

of beliefs. Thus, the emphasis here is on the social rather than the theological. In these terms, Protestants and Catholics alike in the sixteenth century each viewed the other as pollutants of their own particular notion of the body social, as threats to their own conception of ordered society.[202]

So, for example, Holt interprets the Placards Affair as illustrating this social divide. On October 18, 1534, anonymous Calvinists posted placards in prominent places throughout northern France attacking the Catholic mass. According to Holt, what shocked Catholics "was not so much the heterodox doctrine of the Eucharist itself but rather its social implications."[203] For French Catholics, the Eucharist was the fundamental symbol of social bonding. King Francis I reacted violently to this provocation, not because he was a doctrinal zealot—he had heretofore welcomed and promoted Erasmus and other more radical humanists and critics of the church—but because he saw the affair as a threat to social order and his authority.[204]

As helpful as this is, religion and the social are ultimately not inseparable for Holt; there remains a division between "doctrine itself" and its "social implications." By the conclusion of the book, religion has been reinstated as one of a number of separate factors. Holt claims that, by "emphasizing the social importance of religion," he is not trying to downplay "politics, economics, intellectual trends, and other social forces"; he is only trying to restore a missing piece of the puzzle.[205] The missing piece is a peculiar one, however. For Holt, religion is a unique qualification of the social. The equation for Holt appears to be this: religion = the social + a peculiar kind of irrational misreading of the social in terms of God, heaven, and so on. A social order from which this irrational element has been purged remains a possibility. Modern liberal presuppositions thus sneak back into the historical narrative. Despite his attempt to show that religion meant something very different in the sixteenth century than it does in our time, Holt says in his introduction that his book "is simply one historian's 'attempt' at making sense of a complex problem that still plagues the world at the close of the twentieth century: religious wars."[206]

Is there a better way to handle the term religion when dealing with these conflicts? Many historians refer to the inseparability of religious factors from other factors in the wars of religion. R. Po-Chia Hsia, for example, writes, "For the princes who converted to Calvinism, religious and political concerns were inseparable in their personal motivations."[207] Barbara Diefendorf states, "[F]rom my perspective, at least, religious and secular motives were inseparable."[208] According to Diefendorf, processions of the eucharistic host, which sometimes served as the occasion of violence, were not purely religious events but were opportunities to reinforce social boundaries and ask God's intervention in "secular affairs." These processions show how "Catholic beliefs, monarchical politics, and civic identity were mutually reinforcing elements of Parisian culture."[209]

John Bossy has perhaps done the most to highlight the problems with the very categories of religion and society in the sixteenth century. In a 1991 essay entitled "Unrethinking the Sixteenth-Century Wars of Religion," Bossy calls Davis's essay "The Rites of Violence" "the most important contribution to understanding the wars of religion made in our time."[210] What Bossy likes about Davis's work is that she studiously avoids the category of society, and thus avoids an anachronistic reduction of religion to social causes. According to Bossy, sociologists have too long assumed that religion is an ideological cover for more fundamental causes.[211] They assume that those who killed in the name of Christianity did not really understand what they were doing. A Durkheimian says that religion is nothing but the social; a Weberian separates the enchantment of religion from a more basic secular social remainder.[212] Neither allows us to understand events as the participants in those events would. *Pace* Holt, Bossy puts some distance here between his own view and that of Durkheim: "The fact about society is that there is good reason to suppose that no such thing existed in the sixteenth century. I suspect that there was no such thing because there was no such concept....There was nothing we could refer to which [a sixteenth-century person] would not recognize as falling under the heading 'Commonwealth,' or under the heading 'Church' or 'Christianity.' "[213] There was no abstraction called "society" that remained once religion was bracketed off; according to Bossy, the supreme embodiment of Christian "social" reality was the Eucharist.[214] For Bossy, religion is not simply a "manifestation of the social" (Holt's phrase) in the sixteenth-century context. The distinction between the religious and the social only comes about with the birth of modernity in the division of church and state, transcendent and immanent.

To fully grasp this point, we should recall what Bossy says elsewhere about religion: there was also no such concept in the sixteenth century, or at least it was not fully formed until around 1700.[215] Bossy says that the development of the modern idea of society was "a successor effect of the transition in 'religion,' whose history it reproduced. One cannot therefore exactly call Religion and Society twins; but in other respects they are like the sexes according to Aristophanes, effects of the fission of a primitive whole, yearning towards one another across a great divide."[216] In other words, in the sixteenth century, there simply was no coherent way yet to divide religious causes from social causes; the divide is a modern invention. If this is true, then Davis has not entirely escaped anachronism when she claims that the sixteenth-century riots were "essentially religious." Indeed, if we follow Davis in seeing that the goal of the rites of violence was either to restore a lost unity of the body social (Catholics) or to create a new unity of the body social (Protestants), then there is no reason at all for calling the violence "essentially religious" as opposed to social, political, or economic. Rival visions of the social order were at stake, and there is simply no way to separate religious factors from other, supposedly more mundane and rational factors.

Davis and Bossy are right to criticize earlier historiography's attempts to see political, social, and economic factors as more real and more basic than religious factors. But we are not therefore licensed to reach the opposite and equally invalid conclusion that there is something called religion lurking behind more mundane factors that is essentially responsible for the fury of the French civil wars of the sixteenth century. Nor do we solve the problem simply by seeking a middle ground, e.g., assigning equal shares of responsibility to political, religious, economic, and social causes. I think we must conclude that any attempt to assign the cause of the wars in question to religion—as opposed to politics or other secular causes—will get bogged down in hopeless anachronism. The same, of course, is true of attempts to pin the blame on political and economic causes as opposed to religion. We are best served by saying something like what Axel Oxenstierna—Gustavus Adolphus's chancellor and architect of the Swedish intervention in the Thirty Years' War—told the Swedish council of state in 1636: the war was "not so much a matter of religion, but rather of saving the *status publicus,* wherein religion is also comprehended."[217] There is simply no way to isolate religion as the source of the conflict from the whole fabric of the *status publicus.* It is clear, then, that the standard narrative of the wars of religion will not stand up to scrutiny of the term religion.

(D) The Rise of the Modern State Was Not a Cause of the Wars,
but Rather Provided a Solution to the Wars

Should we conclude, therefore, that the term religion should simply be jettisoned in discussing these wars? As Oxenstierna's comment indicates—and the genealogy in chapter 2 showed—religion was not simply absent but was a concept being born in the period covering these wars. It was, furthermore, being born in the context of the rise of the modern state. Oxenstierna could consider religion to be entirely comprehended within the *status publicus* because the church had been wholly absorbed by the Crown in Sweden since King Gustav Vasa in the 1520s.

Hans-Jürgen Goertz has argued that distinctions made between the religious ideas of the Reformation, on the one hand, and social, political, and economic factors, on the other, are misleading and anachronistic. Goertz wants to go beyond both Marxist and Durkheimian approaches by eliminating categories that are foreign to the thinking of the historical actors themselves.[218] Johannes Wolfart is sympathetic with Goertz; he also challenges the standard historiography that segregates the religious history of the Reformation from the political history of the empire.[219] He notes that some scholars have begun to treat the Reformation as being, like religion in Jonathan Z. Smith's view, "solely the creation of the scholar's study."[220] Wolfart, however, thinks that it is not quite right to claim that the distinction between religion and politics was simply absent. Wolfart believes, rightly I think, that it is more accurate to say that the distinction between religion and politics was being born in the sixteenth and seventeenth centuries. In a careful study of the town of Lindau, Wolfart argues that people did discuss the extent of religion and the proper boundaries between spiritual and secular affairs. But such distinctions were extremely fluid and were used to correspond to different configurations of power:

> As ideological figments, they must be considered, along with much else, in the context of that ongoing struggle for power and authority which had divided the Western world into two distinct "jurisdictions" since Constantine hatched imperial Christianity/ Christian imperialism. As a crucial "invention" of this struggle, the Reformation obviously made a significant contribution to early modern and subsequent debates.[221]

The point is not that the distinction between religion and other secular factors was simply absent, but that the distinction was in the process of development as new forms of power—what would become known as the "state"—were developing. The modern idea of religion as a realm of human activity inherently separate from politics and other secular matters depended upon a new configuration of Christian societies in which many legislative and jurisdictional powers and claims to power—as well as claims to the devotion and allegiance of the people—were passing from the church to the new sovereign state. The secular-religious binary helped to facilitate this shift. The noun "secularization" as it first appeared in France in the late sixteenth century meant "the transfer of goods from the possession of the Church into that of the world."[222] At the same time, the new conception of religion would help to "purify" the church of powers and claims that were not its proper function. The new conception of religion helped to facilitate the shift to state dominance over the church by distinguishing inward religion from the bodily disciplines of the state. The new subject is thus able to do due service to both church and state, without conflict. Certain interests promoted this process, while others resisted it.

If this is true, then the idea that the rise of the modern state rescued Europe from the scourge of religious wars becomes highly questionable. The modern state was not simply a response to the advent of religious differ-ence in the Reformation and the subsequent violence that religious differ-ence unleashed. If the Reformation itself was, as Wolfart says, an "invention" of the ongoing struggle for power and authority between church and civil rulers—which had been going on for quite some time before Luther nailed his Ninety-Five Theses on the door at Wittenberg—then the transfer of power from the church to the state appears not so much as a solution to the wars in question, but as a *cause* of those wars. The so-called wars of religion appear as wars fought by state-building elites for the purpose of consolidating their power over the church and other rivals. This view conforms more closely than the wars-of-religion myth to the historical account of the actual rise of the state given by David Held above. The point here is *not* that these wars were really about politics and not really about religion. The point is that the very distinction of politics and religion made possible by the rise of the mod-ern state against the decaying medieval order—the transfer of power from the church to the state—was itself at the root of these wars.

There is a great deal of evidence to suggest that the transfer of power to the emergent state was a cause, not the solution, to the wars of the sixteenth and seventeenth centuries. The process of state building, begun well before the Reformation, was inherently conflictual. Beginning in the late medieval period, the process involved the internal integration of previously scattered powers under the aegis of the ruler, and the external demarcation of territory over against other, foreign states. As Heinz Schilling comments, the invention of sovereignty demanded both the "integration and concentration of all politi-cal, social, economic and other power under the supremacy of the ruler," and "at the same time the process of state-building meant territorial integration and a dissociation from the 'outside' world, which as a rule was implemented in an offensive, not infrequently even aggressive manner. All the states of the early modern age aimed to augment their state territory through expansion and the annexation of as much territory as possible." Schilling continues:

> The internal process of state-building was no different to the external
> one and the accompanying birth of the early modern Europe of the
> great powers was accompanied by massive disruptions. Internally the
> rulers and their state elites used violent means against the estates,

cities, clergy and local associations which laid claim to an independent, non-derived right of political participation which the early modern state could no longer grant under the principle of sovereignty.
Externally in addition to the above-mentioned tendencies of territorial
adjustment between the states, conflicts were mainly over "rank,"
since at this stage there was no generally acknowledged system of
states. Therefore, at the end of the middle ages, Europe entered a long
phase of intense violent upheaval both within and between states.[223]

The link between state building and war has been well documented by
historians of the early modern state. Charles Tilly has shown how building
a state depended on the ability of state-making elites to make war, and the
ability to make war in turn depended on the ability to extract resources from
the population, which in turn depended on an effective state bureaucracy to
secure those resources from a recalcitrant population. As Tilly puts it, "War
made the state, and the state made war."[224] Gabriel Ardant has shown that, in
the period of European state building, the most serious precipitant to violence,
and the greatest spur to the growth of the state, was the attempt to collect taxes
from an unwilling populace.[225] This view of state formation has gained wide
acceptance. It builds on the early twentieth-century work of Otto Hintze[226] and
is confirmed by the more recent work of Perry Anderson,[227] Hendrik Spruyt,[228]
Anthony Giddens,[229] Victor Burke,[230] and others. In his survey of state-making
studies since the 1980s, Thomas Ertman is able to say that "it is now generally
accepted that the territorial state triumphed over other possible political forms
(empire, city-state, lordship) because of the superior fighting ability which it
derived from access to both urban capital and coercive authority over peasant
taxpayers and army recruits."[231] As for explaining variations within the dominant form of the sovereign state, Ertman says that "the work of Hintze, Tilly,
Mann, Downing, and Anderson has already conclusively established that war
and preparations for war tended to stimulate the creation of ever more sophis-
ticated state institutions across the continent"[232] and that war was the "principal force" behind the expansion and rationalization of state apparatuses.[233]
Michael Howard sums up the evidence bluntly: "the entire apparatus of the
state primarily came into being to enable princes to wage war."[234]
    Much of the violence of the so-called wars of religion is explained in terms
of the resistance of local elites to the state-building efforts of monarchs and
emperors. As Howard writes:

The attempts by the dominant dynasties of Europe to exercise dis-
puted rights of inheritance throughout the fourteenth and fifteenth

centuries became consolidated, in the sixteenth century, into a bid by the Habsburgs to sustain a hegemony which they had inherited over most of western Europe against all their foreign rivals and dissident subjects, usually under the leadership of France. The result was almost continuous warfare in western Europe from the early sixteenth until the mid-seventeenth centuries.[235]

Charles V's campaigns against Protestant princes, with some Protestant help, were largely attempts to make of the decentralized Holy Roman Empire a sovereign state with a single church and administration. Resistance from both Protestant and Catholic princes, with the help of Catholic France, was intended both to thwart Charles's attempts at state building and to consolidate the princes' own control over the churches in their realms. The Peace of Augsburg—which gave each prince the power to determine the ecclesial affiliation of his subjects—was not the state's solution to religious violence, but rather represented the victory of one set of state-building elites over another. As Richard Dunn remarks about the Peace of Augsburg:

> The German princes, Catholic and Lutheran, had in effect ganged up against the Habsburgs. They had observed, correctly enough, that Charles V had been trying not only to crush Protestantism but to increase Habsburg power and check the centrifugal tendencies within the empire. The princes, both Lutheran and Catholic, had also been trying to turn the Reformation crisis to their personal advantage, by asserting new authority over their local churches, tightening ecclesiastical patronage, and squeezing more profit from church revenues.[236]

The Habsburgs' position was not substantially different in the Thirty Years' War. Of the many causes of the war, "the most important was the attempt by the Catholic Austrian Habsburg dynasty to resist the challenge to their authority in their hereditary lands, particularly Austria and Bohemia (now part of the Czech Republic) and to gain greater control within the Holy Roman Empire."[237]

In the French civil wars of the sixteenth century, the role played by state-building elites, on the one hand, and resistance to those forces, on the other, was also a major cause of the violence. As Donna Bohanan writes, "The expansion of monarchical authority brought central government into direct conflict with the many groups, duly constituted bodies, and regions in whose interest it was to oppose and obstruct the process of state-building."[238] Arlette Jouanna argues that the rebellion of the nobility—both Catholic and Protestant—in the French wars of religion was motivated by the fear that the trend toward absolutism would upset the proper hierarchy of estates in the mystical body politic of the king. The nobility eventually came around in support of absolutism when the rebellion was taken in an egalitarian direction.[239]

The French wars of religion pitted the French Crown's determination to unite France under *un roi, une foi, une loi* against the nobility, who resisted such threats to their power and privileges. The aggrandizement of the monarchy's power had begun in earnest in the fifteenth century, well before the Reformation, and resistance to this movement was at the heart of the wars of the sixteenth:

> Charles VII acquired the power to tax most of France without consent, and Louis XI grossly tampered with the social system itself. François I instituted reforms which altered the whole character of the administration, both in terms of its general design and in terms of its social basis. By openly acknowledging the principle of venality of office, and vastly increasing the number of office-holders, he set in train social tensions that were to play their part in the crisis of the religious wars.[240]

While the Crown's propagandists like Michel de L'Hôpital strove to establish continuity between the Crown and an idealized medieval monarchy, Huguenot propaganda idealized the nobility as those who defended ancient custom and the political body of France against the usurpations of the growing royal bureaucracy. As Salmon comments, "[T]he basic reason for the war was the distrust of the Crown evidenced by the Protestant nobility."[241]

The reasons for Catholic opposition to the Crown were very similar. The manifesto of the Catholic League committed its members not only to restoring the dignity of the Catholic Church, but to recovering the "perfect freedom" to which the nobles were entitled and abolishing "new taxes and all additions since the reign of Charles IX."[242] Robert Descimon and Elie Barnavi have described the Catholic League in the following terms:

> What was the League...? A movement of religious opposition first of all, the offensive arm of the French Counter Reformation. A purely political opposition also, and in this respect a reaction of the body social against absolutizing centralism: for the nobles an attempt at "feudal" division; for the towns a manifest desire to consolidate their threatened traditional autonomy; for the provinces, the dream of lost liberties, of fiscal privileges, judicial rights, of political autonomy likewise. A movement of social opposition finally where

orders and classes grapple with one another in a confused mêlée,
nobles against the crown, lesser office holders against grand robins;
those without office, commoners, against the nobility, everyone
against the kind of life led by the court, against waste, corruption,
taxes.[243]

As J. H. M. Salmon has noted, the religious wars in France are often
seen as an aberration, an interlude of chaos coming between two periods of
national consolidation, first the centralizing reigns of Charles IX, Louis XI,
and Francis I, then the trend toward absolutism under Henry IV and his
successors. Salmon objects to seeing the religious wars as a discontinuity in
French history, as a curious intermission of chaos between two periods of
increasing order. Salmon argues that "the later sixteenth century is of crucial importance in the general development of the ancient régime. It is the
crucible in which some of the competing forces from an earlier age were con-
sumed in the fire and others blended and transmuted into new compounds: it
is the matrix for all that came after."[244] If Salmon's narration of the fifteenth
through seventeenth centuries is true, then the rise of the absolutist state in
France was not simply the solution to the wars of religion; the rise of the state
was one of the principal causes of the wars. The so-called wars of religion
were the birth pangs of the state, not simply the crisis which required the
state to step in as savior.

The point of this again is *not* that these wars were really about politics and
not about religion, nor that the state is to blame and the church is innocent of
the violence. If the transfer of power from church to state contributed to the
upheavals of the sixteenth and seventeenth centuries, that transfer generally
took the form of the absorption of the church into the apparatus of the state.
The church was, of course, deeply implicated in the violence of the sixteenth
and seventeenth centuries. The point is that the rise of the modern state was
not the solution to the violence of religion. The absorption of church into state
that began well before the Reformation was a crucial component of the rise of
the state and the turmoil of the sixteenth and seventeenth centuries.

Beginning in the fourteenth and fifteenth centuries, rulers looked to
expand their powers by absorbing the powers and revenues of the church:
"Through concordats with the papacy or pressure on their subjects, most later
medieval rulers steadily engrossed greater control over the distribution of
senior ecclesiastical posts in the lands under their control."[245] In Spain and
France, a series of concessions wrung from the papacy over the course of the
fifteenth century and into the first decades of the sixteenth century transferred many church revenues and appointments from the pope to the Crown.

In Spain, a series of concordats between 1482 and 1508 transferred to the king the power to "supplicate" for all major ecclesiastical appointments in both the Old World and the New.[246] In France, the Pragmatic Sanction of Bourges in 1438 took away the pope's right to make appointments to vacant sees and gave it to local cathedral chapters. The Concordat of Bologna in 1516 transferred that right to the French king and gave him virtually unfettered license to make ecclesiastical appointments, both bishops and abbots, in his realm.[247] Francis I proceeded to pack the episcopacy with his clients, largely nobles of the sword who had little or no theological training. Benefices were passed down within families, many bishops rarely if ever set foot in their dioceses, and some held multiple appointments. Cardinal de Tournon, for example, a provincial governor and financier of the Crown, was simultaneously archbishop of Auch, Bourges, Embrun, and Lyon, as well as abbot of thirteen large monasteries and a number of smaller ones.[248] As Salmon notes, "The church was a part of the clientage system."[249] A principal cause of Huguenot revolt was the corruption of the church, by which is meant precisely this absorption of the church into the emergent state.

In the late fifteenth century, the civil authorities in England, Sweden, Denmark, and Germany tried—with only partial success—to limit clerical exemptions from civil courts, limit the power of ecclesiastical courts, and transfer church appointments, revenues, and lands to the civil rulers. As Quentin Skinner points out, the Reformation failed in France and Spain, where the monarchies had largely absorbed the church into their clientage systems and therefore had an interest in maintaining the status quo.[250] As Pope Julius III wrote to Henry II of France, "in the end, you are more than Pope in your kingdoms.... I know no reason why you should wish to become schismatic."[251] Where the Reformation succeeded was in England, Scandinavia, and many German principalities, where breaking with the Catholic Church meant that the church could be used to augment the power of the civil authorities. To cite one example, King Gustav Vasa welcomed the Reformation to Sweden in 1524 by transferring the receipt of tithes from the church to the Crown. Three years later, he appropriated the entire property of the church.[252]

As William Maltby notes, accepting Lutheranism both gave princes an ideological basis for resisting the centralizing efforts of the emperor and gave them the chance to extract considerable wealth from confiscated church properties.[253] Steven Gunn summarizes the situation in these terms:

> The official adoption of reformed religion contributed to the power
> of different rulers in different ways. One, Albrecht of Hohenzollern,
> made a hereditary secular principality for himself from scratch, by

secularizing the Prussian branch of the Teutonic Order, of which
he was the Grand Master. Many others, notably Henry VIII in
England, Gustav Vasa in Sweden, Christian III in Denmark, and a
dozen leading German princes, confiscated church property within
their territories or absorbed into their states adjoining bishoprics or
monastic estates. Most stepped up taxation of the clergy, took control
of clerical promotions, and integrated the church courts' system of
moral controls more closely into their own judicial structures. Most
took a firmer grip on education from school level to the universities, and introduced state-run poor relief to replace the charity of
dissolved monasteries and hospitals.... Secular and ecclesiastical
bureaucracies expanded in parallel and became intertwined, as the
Reformation helped consolidate a more intensive form of state. They
provided the means to regulate, down to parish level, changes which
had the potential to reach every subject.[254]

It is unarguably the case that the reinforcement of ecclesiastical difference
in early modern Europe was largely a project of state-building elites. As
G. R. Elton bluntly puts it, "The Reformation maintained itself wherever the
lay power (prince or magistrates) favoured it; it could not survive wherever the
authorities decided to suppress it."[255]

This is not to say that rulers were insincere in their embrace of the
Reformation. It is to say, however, that the building of the modern state was
not simply a response to religious divisions but was itself deeply implicated in
the production of such differences. This connection is confirmed by the confessionalization thesis, which since the 1970s has redefined historical scholarship
on Germany and much of the rest of Europe in the sixteenth and seventeenth
centuries. The building of strong confessional identities among Protestants
and Catholics in this period was part of the state-building project. As Luther
Peterson summarizes it:

The confessionalization thesis is a fruitful instrument in explaining the transformation of medieval feudal monarchies into modern
states, in particular how the new states changed their inhabitants
into disciplined, obedient and united subjects. According to the
thesis, a key factor in that change is the establishment of religious uniformity in the state: the populace was taught a religious
identity—Catholic, Lutheran, or Calvinist—through doctrinal
statements (confessions and catechisms) and liturgical practices.
This distinguished "us" as a religious and political community from
"other," often neighboring, religious-political societies. The ruler was

sacralized as the defender and—in Protestant lands—leader of the church, rightfully overseeing the church of his land. These state-led churches also aided state development by imposing moral discipline on the communities.[256]

One of the major figures in the study of confessionalization, Heinz Schilling, illustrates how the thesis helps to recast the Reformation not as a purely religious movement that has political effects, but as itself inextricable from broader social and political movements. In his contribution to a volume on Luther and the modern state, Schilling notes a tendency since World War II to draw a connection between Martin Luther and Adolf Hitler because of the tendency of Lutheranism to build confessional states in the early modern period with comprehensive systems of social discipline. As Schilling argues, however, there is no point in singling out Luther and Lutheranism for its influence on German state building, because the rise of the state was a general European phenomenon that predated the Reformation and was evident in territories that remained Catholic. Lutheranism offered certain advantages to princes, increasing their autonomy from the empire. But the building of the Lutheran confessional state is inextricable from the larger trend toward the concentration of state power.[257]

According to Karlheinz Blaschke, the Reformation offered the opportunity for the emerging territorial state to grow both quantitatively, with lands seized from the church, and qualitatively, with the integration of governing and disciplining functions formerly belonging to the church. This was possible and necessary precisely because the medieval sense that the entire structure of social life was bound up with the church was still strong. Nevertheless, the modern state was something new:

> Had the state rejected the opportunity offered by the Reformation, it would have violated the principle of its own development. The thoroughly "modern" (i.e., new) character of this state control over the church, for which there was no precedent and no connection to older institutions, may be contrasted with the medieval view of things with its conception of two powers, temporal and spiritual, which supplied neither material nor formal justification for the new order. The innovation nonetheless spoke to the interests of the territorial state, which seized the opportunities to create the new order of things.[258]

R. Po-Chia Hsia's extensive studies of social discipline in sixteenth- and seventeenth-century Germany have shown that the sharp confessional differences that lent themselves to violence in this period were part and parcel of the state-building process which, it must be emphasized, predated the Reformation:

> The process of political centralization, discernible in the fifteenth century—the adoption of Roman Law, the rise of an academic jurist class, the growth of bureaucracies, and the reduction of local, particularist privileges—received a tremendous boost after 1550. Conformity required coercion. Church and state formed an inextricable matrix of power for enforcing discipline and confessionalism. The history of confessionalization in early modern Germany is, in many ways, the history of the territorial state.[259]

Sharp ecclesial boundaries coincided with the creation of sharp territorial boundaries in the making of the modern state. Church and state were fused to create "obedient, pious, and diligent subjects of their German princes."[260] The means of this discipline were confessions of faith, liturgical uniformity, and moral policing, enforced by frequent visitations of local churches by officials of church and state. According to Hsia, it was generally the officials of state who took the lead in enforcing confessionalization: "Secular authorities such as princes, officials, and magistrates usually played a more crucial role than the clergy in determining the course of confessionalization.... Having become the head of their territorial churches, princes understood the imposition of confessional conformity both as an extension of their secular authority and as the implementation of God's work."[261]

By the seventeenth century, Lutheran clergy were essentially a branch of the civil bureaucracy in most German principalities.[262] The Second Reformation in Germany—the advent of Calvinism—"was a reform imposed from above by princes and a small crust of official-academic elite; confessional struggles often reflected the contest between the centralizing state and the traditional forces of a society based on estates and established privileges."[263] Calvinism for the Hohenzollerns in Prussia "represented a confessional ideology in the making of absolutism."[264] As Hsia points out, this dynamic was not limited to Calvinism, but typified the Catholic Counter-Reformation as well: "Both were reformations from above, emanating from princes, high officials, and the academic elite."[265] The creation of a centralized Bavarian state church under the Wittelsbachs followed this model.[266] Likewise, Catholic institutions, practices, and symbols such as the crucifix and Marian devotions became the basis for the evolving state rituals of the Habsburgs.[267] Regarding Salzburg, Hsia remarks, "The final triumph of Baroque Catholicism in Salzburg represented the final victory of the absolutist state over the peasant communalism of the mountain villages."[268]

As this remark implies, the creation of sharp confessional boundaries did not come without resistance at the local level: "To enforce confessional conformity, local and particular privileges had to be swept aside: estates, towns, cloisters, and nobility resisted confessionalization behind the bulwark of corporate privileges."[269] Hsia notes a considerable gulf between the "amorphous popular religion" of the villages and self-conscious official state confessions. Hsia points to the example of the region surrounding Osnabrück, where as late as 1624 the majority of village clergy could not be classified clearly as either Catholic or Lutheran. In his visitation, the general vicar of the bishop found that, of seventy-three parish priests, nineteen or twenty were clearly Lutheran, thirteen or fourteen were Catholic, and the rest fell into a gray zone in between. During the Thirty Years' War, the official state religion was changed so frequently by conquering armies in many areas that confusion and indifference to confessional boundaries were common among the laity, and those with Protestant and Catholic tendencies often worshipped side by side.[270]

Hsia acknowledges that it would be an oversimplification to say that confessionalization was imposed by the elites; the cooperation of other social groups such as teachers, merchants, more prosperous peasants, and so on was crucial to the eventual success of the project.[271] Hsia acknowledges too that confessional allegiances could also mobilize resistance to the consolidation of princely power.[272] Nevertheless, it is clear from the evidence Hsia provides that the modern state, in Germany at least, was not simply the solution to the problem of confessional conflicts in the sixteenth and seventeenth centuries, but was itself one of the primary creators and enforcers of such conflicts. When Hsia states that "[t]he age of confessional conflicts coincided with the age of absolutism,"[273] he does not mean to say that the wars of religion and the absolutist state were only coincidentally related, nor that the absolutist state was the solution to such wars. Indeed, the state was deeply implicated in the production of the confessional differences that sometimes helped to fuel conflict.

The confessionalization thesis has replaced older ideas associated with Ernst Troeltsch, which ranked the different confessions according to their tendency toward modernity and progress. Troeltsch saw Catholicism as conservative and backward, Lutheranism as slightly more progressive but tending toward absolutism, and Calvinism as most progressive, tending toward the contract theory of the state.[274] Beginning in the 1970s, Schilling and others began to tear down this paradigm and replace it with a view that sees the different confessions, aligned with the growth of the modern state, traveling down parallel paths to modernity. As such, the confessionalization thesis has not been limited to German lands, but has sometimes been applied to Europe as a whole in attempting to understand the emergence of modernity in Europe.

When confessionalization is applied elsewhere, however, it has been criticized for minimizing differences of context and having a top-down bias. Wolfgang Reinhard and others have therefore developed a less state-centered version of confessionalization.[275] Ute Lotz-Heumann and Karl Bottigheimer, for example, have shown that, while the state-centered version of confessionalization fits the English state in the sixteenth and seventeenth centuries, Irish and Old English Catholics in Ireland resisted the English monarchy through the Tridentine reforms of the Catholic Church in Ireland, unaided by any state-building project.[276] Mack Holt has likewise argued that confessionalization without a strong state applies to the case of France during the wars of religion, when the state was not strong enough to impose confessional identities, but confessionalization took place through the local authorities.[277]

Neither of these cases, however, lessens the weight of evidence that the rise of the state—far from being the solution to the wars of the sixteenth and seventeenth centuries—is in fact deeply implicated in the reinforcement of those conflicts. Though we are accustomed to reading the English Civil War through the eyes of Hobbes and Locke, most historians today see it not as the final gasp of religious fanaticism to which the state provided the answer, but as one example of a general European phenomenon of resistance to the ambitions of state-building elites by those who had the most to lose. As Ann Hughes says, the trend among contemporary historians is to see the English Civil War as one episode in the "General European Crisis" of the sixteenth and seventeenth centuries. What unites the disparate episodes of this general crisis is resistance to the growth of centralized monarchies. The English Civil War is fitted into this crisis because of the important role that tensions between local and national interests played in fomenting civil war.[278] As Hughes summarizes, "The civil war is thus, in part at least, Charles's attempt to achieve a financial base and freedom of action comparable to that of continental 'absolutist' monarchs."[279]

The English Civil War is not difficult to fit into the confessionalization paradigm, because the spark that ignited the uprising in Scotland was Charles's attempt to impose a new Book of Canons, a new prayer book, and episcopal church government on recalcitrant Presbyterians. The English Civil War is therefore sometimes classified as a war of religion. Against such a view, Hughes says, "Whilst religious divisions were crucial in motivating people and in poisoning the political atmosphere, it is a mistake to imply such a clear separation between religion and politics."[280] Charles's ecclesiastical innovations were a reflection of the fact that, since Henry VIII's Act of Supremacy, control of the Church of England had been absorbed by the monarchy. The attempt to impose uniformity of worship and episcopal church government was part and parcel of Charles's attempt to consolidate the power of the Crown over its subjects. Charles, for his part, thought that Scottish opposition to his ecclesiastical policies was an act of treason. Scottish rebellion, according to Charles, was "fomented by factious spirits, and those traitorously affected, begun upon pretenses of religion, the common cloak for all disobedience; but now it clearly appears, the aim of these men is not religion (as they falsely pretend and publish) but it is to shake off all monarchical government."[281] The idea that the English Civil War was a "Puritan revolution" has now been widely questioned. Puritan opposition to Charles's "popery" was intertwined with resistance to Charles's centralization of authority over local rights and privileges. In the words of the Grand Remonstrance presented to Charles in 1641, "The root of all this mischief we find to be a malignant and pernicious design of subverting the fundamental laws and principles of government, upon which the religion and justice of this kingdom are firmly established."[282] Many scholars now recognize that Puritan resistance to the monarchy was a conservative and defensive response to the monarchy's attempts to consolidate its power.[283] The Hobbesian idea that the centralization of state power was not the cause of, but rather the solution to, the violence of the civil war is highly doubtful.

In the case of France during the wars of religion, Holt is right to say that the more state-centered version of the confessionalization paradigm does not neatly fit. This is not because the state did not attempt to enforce ecclesiastical uniformity for the sake of social discipline, but is only because the state was not powerful enough to do so effectively. This does not diminish the importance of the comments by Bohanan, Salmon, Jouanna, and others cited above, which identify the attempted expansion of state powers as a cause of the wars of religion. The goal of *un roi, une foi, une loi* meant that ecclesiastical uniformity was an important concomitant to state building. It was also an important irritant to local autonomy. For this reason, Holt emphatically rejects the narrative that locates the end of the wars of religion in the Edict of Nantes in 1598. The liberal tale is that a group of modern-minded men called *politiques* finally saw the futility of fighting over religious doctrine and persuaded Henry IV to set aside the goal of religious unity in favor of the unity of the kingdom. Thus, the modern state was born of toleration for both of the warring religious factions: "In other words, religious piety and zealous faith were forced to take a backseat to modern secular politics. This view is not only anachronistic—there was no such thing as secular politics in the sixteenth century—but it also completely overlooks Henry's goals of religious concord and unity as well as his own understanding of confessional politics."[284] According to Holt, neither the Crown nor its *politique* advisers ever abandoned the goal of uniformity of faith; the Edict of Nantes was just a temporary settlement meant to buy time for winning back the obedience of the Huguenots through conversion. In this regard, Holt sees continuity in the policies of Henry IV, Louis XIII, Richelieu, and Louis XIV. The Edict of Nantes was a dead letter long before it was officially revoked by Louis XIV in 1685. The *politiques* were not modern liberals but preferred uniformity of faith as a means to the unity of the state.[285] Holt comments, "No matter how hard generations of liberal, Protestant historians have tried to separate 'one faith' from 'one law' and 'one king,' in the sixteenth century no such dissolution was possible."[286]

What we have seen so far is sufficient to reject the idea that the advent of the sovereign state—either in its absolutist or liberal form—was the solution to the wars of religion. The transfer of power from the church to the state was clearly a cause, not the solution, of the violence of the sixteenth and seventeenth centuries. The idea that the liberal state solved the wars of religion is even more implausible than the absolutist version of the myth because in historical fact the liberal state does not appear until much later. If "liberalism" in this case is taken to mean the secularization of government, then the very opposite is found in Europe as the so-called wars of religion drew to a close. The state was increasingly *sacralized* in the sixteenth and seventeenth centuries. This process is what Bossy calls the "migration of the holy" from the church to the state. In France, the fifteenth century saw the monarchy borrowing wholesale sacred rituals and formulae from the church to express sacred solidarity with the Crown. The dictum "one king, one faith, one law" was a transmutation of the biblical formula "one God, one faith, one baptism."[287] The feast of Corpus Christi was mined for ceremonies marking the entrance of the king into a city. Previously, entry ceremonies emphasized local customs rather than the glory of the king. The purpose of such ceremonies was to pledge an oath of loyalty to the king in exchange for the king's promise to respect local privileges.[288] This changed dramatically in the late fifteenth century. Charles VIII was welcomed to Rouen with the titles "Lamb of God, saviour, head of the mystical body of France, guardian of the book with seven seals, fountain of life-giving grace to a dry people, and deified bringer of peace."[289] Increasingly elaborate rituals sacralized the monarchy. The coronation of Francis I in 1515 presented the king no longer as a layman but anointed, with priestly vestments and access to the chalice.[290] As the century wore on, what David Potter calls a "royal religion" developed which identified the king not simply as priest but as the very image of God on earth. Pierre de Ronsard in 1555 would write, "In short, the king of the French is a great God."[291] By 1625, the General Assembly of the Clergy of France could proclaim not only that the French kings were ordained by God, but "they themselves were gods,"[292] a sentiment echoed by

Bishop Jacques-Bénigne Bossuet when he declared that kings "are Gods and share in some way in divine independence."[293] The cult of the king reached its zenith under the "Sun King," Louis XIV, at Versailles, where elaborate court rituals were staged to emphasize the close association of the king with the godhead.[294]

The case of France represents the extremes to which the cult of the king could be taken, but the same dynamic is found in German lands, England, and throughout the continent. We have already seen how the dynamic of confessionalization wed kings and princes to symbols of the holy in what Luther Peterson calls the "sacralization" of rulers.[295] The Holy Roman emperors adopted *Plus Ultra* (Yet Farther) as their motto and declared themselves to be blood relations of Roman and Byzantine emperors, the Old Testament patriarchs, and Christ himself. Another Habsburg, Philip II, adopted a device identifying himself with the sun god, Apollo, ruler of a newly born world.[296] In England, the subsumption of the church under the Crown under Henry VIII was followed by a migration of holy symbols to the monarchy. At the same time that Elizabeth I was suppressing celebrations of the feast of Corpus Christi, she was appropriating significant symbolic aspects of the feast with herself substituted for the host. Elizabeth made a frequent practice of being processed around under a canopy modeled after those used for Corpus Christi feasts. A royal cult complete with shrines and pilgrimages grew up around the person of Elizabeth.[297] King James I's treatise *The True Law of Free Monarchies*, written five years before he succeeded Elizabeth, contends, "Kings are called gods by the prophetical King David because they sit upon God his throne in the earth and have the count of their administration to give unto him."[298] As Bossy notes, with James the new strand of "monarcholatry" that had emerged in France definitively passed to England and to the Christian world at large.[299] It would be a short step from here to Hobbes's "mortal god."

Ernst Kantorowicz famously documented how the imagery of the mystical body of Christ was appropriated for use by the emergent state in the late middle ages, culminating in the doctrine of the king's two bodies in Elizabeth I's reign.[300] Kantorowicz also documented the accompanying migration of the idea of martyrdom from the church to the state. If the rise of the modern state did not in fact produce a more peaceful Europe, it did produce a shift in what people were willing to kill and die for. Already in the late medieval period, the language of martyrdom on behalf of the celestial *patria* had begun to shift to martyrdom on behalf of the earthly *patria*. The *communis patria* meanwhile was redefined from either one's locality or Christendom as a whole to the emerging protonational state. The more advanced national monarchies such as France were appropriating liturgical symbolism from the church such that the emerging state was a mystical body politic and a source of *caritas,* which bound one to one's compatriots. Martyrdom *pro fide* was eclipsed by or included in martyrdom *pro patria,* which was extolled as a work of *caritas* on behalf of one's countrymen.[301]

While the future was assured for the praise of death for one's country, Christian martyrdom would be strictly delimited by the theorists of the modern state. Thomas Hobbes assumed the fittingness of dying for the mortal god, Leviathan. Christian martyrdom, however, he restricted only to those who died for proclaiming one single article of faith: "Jesus is the Christ." Those who oppose the laws of the civil state for any other doctrine do so for private ambition and deserve their punishment. A person can only be a martyr, or witness, if he or she proclaims that Jesus is the Christ to infidels. There can be no martyrs in a Christian commonwealth, for one cannot witness to those who already believe.[302] In eliminating any possibility of civil disobedience to the state, Hobbes eliminates the possibility of martyrdom for Christ.

The historical evidence renders component (D) of the myth of the wars of religion—the idea that the modern state saved Europe from religious violence—unbelievable. As we have seen, state building—which began well before the advent of Protestant-Catholic divisions—was a significant cause of the violence. An important aspect of state building was the absorption of the church by the state, which exacerbated and enforced ecclesial differences and therefore contributed to warfare between Catholics and Protestants. In the process, the state did not rein in and tame religion but became itself sacralized. The transfer of power from the church to the state was accompanied by a migration of the holy from church to state.

The myth of the wars of religion concludes in one of two ways: either the baneful influence of religion in the public realm is banished to the private realm by the secularization of the state (liberalism), or religious disunity is overcome by the imposition of religious unity by a powerful state (absolutism). Neither of these ideas can stand up to the historical record. On the one hand, the idea that the liberal state was the solution to the wars of religion is anachronistic. The state was not secularized but sacralized in the sixteenth and seventeenth centuries; religion was not banished but, as John Neville Figgis wrote, "the religion of the State has replaced the religion of the Church."[303] The advent of liberalism in any strong form would come only a century or more after the conclusion of the so-called religious wars. On the other hand, the idea that the absolutist state solved the crisis of the wars of religion by the imposition of a firm unity is plausible only if one ignores the fact that the rise of the centralized sovereign state was a principal *cause* of the wars in question. The notion that the state came on the scene as peace maker requires a quaint and credulous belief that the political theories of state-building elites—represented by Bodin, Hobbes, Rousseau, et al.— are an accurate reflection of the actual history of the state. As Charles Tilly remarks:

> [A] portrait of war makers and state makers as coercive and self-seeking entrepreneurs bears a far greater resemblance to the facts than do its chief alternatives: the idea of a social contract, the idea of an open market in which operators of armies and states offer services to willing customers, the idea of a society whose shared norms and expectations call forth a certain kind of government.[304]

Conclusion

We must conclude that the myth of the wars of religion is finally incredible, which is to say, false. A significant proportion of the violence was between members of the same church, and members of different churches often collaborated (A). It is impossible to separate religious motives from political, economic, and social causes (B and C). And the idea that the advent of the state solved the violence ignores abundant evidence that state building was perhaps the most significant cause of the violence (D).

One might perhaps grant that the myth of the wars of religion as commonly told is implausible, but still try to claim that the inseparability of religion and politics was precisely the problem in the early modern period. In other words, the problem with the early modern state was that it was not yet secularized. We have now learned that violence can be tamed by privatizing religion.

This objection continues to see politics and religion as two essentially different human activities that can be, and should be, sorted out. It imagines that, once the state had laid claim to the holy, the state voluntarily relinquished it by banning religion from direct access to the public square. However, if it is true, as we saw in chapters 1 and 2, that nationalism exhibits many of the characteristics of religion—including, most important for our purposes, the ability to organize killing energies—then what we have is not a separation of religion from politics but rather the substitution of the religion of the state for the religion of the church. The gap that liberal theorists propose between early modern and modern is not as wide as we would like to believe. In his study of Louis XIV, John Wolf writes, "[T]he deification of the person of the king in this theocentric era was accomplished in much the same way and with the same intentions that secular societies of the nineteenth and twentieth centuries have deified the state."[305] After detailing the elaborate ceremonies dedicated to the Sun King, Wolf comments:

> Before we leave these hymns of praise and celebrations, we should note that a study of this literature will call to mind the small-town, pre-motorized age of patriotic celebrations and ceremonies of July 4 or of July 14 (Bastille Day) and other such days that men set aside to instill patriotism and love for the Republic. The words in a society dedicated to popular sovereignty will be different from those used by men who believe that authority comes from God, but the impact is very similar. The orators who extolled the glories of the Republic, the heroism of its soldiers, and the faultless purity of its national policies were creating a secular deity out of the state, and their hearers were thrilled by their words and made more ready to obey the laws that were set above them.[306]

As Eric Hobsbawm has pointed out, ours is an unliturgical age in most respects, with one enormous exception: the public life of the citizen of the nation-state. Citizenship in secular countries is tied to symbols and rituals that have been invented for the purpose of expressing and reinforcing devotion to the nation-state.[307]

The migration of the holy is much easier for a modern person to identify in early modern Europe than in the contemporary liberal nation-state. Civil religion in the contemporary United States is in some respects similar, but in others quite dissimilar, to the worship practices of the Christian churches. When the topic is religion and violence, however, the most relevant aspect of the holy is the ability to organize lethal forces; the argument, after all, is that religion is especially prone to compel believers to die and kill. If it is true that "in the West the power to compel believers to die passed from Christianity to the nation-state, where it largely remains,"[308] then in this most relevant aspect, the migration of the holy from the church to the state is plain to see. If the state had relinquished the holy, we would expect that martyrdom would have faded from human history, at least in the West. As the poet Wilfred Owen would note during World War I, however, "the old Lie: Dulce et Decorum est / Pro patria mori" would carry more weight than ever in the twentieth century and into the twenty-first. Benedict Anderson has remarked that, in modernity, the nation replaces the church as the primary institution that deals with death. Nations provide a new kind of salvation; my death is not in vain if it is for the nation, which lives on into a limitless future.[309] According to Carolyn Marvin and David Ingle, the nation not only gives death meaning, but sacrifice for the nation-state provides the glue that binds a liberal social order together:

> Americans generally see their nation as a secular culture possessed of few myths, or with weak myths everywhere, but none central and organizing. We see American nationalism as a ritual system orga- nized around a core myth of violently sacrificed divinity manifest in the highest patriotic ceremony and the most accessible popular culture.[310]

Any uncomplicated tale of progress from the barbarous religious past to a peaceable secular present must reckon with the staggering amount of energy, resources, and devotion marshaled by the militaries of Western nations, espe- cially the United States.

To say that the foundational myth of the wars of religion is false is not to say that liberal principles are therefore false; the separation of church and state is, to my mind, important to uphold for several reasons, some of them theolog- ical. It is to say, however, that the triumphalist narrative that sees the liberal state as the solution to the violence of religion needs to be abandoned. To reject the myth by no means implies nostalgia for medieval forms of governance, any more than Michel Foucault's *Discipline and Punish* implies nostalgia for corpo- ral punishment.[311] Foucault's famous study shows the modern transition from public torture and execution aimed at the body to imprisonment aimed at the soul as part of a larger movement in modernity toward more invisible—and therefore more effective—types of discipline and power. Foucault's aim is not to hold up medieval practices as a paradigm, but to question the triumphalist narrative that Western modernity prefers to tell about itself, in which barba- rism is progressively conquered by rationality and freedom. Likewise, I want to question the triumphalist view of the liberal state. The shift from church power to state power is not the victory of peaceable reason over irrational reli- gious violence. The more we tell ourselves it is, the more we are capable of ignoring the violence we do in the name of reason and freedom.

In this chapter, it has not been my intention to provide anything like a complete historical account of the European wars of the sixteenth and seven- teenth centuries. To do so would be a monumental undertaking, beyond my competence. The purpose of this chapter instead has been negative: to show that the myth of the wars of religion cannot stand up to historical fact. I am not therefore required to substitute another grand narrative in its place.

Nevertheless, simply to refute the myth is not enough, for to do so raises important questions about why the myth was generated and perpetuated in the first place, if it appears so flimsy in light of the facts. My hypothesis is that the myth of the wars of religion—like the larger myth of religious violence—has been useful for the promotion of Western secular forms of governance as essentially peace making. According to the myth, only by carefully separating the dangerous impulses of religion from the mundane affairs of politics—as the liberal state has done—can a peaceful and prosperous world be finally achieved. In domestic politics, the myth serves both to legitimate devotion to the nation-state and to marginalize actors labeled religious from the public square. In foreign affairs, the myth serves to justify efforts to promote and propagate Western forms of governance in the non-Western world, by violence if necessary. In the next chapter, I will explore these uses of the myth of religious violence.

4

The Uses of the Myth

The first chapter of Martin Marty's *Politics, Religion, and the Common Good* begins with a cautionary tale:

> In the 1940s, what could incite otherwise law-abiding white Christian Americans to treat a group of fellow white Christian citizens like this?
>
> > In Nebraska, one member of this group was castrated.
> > In Wyoming, another member was tarred and feathered.
> > In Maine, six members were reportedly beaten.
> > In Illinois, a caravan of group members was attacked.
> > In other states, sheriffs looked the other way as people assaulted group members.
> > The group's meeting places were also attacked.
> > Members of the group were commonly arrested and then imprisoned without being charged.[1]

Marty reveals that the group in question was the Jehovah's Witnesses whose offense, in the eyes of their fellow citizens, was to circulate pamphlets such as one entitled "Reasons Why a True Follower of Jesus Christ Cannot Salute a Flag." In 1940, the Supreme Court had ruled that all American schoolchildren could be required to salute the U.S. flag. Marty comments that, with war raging in Europe, "The country had to stand together."[2] The Jehovah's Witnesses refused to comply.

Here we have a nation on the brink of war enforcing reverence to its flag and violently persecuting a nonviolent group of people who believe that flag worship is idolatrous. One would think that the lesson Marty would draw from this story would be a warning against the violence of zealous nationalism. Astonishingly, the punch line of the story is a warning about the dangers of religion in public. Within three years, the Supreme Court reversed itself. Marty says:

> But, during the three years before that reversal, it became obvious that religion, which can pose "us" versus "them"—or "them" versus what we think "the state" should be and do—carries risks and can be perceived by others as dangerous. Religion can cause all kinds of trouble in the public arena. The world scene reveals many instances of terror and tragedy created by people acting in the name of religion.[3]

As Marty uses it in this case, the term "religion" refers *not* to ritually putting one's hand over one's heart and reciting a pledge of allegiance to a piece of cloth endowed with totemic powers. The term religion applies only to the Jehovah's Witnesses' refusal to do so. And yet the violence *against* the Jehovah's Witnesses is exhibit A in Marty's warning about the violent tendencies of religion. Marty's own analysis of the religious symbols and rituals that characterize politics—which I examined in chapter 1—is forgotten as soon as he turns to his argument that religion has a tendency to produce violence.

Clearly, Marty disapproves of coercing people to salute the flag. Marty's sympathies are not with those ardent nationalists who would do violence to nonconformists. Much of Marty's book is dedicated to showing that allowing religion a voice in public affairs is—as the title of his second chapter indicates—"worth the risk." Nevertheless, the core of the problem for Marty is something alien and volatile that religion brings to the public arena. The stated thesis of Marty's first chapter is "public religion can be dangerous; it should be handled with care."[4] That view of religion causes him in this case to overlook the violence that can accompany nationalism. The need for the nation to revere its flag and stand together in a time of war appears as something natural and unquestionable, while the Jehovah's Witnesses' religious loyalty to Jesus Christ appears as something provocative of violence, even if they suffered rather than committed it.

In the first three chapters of this book, I have shown that the myth of religious violence is not simply based on empirical fact but is an ideological construction that authorizes certain uses of power. In this fourth and final chapter, I examine what kinds of power the myth authorizes. In other words, I attempt to answer the question, "If the myth of religious violence is so incoherent, why is it so prevalent?" I argue that the idea that religion has a peculiar tendency to produce violence serves certain definite purposes for its consumers in the West. In domestic politics, it serves to marginalize certain types of discourse labeled religious, while promoting the idea that the unity of the nation-state saves us from the divisiveness of religion. In foreign policy, the myth of religious violence helps to reinforce and justify Western attitudes and policies toward the non-Western world, especially Muslims, whose primary point of difference with the West is their stubborn refusal to tame religious passions in the public sphere. We claim to have learned the sobering lessons of religious warfare, while they have not. The myth of religious violence reinforces a reassuring dichotomy between their violence—which is absolutist, divisive, and irrational—and our violence, which is modest, unitive, and rational.

Although the myth authorizes certain uses of power, I do not think that there exists a conscious conspiracy on the part of certain powerful people to construct the myth as deliberate propaganda. The myth of religious violence is simply part of the general conceptual apparatus of Western society. It is one of the ways that the legitimacy of liberal social orders is continually reinforced, from official government actions to the common assumptions of the citizen on the street. The myth is never uncontested, as the Supreme Court cases I examine below make clear. But the myth is pervasive and helps to structure domestic and foreign policy in ways that are often unconscious.

The argument of this chapter proceeds in three sections. In the first section, I examine some domestic uses of the myth of religious violence. In particular, I examine the way the myth has been used by the Supreme Court to justify decisions on Establishment Clause cases since the 1940s. The next two sections deal with foreign policy. In the second section of this chapter, I give some examples of how the myth of religious violence is used to reinforce a dichotomy between the rational and peace-loving West, on the one hand, and irrational and violent non-Western cultures, especially Muslims, on the other. In the third section, I give examples of how the myth of religious violence can be used to justify violence against non-Western Others. I then conclude by briefly considering some implications of this book's argument. All of the examples in this chapter refer to the use of the myth in U.S. domestic and foreign policy, but I believe that the argument has relevance in many other contexts.

Constructing the Wall

Well into the twentieth century, when the term religion appeared in U.S. jurisprudence, it was considered a unitive, not a divisive force. What legal scholar

Frederick Gedicks calls "religious communitarianism" held sway. Religion was considered to be one of the principal binding forces that held a civilized society together. Church and state were separate institutions, but religion was not separate from the culture and political life of the nation. Government was expected to protect the rights of dissenters, but it was not expected to remain neutral with regard to religion. Under the de facto Protestant establishment, government was expected to give public recognition to a generic version of the biblical God and otherwise reinforce the conservative cultural values that religion represented.[5] As Philip Hamburger has documented, Thomas Jefferson's words in a letter to the Danbury Baptist Association about a "wall of separation between Church and State" had little effect on American society before they were quoted by the Supreme Court in 1947: "There is much reason to believe that modern suppositions about the wisdom and influence of Jefferson's words regarding separation have developed largely as part of a twentieth-century myth."[6] When separation of church and state was advocated in the nineteenth and early twentieth centuries, it usually appeared in a Protestant version meant to keep government from providing any aid to Catholic schools.[7]

By the 1940s, however, U.S. jurisprudence regarding religion had begun to shift to what Gedicks calls a "secular individualist" discourse, in which the inherent divisiveness of religion is highlighted. According to Edward Purcell, factors behind this shift included the influence of post-Darwinian naturalism, the prestige of the Enlightenment that accompanied the professionalization of American higher education, and the rise of legal realism.[8] The secularization thesis accepted by so many intellectuals was beginning to manifest itself in jurisprudence. Religion was no longer seen as the glue of society, but as a non-rational and potentially regressive force that must be confined to private life to protect rational public conversation from the subjectivity and divisiveness of religion. The myth of religious violence came for the first time to be invoked in important cases involving the interpretation of the First Amendment.[9]

The first significant Supreme Court case in this regard is the same one cited by Martin Marty: *Minersville School District v. Gobitis* (1940), which upheld compulsory pledging of allegiance to the U.S. flag. Writing for the majority, Justice Felix Frankfurter invoked the specter of religious wars in denying the Jehovah's Witnesses the right to dissent from patriotic rituals:

> Centuries of strife over the erection of particular dogmas as exclusive or all-comprehending faiths led to the inclusion of a guarantee for religious freedom in the Bill of Rights. The First Amendment, and the Fourteenth through its absorption of the First, sought to guard against repetition of those bitter religious struggles by

prohibiting the establishment of a state religion and by securing to every sect the free exercise of its faith.[10]

Such free exercise does not apply to the Jehovah's Witnesses in this case, however, because their dissent threatens the "promotion of national cohesion. We are dealing with an interest inferior to none in the hierarchy of legal values. National unity is the basis of national security."[11] Frankfurter argues that the necessary common sentiment that underlies national unity is promoted by symbols—"We live by symbols"—the most crucial of which is the flag.[12] Although there is disagreement over how best to inculcate patriotism in children, schools have a right to make those decisions without undue interference from either courts or parents: "What the school authorities are really asserting is the right to awaken in the child's mind considerations as to the significance of the flag contrary to those implanted by the parent."[13] In this case, the Supreme Court upheld the right to inculcate patriotism over the right to free exercise of religion. The Court would reverse itself three years later in *West Virginia State Board of Education v. Barnette,* but Frankfurter had succeeded in introducing the idea that First Amendment decisions could be made against a backdrop of some unspecified history of "bitter religious struggles," the antidote to which is the enforcement of national unity.

The Supreme Court decision that made famous Thomas Jefferson's phrase commending a "wall of separation between Church and State" was *Everson v. Board of Education* in 1947. The case challenged the use of public funds in New Jersey to bus children to parochial schools. Although the Court decided to allow this practice, its reasoning moved in the opposite direction. As Justice Robert Jackson wrote in his dissent, "In fact, the undertones of the opinion, advocating complete and uncompromising separation of Church from State, seem utterly discordant with its conclusion yielding support to their commingling in educational matters."[14]

Justice Hugo Black, writing for the majority, invoked the European wars of religion in erecting the wall of separation:

> The centuries immediately before and contemporaneous with the colonization of America had been filled with turmoil, civil strife, and persecutions, generated in large part by established sects determined to maintain their absolute political and religious supremacy. With the power of government supporting them, at various times and places, Catholics had persecuted Protestants, Protestants had persecuted Catholics, Protestant sects had persecuted other Protestant sects, Catholics of one shade of belief had persecuted Catholics of another shade of belief, and all of these had from time to time

persecuted Jews. In efforts to force loyalty to whatever religious group happened to be on top and in league with the government of a particular time and place, men and women had been fined, cast in jail, cruelly tortured, and killed.[15]

Justice Black admits that these events might seem a little distant from letting parochial school kids ride the bus in New Jersey. According to Black:

> [The] words of the First Amendment reflected in the minds of early Americans a vivid mental picture of conditions and practices which they fervently wished to stamp out in order to preserve liberty for themselves and for their posterity. Doubtless their goal has not been entirely reached; but so far has the Nation moved toward it that the expression "law respecting an establishment of religion," probably does not so vividly remind present-day Americans of the evils, fears, and political problems that caused that expression to be written into our Bill of Rights.[16]

Though the New Jersey busing policy had provoked no violence, Black feels it is important to recall the violent persecutions of centuries past, for he insists that the original context and intent of the First Amendment is crucial for understanding how to apply it today, and the original context of the First Amendment was the transplanting of the persecutions of the Old World to the New. Catholics, Quakers, and Baptists were discriminated against and persecuted in the American colonies, while having to pay taxes to support established churches. Black credits Jefferson and Madison with bringing that era to a close with their principled opposition to the 1785 tax to support the established Episcopalian Church in Virginia. Black further credits the Bill of Rights to Jefferson and Madison, and thus argues that the Fourteenth Amendment— which extended the ban on government-established religion from the federal government to the states—is in direct continuity with the First Amendment. In this way, Black draws a continuous line from the wars of religion in Europe to the state-established churches in the United States to the First Amendment to the Fourteenth and finally to the school kids in New Jersey in 1947. Black's opinion concludes, "The First Amendment has erected a wall between church and state. That wall must be kept high and impregnable. We could not approve the slightest breach. New Jersey has not breached it here."[17]

Black's use of the threat of religious violence in *Everson* is remarkable in that he seems to acknowledge that the threat of such violence in the United States had never been so remote. It was necessary for Black to summon the violence of the past because present-day Americans may have forgotten the havoc that religion had previously wrought. This was not the first time that Black had summoned the specter of religious violence. Shortly after his confirmation to the Supreme Court in 1937, Black's membership in the Ku Klux Klan had come to light, provoking public outrage. In a radio address meant to put the matter to rest, Black turned the accusation of bigotry against his opponents and warned that opposition to him would "breed or revive religious discord" that the First Amendment had been intended to quell.[18] As the *New York Herald Tribune* commented on his speech, "The effort of Senator Black to suggest that he is the real protagonist of tolerance and that his enemies are intolerant is perhaps the greatest item of effrontery in a uniquely brazen utterance."[19]

Philip Hamburger has suggested that Black intended in his decision in *Everson* to undercut Catholic criticism of him while simultaneously establishing the foundation for an absolute doctrine of separation of church and state.[20] Whether or not this was Black's intention, the *Everson* case had a tremendous influence on future religion-clause jurisprudence, not because of its decision, but because of its reasoning.[21] According to Gedicks, "With *Everson* the Supreme Court clearly signaled that the de facto establishment would be abandoned as a guide to church-state relations in favor of a philosophy like secular individualism."[22] Gedicks is probably overstating his case here; Black, at least, was certainly no secular individualist. As Hamburger documents, Black represented a brand of nativist Protestantism that was interested in separation of church and state primarily as a tool to keep government from aiding Catholic schools.[23] *Everson* did signal a shift, however, in that the absolute separation of church and state was based on a view of religion as inherently divisive if allowed to intrude into the public sphere. The black legend of the wars of religion and the specter of religious violence would subsequently be used by the Supreme Court in a discourse closer to what Gedicks calls "secular individualism."

Only a year after *Everson*, the Supreme Court used the same logic of separation in banning optional religious education from public school buildings. Whereas the complaint in *Everson* had been brought by a Protestant nativist, the complaint in *McCollum v. Board of Education* was brought by an atheist who objected to a program of nonmandatory religious instruction in Champaign, Illinois, public schools. Children whose parents agreed were released from the secular curriculum for one class period per week and sent to instruction in the Protestant, Catholic, or Jewish faith, depending on the parents' wishes. When the Court banned this practice, many Protestant nativists began to rethink their support for complete separation of church and state, seeing the secularist purposes to which it could be put.[24]

Black wrote the majority opinion in *McCollum,* but this time the myth of religious violence was invoked not by Black but by secularist Felix Frankfurter, in his concurring opinion. Frankfurter contrasts the unitive effects of secular education with the divisive effects of religion:

> The sharp confinement of the public schools to secular education was a recognition of the need of a democratic society to educate its children, insofar as the State undertook to do so, in an atmosphere free from pressures in a realm in which pressures are most resisted and where conflicts are most easily and most bitterly engendered. Designed to serve as perhaps the most powerful agency for promoting cohesion among a heterogeneous democratic people, the public school must keep scrupulously free from entanglement in the strife of sects.[25]

Frankfurter is concerned that the program in Champaign will increase the consciousness of religious differences among the students—especially for those who belong to sects that are unwilling or unable to provide religious instruction in the schools—whereas the purpose of public education is to promote a sense of our common destiny as Americans:

> These are consequences not amenable to statistics. But they are precisely the consequences against which the Constitution was directed when it prohibited the Government common to all from becoming embroiled, however innocently, in the destructive religious conflicts of which the history of even this country records some dark pages.[26]

The threat of religious conflict would become a recurring trope in subsequent Supreme Court cases involving religion. Two landmark cases involving prayer in public schools can serve as examples. In *Engel v. Vitale* in 1962, the Court's decision banning state-sponsored, mandatory, nondenominational prayer in New York schools is based in a narrative of centuries-old civil strife across the Atlantic. Writing for the majority, Hugo Black cited controversies over the Book of Common Prayer in England that "repeatedly threatened to disrupt the peace of that country"[27] in previous centuries. The framers of the U.S. Constitution "knew the anguish, hardship and bitter strife that could come when zealous religious groups struggled with one another to obtain the Government's stamp of approval from each King, Queen, or Protector that came to temporary power."[28] In the 1963 case *Abington School District v. Schempp,* the divisiveness of religion was highlighted in banning school-sponsored prayer and Bible readings in public schools. As Justices Arthur Goldberg and John Marshall Harlan wrote in their concurring opinion, "The practices here involved do not fall within any sensible or acceptable concept of compelled or permitted accommodation and involve the state so significantly and directly in the realm of the sectarian as to give rise to those very divisive influences and inhibitions of freedom which both religion clauses of the First Amendment preclude."[29] In his exhaustive, seventy-three-page concurring opinion in *Abington*, Justice William Brennan also wrote that public school devotional exercises "sufficiently threaten in our day those substantive evils the fear of which called forth the Establishment Clause of the First Amendment."[30] Unlike Hugo Black in *Everson*, Brennan was convinced that the danger is now greater than in the eighteenth century, because religious diversity has led to "the much more highly charged nature of religious questions in contemporary society."[31] According to Brennan, a thoroughly secular public education is the way to deal with this diversity. The function of public education is "the training of American citizens in an atmosphere free of parochial, divisive, or separatist influences of any sort—an atmosphere in which children may assimilate a heritage common to all American groups and religions.... This is a heritage neither theistic nor atheistic, but simply civic and patriotic."[32] A patriotic and united allegiance to the United States is the cure for the divisiveness of religion in public.

In his dissent, Justice Potter Stewart famously warned that the majority decision in *Abington* would be seen "not as the realization of state neutrality, but rather as the establishment of a religion of secularism."[33] In his dissent in *Engel v. Vitale*, Stewart had already noted the long history of government-sanctioned religious practice in the United States, including the fact that the Supreme Court opened its sessions with "God save this Honorable Court." In their concurring opinion in *Abington*, however, Goldberg and Harlan addressed this objection by drawing a sharp line between patriotic invocations of God and religious ones:

> There is of course nothing in the decision reached here that is inconsistent with the fact that school children and others are officially encouraged to express love for our country by reciting historical documents such as the Declaration of Independence which contain references to the Deity or by singing officially espoused anthems which include the composer's professions of faith in a Supreme Being, or with the fact that there are many manifestations in our public life of belief in God. Such patriotic or ceremonial occasions bear no true resemblance to the unquestioned religious exercise that the State has sponsored in this instance.[34]

Goldberg and Harlan offer no reason that patriotic invocations of God bear no true resemblance to religious invocations. But it is clear that what separates religion from what is not religion is *not* the invocation of God. God may be invoked in public ceremonies without such ceremonies thereby becoming religious exercises, provided such ceremonies express "love for our country." Separating religion from nonreligion in this case depends not on the presence or absence of expressions of faith in God, but on the presence or absence of expressions of faith in the United States of America. God without America can be divisive; God with America unifies us all.

One of the most significant Supreme Court cases involving church and state was *Lemon v. Kurtzman* in 1971, in which the Court established what became known as the "Lemon test," three criteria that must be met for any legislative action concerning religion.[35] The three prongs of the test were a distillation of criteria from previous Supreme Court decisions. Also carried over from decisions since *Everson* was the assumption that religion is a potentially divisive and violent force when allowed into the public arena. *Lemon* involved the use of public funds in Rhode Island and Pennsylvania to supplement the salaries of teachers in nonpublic schools, of which the majority were Catholic. Chief Justice Warren Burger, writing for the majority, worried that such state programs had a "divisive political potential" because both those in favor and those opposed would need to rally candidates and voters in support of their cause:

> Ordinarily political debate and division, however vigorous or even partisan, are normal and healthy manifestations of our democratic system of government, but political division along religious lines was one of the principal evils against which the First Amendment was intended to protect.... The potential divisiveness of such conflict is a threat to the normal political process.... The history of many countries attests to the hazards of religion's intruding into the political arena or of political power intruding into the legitimate and free exercise of religious belief.[36]

Here, Burger cited and paraphrased a 1969 *Harvard Law Review* article by Paul Freund entitled "Public Aid to Parochial Schools."[37] Justice Harlan had already cited this article in warning of the dangers of religious strife in *Walz v. Tax Commission* in 1970.[38] In the article, Freund argues for a restrictive view of the kind of aid that can be given to parochial schools. The choice between declaring certain types of aid permissible or forbidden, according to Freund, is a choice between leaving the issue to the political process or defusing it. Ordinarily, Freund says, he would be disposed to leave such "grey-area cases" to the political process. Religious questions, however, are uniquely dangerous: "Although great issues of constitutional law are never settled until they are settled right, still as between open-ended, ongoing political warfare and such binding quality as judicial decisions possess, I would choose the latter in the field of God and Caesar and the public treasury."[39]

In his article, Freund considers the nature of the doctrine of governmental neutrality toward religion that the Court had promulgated since *Everson*. Freund compares the Jehovah's Witnesses' eventual success (*West Virginia State Board of Education v. Barnette*, 1943) in being excused from participating in the Pledge of Allegiance with a Unitarian's success in *Abington* in getting prayers and Bible readings banned from public schools. One might suppose that neutrality would require equal treatment for Unitarians and Jehovah's Witnesses. Not so, in this case, says Freund. Unitarians succeeded in having prayer and devotions banned from all public schools, while Jehovah's Witnesses succeeded only in getting themselves excused from *participation* in the flag salute. The flag salute continued to be employed in public schools even though the Jehovah's Witnesses found the Pledge of Allegiance "at least as unacceptable and religious in nature"[40] as the Unitarians found the Lord's Prayer. Freund finds the difference in the way the Supreme Court has dealt with Unitarians and Jehovah's Witnesses to be entirely appropriate: "Why? Because the prevailing, dominant view of religion classifies the flag salute as secular, in contravention of the heterodox definition devoutly held by the Witnesses. Neutrality, that is, does not assure equal weight to differing denominational views as to what constitutes a religious practice."[41] Freund is equally dismissive of claims that secularism is itself a form of religion. This, he says, is merely a "metaphor," a "play on words or an idiosyncratic characterization, like the Jehovah's Witnesses' view of the flag salute, which is not controlling as a definition of religion."[42]

Freund never offers a definition of religion; none of the Supreme Court cases do either. Nevertheless, Freund appeals to "the prevailing, dominant view of religion," an orthodoxy to counter the Jehovah's Witnesses' "heterodox definition." Crucial to this dominant view—as in Goldberg and Harlan's opinion—is a sharp distinction between religion and patriotism, even patriotic ceremonies like the Pledge of Allegiance that invoke God. Freund is, of course, correct to state that there is a prevailing, dominant view of religion that is consistent with what an Enlightenment figure like Madison would have had in mind in drafting the First Amendment. But Freund does not pause to consider the possibility that the Jehovah's Witnesses' functional view of religion might be more adequate to empirical fact. If the definition of religion were subject to analysis and debate, the Jehovah's Witnesses could call on scholars like Carlton Hayes to defend the idea that nationalism functions as a religion. Freund, however, offers no defense of the prevailing, dominant view of religion other than to say that it is prevailing and dominant. In the case of Unitarians, they must be protected from exposure to prayer to God, even if they are the tiniest minority in a school where everyone else wants public prayer. In the case of the Jehovah's Witnesses, however, the fact that they are a minority is used to dismiss as idiosyncratic and heterodox their objections to the idolatry of flag worship. Religion is the realm of mere opinion, such that the law must remain neutral between Unitarians and evangelicals and leave questions of prayer to the private realm. The definition of religion, however, is fixed and immutable orthodoxy, a fully public part of the way things are.

It is no accident that in the secular individualist world view the definition of religion is negatively but inextricably linked to patriotism. Religion appears as the alter ego of the liberal nation-state; religion—or more precisely, religion in public—is what the liberal nation-state saves us from. Religion is defined as mere opinion, with no rational basis on which disputes can be solved. Religion therefore is inherently divisive and dangerous. What unifies us is the nation-state. In public, our identities as Jehovah's Witnesses and Unitarians and Catholics and atheists no longer take precedence. We are all Americans, and devotional exercises meant to instill love of our country are unitive, not divisive. Such exercises, however, are *not religion*. Patriotism, in this world view, is defined over against public religion. To allow that patriotism might be a type of religion and might carry its own dangers of violence would threaten the very basis of our social order. Religion belongs to the private realm of opinion; patriotism belongs to the public realm of fact. Dissenters from religious orthodoxy must be protected from religion; dissenters from patriotic orthodoxy may be tolerated but not allowed to interfere with the inculcation of the fervent love of country.[43]

The myth of religious violence has continued to be invoked in Supreme Court cases on religion—including by Justices Stephen Breyer,[44] David Souter,[45] and Sandra Day O'Connor[46]—but the examples already cited should suffice. It is not my intention here to provide a thorough review of Supreme Court jurisprudence on religion. Nor do I wish to take exception to particular decisions made by the Supreme Court in these matters. In general, I think the separation of church and state is a good thing for many reasons, some of them theological. My purpose here is only to highlight some influential ways that the myth of religious violence has been found useful in shaping U.S. society. It has been useful in ending certain kinds of practices, for example, prayer in public schools and public funding for parochial schools. But the myth has been generative as well; it has helped to reinforce the importance of devotion to the nation-state.

Perhaps the most remarkable thing about the myth of religious violence in U.S. jurisprudence is the fact that it was made useful at a moment in U.S. history when the violence against which it warned was least likely to occur. Was the Supreme Court seriously concerned in 1971 that a marauding band of enraged Rhode Island Presbyterians would attack St. Agnes grade school and shoot the social studies teacher in the middle of her Mt. Rushmore slide show? The nation had by then elected its first Catholic president, and suspicion of Catholics as agents of a foreign potentate—the pope—although not absent, was at a historical low. Despite dire warnings about the volatility of the issues at hand, none of the Supreme Court opinions was able to point to any actual disruptions of the peace that were less than a couple of centuries old. The Rhode Island and Pennsylvania legislatures had passed the offending legislation several years before *Lemon v. Kurtzman,* without apparently causing more violent disagreement than other funding bills dealing with highways and health care.

Of course, the Supreme Court has never been of one mind on these issues. None of the above decisions was unanimous, Supreme Court decisions on religion-clause cases have been notoriously inconsistent, and several justices have called into question the use of centuries-old tales of religious divisiveness. In *Aguilar v. Felton* (1985), the Supreme Court ruled against using Title I government funds for nonsectarian remedial educational programs for children from low-income families, programs which were conducted by public school teachers but took place in parochial schools. Writing for the majority, Justice Brennan again warns of "the dangers of political divisiveness along religious lines."[47] In his dissent, Warren Burger writes:

> Under the guise of protecting Americans from the evils of an Established Church such as those of the 18th century and earlier times, today's decision will deny countless schoolchildren desperately needed remedial teaching services funded under Title I.... What is disconcerting about the result reached today is that, in the face of the human cost entailed by this decision, the Court does not even attempt to identify any threat to religious liberty posed by the operation of Title I.... It borders on paranoia to perceive the Archbishop of Canterbury or the Bishop of Rome lurking behind programs that are just as vital to the Nation's schoolchildren as textbooks.[48]

Justices Sandra Day O'Connor and William Rehnquist likewise dissented, writing, "The Court's reliance on the potential for political divisiveness as evidence of undue entanglement is also unpersuasive. There is little record[ed] support for the proposition that New York City's admirable Title I program has ignited any controversy other than this litigation."[49]

What these dissenting opinions underscore is that the Supreme Court's use of the myth of religious violence has never been a response to empirical fact as much as it has been a useful narrative that has been produced by and has helped to produce consent to certain changes in the American social order. Stories of the inherent danger and divisiveness of religion helped to facilitate a shift from a predominant religious communitarianism to a predominant secular individualism in American jurisprudence and American culture. To recognize this shift is not necessarily to imply nostalgia for the previous regime. In the older view, religion is the glue that holds the nation together. The recruitment of the churches for the support of U.S. nationalism is, in my view, problematic. However, a shift toward the newer view, in which the nation is held together by allegiance to the nation itself over against the divisiveness of public religion, is also problematic, insofar as it unfairly marginalizes voices labeled religious from public discourse while it simultaneously promotes a secular religion of U.S. nationalism.

The West and the Rest

In addition to its uses in shaping and reflecting domestic politics, the myth of religious violence has been useful in forming and reflecting Western attitudes toward non-Western societies. Today, this is especially true of Western attitudes toward Islamic societies. Muslim societies are said to be peculiarly prone to violence precisely because they have not yet learned to separate religion, which is inherently volatile, from politics. The myth of religious violence is a form of Orientalist discourse that helps to reinforce a dichotomy between the rational West and other, more benighted cultures—Muslims especially— that lag behind.

Bernard Lewis of Princeton has been one of the most influential scholars of Islamic-Western relations since the 1970s. Lewis has been called "perhaps the most significant intellectual influence behind the invasion of Iraq."[50] Vice President Dick Cheney has acknowledged Lewis's influence and credited his 1990 article, "The Roots of Muslim Rage," as anticipating the acts of terror that followed it.[51] It was that article that originated the term "clash of civilizations" that Samuel Huntington would popularize. The article was first presented as the 1990 Jefferson Lecture in the Humanities, the most prestigious honor the U.S. government can confer on a humanities scholar. Lewis begins by quoting Thomas Jefferson's contention "that in matters of religion 'the maxim of civil government' should be reversed and we should rather say, 'Divided we stand, united, we fall.' "[52] Unity of government, in other words, is best preserved by allowing a diversity of religious expressions to flourish, separated from the state. Lewis thus gives notice that the attitudes of Muslims toward the West will be read against the wisdom that the West has acquired concerning religion. According to Lewis, that wisdom comes from Christ's admonition to separate what belongs to God from what belongs to Caesar and, most especially, the experience of the wars of religion:

> Muslims, too, had their religious disagreements, but there was
> nothing remotely approaching the ferocity of the Christian struggles
> between Protestants and Catholics, which devastated Christian
> Europe in the sixteenth and seventeenth centuries and finally drove
> Christians in desperation to evolve a doctrine of the separation of
> religion from the state. Only by depriving religious institutions of
> coercive power, it seemed, could Christendom restrain the mur-
> derous intolerance and persecution that Christians had visited on
> followers of other religions and, most of all, on those who professed
> other forms of their own.[53]

The Muslim world was happily spared such an experience of devastation, but the consequence is that Muslims never learned to assimilate the blessings of secularism. The current result is the clash of civilizations between the secular West and a Muslim world that cannot abide the separation of religion from politics.

Lewis sets up the clash in terms of a dualistic opposition of two monolithic civilizations. Like all religions, Lewis says, Islam has gone through periods when it has inspired hate and violence in its followers. Unfortunately for us, it is currently in such a stage, and much of the hatred is directed at us. At times, this hatred goes beyond hostility toward specific actions and policies and becomes "a rejection of Western civilization as such."[54] Although the struggle between Islam and the Christian West is centuries old, in the late twentieth century it reached a boiling point. Lewis describes it as a reaction to a series of humiliations suffered by "the Muslim": first came his loss of domination in the world to Russia and the West, second came his loss of authority in his country to foreign ideas and rulers, and third came the challenge to his mastery at home, from emancipated women and rebellious children. The result was an "outbreak of rage against these alien, infidel, and incomprehensible forces."[55]

At first, this rage was not focused on the United States. After World War II, the oil industry brought Americans to Muslim lands, and markets brought

American material and cultural products, but the United States was generally admired:

> And then came the great change, when the leaders of a widespread
> and widening religious revival sought out and identified their ene-
> mies as the enemies of God, and gave them "a local habitation and
> a name" in the Western Hemisphere. Suddenly, or so it seemed,
> America had become the archenemy, the incarnation of evil, the
> diabolic opponent of all that is good, and specifically, for Muslims,
> of Islam.[56]

The direct cause of the clash appears here as a "religious revival" in the Muslim world. The following section of the essay, entitled "Some Familiar Accusations," considers other causes, but ends up dismissing all of them as secondary and superficial. European philosophies provided an outlet for anti-Americanism, but did not cause it. The U.S. support for Israel is a factor, but early Soviet support for Israel did not cause such ill will. The U.S. support for oppressive regimes in the Muslim world is also a plausible factor, but such support "has been limited both in extent and—as the Shah discovered—in effectiveness."[57] To accusations of sexism, racism, imperialism, patriarchy, slavery, tyranny, and exploitation, Lewis says, "we have no option but to plead guilty—not as Americans, nor yet as Westerners, but simply as human beings,"[58] for every people throughout history has done such things. Indeed, the United States and the West are only distinct in having tried to remedy these historic ills: "Clearly, something deeper is involved than these specific grievances, numerous and important as they may be—something deeper that turns every disagreement into a problem and makes every problem insoluble."[59] That something deeper is Muslims' religious world view. The confrontation, Lewis tells us, ultimately comes down to a deep struggle against secularism that is explicit and con-scious, and a war against modernity that is largely unconscious:

> It should by now be clear that we are facing a mood and a movement
> far transcending the level of issues and policies and the governments
> that pursue them. This is no less than a clash of civilizations—the
> perhaps irrational but surely historic reaction of an ancient rival
> against our Judeo-Christian heritage, our secular present, and the
> worldwide expansion of both.[60]

Lewis writes of the "backwardness of the Islamic world as compared with the advancing West."[61] For Lewis, the West is a monolithic reality representing modernity, secularism, and rationality, while the Muslim world is an equally monolithic reality that is ancient, that is, lagging behind modernity, because of its essentially religious and irrational character. The West has learned to tame dangerous religious passions by relegating them to the private realm. The Muslim world has not, and so the clash continues.

Although Lewis gives the appearance of being deeply versed in the history of Islam and its relations to the West, actual specific historical events get glossed over in favor of the religious root of the problem. Imperialism, he says, is the one offense of the West against the Muslim world most frequently and vehemently denounced. But the word means something different for Muslim fundamentalists, for whom "the term 'imperialist' is given a distinctly religious significance";[62] what is truly evil is the domination of infidels over true believers. There is something inherent in Muslim civilization that causes them to misread mundane political events in terms of religion. We can bicker over this coup or that tyrant, but the real root of Muslim rage is at the level of an irrational reaction against the marginalization of irrationality in secular civilization. Close scrutiny of historical grievances is therefore not necessary.

Let us take, for example, Lewis's treatment of the 1953 coup in Iran. In his book *The Crisis of Islam,* Lewis acknowledges that the coup is perhaps the most frequently cited example of Western imperialism in the Muslim world. As Stephen Kinzer documents, almost all American historians of the coup agree that the coup defined subsequent Iranian history, leading to the radically anti-American regime that was in power in the late twentieth and early twenty-first century.[63] Indeed, even Secretary of State Madeleine Albright in 1990 admitted the U.S. role in overthrowing Mohammed Mossadegh and acknowledged the continuing resentment against the United States it has caused in Iran.[64] Lewis acknowledges the role of the United States and Britain, but says that the coup at first did not go well. As Lewis tells the story, the success of the coup depended upon a shift from popular demonstrations that opposed the Shah to demonstrations supporting him.[65] "The aftermath," Lewis writes, "by the standards of the region, was remarkably mild."[66] Mossadegh, for example, was allowed to live. From there, Lewis simply skips over the next twenty-six years of U.S. support for the Shah and the operations of his brutal secret police, SAVAK, which tortured and killed tens of thousands of Iranians. No mention is made of CIA collaboration with SAVAK nor the fact that the United States gave the Shah access to virtually the entire array of U.S. weapons, excluding only nuclear weapons. From 1972 to 1976 alone, the Shah purchased more than $9 billion of U.S. weaponry—some of it used ruthlessly to suppress calls for democracy within Iran—in exchange for U.S. access to oil and Iranian support of Israel.[67] Lewis mentions none of this. He resumes the story in 1979 and gives a relatively detailed account of the Shah's itinerary after his overthrow by the Islamist regime. Lewis emphasizes that the United States did not intervene militarily on the Shah's behalf and refused to give him asylum until October 1979, when it became clear he needed medical care. Therefore, Lewis contends, the Shah could hardly be called a puppet of the United States. Lewis concludes his brief analysis of Iranian politics by repeating verbatim the line from his article, quoted above, about "something deeper" involved than these specific grievances. He adds, "What we confront now is not just a complaint about one or another American policy but rather a rejection and condemnation, at once angry and contemptuous, of all that America is seen to represent in the modern world."[68]

The deeper opposition that Lewis sets up is between a rational, secular civilization, on the one hand, and a civilization that has not learned to tame the dangerous, irrational passions of religion in public, on the other. The myth of religious violence thus allows those in the West to shrug off any specific grievances that the Muslim world might have about U.S. foreign policy and U.S. relations with the rest of the world. Most Americans today have never heard of Mohammad Mossadegh, even though he was *Time* magazine's Man of the Year in 1951. When Americans' television screens were suddenly filled with strange people chanting "Death to America!" in 1979, we were at a loss to explain why. The story we have come to accept is that those people over there have had some kind of weird religious revival. We shake our heads at the irrationality and craziness of it all and warn solemnly about the dangers of religious fanaticism. We congratulate ourselves at having solved the problem of religion in public long ago. And we are thereby licensed to overlook the specific grievances that some in the Muslim world might have about U.S. involvement there.

The problematic way that the myth of religious violence tends to construct the Otherness of the non-Western world is not confined to those on the conservative end of the political spectrum. Mark Juergensmeyer, whose work I examined in chapter 1, is clearly opposed to a heavy-handed approach to the "war on terror" and is not in sympathy with the invasion of Iraq.[69] Juergensmeyer sees his work as an attempt to promote understanding of religious actors, and he believes that "we can learn to live with at least some aspects of the religious political agenda."[70] Nevertheless, the idea that religion has a peculiar relationship with violence leads to an asymmetrical relationship between secular and religious actors.

In his 1993 book, *The New Cold War?* and his 2008 book, *Global Rebellion*, which brings the earlier work up to date, Juergensmeyer sees a new Cold War pitting the "resurgence of parochial identities" over against "the secular West."[71] As in Lewis, religious actors come from the past and represent parochial, as opposed to universal, identities. Although he takes pains to avoid demonizing "religious nationalists," Juergensmeyer sees them as essentially "anti-modern."[72]

Religious and secular also name sharply opposed cultures: "Like the old Cold War, the confrontation between these new forms of culture-based politics and the secular state is global in its scope, binary in its opposition, occasionally violent, and essentially a difference of ideologies."[73] Juergensmeyer does not set himself up as a warrior on either side of this binary divide; his intention is clearly to defuse the conflict by promoting understanding of what motivates religious actors. Nevertheless, the way he divides the world in two and reduces conflicts in very different circumstances around the globe to a religious-secular binary is problematic. Furthermore, by contending that this conflict is "essentially a difference of ideologies," his analysis tends, like Lewis's, to distract the reader's attention from close analysis of actual historical events, because the cause of the violence is located "deeper" in the ideological conflict of religion versus the secular.

As we saw in chapter 1, Juergensmeyer makes some attempt to acknowledge the kind of historical work on the concepts of religious and secular that I discussed in chapter 2. He tries to level the playing field between the two contestants by subsuming both religion and secularism under the genus "ideologies of order." However, Juergensmeyer continues to identify religion as peculiarly problematic for the way that it escalates merely mundane war into cosmic war. The conflicts he examines in his book, he writes, began as matters of social and political identity, but were subsequently "religionized."[74] Religion is especially problematic because it introduces the idea of cosmic war, which is "an all-encompassing worldview." Religion "absolutizes the conflict," it "demonizes opponents," it demands only "total victory," it extends conflict out to a time frame that is potentially eternal.[75] Although religion does not simply cause violence, it has a unique capacity to exacerbate it: "Religious violence is especially savage and relentless since its perpetrators see it not merely as part of a worldly political battle but as a part of a scenario of divine conflict."[76] There is a "special relationship between religion and violence."[77]

Despite Juergensmeyer's attempt to be even-handed, then, it is hard to escape the conclusion that actors labeled religious are peculiarly prone to violence in ways that secular actors are not. Even when Juergensmeyer acknowledges that secular nation-states can be authoritarian or can limit freedom of expression, these are either held to be exceptions—as in secular states like Stalin's Soviet Union or Hitler's Germany[78]—or attributed to the role of religion in a secular state. Juergensmeyer says that the U.S. war on terrorism has been elevated by many politicians and commentators above the mundane—"like all images of cosmic war, all-encompassing, absolutizing, and demonizing"—but he attributes the problem to the "role of religion" and the way it has "problematized the conflict."[79] Despite Juergensmeyer's approval of Carlton Hayes's contention that secular nationalism is a religion,[80] religion continues to be used as something essentially other than secularism. In this case, the term religion is used to declare as Other an aspect of secular nationalism we find unappealing. Although secular nationalism can be susceptible to the influence of religion, the true essence of the secular would appear to be mundane, reasonable, and modest. The question then becomes "whether religious nationalism can be made compatible with secular nationalism's great virtues: tolerance, respect for human rights, and freedom of expression."[81] Given the fact that "reason and religion have begun to war with one another on a global plane," however, Juergensmeyer is not optimistic: "there is ultimately no satisfactory ideological compromise between religious and secular views of the grounds for legitimizing public authority."[82]

Despite Juergensmeyer's sincere efforts to defuse conflict, the way that he has set up a dichotomy between the rational, secular West, on the one hand, and religious actors who are peculiarly prone to violence, on the other, can help to reinforce the conflicts he seeks to ameliorate. The conflict becomes explicable in terms of the essential qualities of the two opponents, not in terms of actual historical encounters. So, for example, Juergensmeyer attempts to explain the animosity of the religious Other toward America:

> Why is America the enemy? This question is hard for observers
> of international politics to answer, and harder still for ordinary
> Americans to fathom. Many have watched with horror as their com-
> patriots and symbols of their country have been destroyed by people
> whom they do not know, from cultures they can scarcely identify on
> a global atlas, and for reasons that do not seem readily apparent.[83]

Juergensmeyer lists four reasons "from the frames of reference" of America's enemies. First, the United States often finds itself cast as a "secondary enemy": "In its role as trading partner and political ally, America has a vested interest in shoring up the stability of regimes around the world. This has often put the United States in the unhappy position of being a defender and promoter of secular governments regarded by their religious opponents as primary foes."[84] Juergensmeyer cites as an example the case of Iran, where "America was tarred by its association with the shah."[85] The second reason often given is that the United States is the main source of "modern culture," which includes cultural products that others regard as immoral. Third, corporations that trade internationally tend to be based in the United States. Fourth and finally, the fear of globalization has led to a "paranoid vision of American leaders' global designs."[86]

Juergensmeyer acknowledges, "Like all stereotypes, each of these characterizations holds a certain amount of truth."[87] The fall of the Soviet Union has left the United States as the only military superpower, and it is therefore "an easy target for blame when people have felt that their lives were going askew or were being controlled by forces they could not readily see. Yet to dislike America is one thing; to regard it as a cosmic enemy is quite another."[88] The main problem, according to Juergensmeyer, is "satanization," that is, taking a simple opponent and casting it as a superhuman enemy in a cosmic war. Osama bin Laden, for example, inflated America into a "mythic monster."[89]

The problem with Juergensmeyer's analysis is not just its relatively sanitized account of colonial history. The problem is that history is subordinated to an essentialist account of religion in which the religious Others cannot seem to deal rationally with world events. They employ guilt by association. They have paranoid visions of globalization. They stereotype, and they blame easy targets when their lives are disrupted by forces they do not understand. They blow simple oppositions up into cosmic proportions. As in Lewis, understanding Muslim hostility toward the United States therefore does not require careful scrutiny of America's historical dealings with the Muslim world. Rather, Juergensmeyer turns our attention to the tendency of such religious actors to misunderstand such historical events or blow them out of proportion.

Juergensmeyer's conviction that the struggle between religious actors and secularism is essentially ideological means that analyzing the specific historical grievances of religious Others will take second place behind understanding their religious beliefs. Juergensmeyer's analysis of Iranian Shi'ite militancy in *Global Rebellion* therefore is understood in terms of three perennial themes in the Shi'ite world view: the Shi'ite tradition of struggle against evil, the vesting of political power in the clergy, and the messianic and utopian expectations of Shi'ite Islam. The Shah, his SAVAK, and U.S. support for him are briefly discussed, but the Shah appears only as a recent placeholder in the role of enemy that Shi'ite Islam perpetually requires:

> These three aspects of Shi'ite Islam—its history of struggle against oppression, the political power it has traditionally vested in the clergy, and its tradition of messianic and utopian expectations— made Islam in Iran ripe for revolutionary political exploitation. That the revolution happened so easily was due in part to the vulnerability of its adversaries. Few characters in the Shi'ite drama of the forces of good struggling against the forces of evil have been so effectively thrust into the role of evil as the members of the Pahlavi dynasty— Riza Shah, who established a military dictatorship in 1921, and his son Muhammad Riza Shah, who succeeded him in 1941.[90]

Juergensmeyer does not present the Shah as innocent, but as in Lewis, actual analysis of specific grievances is secondary to a consideration of the archaic religious ideas of Iranian Muslims as the factor that blows mundane matters such as torture and coups and oil trading into a cosmic war. The United States, though also not innocent, similarly finds itself cast in the role of demon by Muslim radicals; the United States is "a fitting target for their religious and political anger."[91] The anger seems to come first, then a target is found: "They had seen the strength of their forces grow as they rallied against an enemy—the Soviet Union. In the 1990s, they needed a new enemy, and the United States fit that bill."[92]

It is, of course, the case that Shi'ite theology is relevant to understanding the theopolitical order that in the twenty-first century rules—badly and oppressively—in Iran. Such theology should be open to criticism. The problem with singling out Shi'ite religion as the unique source of the problem, however, is that isolating religion from other factors that the West divides into political, economic, and social distorts our understanding of the Iranian context. The attempt to impose a Western framework of understanding on Iran means that Shi'ite Islam will inevitably appear as dangerous because it mixes religion and politics. Efforts to separate moderate from militant forms of Shi'ite theology and practice are hampered by the idea that religion as such is inherently prone to violence. Other factors for understanding contemporary Shi'ite militancy—such as the history of U.S.–Iranian relations—are thereby downplayed or ignored. Recognizing this by no means implies that external factors are the sole source of Shi'ite militancy, or that Western involvement is to blame for all that is wrong in Iran. But there is a danger any time that religion is identified as a peculiar type of ideology with a unique tendency to promote violence. For its consumers in the West, the myth of religious violence allows them to concentrate on the inherent irrationality of non-Western Others as the source of conflict with their secular way of life. The danger of Juergensmeyer's analysis, in other words, is that it calls attention to anticolonial violence, which is labeled religious, and calls attention away from colonial or neocolonial violence, which is labeled secular.

Andrew Sullivan's article "This *Is* a Religious War" is another example of how the myth of religious violence appears in public discourse to establish a sharp contrast between *our* peaceableness and *their* violence. The article, which appeared in the *New York Times Magazine* a few weeks after the September 11, 2001, attacks, is representative of the way in which mainstream commentators, both liberal and conservative, tend to deal with the supposed conflict between Western and Islamic civilizations. Sullivan begins by arguing that the rush after September 11 to claim that the conflict is not really about religion is well intentioned but misguided. People want to defuse the conflict by taking religion out of it, but the reality is that Osama bin Laden is quite clear about the religious underpinnings of the struggle. Sullivan quotes bin Laden: "The call to wage war against America was made because America has spearheaded the crusade against the Islamic nation, sending tens of thousands of its troops to the land of the two holy mosques over and above its meddling in its affairs and its politics and its support of the oppressive, corrupt, and tyrannical regime that is in control."[93] Sullivan comments, "Notice the use of the word 'crusade,' an explicitly religious term.... Notice also that bin Laden's beef is with American troops defiling the land of Saudi Arabia—'the land of the two holy mosques' in Mecca and Medina."[94] The words "crusade" and "mosques" indicate that religion is at the root of the problem. According to Sullivan, bin Laden has been quite clear about the religious nature of the conflict, and we should take this seriously.

Despite bin Laden's identification of some very concrete matters of U.S. foreign policy—the stationing of troops in Saudi Arabia and support for the corrupt and authoritarian Saudi regime—Sullivan, like Lewis and Juergensmeyer, calls the reader's attention away from such mundane historical matters to "something deeper" at the root of the problem:

> It seems almost as if there is something inherent in religious monotheism that lends itself to this kind of terrorist temptation. And our bland attempts to ignore this—to speak of this violence as if it did not have religious roots—is some kind of denial. We don't want to denigrate religion as such, and so we deny that religion is at the heart of this. But we would understand this conflict better, perhaps, if we first acknowledged that religion is responsible in some way, and then figured out how and why.[95]

Sullivan then proceeds to analyze "fundamentalism," the "blind recourse to texts embraced as literal truth, the injunction to follow the commandments of God before anything else, the subjugation of reason and judgment and even conscience to the dictates of dogma."[96] The relationship between fundamentalism and religion is not made entirely clear. Fundamentalism seems to indicate what happens when religion is allowed to take a fully public role in society: "This is the voice of fundamentalism. Faith cannot exist alone in a single person. Indeed, faith needs others for it to survive—and the more complete the culture of faith, the wider it is, and the more total its infiltration of the world, the better."[97] Because it needs others, fundamentalism will seek to coerce others violently into its own camp. If you believe that faith is social and that the sin of others can corrupt you as well, then you have no choice but to try to impose your religion on society—by force, if necessary.[98]

The evils of such an arrangement seem obvious to us. We in the West have learned our lesson from the wars of religion: "From the Crusades to the Inquisition to the bloody religious wars of the 16th and 17th centuries, Europe saw far more blood spilled for religion's sake than the Muslim world did."[99] Unfortunately, "[f]rom everything we see, the lessons Europe learned in its bloody history have yet to be absorbed within the Muslim world."[100] The solution to the religious violence that roils the Muslim world is the adoption of Western-style liberalism, with its separation of religion and politics. Sullivan is thus able to use the myth of religious violence and the legend of the European wars of religion to change the subject. The subject is no longer U.S. military support for authoritarianism and tyranny in Saudi Arabia. The subject is now the blessings of peace and freedom that U.S. liberalism could bring to the world, if only the Muslims would learn from us. Unfortunately, their lack of a similar experience with religion means that they will probably be slow to learn: "For unlike Europe's religious wars, which taught Christians the futility of fighting to the death over something beyond human understanding and so immune to any definitive resolution, there has been no such educative conflict in the Muslim world."[101]

As this quote indicates, the problem for Sullivan is at root epistemological. The problem with religion is that authoritative truth is simply not available to us mortals in any form that will produce consensus rather than division. Locke, therefore, emerges as Sullivan's hero, for it was Locke who recognized the limits of human understanding of revelation and enshrined those limits in a political theory. Locke and the founding fathers saved us from the curse of killing in the name of religion: "What the founders and Locke were saying was that the ultimate claims of religion should simply not be allowed to interfere with political and religious freedom."[102] In theory, then, we have the opposition of a cruel fanaticism with a modest and peace-loving tolerance. However, Sullivan's epistemological modesty applies only to the command of God and not to the absolute superiority of "our" political and cultural system over "theirs." As the title of his essay indicates, Sullivan insists that the "war of fundamentalism against faiths of all kinds that are at peace with freedom and modernity"[103] is a "religious war" worth fighting. According to Sullivan, "What is really at issue here is the simple but immensely difficult principle of the separation of politics and religion.... We are fighting for the universal principles of our Constitution—and the possibility of free religious faith it guarantees. We are fighting for religion against one of the deepest strains in religion there is. And not only our lives but our souls are at stake."[104] *Universal* knowledge is available to us after all, and it underwrites the "epic battle" we are currently waging against fundamentalisms of all kinds. On the surface, the myth of religious violence establishes a dichotomy between our peace-loving, secular reasonableness and their irrational religious fanaticism. Under the surface lies a religious devotion to the American vision of a hegemonic liberalism.

Regardless of their intentions, the way that Lewis, Juergensmeyer, and Sullivan use the myth of religious violence helps to reinforce the divide between the West and the rest of the world. These three writers are far from isolated in their use of the myth. The opposition of rational and irrational, secular and religious, which was born of internal struggles in Europe, has been projected onto the rest of the world to superimpose those binary distinctions on a putative divide between the "West and the rest," as Huntington puts it. As Roxanne Euben writes in her study of Islamic fundamentalism, the opposition of Western and Muslim is part of a larger Enlightenment narrative in which defining reason requires its irrational Other:

> Embedded in the Enlightenment's (re-)definition and elevation of reason is the creation and subjection of an irrational counterpart: along with the emergence of reason as both the instrument and essence of human achievement, the irrational came to be defined primarily in opposition to what such thinkers saw as the truths of their own distinctive historical epoch. If they were the voices of modernity, freedom, liberation, happiness, reason, nobility, and even natural passion, the irrational was all that came before: tyranny, servility to dogma, self-abnegation, superstition, and false religion. Thus the irrational came to mean the domination of religion in the historical period that preceded it.[105]

Religion appeared as the alter ego of the new secularist politics being born in the post-Enlightenment West. This opposition was subsequently extended to relations between West and East. The problem with this narrative, according to Euben, is that it is incapable of understanding the appeal of non-Western patterns of thinking on their own terms. It dismisses rather than explains.[106] Such patterns of thinking hardly qualify as thought at all, since they are inherently irrational and violent.

Elizabeth Hurd's *The Politics of Secularism in International Relations* shows how Western secularist discourses have managed to present themselves as neutral tools of descriptive analysis that are valid internationally. Secularist discourse assumes that religion and politics are stable and unchanging categories. Islam is then considered to be inherently dangerous and volatile because it mixes religion and politics. But religion and politics do not designate separate universal and natural spheres of human activity. As Hurd says, "The designation of the religious and the political is itself a political act."[107] At the same time, Hurd refers to secularism as a kind of "theological politics"[108] and calls international relations a "secular church."[109]

Hurd identifies two different types of secularism in the West. The first she labels "laicism." It is marked by a certain Enlightenment hostility toward religion as something inherently dangerous and irrational. There is also, however, especially in the United States, a type of Judeo-Christian secularism which is suspicious not of religion as such but only of the mixing of religion and politics. This second type of secularism sees the separation of religion and politics, God and Caesar, as the special discovery of the Judeo-Christian tradition and its gift to the world.[110] Both types of secularism are capable of appealing to the myth of the wars of religion, laicism to warn of the dangers inherent in religion and Judeo-Christian secularism to show how the West finally learned—especially through the genius of Protestantism—the lesson that Jesus taught when he told the Pharisees to give to God what is God's and give to Caesar what is Caesar's. Hurd argues that both types of secularism are capable of prejudicing the West's view of Islam especially, for Islamic politics is seen as either too infected by religion or insufficiently tutored by the wisdom of the Judeo-Christian tradition of secularism.[111] Hurd lists three policy consequences of Western secularist views of the Islamic world. First, there is a profound skepticism in policy-making circles about the possibility of success for any oppositional politics within Muslim-majority societies that use Islamic language. Secularism is viewed as a prerequisite for democracy. Second, any attempts to renegotiate the boundaries of the religious and the political that actually are taking place in Muslim-majority societies are dismissed as unnatural and ill-fitting attempts to realize a modern secularist ideal. Third, the secularist framing of religion and politics discourages engagement between secularists and moderate "civil Islamists." The only difference between laicists and Judeo-Christian secularists on these policies is that the latter are relatively more pessimistic about the possibility of any Islamic society achieving the separation of religion and politics, whereas laicists hold out the hope that Muslim-majority societies can be modernized, like Turkey was, by the imposition of a Western-style separation of religion and politics.[112]

Secularist discourse is not a grand conspiracy directed by a manipulative class of ruling elites. The theoretical separation of religion and politics is not part of a deliberate plan to assert Western supremacy over non-Western Others. As Melani McAlister says in her study of culture, media, and U.S. foreign policy with regard to the Middle East, national identity and national interests are determined in complex ways through a variety of languages and signs: "Foreign policy is a semiotic activity, not only because it is articulated and transmitted through texts but also because the policies themselves construct meanings."[113] Secularist discourse about religion and politics both helps to shape and is shaped by U.S. policies with regard to the non-Western world. It is not simply intentionally targeted propaganda, however, but works within a field of signs that establishes the boundaries of what is considered normal. As the eminent scholar of Islam John Esposito has pointed out, the use of the Western term religion to describe Islam immediately marks Islam as an "abnormal" religion, precisely because it does not conform to the Western standard of religion as a system of personal belief:

> However, the modern notions of religion as a system of belief for
> personal life and of separation of church and state have become so
> accepted and internalized that they have obscured past beliefs and
> practice and have come to represent for many a self-evident and time-
> less truth. As a result, from a modern secular perspective (a form
> of "secular fundamentalism"), the mixing of religion and politics is
> regarded as necessarily abnormal (departing from the norm), irratio-
> nal, dangerous, and extremist.[114]

In addition to the abnormalization of the Other, secularist discourse—and the myth of religious violence in particular—helps to form consent for foreign policies by diverting attention away from scrutiny of past policies and their effects. For example, McAlister examines the treatment of the Iranian hostage crisis of 1979–1981 by the Western media and U.S. government spokespersons. Most media reports took an ahistorical approach and concentrated on the personal narratives of the hostages and their families. When the question of an explanation for the hostage taking was approached, the standard response was either a posture of appalled bafflement or an attempt to explain the event through religion. (Bafflement and religion are not necessarily opposed, for religion in the dominant view is inherently mysterious, personal, and sui generis.) McAlister shows that "Islam" rather than oil wealth became the prime signifier of the Middle East during and after the hostage crisis. Explanations of the hostage crisis in the media and by U.S. government spokespersons were given through the lens of religion, specifically the dangerous and inherently violent nature of Islam because of its tendency to mix religion and politics. What was thereby ignored was the history of U.S.–Iranian relations.[115] Once the myth of religious violence was invoked, there was no need to examine specific U.S. policies toward Iran—such as the coup and support for the Shah—because a deeper explanation had been found. Once an essential root of the problem had been identified, the treatment of history became of secondary importance, at best. Everyone in the United States knew in 1979 that the Ayatollah Khomeini had imposed a strict Islamic dress code in Iran. Almost no one knew that the first shah (1925–1941) had imposed an equally strict secular dress code that mandated Western dress for men, restricted clerical garb, and banned the veil for women.[116] Discussion of the essential qualities of religion cast a convenient fog of amnesia over any serious public analysis of the roots of Iranian opposition to U.S. policy and its support for the modernization and Westernization of Iran.

The Liberal War of Liberation

In 1971, while the Supreme Court was fretting about the potential explosiveness of supplementing parochial teachers' salaries in Rhode Island, the U.S. military was carpet bombing Vietnamese villages to help bring liberal democracy to Southeast Asia. Is there a connection?

Any connection would not be direct, of course. The myth of religious violence is not a deliberate piece of propaganda meant to justify acts of war. I do not suggest that theories of religion and violence are constructed with this purpose in mind; to the contrary, I believe that most theorists of the link between religion and violence are deeply concerned to understand and limit violence in all its forms. Nevertheless, insofar as the myth of religious violence is used to divide acts of violence into those that are potentially legitimate and those that are always illegitimate, the myth can be used to divert moral scrutiny away from certain acts of violence. The categorization of certain acts of violence as religious renders them subject to immediate disapproval. Violence that is deemed secular, on the other hand, is often necessary and sometimes praiseworthy, especially when used for the purposes of bringing the blessings and peacefulness of liberalism to places like Vietnam, where freedom has been repressed. This is even more the case when secular violence is deemed necessary to contain or prevent religious violence. The twenty-first-century confrontation between the West and the Islamic world provides many examples of this type of rhetoric. In this view, the problem of violence is seen as a function of Muslims' inability to learn the lessons of history and tame the influence of religion in public. Peace will only be achieved when the blessings of liberal democracy have taken root in the Muslim world. As in the cases of Iraq and Afghanistan, war is sometimes necessary to help the process along.

In chapter 1, I examined Charles Kimball's book *When Religion Becomes Evil* and argued that Kimball is unable to sustain a coherent distinction between religious and secular violence. The distinction is crucial to Kimball's book, however, and it reflects broader assumptions in the West about what kinds of violence are at least potentially legitimate and what kinds are not. Nothing in my discussion of Kimball's book takes anything away from the power of his many examples of violent acts committed throughout history by Christians, Muslims, Buddhists, and others. The reader gets a strong sense from the autobiographical comments that Kimball inserts into the narrative that these indictments are motivated by a deep commitment to stop violence and create peace among warring peoples.[117] Unfortunately, Kimball's indictments only apply to *certain kinds* of violence, and the danger is that, by overlooking other kinds of violence, the argument as a whole can be used actually to *legitimate* them.

In his chapter on holy war, for example, Kimball tells the story of the development of Christian thinking and practice on war as a fall from an original commitment to nonviolence to a compromised stance of justifying bloodshed. According to Kimball, the "overwhelming evidence suggests that the followers of Jesus were pacifists for the first three centuries."[118] The ensuing story of Christian attitudes toward war is one of "how the religious ideal is easily compromised and antithetical behavior justified."[119] As the Just War doctrine developed, it served to support those in power and, says Kimball, it "also had no obvious connection with the Christian faith."[120] He quotes historian John Ferguson's conclusion that the Just War doctrine is "a replacement of the teaching of the New Testament by Greek philosophy or Roman law. There is nothing, literally nothing, distinctively Christian about the result."[121] According to Kimball, these justifications of violence came in handy during the Crusades, the era "when the behavior and example of many Christians was furthest removed from the teachings and example of Jesus."[122]

Given this narrative of the Just War tradition as a falling away from the original pacifism of Jesus and the early Christians, one would expect that Kimball—a self-identified Christian—would count himself a pacifist. He says otherwise in the same chapter:

> Perilous situations, at times, may indeed warrant the decisive use of force or focused military action. But such action must not be cloaked in religious language or justified by religion. There is no doubt, in my view, that the attacks of September 11 and the prospect of additional mass murder through terrorism required swift and decisive action. The immediate potential for catastrophe—from the loss of life to widespread suffering resulting from economic and political instability—was, and remains, a real and present danger. While there are legitimate bases for collective military action in the community of nations, an appeal to religion is not one of them.[123]

Though Kimball is not a pacifist, he is clearly trying to limit violence, not justify it. His criticism of the Just War tradition should be read in this light; the
Just War criteria have been used by Christians and others primarily as a way of
giving cover to acts of violence, not restraining violence. He wants to proscribe
religious justifications of violence because he believes that religion, with its
absolutist tendencies, is prone to fan the flames of violence.

The problem is that there remain, in Kimball's view, perfectly legitimate
nonreligious, or secular, ways of justifying violence. Far from a condemnation
of violence, Kimball's analysis results in a selective condemnation of *certain
kinds* of violence, those labeled religious. The problem is not violence as such;
there are still, sometimes, good reasons for bombing and shooting people.
To qualify as good, these reasons must be secular. Secular violence, however
regrettable, is sometimes necessary. Religious violence, on the other hand, is
always reprehensible.

There are two related—and, in Kimball's case, almost certainly unintended—dangers to this hierarchization of kinds of violence. The first is that
beliefs that are characterized as religious may be subordinated in the matter
of violence to beliefs that are secular, thereby weakening the possibility of
religious resistance to violence. The religious believer is admonished "You
have to learn to think for yourself!"[124] and to take a critical distance from religious beliefs because of their tendency to dogmatism and absolutism. Are
secular beliefs subject to such scrutiny? Is patriotism equally prone to absolutism? Kimball would probably want to say that religion is unwelcome in
the public square only when it is being used to justify violence, but if that is
the case, then it falls to secular reason to make the difficult decisions about
when violence is necessary and when it is not. It would be hard to escape the
conclusion that religious beliefs have no place in decisions about the use of
violence. It is possible, then, for a Christian to recognize the normative status
of pacifism in the Christian tradition, but nevertheless trust the judgment
of the putatively secular nation-state in matters of war. If, as Kimball suggests, "dangers abound when people take direction uncritically from religious
authorities,"[125] then it falls to secular authorities to decide when violence is
necessary. Christian beliefs are effectively privatized in deference to loyalty to
the nation-state, so that Christian resistance to the violence of the nation-state
is muted. So, for example, a majority of U.S. Christians supported the 2003
war in Iraq, despite the nearly unanimous condemnation of the war by the
leaders of the major Christian bodies.

The second danger in the hierarchization of types of violence is that there
is a pro-Western bias built into the analysis. Those who have not yet learned to
disassociate religion from the use of force are threats to the peace of the world

and must be dealt with as such. *Their* violence—being tainted by religion—is uncontrolled, absolutist, fanatical, irrational, and divisive. *Our* violence— being secular—is controlled, modest, rational, beneficial, peace making, and sometimes regrettably necessary to contain *their* violence. It is no secret who the primary "they" are today. We in the West are said to be threatened by a Muslim culture whose primary point of difference with ours is its stubborn refusal to tame religious passions in the public sphere. We in the West long ago learned the sobering lessons of religious warfare and have moved toward the secularization of the use of force. Now, we only seek to share our solution with the Muslim world.

Kimball is a scholar of Islam who has spent many years among Muslims and others in the Middle East trying to foster mutual understanding. Despite his sympathy for Muslim ways, however, he is clear that the Muslim world must change, and it must look more like the Western world:

> While many Muslims call for some type of Islamic state, others work
> toward other goals. Given our pluralist, interdependent world, some
> Muslims argue for secular democratic states as the best model for
> the future.... Muslims living in Western democratic countries have
> an especially important role to play in openly discussing and debat-
> ing viable, alternative social and political structures for the future.
> All of the above begs the question: Is it really possible to fashion an
> Islamic state in the twenty-first century? We will likely find out in
> the coming decade. Having spent a great deal of my professional life
> at the intersection of religion and politics in the Middle East, I have
> grave doubts. At some level, any state in which rights and status are
> tied to a particular religious tradition will relegate some of its citi-
> zens to second- and third-class status.[126]

The problem is not simply that Kimball has certain views about what is best for the Muslim world. The problem is that those views help to frame an argu- ment about religion and violence that is meant to pass as an objective, descrip- tive analysis of certain kinds of violent behavior. The framing of the argument is determined by a built-in bias toward condemning only certain kinds of vio- lence. The choice of which kinds of violence are condemnable is based on a deep bias toward the Western Enlightenment way of narrating the world. Violence on behalf of the Muslim *umma* is always reprehensible. Violence on behalf of the Western nation-state is sometimes necessary and often praiseworthy.

This bias is seen in the way that Kimball's warning signs favor a kind of procedural liberalism. According to this view, the problem is not just that var- ious religions hold certain beliefs that can lend themselves to violence. The problem is that religious people take their beliefs too absolutely. Their obedience to authorities is too uncritical or blind. This fanaticism leads to valuing ends over means and other excesses. The problem with religion is a problem of *degree*. In good liberal fashion, we cannot argue about the actual *content* of ultimate beliefs and values, because this is beyond the ken of reason. In liberalism, individuals have a right to believe anything they want, and we cannot adjudicate between true and false. We can merely ask that these beliefs not be taken too seriously in public. At the same time, there is no theoretical limit on the degree of one's obedience to the secular nation-state. Those who make the "ultimate sacrifice" for the flag, to the point of killing and dying for it, are not called "fanatics," but "patriots."

If there is a danger in Kimball's approach that scrutiny will be diverted from violence labeled secular, others are much more direct in using the myth of religious violence to endorse violence on behalf of secular ideals. One of the most egregious examples is Sam Harris's *The End of Faith: Religion, Terror, and the Future of Reason,* a *New York Times* bestseller. The theme of the book is the utter absurdity of religion, now and always. Religion is inherently irrational and in fact antirational. It is therefore also "the most prolific source of violence in our history,"[127] since religions hold to divergent and irreconcilable notions that are not testable by reason: "A glance at history, or at the pages of any newspaper, reveals that ideas which divide one group of human beings from another, only to unite them in slaughter, generally have their roots in religion."[128] Harris regards religion as a transhistorical and transcultural phenomenon, regrettably present in all times and places. He does not, however, provide a definition of religion. Christianity, Islam, Hinduism, Buddhism, Jainism, and the other world religions are clearly included, but Harris also briefly mentions Stalinism and Maoism as "political religions," both cultic and irrational, which adds to the indictment against religion.[129] He does not consider the possibility that Western political religions, such as American civil religion, might qualify as religion, for that would confound his neat dichotomy between liberal reason and religious irrationality.

In examining the causes of violence in the contemporary world, Harris makes clear that religious belief is at the heart of the matter, and not any other merely political or economic causes. Why does Osama bin Laden do what he does? Not because of any psychological malfunction or poverty or personal grievances against the West. He does it because he believes in the literal truth of the Koran: "Why did nineteen well-educated, middle-class men trade their lives in this world for the privilege of killing thousands of our neighbors? Because they believed they would go straight to paradise for doing so. It is rare to find the behavior of human beings so fully and satisfactorily explained. Why have we been reluctant to accept this explanation?"[130] We have been so reluctant, Harris explains, because we too have made concessions to religious faith, to the idea that beliefs can be justified with no evidence whatsoever.

The identification of religious belief as the heart of the problem allows Harris to avoid serious consideration of the causes of colonial and anticolonial violence. Muslim militants' demands for Palestinian statehood and for the withdrawal of U.S. troops from Saudi Arabia, Harris says, are "purely theological grievances" that have to do, respectively, with Muslim "anti-Semitism" and the protection of Muslim holy land from desecration.[131] Westerners try to find rational explanations for Muslim hatred of the West, because we naively assume that other human beings must be as rational as we are.[132] For example, "much of the world now blames Israel for the suicidal derangement of the Palestinians," because we assume that for people to behave that badly they must have good reasons.[133] But they don't have good reasons. No amount of economic and political improvements would alter the basic problem, which is the crazy ideas about God to which the Muslims cling.[134] Harris acknowledges that his approach to the problem of Muslim violence will frustrate many readers, since it ignores the Israeli occupation of the West Bank, it ignores the collusion of Western powers with Middle Eastern dictatorships, and it ignores endemic poverty in the Arab world:

> But I will argue that we can ignore all of these things—or treat them only to place them safely on the shelf—because the world is filled with poor, uneducated, and exploited peoples who do not commit acts of terrorism, indeed who would never commit terrorism of the sort that has become so commonplace among Muslims; and the Muslim world has no shortage of educated and prosperous men and women, suffering little more than their infatuation with Koranic eschatology, who are eager to murder infidels for God's sake. We are at war with Islam.[135]

Harris concedes that the United States and other Western nations have a history of imperialism and death dealing in the Third World. After giving a long list of such acts, Harris states, "Nothing I have written in this book should be construed as a denial of these facts, or as defense of state practices that are manifestly abhorrent."[136] Nevertheless, none of this history gets to the real root of the problem. With regard to the Muslim world especially, "[t]he problem seems to have been located everywhere except at the core of the Muslim faith—but faith is precisely what differentiates every Muslim from every infidel. Without faith,

most Muslim grievances against the West would be impossible even to formulate, much less avenge."[137] As with the term religion, the "core of the Muslim
faith" is an unchanging, ahistorical essence. Actual historical circumstances
are only vehicles for the perennial craziness of Muslim beliefs. Once we have
located such a wellspring of violence, mere details like the Israeli occupation
and settlement of the West Bank; the U.S. occupation of Iraq; U.S. support for
Saddam, the Shah, Hosni Mubarak, and the Saudi royal family; or Abu Ghraib,
Halliburton, and "extraordinary rendition" can all be ignored or placed "safely
on the shelf."

Harris singles out Islam and Muslims for his harshest treatment—"There
are other ideologies with which to expunge the last vapors of reasonableness
from a society's discourse, but Islam is undoubtedly one of the best we've
got"[138]—but not because he believes that Christian beliefs, for example, are any
less ridiculous. Many Christians in the West, however, have learned to ignore
most of their canon and render religion politically innocuous.[139] Muslim societies are at a much less evolved stage of moral development.[140] Secular liberalism, not Christianity, is to be credited with defanging religion in the West,
and secular liberalism is the solution for the Muslim world as well. Harris's
version of liberalism, however, does not consider religious toleration to be a
virtue. Harris makes clear that his target is not only religious extremists, but
religious moderates as well:

> One of the central themes of this book, however, is that religious
> moderates are themselves the bearers of a terrible dogma: they
> imagine that the path to peace will be paved once each of us has
> learned to respect the unjustified beliefs of others. I hope to show
> that the very ideal of religious tolerance—born of the notion that
> every human being should be free to believe whatever he wants
> about God—is one of the principal forces driving us toward the
> abyss.[141]

To rescue the people of the Middle East, whom he likens to brainwashed
hostages,[142] Harris believes we cannot be content to encourage the adoption
of religious freedom in Muslim societies. Islam is not compatible with civil
society;[143] "Islam and Western liberalism remain irreconcilable."[144] Islam
must either be radically transformed or abandoned: "Unless Muslims can
reshape their religion into an ideology that is basically benign—or outgrow it
altogether—it is difficult to see how Islam and the West can avoid falling into
a continual state of war, and on innumerable fronts."[145]

To avert the danger of war caused by religion, religious actors must be
changed. How is this possible? Harris makes clear that it cannot happen

through rational dialogue, since religious beliefs render believers immune to reason. Our only recourse is to violence:

> Some propositions are so dangerous that it may even be ethical to kill people for believing them. This may seem an extraordinary claim, but it merely enunciates an ordinary fact about the world in which we live. Certain beliefs place their adherents beyond the reach of every peaceful means of persuasion, while inspiring them to commit acts of extraordinary violence against others. There is, in fact, no talking to some people. If they cannot be captured, and they often cannot, otherwise tolerant people may be justified in killing them in self-defense. This is what the United States attempted in Afghanistan, and it is what we and other Western powers are bound to attempt, at an even greater cost to ourselves and innocents abroad, elsewhere in the Muslim world. We will continue to spill blood in what is, at bottom, a war of ideas.[146]

Harris's logic is impeccable: if religious people hold irrational beliefs so fervently that they will do violence for them, then there is no use trying to reason with them. They can only be dealt with by force. The myth of religious violence thus becomes a justification for the use of violence. We will have peace once we have bombed the Muslims into being reasonable.

Harris writes, "In our dialogue with the Muslim world, we are confronted by people who hold beliefs for which there is no rational justification and which therefore cannot even be discussed, and yet these are the very beliefs that underlie many of the demands they are likely to make upon us."[147] This is especially a problem if such people gain access to nuclear weapons:

> There is little possibility of our having a *cold* war with an Islamist regime armed with long-range nuclear weapons.... In such a situation, the only thing likely to ensure our survival may be a nuclear first strike of our own. Needless to say, this would be an unthinkable crime—as it would kill tens of millions of innocent civilians in a single day—but it may be the only course of action available to us, given what Islamists believe.[148]

Muslims then would likely misinterpret this act of "self-defense" as a genocidal crusade, thus plunging the whole world into nuclear holocaust: "All of this is perfectly insane, of course: I have just described a plausible scenario in which much of the world's population could be annihilated on account of religious ideas that belong on the same shelf with Batman, the philosopher's stone, and unicorns."[149] The absurdity of so many of us dying "for the sake of myth" does not mean it won't happen, however. It is increasingly likely, according to Harris. But he is clear that, if we have to slaughter millions through a nuclear first strike, it will be the fault of the Muslims and their crazy religious beliefs.

Before we get to that point, Harris contends, we must encourage civil society in Islamic countries, but we cannot trust them to vote it in. If we allow them the freedom to vote, they will vote to enslave themselves to sharia. We have had to support corrupt and oppressive regimes in the Muslim world to try to keep a lid on their irrationality: "This is a terrible truth that we have to face: the only thing that currently stands between us and the roiling ocean of Muslim unreason is a wall of tyranny and human rights abuses that we have helped to erect. This situation must be remedied, but we cannot merely force Muslim dictators from power and open the polls."[150] The remedy is as follows:

> It seems all but certain that some form of benign dictatorship will generally be necessary to bridge the gap. But benignity is the key— and if it cannot emerge from within a state, it must be imposed from without. The means of such imposition are necessarily crude: they amount to economic isolation, military intervention (whether open or covert), or some combination of both. While this may seem an exceedingly arrogant doctrine to espouse, it appears we have no alternatives.[151]

This type of double standard with regard to violence runs throughout Harris's book. He condemns the irrational religious torture of witches,[152] but provides his own argument for torturing terrorists.[153] He rejects the idea that our violence is equivalent to their violence: "Any honest witness to current events will realize that there is no moral equivalence between the kind of force civilized democracies project in the world, warts and all, and the internecine violence that is perpetrated by Muslim militants, or indeed by Muslim governments."[154] What allows Harris to maintain this double standard is the distinction between religious violence and secular violence. Violence labeled religious is always irrational, peculiarly virulent, and reprehensible. Violence labeled secular, on the other hand, no matter how regrettable, is often necessary and sometimes even praiseworthy for the job it does defending us from religious violence.

The blunt crudity of Harris's book should not lead us to assume that his is a voice from the fringe. Indeed, Harris might be correct when he says that he is merely enunciating ordinary facts about the world in which we live, at least as those "facts" are constructed by dominant secularist myths. *The End of Faith* won the 2005 PEN award for nonfiction. The book's appearance on the

New York Times bestseller list was replicated by Harris's second book, *Letter to a Christian Nation. The End of Faith* is not only popular with a general audience, but has been enthusiastically endorsed by such academic superstars as Alan Dershowitz (Harvard), Peter Singer (Princeton), and Richard Dawkins (Oxford).[155] That the same Peter Singer who believes it is unjustifiable to kill nonrational animals for food[156] would endorse Harris's treatment of putatively nonrational Muslims is a testament to the power of the myth of religious violence.

Christopher Hitchens provides another prominent example of using the myth of religious violence to provide a secularist justification for violence against religious actors. Hitchens is an author and ubiquitous commentator who has made a dramatic public shift from leftist to conservative politics. He broke with the Left in order to support the invasion of Iraq in 2003. He believes that his fellow secularists on the Left should overcome their opposition to war and recognize the dire threat to secularism that Islamist politics represents. Although the regime of Saddam Hussein that was overthrown in 2003 is generally considered to be secular, Hitchens argues that it was religious and deserved, therefore, to be vanquished.

Hitchens makes his arguments about religion at greatest length in his bestselling book *God Is Not Great,* which is subtitled—with typical British understatement—*How Religion Poisons Everything.* A chapter entitled "Religion Kills" makes the standard argument with examples from around the globe of religious violence: "Violent, irrational, intolerant, allied to racism and tribalism and bigotry, invested in ignorance and hostile to free inquiry, contemptuous of women and coercive toward children: organized religion ought to have a great deal on its conscience."[157] Exactly what qualifies as religion is not entirely clear, however, as the example of Saddam Hussein's Baathist regime shows. Though the Baath Party was a secularist party with socialist leanings, founded by a Christian and open to people of all religions, and although Saddam Hussein had marginalized the public power of Muslim clerics throughout his regime, Hitchens claims that those who regard his regime as secular are deluded because Saddam tried to appropriate some Islamic symbols and claim the mantle of defender of Islam against Western invaders.

The line between religious and secular is even more blurred in Hitchens's chapter on totalitarianism. In this chapter, Hitchens attempts to answer the objection that secular regimes such as those of Stalin and Hitler can be just as brutal or worse than religious regimes. Hitchens responds by denying that such regimes are secular. According to Hitchens, they are religious precisely because they are totalitarian. At the heart of totalitarianism is the demand that one relinquish control of one's life entirely to the state or supreme leader.

And for most of human history, says Hitchens, "the idea of the total or absolute state was intimately bound up with religion."[158] This is true across history in all places; Hitchens lists China, India, Persia, the Aztecs and Incas,
and the medieval courts of Spain, Russia, and France. Religion is once again
a transhistorical and transcultural phenomenon, always and everywhere
essentially the same and essentially distinct from politics, which nevertheless tries to work its poison into political realities. Hitchens contends that
"the object of perfecting the species—which is the very root and source of
the totalitarian impulse—is in essence a religious one."[159] Secular totalitarian regimes are therefore religious, because they have simply taken religion
and transmuted it into a different form. Even when—like Stalin's regime—
they claim to be atheist and actively work to extirpate religion from society,
root and branch, totalitarian regimes thereby show themselves to be truly
religious: "All that the totalitarians have demonstrated is that the religious
impulse—the need to worship—can take even more monstrous forms if it
is repressed."[160]

Hitchens thus seems to employ a functionalist conception of religion, but
he does not do so consistently. For most of his book, what Hitchens means
by religion seems to be limited to some substantivist list of world religions:
Christianity, Islam, Judaism, Hinduism, Buddhism, and Confucianism all
come in for criticism and dismissal. When it helps to make his case against
religion, however, things like Kim Jong-il's militantly atheist regime in North
Korea count as religion too.[161] But Hitchens refuses to employ a functionalist view of religion when it comes to ideologies and institutions of which he
approves. There is no recognition that secular nationalism, with its rites and
sacrifices, can be religious too. Such a recognition would threaten Hitchens's
absolute distinction between religion and the secular. But the distinction
is based on little more than the distinction between those things of which
Hitchens approves and those of which he does not. Religion poisons everything because Hitchens identifies everything poisonous as religion. Likewise,
everything good ends up on the other side of the religious-secular divide. For
example, Hitchens writes of Martin Luther King, Jr., "In no real as opposed
to nominal sense, then, was he a Christian."[162] Hitchens bases this remarkable conclusion on the fact that King was nonviolent and preached forgiveness
and love of enemies, as opposed to the Bible, which in both the Old and New
Testaments is marked by a vengeful God.[163] Here, what is not violent cannot
possibly be religious, because religion is *defined* as violent.

And yet, despite his attempt to recruit Martin Luther King, Jr. to his
side, and despite his apparent desire to claim the mantle of nonviolence and

forgiveness for the secular, Hitchens has some very approving things to say about killing people:

> And I say to the Christians while I'm at it, "Go love your own ene-
> mies; by the way, don't be loving mine." ... I think the enemies of civ-
> ilization should be beaten and killed and defeated, and I don't make
> any apology for it. And I think it's sickly and stupid and suicidal to
> say that we should love those who hate us and try to kill us and our
> children and burn our libraries and destroy our society. I have no
> patience with this nonsense.[164]

So much for Martin Luther King. Hitchens has been very vocal in his support for the wars in Afghanistan and Iraq.[165] He sees them as part of a larger war against Islamic radicals, and he faces that war with a certain relish:

> We can't live on the same planet as them, and I'm glad because
> I don't want to. I don't want to breathe the same air as these psycho-
> paths and murders [sic] and rapists and torturers and child abusers.
> It's them or me. I'm very happy about this because I know it will be
> them. It's a duty and a responsibility to defeat them. But it's also a
> pleasure. I don't regard it as a grim task at all.[166]

Likewise: "Cluster bombs are perhaps not good in themselves, but when they are dropped on identifiable concentrations of Taliban troops, they do have a heartening effect."[167] The fact that "religion kills" cannot alone be an indict-ment against religion, then, because killing in and of itself is not necessarily a bad thing. The problem with religion is that it kills for the wrong reasons. Killing for the right reasons can be not only justifiable but pleasing.

The right reasons to kill are those reasons labeled secular. In "Bush's Secularist Triumph," Hitchens applauds what George W. Bush has done for secularism in invading Iraq.[168] Hitchens reminds us, "Secularism is not just a smug attitude. It is a possible way of democratic and pluralistic life that only became thinkable after several wars and revolutions had ruthlessly smashed the hold of the clergy on the state."[169] The same ruthlessness must be employed now in defense of secularism, the defense of which Hitchens contends is now "a matter of survival."[170] The game is zero-sum: "It is not possible for me to say, Well, you pursue your Shiite dream of a hidden imam and I pursue my study of Thomas Paine and George Orwell, and the world is big enough for both of us. The true believer cannot rest until the whole world bows the knee."[171] The true believer Hitchens has in mind is, of course, the Islamist. But Hitchens's message is that the true believer in secularism can also not rest until the whole world has been made safe for secularism. The United States in particular has a mission to spread the good news of secularism to the whole world, and Americans must not shy away from using military means to accomplish that mission. Thus, again, is the myth of religious violence employed not to resist violence, but to justify it, and indeed to celebrate it, so long as such violence is secular.

Using the myth of religious violence to support war is not limited to the right wing of the political spectrum. An example from the left is Paul Berman, a professor of journalism at New York University and a contributing editor to the *New Republic*. Berman's *Terror and Liberalism,* which also made the *New York Times* bestseller list, is an attempt by someone who describes himself as "pro-war and left-wing"[172] to justify the wars in Afghanistan and Iraq on liberal grounds. According to Berman, the secret to liberalism's success is discovering how finally to sequester religious passions. He tells a version of the tale of the wars of religion:

> The whole purpose of liberalism was to put religion in one corner,
> and the state in a different corner, and to keep those corners apart.
> The liberal idea arose in the seventeenth century in England and
> Scotland, and the philosophers who invented it wanted to prevent
> the English Civil War, which had just taken place, from breaking out
> again. So they proposed to scoop up the cause of that war, which was
> religion, and, in the gentlest way, to cart it off to another place, which
> was the sphere of private life, where every church and sect could
> freely rail at each of the others.[173]

During the nineteenth century, liberalism seemed to be driving the West ever forward; "during those hundred years, the Western countries seemed to have discovered the secret of human advancement."[174] What was the basis of that secret? "It was the recognition that all of life is not governed by a single, all-knowing and all-powerful authority—by a divine force."[175] It was the belief that each sphere of life could operate independently of the others.

Unfortunately, the twentieth century saw the resurgence of irrationality in the form of totalitarian systems that demanded that all spheres of life be brought into submission to the totality. Totalitarianism, according to Berman, is a variation on the central religious myth, the ur-myth of Western civilization, which comes from the Bible: there is a people of God, under attack from sinister forces, but the coming society will be purified by a violent act of God and unified under the one God.[176] Thus does Berman include antiliberal political movements, even those that are expressly atheistic, under the rubric of religion. On similar grounds, Berman includes the secular socialist Baath movement under religion. According to Berman, Baath socialism also told a version of the same religious ur-myth, with the Arab nation taking the place of the people of God.[177] "The Baathi and the Islamists were two branches of a single impulse, which was Muslim totalitarianism—the Muslim variation on the European idea."[178]

Communism and fascism serve Berman primarily as object lessons in how various liberal appeasers underestimated their threats. Now that Islamism has become the latest in this line of totalitarianisms, Berman's book is primarily directed against those liberals who would again underestimate the threat or try to explain it away by pointing to certain sociological facts or the history of Western imperialism. Berman is adamant in contending that no such explanation is possible. In a chapter entitled "Wishful Thinking," Berman excoriates liberals whose own rationality leads them to assume that others are rational too. Because of liberals' rationality, they assume, for example, that Palestinians must have some legitimate reasons for using violence against the Israeli occupation. Indeed, says Berman, the more extreme the violence—including especially suicide bombings—the more liberals assume that the Palestinians have been pushed to such desperation by the extremity of Israel's oppression of them. But Berman assures us that the only explanation for Palestinian behavior is "mass pathology,"[179] based on some crazy theological ideas. There was no logic to the Palestinian turn to suicide attacks. They certainly could not hope to gain concessions from the Israelis, for the attacks only hardened Israel's hard line. Israelis turned to Ariel Sharon, who "had never believed in negotiating, anyway."[180] Sharon cracked down, and even innocent bystanders were killed: "Still, this policy of his conformed to an obvious logic of military reasoning. A conventional logic: to smother violence under a blanket of greater violence."[181] This is logic we can understand: "But what was the logic of the suicide attacks?"[182] They obeyed no logic and had no prospect for success: "Suicide terror against the Israelis was bound to succeed in one realm only, and this was the realm of death—the realm in which a perfect Palestinian state could luxuriate in the shade of a perfect Koranic tranquility, cleansed of every iniquitous thought and temptation and of every rival faith and ethnic group."[183] But liberals, with their naive faith in human nature, persisted in thinking that Palestinian suicide attacks must be "a rational response to real-life conditions."[184]

For Berman, the Israeli logic of crushing the Palestinians under a "blanket of greater violence" is perfectly rational, if perhaps regrettable, while the futility of the Palestinian attacks against a superior force is evidence of madness. Berman is right to refuse any justifications for attacks on civilians. But he goes further to insist that any explanations are also impossible. This move guarantees that the blanket of greater violence imposed by the Israeli occupation is always seen as a response to—and never an aggravating factor in—the futility and madness of Palestinian violence. Berman rules out a priori any serious consideration of the actual root causes and history of the Israeli-Palestinian conflict by declaring one side to be mad before any empirical work is done.

In looking for the causes of radical Islamism, Berman goes no further than to read the works of Sayyid Qutb, one of the chief intellectual influences on radical Islam. Berman's detailed reading of Qutb, which spans two chapters of Berman's book, is apparently all that is needed to understand Islamism. Qutb's big idea is the antiliberal one that there should be no split between sacred and secular; all of life should be brought into unity under God. Here is the key to understanding the current clash; they reject liberalism's big idea of keeping religion and the secular separate. The war of Islamism versus the West is a war of ideas. This is evident in Berman's narration of the wars in Afghanistan and Iraq, in which he refers to "Islamists and Baathi" together, as if they were simply on the same side, the "totalitarian" side:

> Their ideology was mad. In wars between liberalism and totalitarianism, the totalitarian picture of war is always mad. (Or, to be more precise, the totalitarian picture rests on a mad platform—even if the totalitarian side in a war may also invoke some of the more conventional causes and aims of war.) The Nazis pictured the Second World War as a biological battle between the superior race (them) and the mongrel and inferior races (us).... Islamism's medieval image of jihadi warriors waving scimitars at the Zionist-Crusader conspiracy was no less fanciful, and no less demented. The reality of the Terror War, then—the real-life vista that first became evident in those early days of the Afghan War—was neither policelike, nor civilizational, nor cosmic. It was an event in the twentieth-century mode. It was the clash of ideologies. It was the war between liberalism and the apocalyptic and phantasmagorical movements that have risen up against liberal civilization ever since the calamities of the First World War.[185]

Although Berman grants parenthetically that totalitarians may invoke some conventional causes and aims of war, such conventional reasons are clearly mere adjuncts to the clash of ideologies. Any attempt to read the rise of Islamism against the complicated history of colonialism, the importance of oil, the variety of Muslim responses to the Cold War, or the role of the United States in the Middle East is of secondary importance at best and dangerous liberal naïveté at worst.

Concentrating on the war of ideas allows Berman to marginalize critiques of imperialism and other material causes, but it also allows him to say that the "terror war" will be fought primarily without weapons. The terror war, he says, will be fought principally on the level of philosophies and theories, and its media will be books, magazines, lectures, and conferences.[186] He lays out a vision of a "liberal war of liberation, partly military but ultimately intellectual, a war of ideas, fought around the world."[187] If the opposition is mad, however, and subject to inexplicable bouts of mass pathology, it is hard to see how such a war could be fought through rational persuasion. Sam Harris has drawn out the logical conclusion of Berman's book, which Harris cites. If people's behavior has no rational basis, one cannot hope to reason with them. One can only deal with them by force. Although Berman would prefer to fight with books, he puts his justifications of the Gulf War, the war in Afghanistan, and the Iraq War[188] in the context of a wider argument about the need for liberalism to flex its military might. Berman considers Lincoln's Gettysburg Address in this light. Lincoln spoke about death without glorifying it as a totalitarian would. But nevertheless Lincoln "spoke about death as 'the last full measure of devotion,' which the Union soldiers had given. . . . 'From these honored dead we take increased devotion,' he said. He was explaining that a liberal society must be, when challenged, a warlike society; or it will not endure."[189] Berman continues on to say that a liberal society is different from other societies because it shuns absolutes, "but liberalism does not shun every absolute."[190] The absolute that it does not shun but requires is the "absolute commitment to solidarity and self-government,"[191] even unto death. In chapter 1, we saw how absolutism is said to be one of the principal reasons that religion has a tendency toward violence. For Berman, the absolutism of liberalism does not make liberalism a religion, however, because it is absolutism in defense of the shunning of absolutes. But the division of the world between us and them is as sharp in Berman's vision as in the totalitarian picture of the world. And those killed in the "liberal war of liberation" are not any less dead.

Berman and others who make this sort of argument are simply articulating a strand of thinking that has been prominent in U.S. foreign policy for at least a century. Berman's liberal war of liberation is just one expression of a foreign policy that is commonly labeled "Wilsonian," since President Woodrow Wilson made its terms explicit. Wilson was convinced that the future peace and prosperity of the world depended on the extension of liberal principles of government—along with open markets—to the entire world. The liberal tradition on which Wilson drew assumes that liberal democratic governments are inherently more peaceable than other types of government, in part because the former have learned to separate religion from politics. Liberal democracy and free markets also reinforce each other and lead to peaceful relations among countries that are based on trade rather than war. This does not mean, however, that liberals need be reluctant to use military power to further the spread of liberal ideals. In the American tradition which Wilson articulated, it was assumed that the United States—and in particular U.S. military might—had a special mission of bringing liberal ideals to the rest of the world.[192] This is a remarkably ambitious project. As John Lukács remarked, "If we judge events by their consequences, the great world revolutionary was Wilson rather than Lenin."[193]

Liberal ideas have by no means been the only influence on U.S. foreign policy, but they have been the dominant one.[194] Classical liberals have often been opposed by "realists," who view foreign policy through the lens of more narrowly defined balances of power. Liberals themselves—though agreeing on the spread of liberal ideals—are divided between what Colin Dueck calls "crusaders" and "exemplarists," that is, those who tend to favor international intervention, on the one hand, and those who are more reluctant to intervene and prefer to lead by example, on the other. When military intervention occurs, however, unless it is a matter of obvious self-defense, Americans tend to favor military action, as Dueck says, "either for liberal reasons, or not at all."[195] Although military intervention may be pursued for material self-interest—oil, especially—or for other more narrowly defined strategic goals, Americans prefer to justify military intervention in terms of idealistic, Wilsonian goals. Wilsonian rhetoric is not an independent variable or cause of U.S. military intervention, but is rather a "permissive cause," or filter, as Dueck says: "Classical liberal assumptions have a kind of filtering effect upon the process by which foreign policy officials within the United States formulate national goals and perceive international conditions."[196] Whether the United States *really* invaded Iraq to guarantee access to oil or to make the world more free is probably an insoluble question. What is clear, however, is that the latter type of rhetoric is crucial both in formulating policy and in securing assent to those policies.

Liberals, including those in Europe, often prefer to see the fact that Americans go to church as the cause of American violence abroad; the United States is a religious country and therefore violent. It is true, of course, that there are significant Christian justifications for U.S. interventions abroad. There are, for example, streams of Christian Zionism within American evangelicalism that use dispensationalist biblical interpretation to support U.S. backing of Israel and the Iraq War. Such groups within the churches render significant support for U.S. foreign adventures; Christian churches are often deeply implicated in supporting America's war efforts. Such support, however, has had a negligible effect on the formation of U.S. foreign policy. As Dueck points out, the United States goes to war for liberal reasons, for freedom and democracy and free markets; it does not go to war for Christian reasons. For most of the past century, Christian theological arguments have had minimal influence on the actual making and marketing of U.S. foreign policy. No U.S. president, no matter how personally devout, would argue for war based on explicitly Christian principles. Even within the George W. Bush administration, foreign policy has been directed by neoconservatives based on Wilsonian principles. The architects of the Iraq War were not evangelical Christians, but men such as Paul Wolfowitz, Dick Cheney, Richard Perle, and Donald Rumsfeld.[197]

Despite the frequency with which the Bush Doctrine is seen as a radical departure from traditional U.S. foreign policy—especially for its apparent expansion of the idea of preemptive war—many scholars emphasize the continuity between the foreign policy of George W. Bush and the Wilsonian tradition.[198] Bush has tended to stress that the Iraq War is a war of liberation, especially as other justifications for the war, such as weapons of mass destruction, became less plausible.[199] For example, Bush cited Woodrow Wilson's Fourteen Points in defending the Iraq War before the National Endowment for Democracy on November 6, 2003. The speech is saturated with Wilsonian language: "Every nation has learned, or should have learned, an important lesson: Freedom is worth fighting for, dying for, and standing for—and the advance of freedom leads to peace."[200] The liberal war of liberation is no less clear in Bush's "National Security Strategy," published in September 2002. There, we are told that the great twentieth-century struggle between liberty and totalitarianism has been won, and a "single sustainable model" has emerged: freedom, democracy, and free enterprise.[201] "These values of freedom are right and true for every person, in every society—and the duty of protecting these values against their enemies is the common calling of freedom-loving people across the globe and across the ages."[202] Preemptive war is one of the tools we need in such a struggle, for "we recognize that our best defense is a good offense."[203]

Conclusion

Despite the incoherence of attempts to identify a transhistorical and transcultural essence of religion, separate from politics, with a peculiar tendency to promote violence that is absent from secular realities, the myth of religious violence has proven to be an extraordinarily pervasive story in Western culture. The reason it is so prevalent is that it is so useful. For its many avid consumers in the West, the myth of religious violence serves on the domestic scene to marginalize discourses and practices labeled religious, especially those associated with Christian churches and, particularly in Europe, with Muslim groups. The myth helps to reinforce adherence to a secular social order and the nation-state that guarantees it. In foreign affairs, the myth of religious violence contributes to the presentation of non-Western and nonsecular social orders as inherently irrational and prone to violence. In doing so, it helps to create a blind spot in Western thinking about Westerners' own complicity with violence; the history of our interactions with the non-Western world need not be investigated too closely, for the true roots of "rage" against the West are the violent impulses in religion that nonsecularist actors have failed to tame. The myth of religious violence is also useful, therefore, for justifying secular violence against religious actors; their irrational violence must be met with rational violence. We must share the blessings of secularism with them. If they are not sufficiently rational to be open to persuasion, we must regrettably bomb them into the higher rationality.

The myth of religious violence should finally be seen for what it is: an important part of the folklore of Western societies. It does not identify any facts about the world, but rather authorizes certain arrangements of power in the modern West. It is a story of salvation from mortal peril by the creation of the secular nation-state. As such, it legitimates the direction of the citizen's ultimate loyalty to the nation-state and secures the nation-state's monopoly on legitimate violence. In the United States, it helps to foster the idea that secular social orders are inherently peaceful, such that we become convinced that the nation that spends more on its military than do all the other nations of the world combined is in fact the world's most peaceloving country. The myth also helps to identify Others and enemies, both internal and external, who threaten the social order and who provide the requisite villains against which the nation-state is said to protect us.

The myth of religious violence is false, and it has had a significant negative influence. The myth should be retired from respectable discourse. To do so would offer some important benefits.

First, it would free the valuable empirical work on violence done by Mark Juergensmeyer, Scott Appleby, and other scholars, such as those cited in chapter 1, from being hobbled by the religious-secular distinction. Rather than attempt to come up with reasons that a universal and timeless feature of human society called religion has a peculiar tendency to promote violence, the question for researchers would be, "Under what circumstances do ideologies and practices of all kinds promote violence?" Empirical investigations into violent uses of nationalism, the sacrificial atonement of Christ, the invisible hand of the market, jihad, Marxist utopias, and the view of the United States as worldwide liberator would not be hampered by an a priori division of such ideologies and practices into religious and secular. The illusory search for religion as if it were a constant in human society across all times and places would be dropped in favor of a more resolutely historical approach. Investigation into the link between religion and violence would then become investigation into the ways in which the twin terms religious and secular have been used to authorize different practices of power in the modern world. Included would be investigating how the construction of certain practices as religious has authorized certain kinds of violence labeled secular.

Second, abandoning the myth of religious violence would also help us to see that Western-style secularism is a contingent and local set of social arrangements and not the universal solution to the universal problem of religion. The range of options available to any given society, including our own, is not exhausted by a choice between theocracy on the one hand and militant secularism on the other. Abandoning the myth would mean that decisions in the United States, France, and other Western countries about the participation of churches, mosques, and other groups and individuals in civic life could be approached with more pragmatism than paranoia. With regard to Muslim countries, Western governments could adopt a more open approach to Muslim experiments with government that do not enforce a strict separation of mosque and state.

Third, more generally, eliminating the myth of religious violence would rid the West of one significant obstacle to understanding the non-Western, especially Muslim, world. Stereotypical images of "religious fanatics" wired for violence by their deepest beliefs have helped to poison Western dealings with the Muslim world. To eliminate the myth would help to open Western eyes to the complexity and crosscurrents within the Muslim world. Muslim cultures are not simply predetermined by some ahistorical religious depth. Different theopolitical identities are constantly being created and negotiated in ways for which essentialized accounts of religion cannot account.

Fourth, doing away with the myth of religious violence would help to eliminate one of the justifications for military action against religious actors. If the unreasonableness of an opponent were not determined a priori, the resort to violence might be forestalled long enough to permit a more peaceable outcome.

Fifth and finally, abandoning the myth of religious violence would help to rid citizens of the United States of one of the principal obstacles to having any serious public dialogue over the causes of opposition to U.S. policies abroad. President George W. Bush raised the question "Why do they hate us?" after the September 11 attacks, only to answer it with "They hate our freedoms."[204] As we have seen, the myth of religious violence allows its users to ignore or dismiss American actions as a significant cause of hatred of the United States because the true cause is located in the inherent irrationality, absolutism, and violent tendencies of religious actors. They are so essentially evil that our very goodness—our freedoms—is what they hate about us. This kind of self-serving nonsense generally passes in the United States for informed and sober analysis of global reality in the post-9/11 world. There might be insane people out there who hate freedom, but the well of resentment from which anti-American militancy draws is much deeper and broader than such insanity, and the solution to it is unlikely to be military. If there is ever going to be an end to terrorism, we will need to begin to understand its roots in the much larger context of anti-American sentiment. And understanding that context will require a hard look at U.S. foreign policies and their effects over the course of the twentieth century, not as the sole cause of anti-American sentiment, but as a significant factor that cannot be ignored or safely shelved, as Sam Harris and many others would prefer.

While justifying or excusing American misdeeds is not uncommon—the direct and intentional incineration of hundreds of thousands of civilians at Dresden and Hiroshima is justified on the basis of some utilitarian calculation, for example, or U.S. support for terrorism in Africa in the 1970s and 1980s is excused as a byproduct of the Cold War—the most common response to American misdeeds abroad is to overlook them, either by simple amnesia or by distraction of the kind detailed above. Even if past deeds are not simply forgotten, their importance is downplayed as we search for deeper causes, such as religious beliefs. A realistic approach to the causes of anti-American resentment in the Muslim world would need to take a hard look at U.S. dealings with that world: the Iranian coup in 1953 and subsequent support for the Shah; support for Saddam Hussein in the 1970s and 1980s; virtual carte blanche for forty years of Israeli occupation and settlement of Palestinian land; sanctions in the 1990s that UNICEF estimated killed 500,000 Iraqi children, a price U.S. ambassador to the United Nations Madeleine Albright declared "worth it";[205] support for corrupt and dictatorial regimes in Egypt, Saudi Arabia, Pakistan, and Indonesia; the invasion and occupation of Afghanistan and Iraq; postwar profiteering in Iraq; the torturing of prisoners at Abu Ghraib and by "extraordinary rendition" to friendly regimes—these facts and more need close examination.

To refuse to ignore these facts is not thereby to find in them the sole explanation for opposition to the United States, much less to excuse terrorism. The problems of Muslim-majority societies cannot all be blamed on others. Painting the Islamic world as a passive victim of Western aggression would be just as unhelpful as ignoring the history of Muslim-Western interactions. There are clearly unhealthy dynamics within Muslim societies that also must be examined. Islam serves as a rallying point for not only anti-imperialist projects but imperialist projects as well. Muslim theologies are clearly relevant to the overall picture of Muslim militancy, and theologies are not immune to critique. But theologies do not exist unalloyed before they are mixed with politics. There is no "religion" that harbors an unchanging impulse toward absolutism; to blame violence on religion as such makes it difficult or impossible to distinguish good theology from bad theology, or peaceable forms of Islam from malignant forms.

Religious beliefs do not lurk essentially unchanged underneath historical circumstances, waiting to unleash their destructive power on history. And yet much Western commentary on contemporary Muslim militancy sees it as the intrusion of deep, archaic religious impulses into the modern world. As Mahmood Mamdani points out, such a reading fails to see what modern Muslim militancy is. It is the result of a distinctly modern encounter with colonial power. Afghanistan became the crucible of Muslim militancy first as the result of resistance to Soviet occupation. Furthermore, that resistance was largely orchestrated by the United States. The creation and support of the *mujahideen* was the largest covert operation in CIA history, far outstripping support for the Nicaraguan Contras. The United States did not merely fund the *mujahideen,* but played a key role in training them both tactically and ideologically. The launching of a jihad against the Soviet Union was a key part of U.S. strategy under CIA chief William Casey. He hoped to unite a billion Muslims against the Soviet Union and Marxism worldwide by borrowing from Islamic theology. The key tradition was jihad, which as Mamdani points out had been largely dormant in the preceding 400 years. The tradition of jihad was revived with significant U.S. help in the 1980s. Operating through the Pakistani intelligence services, the United States also recruited Osama bin Laden. None of this history is of much interest in American public discourse. Americans prefer to talk about Muslim militancy as a religious revival from a bygone era. But, as Mamdani remarks:

> [E]ven if it evokes pre-modernity in its particular language and specific practices, the Taliban is the result of an encounter of a premodern people with modern imperial power. Given to a highly decentralized and localized mode of life, the Afghani people have been subjected to two highly centralized state projects in the past few decades: first, Soviet-supported Marxism, then, CIA-supported Islamization.[206]

Jihad was subsequently exported to other parts of the Islamic world. The point is not that Islamization is a creation of the CIA. The point is rather that there is no pristine religion called Islam that can be separated from Muslim encounters with Western power. Understanding the theopolitical project of Muslim radicals is not a matter of understanding the timeless essence of religion, but rather requires analysis of how different theologies have been formed in encounters with modern forms of power. As Mamdani says, "Contemporary 'fundamentalism' is a modern political project, not a traditional cultural leftover."[207]

I am certainly not arguing that Muslim radicalism is really political and not really religious. As I have argued at length throughout this book, especially in chapter 2, there is no coherent way to separate a universal essence of religion from that of politics. To attempt to do so in this case would severely distort the nature of Muslim radicalism by imposing an alien theoretical framework on it. Muslim radicalism is best understood as a theopolitical project, which means that any attempt to isolate religion from the political and social contexts of Muslim radicalism will fail to grasp the full reality of Muslim anti-Western sentiment.

This book has been an attempt to help us in the West see into a significant blind spot that we have created for ourselves. In constructing artificial distinctions between religious and secular violence, types of violence and exclusion labeled secular have escaped full moral scrutiny. In doing away with the myth of religious violence, we are not, of course, thereby licensed to create new blind spots, to ignore or excuse antisecular violence as justifiable. We must restore the full and complete picture of violence in our world, to level the playing field so that violence of all kinds is subject to the same scrutiny. This does not mean that all violence is therefore morally equivalent. To level the playing field is not to declare that the contest will result in a tie before it has even begun. It is rather to agree to call fouls committed by any and all participants and to penalize them equally. Understanding and defusing violence in our world requires clear moral vision, of not only the faults of others but our own.

Violence feeds on the need for enemies, the need to separate *us* from *them*. Such binary ways of dividing the world make the world understandable for us, but they also make the world unlivable for many. Doing away with the myth of religious violence is one way of resisting such binaries and, perhaps, turning some enemies into friends.

Notes

INTRODUCTION

1. "The specific political distinction to which political actions and motives can be reduced is that between friend and enemy"; Carl Schmitt, *The Concept of the Political* (New Brunswick, NJ: Rutgers University Press, 1976), 26.

2. One such book is Keith Ward's *Is Religion Dangerous?* (Grand Rapids, MI: Eerdmans, 2007). The introduction to the book, entitled "What Is Religion?" takes on the question of definition and shows how fraught it is. Ward takes one common definition of religion from the *Shorter Oxford English Dictionary* and shows how belief in Superman and the constitution of the Labour Party would count as religions. Ward remarks, "If you do not know what 'religion' is, you can hardly decide whether it is dangerous or not" (9). But Ward then changes the subject and leaves the question unexplored. In the first chapter, he writes, "At last, having discussed and then side-stepped the almost insuperable difficulties in saying what a religion is, I can get around to the question of whether religion is dangerous" (27). The assumption is that there must be something out there, even if we have trouble defining it. The rest of the book is a defense of religion from the charge of violence.

3. Linda M. G. Zerilli, "Doing without Knowing: Feminism's Politics of the Ordinary," *Political Theory* 26, no. 4 (August 1998): 443, quoted in Elizabeth Shakman Hurd, *The Politics of Secularism in International Relations* (Princeton, NJ: Princeton University Press, 2008), 109.

4. The only one of the nine who gives a definition of violence is Charles Selengut, who borrows John Hall's definition of violence as "'actions that inflict, threaten or cause injury' and such action[s] may be 'corporal, written or verbal'"; Charles Selengut, *Sacred Fury: Understanding*

Religious Violence (Walnut Creek, CA: AltaMira, 2003), 9. Selengut thus expands the definition beyond physical injury.

5. Samuel Huntington, "If Not Civilizations, What?" *Foreign Affairs* 72 (November–December 1993): 192.

CHAPTER I

1. R. Scott Appleby, *The Ambivalence of the Sacred: Religion, Violence, and Reconciliation* (Lanham, MD: Rowman and Littlefield, 2000), 2.

2. Leo D. Lefebure, *Revelation, the Religions, and Violence* (Maryknoll, NY: Orbis, 2000), 14.

3. Martin E. Marty, with Jonathan Moore, *Politics, Religion, and the Common Good* (San Francisco, CA: Jossey-Bass, 2000), 28.

4. Lefebure, *Revelation*, 13.

5. Ibid. See especially Lefebure's discussion of Girard in *Revelation*, 16–24. According to Lefebure, Girard's mimetic theory "does illumine a wide range of aspects of religion and culture," but it lacks the empirical evidence necessary to extend the theory to all times and all places. Nowhere does Lefebure explain what the term religion picks out that is distinctive from culture or the nonreligious aspects of culture. Religion and culture are simply thrown together into the type of conceptual soup apparent in the following sentences:

> The theory of the primal murders and the primordial origin of religion and all human culture in the surrogate victim mechanism is highly speculative because we lack adequate data from the period that Girard takes as foundational for all human culture. Girard seeks to reconstruct a form of mimesis prior to symbols, a mimesis that would be the first origin of human consciousness and culture and religious symbolism. (21)

6. One argument that does not fall neatly into any of the three types is Hector Avalos, *Fighting Words: The Origins of Religious Violence* (Amherst, NY: Prometheus, 2005). Avalos argues that violence is caused by fighting over scarce goods, and religion causes violence because it creates scarcity of certain goods. One could perhaps assimilate this argument to the section on the divisiveness of religion. At any rate, the differences in his explanation for why religion causes violence do not save Avalos from the same problems encountered by the other thinkers I examine. Religion remains a transhistorical and transcultural concept, and the problems with the definition of religion remain unexamined and unresolved. Avalos defines religion as "a mode of life and thought that presupposes the existence of, and relationship with, unverifiable forces and/or beings" (ibid., 19). I discuss the problems with such essentialist definitions in the present chapter and chapter 2.

7. Some examples include Oliver McTernan, *Violence in God's Name: Religion in an Age of Conflict* (Maryknoll, NY: Orbis, 2003); Jack Nelson-Pallmeyer, *Is Religion Killing Us? Violence in the Bible and the Quran* (Harrisburg, PA: Trinity Press International, 2003); and Jessica Stern, *Terror in the Name of God: Why Religious Militants Kill* (New York: Ecco, 2003). Despite its title, Hent de Vries's fascinating

book *Religion and Violence: Philosophical Perspectives from Kant to Derrida* (Baltimore, MD: Johns Hopkins University Press, 2002) does not fit into this genre of literature. De Vries defines religion very broadly: "'religion' is the relation between the self (or some selves) and the other—some Other" (1). De Vries's engagement with philosophical texts supports the argument I make in this chapter and chapter 2, because it questions Enlightenment ways of defining and quarantining religion.

8. Examples include Paul Boyer, *When Time Shall Be No More: Prophecy Belief in Modern American Culture* (Cambridge, MA: Harvard University Press, 1992); Martin Dillon, *God and the Gun: The Church and Irish Terrorism* (London: Routledge, 1999); Michael Barkun, *Religion and the Racist Right: The Origins of the Christian Identity Movement* (Chapel Hill: University of North Carolina Press, 1996); and Peter Marsden, *The Taliban: War, Religion, and the New World Order in Afghanistan* (Oxford: Oxford University Press, 1998).

9. John Hick, "The Non-Absoluteness of Christianity," in *The Myth of Christian Uniqueness: Toward a Pluralistic Theology of Religions*, ed. John Hick and Paul F. Knitter (Maryknoll, NY: Orbis, 1987), 16–20. Hick also makes this argument in *An Interpretation of Religion* (London: Macmillan, 1989), 371: "the dogma of the deity of Christ—in conjunction with the aggressive and predatory aspect of human nature—has contributed historically to the evils of colonialism, the destruction of indigenous civilizations, anti-Semitism, destructive wars of religion and the burnings of heretics and witches."

10. Hick, "The Non-Absoluteness of Christianity," 17.

11. Ibid., 34; and John Hick, *Problems of Religious Pluralism* (New York: St. Martin's, 1985).

12. John Hick, *God and the Universe of Faiths* (New York: St. Martin's, 1973), 133. He reiterates this position in *An Interpretation of Religion*, 21.

13. Hick, *God*, 133.

14. The debate began in earnest with Wilfred Cantwell Smith's *The Meaning and End of Religion* (New York: Macmillan, 1962), which traces the history of the term and finds that religion is a modern invention. Timothy Fitzgerald has made the most forceful case for the incoherence of the term in *The Ideology of Religious Studies* (Oxford: Oxford University Press, 2000). See also Derek Peterson and Darren Walhof, eds., *The Invention of Religion: Rethinking Belief in Politics and History* (Piscataway, NJ: Rutgers University Press, 2003).

15. Hick, *An Interpretation of Religion*, 3.

16. Ibid., 4.

17. Ibid.

18. Ibid., 5.

19. Ibid., 5–6.

20. Ibid., 5, 22, 32, 33, 308, for example.

21. Ibid., 5.

22. Charles Kimball, *When Religion Becomes Evil* (San Francisco, CA: HarperSanFrancisco, 2002), 6.

23. Ibid., 15.

24. Fitzgerald, *The Ideology*, 17.

25. Kimball, *When Religion*, 18.

26. Ibid., 22–23.

27. Ibid., 21–23.

28. Sarah Thal, "A Religion That Was Not a Religion: The Creation of Modern Shinto in Nineteenth-Century Japan," in *The Invention of Religion*, ed. Peterson and Walhof, 100–114; and M. R. Mullins, Shimazono Susumu, and Paul L. Swanson, eds., *Religion and Society in Modern Japan* (Berkeley, CA: Asian Humanities Press, 1993).

29. For example, G. Cooper writes, "No tribe has a word for 'religion' as a separate sphere of existence. Religion permeates the whole of life, including economic activities, arts, crafts and ways of living"; G. Cooper, "North American Traditional Religion," in *The World's Religions*, ed. Stewart Sutherland (London: Routledge, 1988), as quoted in Fitzgerald, *The Ideology*, 81.

30. Kimball, *When Religion*, 38.

31. Carlton Hayes, *Nationalism: A Religion* (New York: Macmillan, 1960); Peter van der Veer, "The Moral State: Religion, Nation, and Empire in Victorian Britain and British India," in *Nation and Religion: Perspectives on Europe and Asia*, ed. Peter van der Veer and Hartmut Lehmann (Princeton, NJ: Princeton University Press, 1999), 3–9; Talal Asad, "Religion, Nation-State, Secularism," in *Nation and Religion*, ed. van der Veer and Lehmann, 178–91; Carolyn Marvin and David W. Ingle, *Blood Sacrifice and the Nation: Totem Rituals and the American Flag* (Cambridge: Cambridge University Press, 1999).

32. Carolyn Marvin and David W. Ingle, "Blood Sacrifice and the Nation: Revisiting Civil Religion," *Journal of the American Academy of Religion* 64, no. 4 (Winter 1996): 768.

33. Kimball, *When Religion*, 36.

34. Former U.S. State Department official Francis Fukuyama's book *The End of History and the Last Man* (New York: Free Press, 1992) makes the argument that the fall of communism signaled the definitive triumph of liberalism and capitalism in world history.

35. Richard E. Wentz, *Why People Do Bad Things in the Name of Religion* (Macon, GA: Mercer University Press, 1993), 67.

36. Ibid., 68.

37. Ibid., 70.

38. Ibid., 13.

39. Ibid., 14.

40. Ibid., 18.

41. Ibid., 21.

42. Ibid., 37.

43. Marty, *Politics, Religion, and the Common Good*, 25–26.

44. Ibid., 9.

45. Ibid., 10.

46. Ibid., 14.

47. Ibid., 10–14.

48. Ibid., 25, 27.

49. Mark Juergensmeyer, *Terror in the Mind of God: The Global Rise of Religious Violence* (Berkeley: University of California Press, 2000), xi.

50. Ibid., xii.

51. Ibid., 6.

52. Ibid., 119–20.

53. Ibid., 123.

54. Ibid.

55. Ibid., 132–33.

56. Ibid., 144.

57. Ibid., 125.

58. Ibid., 146.

59. Ibid., 153.

60. Ibid., 154.

61. Ibid., 161–63.

62. Ibid., 148–49.

63. Ibid., 149.

64. Ibid., 155.

65. Ibid.

66. Ibid., 217.

67. Mark Juergensmeyer, *The New Cold War? Religious Nationalism Confronts the Secular State* (Berkeley: University of California Press, 1993), 15. Here, Juergensmeyer footnotes Carlton Hayes's book *Nationalism: A Religion*, which I will discuss further in chapter 2.

68. Juergensmeyer, *Terror*, 217. Although Juergensmeyer does not divide his summary into four separate points, I have done so in order to clarify my response to each point.

69. Ibid., 216–17.

70. Ibid., 229. In another essay, Juergensmeyer acknowledges the similarity between the demonizing, absolutizing language of the U.S. on terrorism and that of the religious violence of the terrorists. In the face of this threat to the distinction between religious and secular violence, Juergensmeyer simply blames the demonizing language of the war on terrorism on the influence of religion, despite the fact that the war on terrorism is being fought for the defense of liberalism and secularity. Once again, for Juergensmeyer, if it's violent, it must be religious; see Mark Juergensmeyer, "Is Religion the Problem?" *Hedgehog Review* 6, no. 1 (Spring 2004): 31–32.

71. Juergensmeyer, *Terror*, 169–70.

72. According to Girard, "There is no society without religion because without religion society cannot exist." Even secular societies are religious; René Girard, *Violence and the Sacred,* trans. Patrick Gregory (Baltimore, MD: Johns Hopkins University Press, 1977), 221.

73. Juergensmeyer tries to tighten the link between war and religion by saying that "the task of creating a vicarious experience of warfare—albeit one usually imagined as residing on a spiritual plane—is one of the main businesses of religion." In the next sentence, however, he acknowledges that "[v]irtually all cultural traditions

have contained martial metaphors"; Juergensmeyer, *Terror*, 156. How then are we supposed to distinguish religion from other cultural traditions?

74. Ibid., 37.

75. Ibid., 41.

76. Ibid., xii, 30–36.

77. Ibid., 127, 164–65.

78. Ibid., 11.

79. Juergensmeyer, *Global Rebellion: Religious Challenges to the Secular State, from Christian Militias to al Qaeda* (Berkeley: University of California Press, 2008), 23.

80. Ibid., 24.

81. Ibid., 23. The quote is repeated verbatim.

82. Juergensmeyer, *Global Rebellion*, 19–20; and Juergensmeyer, *The New Cold War?* 30–31.

83. Juergensmeyer, *Global Rebellion*, 252.

84. Ibid., 39.

85. Ibid., 253.

86. Ibid., 255.

87. Juergensmeyer, *Terror*, 30–36.

88. Pierce's novel describes a battle between patriotic freedom fighters and the U.S. government. Although Pierce scorned Christian Identity, he founded another group called the Cosmotheist Community (ibid., 30–33).

89. David C. Rapoport, "Some General Observations on Religion and Violence," in *Violence and the Sacred in the Modern World*, ed. Mark Juergensmeyer (London: Frank Cass, 1992), 120.

90. Ibid., 121–24.

91. Ibid., 121.

92. Ibid., 125.

93. Ibid., 126.

94. Ibid.

95. Nicolo Machiavelli, quoted in ibid., 127.

96. Ibid., 134.

97. Ibid., 135.

98. Girard, *Violence*, 315.

99. See the glossary in René Girard, *The Girard Reader*, ed. James G. Williams (New York: Crossroad, 1996), 289, 292.

100. Girard, *Violence*, 37.

101. Ibid., 14–22.

102. Ibid., 23.

103. Ibid., 259.

104. Ibid., 262.

105. "Only the introduction of some transcendental quality that will persuade men of the fundamental difference between sacrifice and revenge, between a judicial system and vengeance, can succeed in bypassing violence" (ibid., 24).

106. Ibid., 221.

107. Girard, *The Girard Reader*, 16–19.

108. René Girard, *Things Hidden since the Foundation of the World* (Palo Alto, CA: Stanford University Press, 1987), 224–62.

109. Bhikhu Parekh, "The Voice of Religion in Political Discourse," in *Religion, Politics, and Peace*, ed. Leroy Rouner (Notre Dame, IN: University of Notre Dame Press, 1999), 72.

110. See Bhikhu Parekh, *Rethinking Multiculturalism: Cultural Diversity and Political Theory* (Cambridge, MA: Harvard University Press, 2000).

111. Parekh, "The Voice of Religion in Political Discourse," 73.

112. Ibid., 70.

113. Ibid., 64–65.

114. Ibid., 70.

115. Ibid., 74.

116. Appleby, *The Ambivalence of the Sacred*, 4.

117. Ibid., 5.

118. Ibid., 6.

119. Ibid., 11.

120. Ibid., 8–9.

121. Ibid., 28.

122. Ibid. These phrases come from Otto by way of Appleby's quotation of him.

123. Ibid., 29.

124. Ibid., 30.

125. Rudolf Otto, *The Idea of the Holy: An Inquiry into the Non-Rational Factor in the Idea of the Divine and Its Relation to the Rational*, trans. John W. Harvey (New York: Oxford University Press, 1958), 5–6. At least in its "higher" forms, *das Heilige* is the numinous "completely permeated and saturated" with morality and rationality (109). Otto counts Christianity, especially in its Protestant variations, as one of these higher forms, superior to other religions; see, for example, 1, 56, 175.

126. Ibid., 7.

127. Ibid., 112–13.

128. Ibid., 12.

129. Ibid., 16.

130. Appleby, *The Ambivalence of the Sacred*, 15.

131. Ibid., 4.

132. Ibid., 110.

133. Ibid., 59.

134. Ibid., 61.

135. Ibid.

136. Ibid., 107.

137. Ibid., 60.

138. Ibid., 67.

139. Ibid., 68.

140. Ibid., 69.

141. Charles Selengut, *Sacred Fury: Understanding Religious Violence* (Walnut Creek, CA: AltaMira, 2003), 228.

142. Ibid., 6.

143. Ibid., 8.

144. Ibid., 19.

145. Ibid., 21.

146. Ibid., 14.

147. Ibid., 44.

148. Ibid., 81.

149. Ibid., 84.

150. Ibid., 64–80.

151. Ibid., 9–10.

152. Ibid., 20.

153. Ibid., 25.

154. Ibid., 26.

155. Ibid., 49.

156. Ibid., 55–58.

157. Ibid., 155–56.

158. Ibid., 157–58.

159. Ibid., 158–59.

160. Ibid., 158.

161. Ibid., 159.

162. Sheryl Gay Stolberg, "Given New Legs, Old Proposal Is Back," *New York Times*, June 4, 2003: A28.

163. Carolyn Marvin and David W. Ingle, *Blood Sacrifice and the Nation: Totem Rituals and the American Flag* (Cambridge: Cambridge University Press, 1999).

CHAPTER 2

1. Brian C. Wilson, "From the Lexical to the Polythetic: A Brief History of the Definition of Religion," *What Is Religion? Origins, Definitions, and Explanations*, ed. Thomas A. Idinopulos and Brian C. Wilson (Leiden: Brill, 1998).

2. Arthur L. Greil and David G. Bromley, "Introduction," in *Defining Religion: Investigating the Boundaries between the Sacred and the Secular*, ed. Arthur L. Greil and David G. Bromley (Oxford: JAI, 2003), 3–6.

3. Jonathan Z. Smith, *Imagining Religion: From Babylon to Jonestown* (Chicago: University of Chicago Press, 1982), xi.

4. Talal Asad, "Reading a Modern Classic: W. C. Smith's *The Meaning and End of Religion*," *History of Religions* 40, no. 3 (February 2001): 221.

5. Kimball, *When Religion*, 1.

6. Leroy S. Rouner, "Introduction," in *Religion, Politics, and Peace*, ed. Leroy Rouner (Notre Dame, IN: University of Notre Dame Press, 1999), 2.

7. Wilfred Cantwell Smith, *The Meaning and End of Religion* (New York: Macmillan, 1962), 18–19.

8. Quentin Skinner, *The Foundations of Modern Political Thought*, 2 vols. (Cambridge: Cambridge University Press, 1978), 2:349–50.

9. Smith, *Meaning and End*, 54–55.

10. Ibid., 19–21.

11. Cicero, *The Nature of the Gods*, trans. P. G. Walsh (New York: Clarendon, 1997).

12. S. N. Balagangadhara, *"The Heathen in His Blindness..."*: *Asia, the West, and the Dynamic of Religion* (Leiden: Brill, 1994), 37–43.

13. Paul J. Griffiths, "The Very Idea of Religion," *First Things*, no. 103 (May 2000): 31.

14. Smith, *Meaning and End*, 25–26.

15. Wilfred Cantwell Smith notes that Lactantius used the term *vera religio* often, but "[f]or Lactantius it is clearly a personal ideal, 'true religion' and not 'the true religion': he equates it with piety...and justice"; see Smith, *Meaning and End*, 213n45. This usage accords with Augustine's use of the term.

16. Augustine, *De Vera Religione*, 1–10, English translation in *Augustine: Earlier Writings*, trans. John H. S. Burleigh (Philadelphia: Westminster, 1953), 225–31.

17. Ibid., 69 (260).

18. Ibid., 108–9 (279–80).

19. Ibid., 113 (282).

20. Augustine, *City of God*, trans. Henry Bettenson (Harmondsworth, England: Penguin, 1972), X.1 (373).

21. Smith, *Meaning and End*, 32.

22. John Bossy, "Some Elementary Forms of Durkheim," *Past and Present* 95 (May 1982): 4.

23. About 1400, a nun writes, "Somtyme am I prioresse...and go thrugh alle regiouns, Sekyng alle religiouns"; "Religion," *Oxford English Dictionary*, 2nd ed. (Oxford: Clarendon, 1989); see also Smith, *Meaning and End*, 31.

24. The works are *Contra impugnantes Dei cultum et religionem* (1257) and *Contra retrahentes a religionis ingressu* (1270). They are published in English as *An Apology for the Religious Orders, by Saint Thomas Aquinas, Being a Translation of Two of the Minor Works of the Saint*. Edited, with Introduction, by the Very Rev. Father John Procter (London, 1902); Smith, *Meaning and End*, 215n53.

25. Thomas Aquinas, *Summa Theologiae*, ed. Blackfriars (New York: McGraw-Hill, 1964), II–II.80.1.

26. Ibid., II–II.81.5.

27. Ibid., II–II.81.1.

28. Michael J. Buckley, S.J., "The Study of Religion and the Rise of Atheism: Conflict or Confirmation?" in *Fields of Faith: Theology and Religious Studies for the Twenty-First Century*, ed. David F. Ford, Ben Quash, and Janet Martin Soskice (Cambridge: Cambridge University Press, 2005), 6.

29. Aquinas, *Summa Theologiae*, II–II.81.3. Buckley says that, for Aquinas, *religio* "can be pagan or Christian, private or social, as long as it directs one to the service and reverence of God"; Buckley, "The Study of Religion," 6. But nowhere

does Aquinas say this. He might perhaps recognize in pagan worship an incomplete longing for the true God, but proper *religio* shows "reverence to one God," not many.

30. Ibid., II–II.81.3 ad 1. In the reply to objection 3, Aquinas states, "The worship of religion is paid to images, not as considered in themselves, nor as things, but as images leading us to God incarnate." This is not a statement that can be easily transferred outside the Christian context.

31. Talal Asad, *Genealogies of Religion: Discipline and Reasons of Power in Christianity and Islam* (Baltimore, MD: Johns Hopkins University Press, 1993), 45n29.

32. See Aquinas's treatise on habits and virtues in *Summa Theologiae*, I–II.49–70.

33. Asad, *Genealogies of Religion*, 134.

34. Aquinas, *Summa Theologiae*, II–II.81.1 ad 5.

35. Ibid., II–II.81.8. Michael Buckley is right to correct my earlier reading of this passage ("'A Fire Strong Enough to Consume the House': The Wars of Religion and the Rise of the State," *Modern Theology* 11, no. 4 [October 1995]: 403–4) in which I had said that *religio* for Aquinas refers to the liturgical practices of the church. Buckley rightly points out that, although these are included, Aquinas's concept of *religio* also includes personal devotions and other acts of service to God; Buckley, "The Study of Religion," 5–6.

36. Aquinas, *Summa Theologiae*, II–II.81.8.

37. Ibid., II–II.81.7.

38. Ibid., I–II.51.2–3.

39. Ibid., I.76.1.

40. J. C. Schmitt, "Le geste, la cathédrale et le roi," *L'Arc* 72, quoted in Asad, *Genealogies of Religion*, 138.

41. Aquinas, *Summa Theologiae*, I–II.65.1 *sed contra*.

42. Ibid., I–II.61.4 ad 1.

43. Ibid., II–II.81.4 ad 2.

44. Ibid., II–II.81.1 ad 1.

45. Ernst Feil, "From the Classical *Religio* to the Modern *Religion*: Elements of a Transformation between 1550 and 1650," in *Religion in History: The Word, the Idea, the Reality*, ed. Michel Despland and Gérard Vallée (Waterloo, ON: Wilfred Laurier University Press, 1992), 35.

46. Thomas Aquinas, *On Kingship to the King of Cyprus*, trans. Gerald B. Phelan (Toronto: Pontifical Institute of Mediaeval Studies, 1949), 60 (bk. II, ch. 3). See also the treatise on law in the *Summa Theologiae*, where Aquinas shows that an effect of law is to make people good: "Since then every man is a part of the state [*civitatis*], it is impossible that a man be good, unless he be well proportionate to the common good: nor can the whole be well consistent unless its parts be proportionate to it. Consequently the common good of the state [*civitatis*] cannot flourish, unless the citizens be virtuous, at least those whose business it is to govern" (I–II.92.1 ad 3).

47. Aquinas, *Summa Theologiae*, I–II.105.1 ad 2.

48. Ibid., II–II.50.1 ad 1.

49. Aquinas, *On Kingship*, 60 (bk. II, ch. 3).

50. Aquinas, *Summa Theologiae*, II–II.10.10.

51. On this point, see Asad, *Genealogies of Religion*, 28–29.

52. Smith, *Meaning and End*, 19.

53. Nicholas de Cusa, *De Pace Fidei*, trans. and ed. John P. Dolan, in *Unity and Reform: Selected Writings of Nicholas de Cusa* (Notre Dame, IN: University of Notre Dame Press, 1962), 219.

54. Ibid.,197.

55. Ibid., 198.

56. Ibid.

57. Ibid., 198–99.

58. Ibid., 203.

59. Marsilio Ficino, *De Christiana Religione*, quoted in Smith, *Meaning and End*, 33.

60. Smith, *Meaning and End*, 33–34; see also Peter Harrison, *"Religion" and the Religions in the English Enlightenment* (Cambridge: Cambridge University Press, 1990), 13.

61. Postel writes, "Postquam in principiis convenimus, non potuerit fieri quin et ad vera veniamus axiomata, et ad finales veritates. Nullus sit amplius papista, nullus Lutheranus, omnes ab expetita salute de IESU nomen capiamus"; Guillaume Postel, Πανθενωσια,[Panthenosia] quoted in William J. Bouwsma, *Concordia Mundi: The Career and Thought of Guillaume Postel (1510–1581)* (Cambridge, MA: Harvard University Press, 1957), 194n70.

62. Ibid., 130.

63. Ibid., 173.

64. Bouwsma, *Concordia Mundi*, 174–75.

65. Richard McCoy, *Alterations of State: Sacred Kingship in the English Reformation* (New York: Columbia University Press, 2002), 2.

66. Ibid., 63. Bossy notes that the Book of Common Prayer adopted the meaning of religion as "the correct mode of Christian piety contrasted with the superstitious mode practised by monks and friars"; Bossy, "Some Elementary Forms of Durkheim," 5–6.

67. Graham Ward, *True Religion* (Oxford: Blackwell, 2003), 22.

68. Harrison, *"Religion" and the Religions*, 19–23.

69. Ibid., 23–24.

70. Smith, *Meaning and End*, 39.

71. Harrison, *"Religion" and the Religions*, 25.

72. Bossy, "Some Elementary Forms of Durkheim," 6.

73. See Jean Bodin, *Colloquium of the Seven about Secrets of the Sublime*, trans. Marion L. D. Kuntz (Princeton, NJ: Princeton University Press, 1975). Bossy thinks the translator is mistaken in letting Bodin's characters refer to *the* Christian or Jewish religion; Bossy, "Some Elementary Forms of Durkheim," 6–7. Ernst Feil agrees that Bodin does not yet have a modern concept of religion, but his use of *religio naturalis* suggests changes soon to come; Feil, "Classical *Religio*," 38–39.

74. Bossy, "Some Elementary Forms of Durkheim," 5–6.

75. Ibid., 6–7.

76. Sir Thomas Browne, quoted in ibid., 7–8.

77. John Bossy, *Christianity in the West 1400–1700* (Oxford: Oxford University Press, 1985), 170.

78. Ibid., 171.

79. Lord Herbert of Cherbury, *De Religione Laici*, trans. and ed. Harold R. Hutcheson (New Haven, CT: Yale University Press, 1944), 129.

80. Edward, Lord Herbert of Cherbury, *De Veritate*, trans. Meyrick H. Carré (Bristol, England: Arrowsmith, 1937), 121.

81. Herbert, *De Religione Laici*, 133.

82. Herbert, *De Veritate*, 303.

83. Ibid.

84. Herbert was not solely concerned with civil peace, but had some theological concerns as well. His schema of the common notions was motivated in part by his revulsion at the idea that a good God could damn the majority of humankind to the fires of hell for ignorance of the Christian tenets for salvation; see Harrison, *"Religion" and the Religions*, 65.

85. Herbert, *De Veritate*, 298.

86. As Peter Harrison points out, this distinction helps Herbert to escape some of the more facile objections to his ideas; Harrison, *"Religion" and the Religions*, 70.

87. Herbert, *De Religione Laici*, 129.

88. Ibid., 123.

89. Herbert, *De Veritate*, 305.

90. Herbert, *De Religione Laici*, 105–13.

91. Ibid., 113.

92. Ibid.

93. Ibid., translation altered. In the text, the translator has rendered "haut aliam tamen induunt vicissitudinem, quam unde procuretur totum" as "yet they assume no change other than one whence the whole may be taken care of." I find it hard to make sense of this too-literal translation, so I have used instead the translator's suggestion in a footnote for the meaning of the phrase.

94. Ibid., 113–19.

95. For example, Herbert, *De Veritate*, 122, 126, 146, 291.

96. Ibid., 301–2.

97. Harrison, *"Religion" and the Religions*, 71.

98. Herbert was also a soldier of fortune who fought for the Prince of Orange in several campaigns in the 1610s; see the editor's introduction to *De Veritate*, 9–10.

99. Lord Herbert of Cherbury, "On the King's Supremacy in the Church," in Herbert, *De Religione Laici*, appendix B, 184.

100. Ibid., 185.

101. Herbert, *De Religione Laici*, 127. The editor remarks in a footnote here that a German commentator on this passage "exclaims, very justly, 'Also auch im Bereiche der Herbert'schen Vernunftkirche ist eine Censur des freien Gedankens nicht ausgeschlossen!'" [And so also in the domain of Herbert's Church of Reason a censor of free thinking is not out of the question!]; ibid., 127n42.

102. John Locke, *A Letter Concerning Toleration* (Indianapolis, IN: Bobbs-Merrill, 1955), 18.

103. Ibid., 18.

104. Ibid., 25–26, 31.

105. "For every church is orthodox to itself; to others, erroneous or heretical. For whatsoever any church believes it believes to be true; and the contrary unto those things it pronounces to be error. So that the controversy between these churches about the truth of their doctrines and the purity of the worship is on both sides equal; nor is there any judge, either at Constantinople or elsewhere upon earth, by whose sentence it can be determined" (Ibid., 25).

106. Ibid., 31. "The care, therefore, of every man's soul belongs unto himself, and is to be left unto himself" (ibid., 30).

107. Ibid., 31. Every individual's private search does not begin and end with introspection, however, as it does for Herbert. Locke criticized Herbert's idea of innate notions; John Locke, *An Essay Concerning Human Understanding* (Oxford: Clarendon, 1979), I.ii.15–21.

108. Locke, *Concerning Toleration*, 17.

109. Ibid.

110. Ibid.

111. Ibid., 16.

112. Ibid., 20.

113. Ibid., 22–23.

114. See Bossy, *Christianity in the West*, 57–75.

115. One example of the religious-secular binary: "In the variety and contradiction of opinions in religion, wherein the princes of the world are as much divided as in their secular interests, the narrow way would be much straitened"; Locke, *Concerning Toleration*, 19.

116. Edward I. Bailey, "The Implicit Religiosity of the Secular: A Martian Perspective on the Definition of Religion," in *Defining Religion*, ed. Greil and Bromley, 64. Bailey's comment refers directly to his 1969 interviews with the governing body of a church-related primary school, but more broadly it refers to his analysis of the transition from medieval to modern uses and misuses of the secular; see 58–64.

117. Ezra Kopelowitz, "Negotiating with the Secular: Forms of Religious Authority and Their Political Consequences," in *Defining Religion*, ed. Greil and Bromley, 86–87.

118. Locke, *Concerning Toleration*, 27.

119. The phrase is from John Neville Figgis, *From Gerson to Grotius, 1414–1625* (New York: Harper Torchbook, 1960), 5.

120. Locke, *Concerning Toleration*, 51.

121. William E. Arnal, "Definition," in *Guide to the Study of Religion*, ed. Willi Braun and Russell T. McCutcheon (London: Cassell, 2000), 31. For Asad's comments on the rise of religion and the rise of the state, see *Genealogies of Religion*, 27–29, 39–43.

122. Arnal, "Definition," 31.

123. Ibid., 32.

124. William Arnal, "The Segregation of Social Desire: 'Religion' and Disney World," *Journal of the American Academy of Religion* 69, no. 1 (March 2001): 5.

125. Ibid., 7–8.

126. Smith, *Meaning and End*, 18–19. Smith goes on to say that the case of Islam might be a partial exception to his "no," but only because of a link with Judeo-Christian developments in the origin of Islam.

127. All the above examples are from David Chidester, "Colonialism," in *Guide*, ed. Braun and McCutcheon, 427–28, except for that of Pedro Cieza, which is from Jonathan Z. Smith, "Religion, Religions, Religious," in *Critical Terms for Religious Studies*, ed. Mark C. Taylor (Chicago: University of Chicago Press, 1998), 269.

128. David Chidester, *Savage Systems: Colonialism and Comparative Religion in Southern Africa* (Charlottesville: University of Virginia Press, 1996), 35–69, 103–23.

129. Ibid., 46–56.

130. Chidester, "Colonialism," 428–29.

131. Derek R. Peterson and Darren R. Walhof, "Rethinking Religion," in *The Invention of Religion: Rethinking Belief in Politics and History*, ed. Derek R. Peterson and Darren R. Walhof (New Brunswick, NJ: Rutgers University Press, 2002), 7.

132. Derek R. Peterson, "Gambling with God: Rethinking Religion in Colonial Central Kenya," in *Invention of Religion*, ed. Peterson and Walhof, 38.

133. Smith, *Meaning and End*, 61.

134. Balagangadhara, *The Heathen in His Blindness*, 126–27.

135. Smith, *Meaning and End*, 55–56, 64–65; quote at 56.

136. Louis Dumont, *Homo Hierarchicus: The Caste System and Its Implications* (Chicago: University of Chicago Press, 1980), 228, quoted in Timothy Fitzgerald, *The Ideology of Religious Studies* (New York: Oxford University Press, 2000), 144–46.

137. Quoted in Peter Beyer, "Defining Religion in Cross-National Perspective: Identity and Difference in Official Conceptions," in *Defining Religion*, ed. Greil and Bromley, 180.

138. Richard King, *Orientalism and Religion: Postcolonial Theory, India and "the Mystic East"* (London: Routledge, 1999), 99. Some contemporary Hindu nationalists would go even further. L. K. Advani, one of the principal ideologues of the BJP, has said, "Muslims, Christians, and Sikhs living in India should be referred to as 'Mohammadi Hindus,' 'Christian Hindus,' and 'Sikh Hindus' "; quoted in Richard S. Cohen, "Why Study Indian Buddhism?" in *Invention of Religion*, ed. Peterson and Walhof, 26.

139. Fitzgerald, *The Ideology*, 153.

140. Frits Staal, *Rules without Meaning: Ritual, Mantras, and the Human Sciences* (New York: Lang, 1989), 397, quoted in Balagangadhara, *The Heathen in His Blindness*, 315.

141. R. N. Dandekar, "Hinduism," in *Historia Religionum: Handbook for the History of Religions*, ed. E. Jouco Bleeker and Geo Widengren, 2 vols. (Leiden: Brill, 1969), 2:237, quoted in Balagangadhara, *The Heathen in His Blindness*, 15.

142. Simon Weightman, "Hinduism," in *A Handbook of Living Religions*, ed. John R. Hinnells (Harmondsworth, England: Penguin, 1984), quoted in Balagangadhara, *The Heathen in His Blindness*, 15.

143. Ibid.

144. James Mill, quoted in Balagangadhara, *The Heathen in His Blindness*, 116.

145. Balagangadhara, *The Heathen in His Blindness*, 116.

146. Ronald Inden, *Imagining India* (Oxford: Blackwell, 1990), 165–72. The East India Company had a lively interest in the new nineteenth-century "science" of religion; Friedrich Max Müller's landmark translation of the Rig Veda from 1849 to 1862 was financed by the East India Company; Russell T. McCutcheon, "The Imperial Dynamic in the Study of Religion: Neocolonial Practices in an American Discipline," in *Post-Colonial America*, ed. C. Richard King (Chicago: University of Illinois Press, 2000), 280.

147. Inden, *Imagining India*, 90–92.

148. Balagangadhara, *The Heathen in His Blindness*, 143–47.

149. King, *Orientalism and Religion*, 96–142. The emphasis on texts was heretofore quite foreign to Indian culture until Westerners elevated the Vedas into the Hindu "bible." King describes how the Orientalists created Hinduism as a textual religion, in the image of Protestant Christianity.

150. Ibid., 121–23.

151. Ibid., 105.

152. Inden, *Imagining India*, 128.

153. Ibid., 127–30.

154. The essentially private nature of religion can be found in the proclamation of Queen Victoria when India formally became a British colony in 1858:

> Firmly relying ourselves on the truth of Christianity, and acknowledging with gratitude the solace of religion, we disclaim alike the right and the desire to impose our convictions on any of our subjects. We declare it to be our royal will and pleasure, that none be in anywise favoured, none molested or disquieted, by reason of their religious faith or observances; but that all shall alike enjoy the equal and impartial protection of the law. And we do strictly charge and enjoin all those who may be in authority under us, that they abstain from all interference with the religious belief, or worship, of any of our subjects on pain of our severest displeasure. (Quoted in Balagangadhara, *The Heathen in His Blindness*, 140)

155. King, *Orientalism and Religion*, 103–4.

156. Sanjay Joshi, "Republicizing Religiosity: Modernity, Religion, and the Middle Class," in *Invention of Religion*, ed. Peterson and Walhof, 79–99.

157. Cohen, "Why Study Indian Buddhism?" 27. BJP stands for the Bhartiya Janta Party, India's largest political party.

158. Philip Almond, *The British Discovery of Buddhism* (Cambridge: Cambridge University Press, 1988), 13. According to Wilfred Cantwell Smith, the first use of the term "Boudhism" appeared in 1801; Smith, *Meaning and End*, 61.

159. Tomoko Masuzawa, *The Invention of World Religions; or, How European Universalism Was Preserved in the Language of Pluralism* (Chicago: University of Chicago Press, 2005), 122.

160. King, *Orientalism and Religion*, 144.

161. Almond, *The British Discovery*, 1–32; Masuzawa, *Invention of World Religions*, 125–38; also King, *Orientalism and Religion*, 143–48. Almond's account has been justly criticized for overemphasizing the role of European scholars in the

construction of "Buddhism" to the exclusion of Asian actors; see Charles Hallisey, "Roads Taken and Not Taken in the Study of Theravāda Buddhism," in *Curators of the Buddha: The Study of Buddhism under Colonialism*, ed. Donald Lopez, Jr. (Chicago: University of Chicago Press, 1995).

162. Martin Southwold, "Buddhism and the Definition of Religion," quoted in Balagangadhara, *The Heathen in His Blindness*, 286.

163. Ibid., 284–85.

164. Donald S. Lopez, Jr., *Prisoners of Shangri-La: Tibetan Buddhism and the West* (Chicago: University of Chicago Press, 1998), 25–41.

165. L. Austine Waddell, quoted in ibid., 40.

166. Ibid., 40.

167. Ibid., 184–85.

168. Ibid., 185–201.

169. Cohen, "Why Study Indian Buddhism?" 24.

170. Ibid., 20–21.

171. Ibid., 26–27.

172. Sarah Thal, "A Religion That Was Not a Religion," in *Invention of Religion*, ed. Peterson and Walhof, 100–104.

173. Quoted in ibid., 104.

174. Ibid., 104–11. An abbreviated version of this history is found in Beyer, "Defining Religion in Cross-National Perspective," 172–74. Beyer uses the term "state Shinto" in place of "shrine Shinto." For a much more detailed history of the distinction of Shinto from religion, see D. C. Holtom, *The National Faith of Japan: A Study in Modern Shinto* (London: Kegan, Paul, Trench, Trubner, 1938).

175. Ibid., 111. The internal quote is from a directive of the supreme commander of the Allied Powers in Japan, December 15, 1945.

176. Quoted in Fitzgerald, *The Ideology*, 170.

177. Fitzgerald, *The Ideology*, 161–97.

178. Beyer, "Defining Religion in Cross-National Perspective," 173–74.

179. Ibid., 174–75.

180. Smith, *Meaning and End*, 69.

181. Beyer, "Defining Religion in Cross-National Perspective," 175–77.

182. Masuzawa, *Invention of World Religions*, 319.

183. Charles F. Keyes, ed., *Asian Visions of Authority: Religion and the Modern States of East and Southeast Asia* (Honolulu: University of Hawaii Press, 1994), 4, quoted in Fitzgerald, *The Ideology*, 164.

184. Daniel Dubuisson, *The Western Construction of Religion: Myths, Knowledge, and Ideology*, trans. William Sayers (Baltimore, MD: Johns Hopkins University Press, 2003), 6. Dubuisson suggests dropping "religion" and using the term "cosmographic formation," which would include not only Catholicism, Islam, and Vedic practice, but also Platonism, Marxism, atheism, nationalism, and all other formations that offer comprehensive conceptions of the world; ibid., 17–22.

185. Ibid., 21.

186. Huston Smith, *The Religions of Man* (New York: Harper and Row, 1958), 7–8, quoted in McCutcheon, "The Imperial Dynamic in the Study of Religion," 287.

187. McCutcheon, "The Imperial Dynamic in the Study of Religion," 281.

188. Smith, *Meaning and End*, 19, 50.

189. Ibid., 18; see also 20, 142–43.

190. Asad, "Reading a Modern Classic," 214–17.

191. Dubuisson, *Western Construction of Religion*, 42.

192. Jan Bremmer, *Greek Religion* (Oxford: Oxford University Press, 1994), 5.

193. Timothy Fitzgerald, "A Response to Saler, Benavides, and Korom," *Religious Studies Review* 27, no. 2 (April 2001): 114.

194. Fitzgerald, *The Ideology*, 12.

195. Nicholas Lash, *The Beginning and the End of "Religion"* (Cambridge: Cambridge University Press, 1996), 168.

196. Fitzgerald, *The Ideology*, 24–25.

197. Arnal, "Definition," 27–28.

198. Peter B. Clarke and Peter Byrne, *Religion Defined and Explained* (New York: St. Martin's, 1993), 7, quoted in ibid., 24.

199. Émile Durkheim, *The Elementary Forms of Religious Life*, trans. Carol Cosman (Oxford: Oxford University Press, 2001), 46.

200. Durkheim writes, "Religious force is the feeling the collectivity inspires in its members, but projected outside and objectified by the minds that feel it. It becomes objectified by being anchored in an object which then becomes sacred, but any object can play this role" (ibid., 174).

201. See Durkheim's comments on flags as sacred in ibid., 154, 165, 174.

202. Fitzgerald, *The Ideology*, 17.

203. W. Cole Durham, Jr., and Elizabeth A. Sewell, "Definition of Religion," in *Religious Organizations in the United States: A Study of Legal Identity, Religious Freedom and the Law*, ed. James A. Serritella et al. (Durham, NC: Carolina Academic Press, 2006), 3–5.

204. Greil and Bromley, "Introduction," 3.

205. Herbert Schneider, quoted in Timothy Fitzgerald, "Experience," in *Guide*, ed. Braun and McCutcheon, 135.

206. Robert H. Sharf, "The Zen of Japanese Nationalism," in *Curators of the Buddha*, ed. Lopez, 116–21.

207. Dorothee Sölle, "Thou Shalt Have No Other Jeans before Me," in *Observations on the Spiritual Situation of the Age*, ed. Jürgen Habermas (Cambridge, MA: MIT Press, 1984), 159.

208. Russell W. Belk, Melanie Wallendorf, and John F. Sherry, Jr., "The Sacred and the Profane in Consumer Behavior: Theodicy on the Odyssey," *Journal of Consumer Research* 16 (June 1989): 1–38. Although the authors continue to regard consumerism as secular rather than "formally religious," they contend that in contemporary society the secular is sacralized and religion is secularized, which indicates a functionalist approach to the definition of religion.

209. David R. Loy, "The Religion of the Market," *Journal of the American Academy of Religion* 65, no. 2 (Summer 1997): 275.

210. Ibid.

211. Ibid., 277–78.

212. Karl Marx, *The Marx-Engels Reader,* 2nd ed., ed. Robert C. Tucker (New York: Norton, 1978), 103–4.

213. Karl Marx, *Grundrisse,* trans. Martin Nicolaus (Harmondsworth, England: Penguin, 1973), 221.

214. Georg Simmel, *The Philosophy of Money,* trans. Tom Bottomore and David Frisby (London: Routledge and Kegan Paul, 1978), 129, 228–38.

215. Norman O. Brown, *Life against Death: The Psychoanalytical Meaning of History* (New York: Vintage, 1959), 252.

216. More examples are given in Eugene McCarraher, "The Enchanted Earthly City: Augustine, Politics, and the Fetishes of Modernity," in *Augustine and Politics,* ed. Kim Paffenroth, Kevin Hughes, and John Doody (Lanham, MD: Lexington, 2005), from which the above examples of Marx, Simmel, and Brown are also taken.

217. Robert H. Nelson, *Economics as Religion: From Samuelson to Chicago and Beyond* (University Park: Pennsylvania State University Press, 2001), 23. See also Nelson's earlier book *Reaching for Heaven on Earth: The Theological Meaning of Economics* (Savage, MD: Rowman and Littlefield, 1991).

218. Alex Berenson, "Deregulation: A Movement Groping in the Dark," *New York Times* (February 4, 2001): 4.6.

219. Emilio Gentile, *Politics as Religion,* trans. George Staunton (Princeton, NJ: Princeton University Press, 2006), xiv.

220. Ibid., 1.

221. Gentile addresses the objections of substantivist views of religion that would confine the term to beliefs in supernatural divinities. Gentile points out that Buddhism has no god, whereas Nazism does, and he concludes that functionalist definitions have far more to offer a political scientist; ibid., 3–9.

222. Ibid., xv.

223. An English version is Erich Vogelin, *Political Religions,* trans. T. J. DiNapoli and E. S. Easterly III (Lewiston, NY: Mellen, 1986).

224. Gentile, *Politics as Religion,* 11–15. Gentile cites examples of this view from Benedetto Croce, Durkheim, Claude Rivire, Salvador Giner, Manuel García Pelayo, and Jean-Pierre Sirroneau.

225. Max Stirner, quoted in Gareth Stedman Jones, "How Marx Covered His Tracks: The Hidden Link between Communism and Religion," *Times Literary Supplement,* no. 5175 (June 7, 2002): 14.

226. Ludwig Feuerbach, quoted in Gentile, *Politics as Religion,* 30.

227. Arthur Koestler in Richard Crossman, ed., *The God That Failed* (New York: Harper and Row, 1949), 16.

228. Joseph Schumpeter, *Capitalism, Socialism, and Democracy,* 3rd ed. (New York: Harper and Row, 1962), 5.

229. A. J. P. Taylor, quoted in Jones, "How Marx Covered His Tracks," 13.

230. Leszek Kolakowski, *Main Currents of Marxism: Its Origins, Growth, and Dissolution,* 3 vols. (Oxford: Oxford University Press, 1981), 1:9–39.

231. Antonio Gramsci, quoted in Gentile, *Politics as Religion,* 31.

232. Benito Mussolini, quoted in ibid.

233. Some prominent examples are Uriel Tal, *Religion, Politics, and Ideology in the Third Reich: Selected Essays* (London: Routledge, 2004); Emilio Gentile, *The Sacralization of Politics in Fascist Italy* (Cambridge, MA: Harvard University Press, 1996); Hans Maier, ed., *Totalitarianism and Political Religions* (London: Routledge, 2004). The journal *Totalitarian Movements and Political Religions* is primarily dedicated to the study of fascism and communism, though other examples, such as militant Islam, come in for scrutiny as well. Gentile gives a good digest of reflections on Italian fascism and German Nazism as religions in *Politics as Religion*, 33–38, 45–109.

234. Ninian Smart, *The Religious Experience of Mankind* (New York: Scribner's, 1969), 5.

235. Ibid., 11.

236. Ninian Smart, *The World's Religions: Old Traditions and Modern Manifestations* (Cambridge: Cambridge University Press, 1989), 25.

237. Gentile, *Politics as Religion*, xvi.

238. Eric Hobsbawm, "Introduction: Inventing Traditions," in *The Invention of Tradition*, ed. Eric Hobsbawm and Terence Ranger (Cambridge: Cambridge University Press, 1983), 12.

239. Carlton J. H. Hayes, *Essays on Nationalism* (New York: Macmillan, 1926), 94–95.

240. Carlton J. H. Hayes, *Nationalism: A Religion* (New York: Macmillan, 1960).

241. Hayes, *Essays on Nationalism*, 100.

242. Benedict Anderson, *Imagined Communities: Reflections on the Origin and Spread of Nationalism*, rev. ed. (London: Verso, 1991), 9–12.

243. Jean-Jacques Rousseau, *The Social Contract*, trans. Willmoore Kendall (South Bend, IN: Gateway, 1954), 154. According to Rousseau, the church has corrupted the true essence of Christianity, which is thoroughly interior and otherworldly: "Christianity is a religion of the spirit through and through; it is concerned with things laid up in heaven, to the exclusion of all else. The Christian's fatherland, for that reason, is not of this world" (ibid., 156).

244. Ibid., 160.

245. Hayes, *Essays on Nationalism*, 101–4.

246. Gentile, *Politics as Religion*, 26–29.

247. Ibid., 17–18.

248. Pauline Maier, *American Scripture: Making the Declaration of Independence* (New York: Knopf, 1997), 186–87.

249. Ibid., 189–90.

250. Gentile, *Politics as Religion*, 21.

251. I treat this subject at greater length in "Messianic Nation: A Christian Theological Critique of American Exceptionalism," *University of St. Thomas Law Journal* 3, no. 2 (Fall 2005): 261–80.

252. Herman Melville, *White Jacket; or, The World in a Man-of-War* (Evanston and Chicago, IL: Northwestern University Press and Newberry Library, 1970), 150–51.

253. For a summary of the debate, see J. A. Mathisen, "Twenty Years after Bellah: Whatever Happened to American Civil Religion?" *Sociological Analysis* 2 (1989): 129–46.

254. Robert N. Bellah, "Civil Religion in America," in *American Civil Religion*, ed. Donald E. Jones and Russell E. Richey (San Francisco, CA: Mellen Research University Press, 1990), 21. This article originally appeared in the Winter 1967 issue of *Daedalus*, the journal of the American Academy of Arts and Sciences.

255. Ibid., 28–30.

256. Will Herberg, "American Civil Religion: What It Is and Whence It Comes," in *American Civil Religion*, ed. Jones and Richey, 77.

257. Ibid., 76–77.

258. Hayes, *Essays on Nationalism*, 107–8.

259. Francis Bellamy, quoted in Cecilia O'Leary, *To Die For: The Paradox of American Patriotism* (Princeton, NJ: Princeton University Press, 1999), 178.

260. Carolyn Marvin and David W. Ingle, "Blood Sacrifice and the Nation: Revisiting Civil Religion," *Journal of the American Academy of Religion* 64, no. 4 (Winter 1996), 767. It is worth noting that Marvin and Ingle wrote this *before* the surge in patriotism following the attacks of September 11, 2001.

261. Carolyn Marvin and David W. Ingle, *Blood Sacrifice and the Nation: Totem Rituals and the American Flag* (Cambridge: Cambridge University Press, 1999).

262. Bill Clinton, quoted in ibid., 138, 140.

263. Marvin and Ingle, "Blood Sacrifice and the Nation," 769.

264. Smith, "Religion, Religions, Religious," 281.

265. William Rehnquist, quoted in Marvin and Ingle, *Blood Sacrifice and the Nation*, 30.

266. Marvin and Ingle, "Blood Sacrifice and the Nation," 770.

267. "By 'religion' we mean a system of cosmological propositions grounded in a belief in a transcendent power expressed through a cult of divine being and giving rise to a set of ethical prescriptions" (ibid., 768).

268. Abraham Lincoln, quoted in Gentile, *Politics as Religion*, 2.

269. George W. Bush, quoted in Ron Hutcheson, "Even amid Security, Nation Feels Its Freedom," *St. Paul Pioneer Press* (July 5, 2002): 1A.

270. Martin E. Marty, with Jonathan Moore, *Politics, Religion, and the Common Good* (San Francisco, CA: Jossey-Bass, 2000), 43.

CHAPTER 3

1. William T. Cavanaugh, "'A Fire Strong Enough to Consume the House': The Wars of Religion and the Rise of the State," *Modern Theology* 11, no. 4 (October 1995): 397–420. The essay was later incorporated into chapter 1 of my book *Theopolitical Imagination* (London: Clark, 2002).

2. Benedict de Spinoza, *Theologico-Political Treatise*, in *Works of Spinoza*, trans. R. H. M. Elwes, 2 vols. (New York: Dover, 1951), 1:7; see also 1:5–6.

3. Ibid., 7.

4. Ibid., 241–56. "When I said that the possessors of sovereign power have rights over everything, and that all rights are dependent on their decree, I did not merely mean temporal rights, but also spiritual rights" (ibid., 245).

5. Ibid., 245–66.

6. Henry Morley, ed., *Ideal Commonwealths: Comprising More's Utopia, Bacon's New Atlantis, Campanella's City of the Sun, and Harrington's Oceana* (Port Washington, NY: Kennikat, 1968).

7. Thomas Hobbes, *Behemoth; or, The Long Parliament*, ed. Ferdinand Tönnies (Chicago: University of Chicago Press, 1990), 95.

8. Ibid., 62. See also his attack on scholasticism, 40–45.

9. Ibid., 55. Hobbes is especially severe with Presbyterian preachers; one of the characters claims that the Presbyterian ministers incited the war and "are therefore guilty of the death of all that fell in that war." He continues on to suggest that it would have been better for the king to kill 1,000 Presbyterian preachers before they preached sedition than to suffer the 100,000 casualties that occurred in the war that they incited (ibid., 95).

10. Ibid., 46.

11. Ibid., 64.

12. Ibid., 1–21.

13. The famous frontispiece of the original edition of Hobbes's *Leviathan* shows, on the lower right, a church council arguing a dispute and weapons with theological concepts engraved upon them. Above these two panels are lightning bolts indicating God's displeasure with theological warfare. This conflict is resolved above by Leviathan, who holds the sword of state in one hand and the crosier of church power in the other; see Arnold Rogow, *Thomas Hobbes: Radical in the Service of Reaction* (London: Norton, 1986), 159.

14. John Locke, *A Letter Concerning Toleration* (Indianapolis: Bobbs-Merrill, 1955), 57.

15. Ibid., 15.

16. Ibid., 14–16.

17. See John Locke, *An Essay Concerning Human Understanding*, ed. Peter Nidditch (Oxford: Clarendon, 1979).

18. Locke, *Concerning Toleration*, 17–18.

19. Ibid., 57–58.

20. Ibid., 17.

21. Ibid., 22–23.

22. James M. Byrne singles out the religious wars, especially the Thirty Years' War, as the most important influence on the Enlightenment's view of religion; see his *Religion and the Enlightenment: From Descartes to Kant* (Louisville, KY: Westminster John Knox, 1996), 28–30.

23. J. G. A. Pocock, *Barbarism and Religion*, vol. 1: *The Enlightenments of Edward Gibbon, 1737–1764* (Cambridge: Cambridge University Press, 1999), 111–12.

24. Baron d'Holbach, *Common Sense; or, Natural Ideas Opposed to Supernatural*, in *The Enlightenment: A Sourcebook and Reader*, ed. Paul Hyland (London: Routledge, 2003), 88.

25. Ibid., 89.

26. Voltaire, *Philosophical Dictionary*, trans. Peter Gay (New York: Harcourt, Brace and World, 1962), 267–69.

27. Ibid., 448. The example of "theological religion" he gives to contrast with the sobriety of state religion is a fanciful account of two parties who come to the Dalai Lama asking him to settle a dispute about the divinity of Fo (the Buddha). The Dalai Lama gives each of them some of his own feces, which the two parties revere, but when the lama decides in favor of one of the parties, they proceed to "assassinating and exterminating and poisoning each other." The Dalai Lama laughs and continues to hand out the contents of his stool to his grateful adherents (ibid.).

28. Ibid., 445.

29. As S. J. Barnett points out, in the Enlightenment:

[A]lmost all those radical in religion or politics also recognized the vital role of the Church in preserving the status quo. Thus Voltaire, famed as a deist, could crusade against all organized religion, yet he also argued that religious observance was to be tolerated and even supported amongst the masses. It was to be tolerated, however, not because of its value as legitimate divine worship, but as an aid in the maintenance of social stability, including the maintenance of the social and economic status of the philosophes themselves, who, for the most part, were drawn from the moneyed classes. (S. J. Barnett, *The Enlightenment and Religion: The Myths of Modernity* [Manchester, England: Manchester University Press, 2003], 17)

Barnett quotes Voltaire's letter to Frederick the Great, "Your majesty will do the human race an eternal service in extirpating this infamous superstition [Christianity]. I do not say among the rabble, who are not worthy of being enlightened and who are apt for every yoke; I say among the well-bred, among those who wish to think" (quoted in ibid., 40).

30. Voltaire, *The Age of Louis XIV*, trans. Martyn P. Pollack (London: Dent, 1961), 394–415; see also 1–19.

31. Jean-Jacques Rousseau, *The Social Contract*, trans. Willmoore Kendall (South Bend, IN: Gateway, 1954), 149.

32. Ibid.

33. Ibid.

34. Ibid., 150.

35. Ibid., 155.

36. Ibid., 154.

37. Ibid., 155.

38. Ibid., 153.

39. Ibid., 160.

40. Ibid., 161.

41. Ibid., 160.

42. Quentin Skinner, *The Foundations of Modern Political Thought* (Cambridge: Cambridge University Press, 1978), 2:352.

43. The paragraph cited above continues: "With Bodin's insistence in his *Six Books* that it ought to be obvious to any prince that 'wars made for matters of religion'

are not in fact 'grounded upon matters directly touching his estate,' we hear for the first time the authentic tones of the modern theorist of the State" (ibid.).

44. See Jean Bodin, *Six Books of the Commonwealth*, trans. and ed. M. J. Tooley (Oxford: Basil Blackwell, n.d.), 140–42.

45. Mack P. Holt, *The French Wars of Religion, 1562–1629* (Cambridge: Cambridge University Press, 1995), 126.

46. Ibid., 168–69.

47. Jeffrey Stout, *The Flight from Authority: Religion, Morality, and the Quest for Autonomy* (Notre Dame, IN: University of Notre Dame Press, 1981), 235–38. On p. 237, Stout quotes the same passage from Skinner that I have quoted above.

48. Ibid., 234–35.

49. Ibid., 241. For more examples of the foundational importance that the wars of religion have for Stout, see pp. x, 3, 46, and 270.

50. Ibid., 241.

51. The only early modern exception, and it is an ambiguous one, is the Dutch republic.

52. The Edict of Nantes is sometimes regarded as the advent of the principle of toleration in France, but it only allowed for a temporary coexistence of Huguenots and Catholics, while Henry IV pursued a policy aimed at the eventual return of church uniformity in France; see Holt, *The French Wars of Religion*, 162–72. At any rate, the Edict of Nantes was a dead letter long before it was officially revoked in 1685.

53. Georg Schmidt, "The Peace of Westphalia as the Fundamental Law of the Complementary Empire-State," in *1648: War and Peace in Europe*, ed. Klaus Bussmann and Heinz Schilling, 3 vols. (Münster: Veranstaltungsgesellschaft 350 Jahre Westfalischer Friede, 1998), 1:451–52.

54. Judith Shklar, *Ordinary Vices* (Cambridge, MA: Harvard University Press, 1984), 5.

55. Ibid., 7–44.

56. John Rawls, *Political Liberalism* (New York: Columbia University Press, 1993), xxivn10.

57. Ibid., xx.

58. Ibid., xxiv.

59. Ibid., xxv.

60. Ibid., xxvi.

61. Ibid., xxii.

62. Kathleen M. Sullivan, "Religion and Liberal Democracy," *University of Chicago Law Review* 59 (1992): 197.

63. Ibid., 198.

64. Michael W. McConnell, "Religious Freedom at a Crossroads," *University of Chicago Law Review* 59 (1992), 115–194.

65. Ibid.

66. Ibid.

67. Ibid., 222.

68. Ibid., 199.

69. Ibid.

70. Ibid., 200.

71. Thomas Hobbes, *Leviathan; or, The Matter, Forme and Power of a Commonwealth Ecclesiasticall and Civil* (New York: Collier, 1962), 100.

72. In addition to the passages cited above, Sullivan uses the phrase four more times in this article, on pp. 199, 200 (citing Rawls), and 222.

73. James Madison, "Memorial and Remonstrance against Religious Assessments," *The Papers of James Madison,* ed. William T. Hutchinson and William M.E. Rachal (Chicago: University of Chicago Press, 1972), 8:298–304, §11.

74. Edwin S. Gaustad, *Faith of Our Fathers: Religion and the New Nation* (New York: Harper and Row, 1987), 12. Gaustad continues:

> The truths that were self-evident to Thomas Jefferson were far from self-evident to the churchmen and the statesmen of an earlier age. On the contrary, what was self-evident to the vast majority of the colonists and their leaders (religious and political) was that society survived only as church and state worked and worshiped together, only as values were shared, only as common assumptions about human nature and the nature of God and the universe underlay all action—or at least all rationalization. (Ibid., 12–13)

75. As I will show in chapter 4, Sullivan is not alone among legal scholars in assuming that religious conflicts are peculiarly dangerous. In that chapter, I will examine this argument in Supreme Court cases concerning the First Amendment.

76. Howard Zinn, *A People's History of the United States* (New York: Harper and Row, 1980), 59.

77. See George Will, "Conduct, Coercion, and Belief," *Washington Post* (April 22, 1990): B7; Will writes that America's founders "wished to tame and domesticate religious passions of the sort that convulsed Europe. They aimed to do so not by establishing religion, but by establishing a commercial republic—capitalism. They aimed to submerge people's turbulent energies in self-interested pursuit of material comforts."

78. Dinesh D'Souza, *What's So Great about America* (Washington, DC: Regnery, 2002), 89–94. D'Souza says that two factors tamed religious passions in America. The first is that no one sect was strong enough to gain the upper hand. "A second reason the American founders were able to avoid religious oppression and conflict is that they found a way to channel people's energies away from theological quarrels and into commercial activity" (90).

79. Francis Fukuyama, *The End of History and the Last Man* (New York: Free Press, 1992), 259–60. Fukuyama's grasp of history is shaky here: the English Civil War in the seventeenth century was an intra-Protestant affair, not Catholic versus Protestant.

80. Ibid., 271; italics in the original. When Fukuyama writes "as we saw" in this passage, he apparently means "as I previously asserted." Nowhere in the book does Fukuyama actually discuss the historical specifics of the English Civil War or present any evidence to support his reading of that conflict.

81. Ibid., 260–61. Fukuyama quotes Schumpeter to the effect that the pursuit of profit in a capitalist world absorbs so much energy that there is little left for making war.

82. Ibid., 11.

83. Stephen Toulmin, *Cosmopolis: The Hidden Agenda of Modernity* (Chicago: University of Chicago Press, 1990), 54.

84. Ibid., 70.

85. Ibid., 91. Toulmin is wrong to put the tilt in the balance so late. As I will point out later in this chapter, the balance was already shifted in favor of civil authorities much earlier.

86. This despite Toulmin's acknowledgment that the Peace of Westphalia only reinforced the policy of allowing the prince to determine the ecclesial affiliation of his subjects, a policy established by the Peace of Augsburg nearly a century before.

87. Many more examples of the myth of the European religious wars can be found in both academic and journalistic publications. Theologian Wolfhart Pannenberg tells the familiar tale in his *Christianity in a Secularized World,* trans. John Bowden (New York: Crossroad, 1989), 11–12: "In this period of confessional wars...people realized that religious passion destroys social peace." See also Wolfhart Pannenberg, *Ethics,* trans. Keith Crim (Philadelphia: Westminster, 1981), 16–20. For another reference to the standard story by a theologian, see David Fergusson, *Community, Liberalism, and Christian Ethics* (Cambridge: Cambridge University Press, 1998), 76. For more examples in liberal political science, see William Galston, "Religious Violence or Religious Pluralism: Islam's Essential Choice," *Philosophy & Public Policy Quarterly* 25, no. 3 (Summer 2005): 12–17; and Paul Berman, *Terror and Liberalism* (New York: Norton, 2003), 79–80. Political theorist William Connolly notes that the story of the religious wars is the standard story told by secularists, and he points out that this is not the only story that could be told about the origins and legitimacy of secularism; William E. Connolly, *Why I Am Not a Secularist* (Minneapolis: University of Minnesota Press, 1999), 20–21. For a more journalistic example, see Thomas Cahill, "The One True Faith: Is It Tolerance?" *New York Times* (February 3, 2002): 4.1: "The forces of the Enlightenment that exalted tolerance in the West were given their impetus by the European wars of the 16th and 17th centuries in which Christian was pitted against Christian—wars over points of doctrine that must have looked exceedingly abstruse, even absurd, to non-Christians, who could see only similarities between the warring systems."

88. Pocock, *Barbarism and Religion,* 100.

89. Ibid., 7.

90. David Held, *Democracy and the Global Order: From the Modern State to Cosmopolitan Governance* (Stanford, CA: Stanford University Press, 1995), 37; italics in the original.

91. Ibid., 33.

92. Ibid., 37.

93. Richard S. Dunn, *The Age of Religious Wars 1559–1689* (New York: Norton, 1970), 6.

94. Ibid., 6–7. Also see James D. Tracy, *Emperor Charles V, Impresario of War: Campaign Strategy, International Finance, and Domestic Politics* (Cambridge: Cambridge University Press, 2002), 45–47, 306.

95. Wim Blockmans, *Emperor Charles V 1500–1558* (London and New York: Arnold Publishers and Oxford University Press, 2002), 77. These wars were essentially a continuation of French attacks on the Holy Roman Empire in 1494 and 1498.

96. Ibid., 139.

97. Ibid., 41; Tracy, *Emperor Charles V, Impresario of War*, 307.

98. Klaus Jaitner, "The Popes and the Struggle for Power during the Sixteenth and Seventeenth Centuries," in *1648: War and Peace in Europe*, ed. Bussmann and Schilling, 1:62.

99. Tracy, *Emperor Charles V, Impresario of War*, 209–15. Both of these men would later ally with the Schmalkaldic League in March 1552; William Maltby, *The Reign of Charles V* (New York: Palgrave, 2002), 63. Several months later, however, Albrecht-Alcibiades was back on Charles's side in an attempt to recover the towns of Lorraine for the empire (Blockmans, *Emperor Charles V*, 75).

100. Maltby, *The Reign of Charles V*, 62.

101. Ibid., 56.

102. Blockmans, *Emperor Charles V*, 94.

103. Maltby, *The Reign of Charles V*, 58.

104. Ibid., 53.

105. Blockmans, *Emperor Charles V*, 95.

106. Ibid., 110.

107. Maltby, *The Reign of Charles V*, 112–13.

108. Ibid., 62–64.

109. Dunn, *The Age of Religious Wars*, 49.

110. Ibid., 50–51.

111. Tracy, *Emperor Charles V, Impresario of War*, 32–34, 46; also see 33n47.

112. Henry Heller, *Iron and Blood: Civil Wars in Sixteenth-Century France* (Montreal: McGill-Queen's University Press, 1991), 53, 61–62.

113. Raymond de Fourquevaux, quoted in Henry Kamen, *Early Modern European Society* (London: Routledge, 2000), 75.

114. Heller, *Iron and Blood*, 63; Kamen, *Early Modern European Society*, 75.

115. Heller, *Iron and Blood*, 63–65.

116. J. H. M. Salmon, *Society in Crisis: France in the Sixteenth Century* (New York: St. Martin's, 1975), 198. Salmon reports that Turenne almost converted to Protestantism two years later, but did not for fear it would impede his future advancement. He did become a Calvinist later in life.

117. Holt, *The French Wars of Religion*, 99. Also see Salmon, *Society in Crisis*, 176, 197.

118. Salmon, *Society in Crisis*, 197–98.

119. Holt, *The French Wars of Religion*, 103.

120. Ibid., 117–19.

121. Salmon, *Society in Crisis*, 204–5. Salmon notes that even Huguenot champion Henri de Condé considered an alliance with Guise; ibid., 204.

122. Ibid., 234.

123. Ibid., 244.

124. Ibid., 183–85.

125. Salmon, *Society in Crisis*, 257; Holt, *The French Wars of Religion*, 130–32.

126. Holt, *The French Wars of Religion*, 117–18. German Catholics also supported Dutch Protestants against the Spanish. The Catholic duke Wilhelm of Jülich, Cleves, and Berg actively supported William of Orange in his armed rebellion that began in 1568. William of Orange also exercised flexible ecclesial politics. In the period 1576–1585, when he needed the support of Catholic nobles in the southern provinces of the Netherlands, he defended Catholicism and suppressed Calvinism in the south, while supporting Calvinism and proscribing Catholicism in the north; Jonathan Israel, "The Dutch-Spanish War and the Holy Roman Empire (1568–1648)," in *1648: War and Peace in Europe,* ed. Bussmann and Schilling, 112–14.

127. Salmon, *Society in Crisis*, 234.

128. Holt, *The French Wars of Religion*, 50–51.

129. Heller, *Iron and Blood*, 95.

130. Ibid., 209–11.

131. Ibid., 91–92.

132. Ibid., 127.

133. Salmon, *Society in Crisis*, 277.

134. Heller, *Iron and Blood*, 126.

135. Holt, *The French Wars of Religion*, 156–57.

136. Salmon, *Society in Crisis*, 282–91.

137. Ibid., 243–57.

138. The Swiss Reformed cities refused to join the Protestant Union because of their alliance obligations to the Swiss Confederation's Catholic regions; Kaspar von Greyerz, "Switzerland during the Thirty Years' War," in *1648: War and Peace in Europe,* ed. Bussmann and Schilling, 135.

139. Geoffrey Parker, ed., *The Thirty Years' War* (London: Routledge, 1984), 59–64.

140. Ibid., 29–33.

141. Robert Oresko, "The House of Savoy and the Thirty Years' War," in *1648: War and Peace in Europe,* ed. Bussmann and Schilling, 143–44.

142. Dunn, *The Age of Religious Wars*, 71.

143. Parker, *The Thirty Years' War*, 94.

144. Ibid., 136.

145. Oresko, "The House of Savoy and the Thirty Years' War," 144–45.

146. Parker, *The Thirty Years' War*, 70–71.

147. Ibid., 76.

148. James B. Collins, *The State in Early Modern France* (Cambridge: Cambridge University Press, 1995), 29.

149. Ibid., 115.

150. R. Po-Chia Hsia, *Social Discipline in the Reformation: Central Europe 1550–1750* (London: Routledge, 1989), 85. In my earlier article on the wars of religion, I called Wallenstein a "Bohemian Protestant" (Cavanaugh, "A Fire Strong Enough to Consume the House," 402). This is inaccurate. He was born a Protestant in Bohemia, but became a Catholic—though not a very zealous one—at age twenty-three.

151. Parker, *The Thirty Years' War*, 194.

152. Dunn, *The Age of Religious Wars*, 71–72.

153. Parker, *The Thirty Years' War*, 195.

154. Quoted in ibid.

155. Ibid., 123. Parker notes that the Swedish declaration of June 1630 makes no mention of saving the Protestant cause in its list of reasons for invading (ibid., 121).

156. Herbert Langer, "The Royal Swedish War in Germany," in *1648: War and Peace in Europe*, ed. Bussmann and Schilling, 189.

157. Parker, *The Thirty Years' War*, 127–28.

158. Ibid. Richelieu did stipulate that Catholic worship should be tolerated in territories conquered by Sweden, but as Parker points out, he had no way of forcing Sweden to comply (ibid., 124, 262n6).

159. Konrad Repgen, "Negotiating the Peace of Westphalia: A Survey with an Examination of the Major Problems," in *1648: War and Peace in Europe*, ed. Bussmann and Schilling, 355.

160. Parker, *The Thirty Years' War*, 142.

161. Ibid., 144; Oresko, "The House of Savoy and the Thirty Years' War," 146.

162. Parker, *The Thirty Years' War*, 142–43.

163. Quoted in ibid., 182.

164. Jaitner, "The Popes and the Struggle for Power," 65. As Jaitner remarks, the pope's "call to fight against heretics and heresies in the Empire was merely rhetorical with no concrete consequences" (ibid.).

165. Parker, *The Thirty Years' War*, 174.

166. Ann Hughes, *The Causes of the English Civil War*, 2nd ed. (London: Macmillan, 1998), 42.

167. Such was the case in the Palatinate and Brandenburg-Prussia; Eric W. Gritsch, *A History of Lutheranism* (Minneapolis, MN: Fortress, 2002), 110–11.

168. Herbert J. A. Bouman, "Retrospect and Prospect," *Sixteenth-Century Studies* 8, no. 4 (1977): 84–104; David C. Steinmetz, *Reformers in the Wings: From Geiler von Kayserberg to Theodore Beza*, 2nd ed. (Oxford: Oxford University Press, 2001).

169. John Bossy, "Unrethinking the Sixteenth-Century Wars of Religion," in *Belief in History: Innovative Approaches to European and American Religion*, ed. Thomas Kselman (Notre Dame, IN: University of Notre Dame Press, 1991), 268.

170. Michel de Montaigne, "Apology for Raymond Sebond," in *The Complete Essays of Montaigne*, ed. Donald M. Frame (Stanford, CA: Stanford University Press, 1965), 323, quoted in Holt, *The French Wars of Religion*, 74.

171. Jean-H. Mariéjol, *La Réforme et la Ligue, l'Edit de Nantes (1559–1598)*, quoted in Mack P. Holt, "Putting Religion Back into the Wars of Religion," *French Historical Studies* 18, no. 2 (Autumn 1993): 526.

172. Lucien Romier, "A Dissident Nobility under the Cloak of Religion," in *The French Wars of Religion: How Important Were Religious Factors?* ed. J. H. M. Salmon (Lexington, MA: Heath, 1967), 26.

173. James Westfall Thompson, *The Wars of Religion in France 1559–1576: The Huguenots, Catherine de Medici, Philip II*, 2nd ed. (New York: Ungar, 1957), 142.

174. "As we look back on this dismal story of the French Religious Wars, what are our reflections?...Undoubtedly, the root of the trouble was the weakness of the monarchy"; J. E. Neale, *The Age of Catherine de Medici* (New York: Harper and Row, 1962), 100–102, quoted in Holt, "Putting Religion Back into the Wars of Religion," 525.

175. Sir John Neale, "The Failure of Catherine de Medici," in *The French Wars of Religion*, ed. Salmon, 35.

176. Henri Drouot, *Mayenne et la Bourgogne: Etude sur la Ligue (1587–1596)*, 2 vols. (Paris: Picard, 1937), 1:33, quoted in Holt, "Putting Religion Back into the Wars of Religion," 529.

177. Henri Hauser, "Political Anarchy and Social Discontent," in *The French Wars of Religion*, ed. Salmon, 32–33.

178. Georges Livet, *Les Guerres de religion* (Paris, 1962), 4, quoted in Holt, "Putting Religion Back into the Wars of Religion," 530.

179. See Robert M. Kingdon, *Geneva and the Coming of the Wars of Religion in France* (Geneva: Droz, 1956); and N. M. Sutherland, *The Massacre of St. Bartholomew and the European Conflict, 1559–1572* (New York: Barnes and Noble, 1973).

180. Natalie Zemon Davis, *Society and Culture in Early Modern France* (Stanford, CA: Stanford University Press, 1975), 157. Chapter 6 of this book originally appeared as "The Rites of Violence: Religious Riot in Sixteenth-Century France," *Past & Present*, no. 59 (May 1973).

181. Ibid., 160.

182. Ibid., 178.

183. Ibid., 181.

184. Ibid., 186.

185. Ibid., 164.

186. Denis Crouzet, *Les guerriers de Dieu: La violence au temps des troubles de religion* (Seyssel, France: Champ Vallon, 1990).

187. Holt, "Putting Religion Back into the Wars of Religion," 539.

188. Ibid.

189. Barbara Diefendorf, *Beneath the Cross: Catholics and Huguenots in Sixteenth-Century Paris* (New York: Oxford University Press, 1991), 6:

> Crouzet's radical thesis will inevitably cause controversy as historians try to decide just how—or if—it can be reconciled with the more familiar interpretations of the religious wars. Must we go from an overly political interpretation of the period to one that seems to offer very little room for politics, at least as traditionally viewed? I hope that when the dust settles my own work will help demonstrate that there is a middle ground.

In his review article on Crouzet's book, M. Greengrass asks a question similar to Diefendorf's: "Can one, however, be convinced by an account of religious change which so thoroughly abandons economic, social and institutional causation in favour of collective psychology?" M. Greengrass, "The Psychology of Religious Violence," *French History* 5, no. 4 (1991): 472.

190. Holt, "Putting Religion Back into the Wars of Religion," 543. Holt is paraphrasing from Richet's *De la Réforme à la Révolution: Etudes sur la France moderne* (Paris: Aubier, 1991).

191. Michael Wolfe, *The Conversion of Henry IV: Politics, Power, and Religious Belief in Early Modern France* (Cambridge, MA: Harvard University Press, 1993), 5.

192. Heller, *Iron and Blood*, 136, as quoted in Holt, "Putting Religion Back into the Wars of Religion," 545.

193. Heller, *Iron and Blood*, 60, as quoted in Holt, "Putting Religion Back into the Wars of Religion," 546.

194. Henry Heller, "Putting History Back into the Religious Wars: A Reply to Mack P. Holt," *French Historical Studies* 19, no. 3 (Spring 1996): 854–55.

195. Ibid., 855.

196. Ibid. As a positive example, Heller holds up William Bouwsma's work on John Calvin for the way it gets at the psychodynamic elements *behind* or *beneath* Calvin's theology: "Indeed, the way in which Bouwsma is able to slip below Calvin's theological rationalism and suggest the confrontation between father and son which underlay it represents an extraordinary *tour de force.*"

197. Mack P. Holt, "Religion, Historical Method, and Historical Forces: A Rejoinder," *French Historical Studies* 19, no. 3 (Spring 1996): 864.

198. Ibid.

199. Ibid., 865.

200. Ibid., 865–66.

201. Holt, *The French Wars of Religion*, 1.

202. Ibid., 2. By "contemporary," Holt of course means pertaining to the sixteenth century.

203. Ibid., 19.

204. Ibid., 17–21.

205. Ibid., 190–91:

But by "putting religion back" into the story, it is equally clear that politics, economics, intellectual trends, and other social forces still have their proper place. Moreover, I do not mean to suggest that explicitly political decisions—such as the decision by the royal council to murder the Huguenot nobles on St. Bartholomew's Day, Henry III's decision to assassinate the Guises, or Henry IV's abjuration of Protestantism—did not significantly shape the outcome of the religious wars. While the sense of religious community that was endemic throughout society from top to bottom may have been the foundation of the conflict, political decisions at court were clearly crucial in triggering the popular violence as well as the military campaigns. Without high politics there is, in fact, no story at all, since it was politics that was responsible for both beginning and ending the long conflict. Moreover, the socio-economic tensions that were so much a part of the hierarchical society of the pre-modern world were also exacerbated by the civil wars, and these tensions occasionally spilled over into the arena of warfare: the popular uprisings in 1579 and 1593 being the most visible examples. Thus, I have not tried to downplay the impact of other factors that were clearly crucial to the wars of religion by emphasizing the social importance of religion; I have simply tried to restore a crucial piece of the puzzle that has been missing for far too long.

206. Ibid., 6. Similarly, Diefendorf closes the introduction to her book by citing parallels between the "emotional outbursts" of sixteenth-century religious actors and the "religious fervor" that is linked with violence today: the "inflammatory rhetoric" of Hindu fundamentalism, the "hysterical pitch" of the crowds at the Ayatollah Khomeini's funeral, and so on. "The use of religion to serve political ends—and vice versa—is by no means a purely historical phenomenon" (Diefendorf, *Beneath the Cross*, 8). Despite all of their careful historical work, Holt and Diefendorf cannot quite escape the liberal narrative that religion is an independent factor with a peculiar tendency, in the sixteenth century and in the twenty-first, to promote war.

207. Hsia, *Social Discipline*, 34.

208. Diefendorf, *Beneath the Cross*, 6.

209. Ibid., 38.

210. Bossy, "Unrethinking the Sixteenth-Century Wars of Religion," 280.

211. Bossy says that the media report violence in the same way: people do not really fight for religion, but must be fighting for something else (ibid., 278). Whatever the case when Bossy was writing, this does not seem to be the case with the media today, especially since the attacks of September 11, 2001.

212. Ibid., 279.

213. Ibid., 278.

214. Ibid., 280.

215. John Bossy, *Christianity in the West 1400–1700* (Oxford: Oxford University Press, 1985), 170–71.

216. Ibid., 171.

217. Axel Oxenstierna, quoted in Parker, *The Thirty Years' War*, 122.

218. Hans-Jürgen Goertz, *Pfaffenhaß und groß Geschrei* (Munich: Beck, 1987), 25.

219. Johannes C. Wolfart, *Religion, Government, and Political Culture in Early Modern Germany: Lindau 1520–1628* (New York: Palgrave, 2002), 6, 35.

220. Ibid., 49. Wolfart is quoting Jonathan Z. Smith, *Imagining Religion: From Babylon to Jonestown* (Chicago: University of Chicago Press, 1982), xi.

221. Wolfart, *Religion, Government, and Political Culture*, 49.

222. Walther von Wartburg, "Saeculum, séculariser," in his *Französiches etymologisches Wörterbuch* (Bonn: F. Klopp 1964), 11:44–46, quoted in Jan N. Brenner, "Secularization: Notes toward a Genealogy," in *Religion: Beyond a Concept*, ed. Hent de Vries (New York: Fordham University Press, 2008), 433.

223. Heinz Schilling, "War and Peace at the Emergence of Modernity: Europe between State Belligerence, Religious Wars, and the Desire for Peace," in *1648: War and Peace in Europe*, ed. Bussmann and Schilling, 14.

224. Charles Tilly, "Reflections on the History of European State-Making," in *The Formation of National States in Western Europe*, ed. Charles Tilly (Princeton, NJ: Princeton University Press, 1975), 42.

225. Gabriel Ardant, "Financial Policy and Economic Infrastructure of Modern States and Nations," in *The Formation of National States in Western Europe*, ed. Tilly, 164–242. The common people came into the emergent state's purview mainly as a source of money and recruits for the purpose of making war; see David Warren Sabean, *Power in the Blood: Popular Culture & Village Discourse in Early Modern Germany* (Cambridge: Cambridge University Press, 1984), 201–2.

226. Otto Hintze, *The Historical Essays of Otto Hintze*, ed. Felix Gilbert (New York: Oxford University Press, 1975). For example, "All state organization was originally military organization, organization for war" (181).

227. Perry Anderson, *Lineages of the Absolutist State* (London: New Left, 1974).

228. Hendrik Spruyt, *The Sovereign State and Its Competitors* (Princeton, NJ: Princeton University Press, 1994).

229. Anthony Giddens, *The Nation-State and Violence* (Berkeley, CA: University of California Press, 1987).

230. Victor Lee Burke, *The Clash of Civilizations: War-Making & State Formation in Europe* (Cambridge: Polity, 1997).

231. Thomas Ertman, *Birth of the Leviathan: Building States and Regimes in Medieval and Early Modern Europe* (Cambridge: Cambridge University Press, 1997), 4.

232. Ibid., 26. Ertman's project builds on this consensus in offering what he says is a better account of the factors which predict whether or not a state will have an absolutist or constitutional framework. Ertman contends that Hintze, Tilly, Downing, and Mann do not adequately account for the "nonsimultaneity" of the process, that is, that not all states were affected by war making at the same time (ibid., 15, 26–27).

233. Ibid., 4.

234. Michael Howard, *The Invention of Peace: Reflections on War and International Order* (New Haven, CT: Yale University Press, 2000), 15.

235. Ibid.

236. Dunn, *The Age of Religious Wars*, 49.

237. Jeremy Black, "Warfare, Crisis, and Absolutism," in *Early Modern Europe: An Oxford History*, ed. Euan Cameron (Oxford: Oxford University Press, 1999), 209–10.

238. Donna Bohanan, *Crown and Nobility in Early Modern France* (New York: Palgrave, 2001), 32.

239. Arlette Jouanna, *Le devoir de révolte: La noblesse française et la gestation de l'état modern, 1559–1661* (Paris: Fayard, 1989). See also Bohanan, *Crown and Nobility*, 27–29.

240. Salmon, *Society in Crisis*, 59–60.

241. Ibid., 168–69.

242. Quoted in Salmon, *Society in Crisis*, 238; also see 201.

243. Elie Barnavi and Robert Descimon, *La Sainte ligue, le juge et la potence* (Paris: Hachette, 1985), quoted in Heller, *Iron and Blood*, 106.

244. Salmon, *Society in Crisis*, 13.

245. Steven Gunn, "War, Religion, and the State," in *Early Modern Europe*, ed. Cameron, 124.

246. Skinner, *Foundations of Modern Political Thought,* 2:59–60; Maltby, *The Reign of Charles V,* 14.

247. Holt, *The French Wars of Religion,* 10–12. The pope retained the right of veto if a candidate was manifestly unqualified, but in practice that right was seldom used.

248. Salmon, *Society in Crisis,* 80–82.

249. Ibid., 81. Salmon notes too that, under Francis I, the units of administration of church and state corresponded at the level of the parish; "the village curé was the means by which the government of both church and state made known its will" (ibid., 79).

250. Skinner, *Foundations of Modern Political Thought,* 2:58–64.

251. Pope Julius III, quoted in David Potter, *A History of France 1460–1560: The Emergence of a Nation State* (New York: St. Martin's, 1995), 227.

252. Skinner, *Foundations of Modern Political Thought,* 2:60–61.

253. Maltby, *The Reign of Charles V,* 25.

254. Gunn, "War, Religion, and the State," 126.

255. G. R. Elton, "The Age of the Reformation," in *New Cambridge Modern History,* ed. Peter Burke, 13 vols. (Cambridge: Cambridge University Press, 1958), 2:5, quoted in Dunn, *The Age of Religious Wars,* 6.

256. Luther D. Peterson, "Johann Pfeffinger's Treatises of 1550 in Defense of Adiaphora: 'High Church' Lutheranism and Confessionalization in Albertine Saxony," in *Confessionalization in Europe, 1555–1700: Essays in Honor of Bodo Nischan,* ed. John M. Headley, Hans J. Hillerbrand, and Anthony J. Papalas (Aldershot, England: Ashgate, 2004), 104–5.

257. Heinz Schilling, "The Reformation and the Rise of the Early Modern State," in *Luther and the Modern State in Germany,* ed. James D. Tracy (Kirksville, MO: Sixteenth Century Journal Publishers, 1986), 21–30.

258. Karlheinz Blaschke, "The Reformation and the Rise of the Territorial State," in *Luther and the Modern State in Germany,* ed. Tracy, 67–68.

259. Hsia, *Social Discipline in the Reformation,* 6.

260. Ibid., 2.

261. Ibid., 177.

262. Ibid., 17–19.

263. Ibid., 36.

264. Ibid., 57.

265. Ibid., 44.

266. Ibid., 39–44.

267. Ibid., 54–55.

268. Ibid., 70.

269. Ibid., 177.

270. Ibid., 131–42, 174–75.

271. Ibid., 143. See also Marc R. Forster, *The Counter-Reformation in the Villages: Religion and Reform in the Bishopric of Speyer 1560–1720* (Ithaca, NY: Cornell University Press, 1992).

272. Hsia, *Social Discipline in the Reformation*, 6.

273. Ibid., 53.

274. Ernst Troeltsch, *Protestantism and Progress: The Significance of Protestantism for the Rise of the Modern World* (Philadelphia: Fortress, 1986); also see Thomas A. Brady, Jr., "Confessionalization: The Career of a Concept," in *Confessionalization in Europe*, ed. Headley et al., 3–4.

275. Brady, "Confessionalization: The Career of a Concept," 5–17.

276. Ute Lotz-Heumann and Karl S. Bottigheimer, "The Irish Reformation in European Perspective," *Archiv für Reformationsgeschichte* 87 (1998): 268–309.

277. Mack P. Holt, "Confessionalization beyond the Germanies: The Case of France," in *Confessionalization in Europe*, ed. Headley et al., 257–73.

278. Hughes, *The Causes of the English Civil War*, 10–25.

279. Ibid., 25. Here, Hughes is summing up the view of Conrad Russell in his book *The Causes of the English Civil War* (Oxford: Clarendon, 1990). Much of Russell's analysis is from the monarchy's point of view. As Hughes points out, other historians put more of the blame on James's and Charles's profligacy and mismanagement. The general point of the tension between localism and the centralizing efforts of the Crown is not in dispute; Hughes, *The Causes of the English Civil War*, 25–30.

280. Ibid., 111.

281. King Charles I, proclamation of February 1639, quoted in ibid., 89.

282. S. R. Gardiner, ed., *The Constitutional Documents of the Puritan Revolution* (London, 1906), 206–7, quoted in Hughes, *The Causes of the English Civil War*, 85.

283. Hughes, *The Causes of the English Civil War*, 58–59, 90–97.

284. Holt, *The French Wars of Religion*, 163.

285. Ibid., 3–4, 126, 168–69.

286. Ibid., 4.

287. Potter, *A History of France 1460–1560*, 32.

288. Ibid., 43–44.

289. Bossy, *Christianity in the West*, 154–55.

290. Potter, *A History of France 1460–1560*, 40.

291. Ibid., 31; for reference to the "royal religion," see 43 and 285.

292. Holt, *The French Wars of Religion*, 9.

293. Jacques-Bénigne Bossuet, *Politics Drawn from the Very Words of Holy Scripture*, trans. P. Riley (Cambridge: Cambridge University Press, 1990), 82.

294. John B. Wolf, *Louis XIV* (New York: Norton, 1968), 357–78.

295. Peterson, "Johann Pfeffinger's Treatises," 104–5.

296. Gunn, "War, Religion, and the State," 116–17; see also Tracy, *Emperor Charles V, Impresario of War*, 26–27.

297. Richard McCoy, *Alterations of State: Sacred Kingship in the English Reformation* (New York: Columbia University Press, 2002), 58–66. At her coronation, Elizabeth expressly ordered the presider not to elevate the host, to eliminate competition between the two objects of reverence.

298. King James I, *The True Law of Free Monarchies*, excerpted in *The Norton Anthology of English Literature*. Available at: http://www2.wwnorton.com/college/english/nael/17century/topic_3/truelaw.htm#top.

299. Bossy, *Christianity in the West*, 159.

300. Ernst H. Kantorowicz, *The King's Two Bodies: A Study in Medieval Political Theology* (Princeton, NJ: Princeton University Press, 1957); see especially 7–23, 193–232.

301. Ibid., 232–72. To "die for France" becomes a significant theme from the late fifteenth century onward; see Potter, *A History of France 1460–1560*, 18–19.

302. Hobbes, *Leviathan*, 363–66.

303. John Neville Figgis, *From Gerson to Grotius, 1414–1625* (New York: Harper Torchbook, 1960), 124.

304. Charles Tilly, "War Making and State Making as Organized Crime," in *Bringing the State Back In*, ed. Peter B. Evans, Dietrich Rueschemeyer, and Theda Skocpol (Cambridge: Cambridge University Press, 1985), 169.

305. Wolf, *Louis XIV*, 383.

306. Ibid., 377.

307. Eric Hobsbawm, "Introduction: Inventing Traditions," in *The Invention of Tradition*, ed. Eric Hobsbawm and Terence Ranger (Cambridge: Cambridge University Press, 1983), 12.

308. Carolyn Marvin and David W. Ingle, "Blood Sacrifice and the Nation: Revisiting Civil Religion," *Journal of the American Academy of Religion* 64, no. 4 (Winter 1996), 769.

309. Anderson, *Imagined Communities: Reflections on the Origin and Spread of Nationalism*, (New York: Verso, 1991), 9–12.

310. Carolyn Marvin and David W. Ingle, *Blood Sacrifice and the Nation: Totem Rituals and the American Flag* (Cambridge: Cambridge University Press, 1999), 3.

311. Michel Foucault, *Discipline and Punish: The Birth of the Prison*, trans. Alan Sheridan (New York: Vintage, 1977).

CHAPTER 4

1. Martin E. Marty, with Jonathan Moore, *Politics, Religion, and the Common Good* (San Francisco, CA: Jossey-Bass, 2000), 23.

2. Ibid., 24.

3. Ibid.

4. Ibid., 23.

5. Frederick Mark Gedicks, *The Rhetoric of Church and State: A Critical Analysis of Religion Clause Jurisprudence* (Durham, NC: Duke University Press, 1995), 10–19.

6. Philip Hamburger, *Separation of Church and State* (Cambridge, MA: Harvard University Press, 2002), 11.

7. Ibid., 191–284.

8. Edward Purcell, *The Crisis of Democratic Theory: Scientific Naturalism and the Problem of Value* (Lexington: University of Kentucky Press, 1973).

9. Ibid., 12–13. I am not aware of any use by the Supreme Court of the idea that religion has a peculiar tendency to produce conflict before the *Minersville* case in 1940. I have read through the few significant Supreme Court religion clause

cases prior to *Minersville*—*Permoli v. Municipality No. 1 of the City of New Orleans* (1845), *Watson v. Jones* (1871), *Bradfield v. Roberts* (1899), *Reuben Quick Bear v. Leupp* (1908), *Gonzalez v. Roman Catholic Archbishop of Manila* (1929), *Cantwell v. State of Connecticut* (1940)—and have found no version of the myth of religious violence. The closest is from *Cantwell*, when Justice Roberts, writing for the majority, states:

> In the realm of religious faith, and in that of political belief, sharp differences arise. In both fields the tenets of one man may seem the rankest error to his neighbor. To persuade others to his own point of view, the pleader, as we know, at times, resorts to exaggeration, to vilification of men who have been, or are, prominent in church or state, and even to false statement. But the people of this nation have ordained in the light of history, that, in spite of the probability of excesses and abuses, these liberties are, in the long view, essential to enlightened opinion and right conduct on the part of the citizens of a democracy. (*Cantwell v. State of Connecticut*, 310 U.S. 296 [1940], 310)

Here, Justice Roberts does not single out religion as prone to cause differences, but puts "religious faith" and "political belief" on the same footing.

   10. *Minersville School District v. Gobitis*, 310 U.S. 586 (1940), 593.

   11. Ibid., 595.

   12. Ibid., 596. Frankfurter writes:

> The ultimate foundation of a free society is the binding tie of cohesive sentiment. Such a sentiment is fostered by all those agencies of the mind and spirit which may serve to gather up the traditions of a people, transmit them from generation to generation, and thereby create that continuity of a treasured common life which constitutes a civilization. "We live by symbols." The flag is the symbol of our national unity, transcending all internal differences, however large, within the framework of the Constitution.

   13. Ibid., 599. For the Court to intervene "would amount to no less than the pronouncement of pedagogical and psychological dogma in a field where courts possess no marked and certainly no controlling competence" (ibid., 598–99).

   14. *Everson v. Board of Education of Ewing Township*, 330 U.S. 1 (1947), 19.

   15. Ibid., 8–9.

   16. Ibid., 8.

   17. Ibid., 18.

   18. Hugo Black, quoted in Hamburger, *Separation of Church and State*, 430.

   19. Quoted in Hamburger, *Separation of Church and State*, 431–32.

   20. Hamburger, *Separation of Church and State*, 461–62.

   21. Philip B. Kurland, "The Religion Clauses and the Burger Court," *Catholic University Law Review* 34 (1984): 7: "On the whole, the Court followed the line of Mr. Justice Black's argument in *Everson*—the school bus case—rather than his judgment."

   22. Gedicks, *The Rhetoric of Church and State*, 20.

   23. Hamburger, *Separation of Church and State*, 399–434.

   24. Ibid., 474–78.

25. *McCollum v. Board of Education,* 333 U.S. 203 (1948), 216–17. Later in his opinion, Frankfurter again emphasizes national unity over religious diversity:

> The public school is at once the symbol of our democracy and the most per-vasive means for promoting our common destiny. In no activity of the State is it more vital to keep out divisive forces than in its schools, to avoid confus-ing, not to say fusing, what the Constitution sought to keep strictly apart. "The great American principle of eternal separation"—Elihu Root's phrase bears repetition—is one of the vital reliances of our Constitutional system for assuring unities among our people stronger than our diversities. (Ibid., 231)

26. Ibid., 228. Frankfurter cites none of these pages, but instead, in a footnote to his comment, cites the differing opinions of the amicus briefs filed by different religious groups as evidence of the inherent divisiveness of religion; see footnote 19 to Frankfurter's opinion.

27. *Engel v. Vitale,* 370 U.S. 421 (1962), 426.

28. Ibid., 429.

29. *Abington Township School District v. Schempp,* 374 U.S. 203 (1963), 307.

30. Ibid., 241.

31. Ibid.

32. Ibid., 242.

33. Ibid., 313.

34. Ibid., 307–8.

35. "First, the statute must have a secular legislative purpose; second, its principal or primary effect must be one that neither advances nor inhibits reli-gion.... finally, the statute must not foster 'an excessive government entanglement with religion' "; *Lemon v. Kurtzman,* 403 U.S. 602 (1971), 612–13.

36. Ibid., 622.

37. Paul A. Freund, "Public Aid to Parochial Schools," *Harvard Law Review* 82 (1969): 1680–92. The first sentence in my quote from Burger's decision appears to be a paraphrase of Freund's statement on p. 1692: "While political debate and division is normally a wholesome process for reaching viable accommodations, political division on religious lines is one of the principal evils that the first amendment sought to forestall."

38. In his concurring opinion in *Walz,* Harlan wrote:

> What is at stake as a matter of policy is preventing that kind and degree of government involvement in religious life that, as history teaches us, is apt to lead to strife and frequently strain a political system to the breaking point. While these concepts are at the "core" of the Religion Clauses, they may not suffice by themselves to achieve in all cases the purposes of the First Amendment. As Professor Freund has only recently pointed out in Public Aid to Parochial Schools, 82 Harv. L. Rev. 1680 (1969), governmental involvement, while neutral, may be so direct or in such degree as to engender a risk of politicizing religion. Thus, as the opinion of THE CHIEF JUSTICE notes, religious groups inevitably represent certain points of view and not

infrequently assert them in the political arena, as evidenced by the continuing debate respecting birth control and abortion laws. Yet history cautions
that political fragmentation on sectarian lines must be guarded against.
(*Walz v. Tax Commission of the City of New York*, 397 U.S. 664 [1970], 695)

39. Freund, "Public Aid to Parochial Schools," 1692.

40. Ibid., 1686.

41. Ibid.

42. Ibid., 1690.

43. Legal scholar William Marshall argues that the recognition of the similarity between nationalism and religion actually *strengthens* the case for greater legal
constraints on religion in public. He writes:

> [R]eligion's unique relationship to one of humanity's deepest fears sug-
> gests that it possesses an inherent volatility that secular ideologies do not.
> Moreover, the argument that there are special concerns posed by religion's
> involvement in politics is buttressed, rather than weakened, by the reali-
> zation that nationalism may also pose the risk of intolerance and persecu-
> tion. Nationalism arguably approaches religion in its ability to maintain a
> fervent hold on its adherents. Therefore, keeping religion out of the political
> sphere assures that these powerful forces do not combine and increase their
> dangers. (William P. Marshall, "The Other Side of Religion," *Hastings Law
> Journal* 44 [April 1993]: 859n80)

The assumption that nationalism is secular, despite its similarity to religion, ensures
that Marshall treats nationalism as a given. Nationalism is simply assumed to be
part of the way things are, and there clearly is not room in public for more than one
totalizing and violent ideology. Marshall's article, he says, is an attempt to investigate "whether there is something about the nature of religion itself that justifies the
special constraints placed upon it" (ibid., 844). Although he never defines religion,
he relies heavily on Rudolf Otto to argue that religion is a fearful human response to
the encounter with the *mysterium tremendum*: "Because fear is a primary motivation
for the adoption of a belief structure, the believer may be upset by any suggestion that
her adopted belief system is fallible" (ibid., 858). This accounts for the need to keep
religion out of the public sphere.

44. Justice Breyer wrote a separate dissent in *Zelman v. Simmons-Harris*, 536
U.S. 639 (2002), as he says, "to emphasize the risk that publicly financed voucher
programs pose in terms of religiously based social conflict. I do so because I believe
that the Establishment Clause concern for protecting the Nation's social fabric from
religious conflict poses an overriding obstacle to the implementation of this well-
intentioned school voucher program."

45. Justice Souter, writing for the majority in banning displays of the Ten
Commandments in courtrooms, *McCreary County et al. v. American Civil Liberties
Union of Kentucky et al.*, 545 U.S. 844 (2005), says:

> Given the variety of interpretative problems, the principle of neutrality
> has provided a good sense of direction: the government may not favor one

religion over another, or religion over irreligion, religious choice being the prerogative of individuals under the Free Exercise Clause. The principle has been helpful simply because it responds to one of the major concerns that prompted adoption of the Religion Clauses. The Framers and the citizens of their time intended not only to protect the integrity of individual conscience in religious matters, *Wallace v. Jaffree*, 472 U.S., at 52–54, and n. 38, but to guard against the civic divisiveness that follows when the Government weighs in on one side of religious debate; nothing does a better job of roiling society, a point that needed no explanation to the descendants of English Puritans and Cavaliers (or Massachusetts Puritans and Baptists). *E.g., Everson, supra,* at 8 ("A large proportion of the early settlers of this country came here from Europe to escape [religious persecution]"). A sense of the past thus points to governmental neutrality as an objective of the Establishment Clause, and a sensible standard for applying it.

46. Justice O'Connor, concurring in ibid.:

Reasonable minds can disagree about how to apply the Religion Clauses in a given case. But the goal of the Clauses is clear: to carry out the Founders' plan of preserving religious liberty to the fullest extent possible in a pluralistic society. By enforcing the Clauses, we have kept religion a matter for the individual conscience, not for the prosecutor or bureaucrat. At a time when we see around the world the violent consequences of the assumption of religious authority by government, Americans may count themselves fortunate: Our regard for constitutional boundaries has protected us from similar travails, while allowing private religious exercise to flourish.

47. *Aguilar v. Felton*, 473 U.S. 402 (1985), 414. The Supreme Court reversed this decision in *Agostini v. Felton*, 521 U.S. 203 (1997).

48. Burger in *Aguilar v. Felton*, 419–20.

49. O'Connor and Rehnquist in ibid., 429.

50. Jacob Weisberg, "Party of Defeat," *Slate*. Rev. March 14, 2007. Available at: http://www.slate.com/id/2161800 (accessed June 13, 2008).

51. "Vice President's Remarks at the World Affairs Council of Philadelphia Luncheon Honoring Professor Bernard Lewis." Available at: http://www.whitehouse.gov/news/releases/2006/05/20060501-3.html (accessed June 13, 2008).

52. Bernard Lewis, "The Roots of Muslim Rage," *Atlantic Monthly* (September 1990): 1. The page numbers refer to the online version. Available at: http://www.theatlantic.com/doc/print/199009/muslim-rage (accessed May 31, 2008).

53. Ibid., 11; see also 1.

54. Ibid., 2.

55. Ibid., 4.

56. Ibid., 5–6.

57. Ibid., 7.

58. Ibid., 8.

59. Ibid., 7.

60. Ibid., 13.

61. Ibid., 11.

62. Ibid., 9.

63. Stephen Kinzer, *All the Shah's Men: An American Coup and the Roots of Middle East Terror* (Hoboken, NJ: Wiley, 2003), 212–15. Kinzer cites historian after historian who reads the coup as the defining moment in modern Iranian history, leading eventually to the overthrow of the Shah and the installation of the Islamist regime.

64. In a speech in Washington, Albright said:

> In 1953 the United States played a significant role in orchestrating the overthrow of Iran's popular prime minister, Mohammad Mossadegh.... The Eisenhower administration believed its actions were justified for strategic reasons. But the coup was clearly a setback for Iran's political development. And it is easy to see now why many Iranians continue to resent this intervention by America in their internal affairs. (Quoted in ibid., 212)

65. Bernard Lewis, *The Crisis of Islam: Holy War and Unholy Terror* (New York: Modern Library, 2003), 73–74.

66. Ibid., 74.

67. Melani McAlister, *Epic Encounters: Culture, Media, & U.S. Interests in the Middle East since 1945* (Berkeley: University of California Press, 2005), 203–4.

68. Lewis, *Crisis of Islam,* 76.

69. For example, see his comments in Juergensmeyer, *Global Rebellion: Religious Challenges to the Secular State, from Christian Militias to Al Qaeda* (Berkeley: University of California Press, 2008), 250.

70. Ibid., 8.

71. Mark Juergensmeyer, *The New Cold War? Religious Nationalism Confronts the Secular State* (Berkeley: University of California Press, 1993), 1–2.

72. Ibid., 5.

73. Ibid., 2. He repeats this sentence almost verbatim in *Global Rebellion,* 2.

74. Juergensmeyer, *Global Rebellion,* 253. I give the full quote in chapter 1.

75. Ibid., 255.

76. Ibid., 254–55.

77. Juergensmeyer, *The New Cold War?* 8.

78. Juergensmeyer, *Global Rebellion,* 225. Juergensmeyer cites American press coverage of the Iraq War as an example of secular limitation of freedom of expression, but says that secular nations are prone to these limits in exceptional circumstances such as a time of revolution or war. Such limits are endemic in religious nationalism, on the other hand; ibid., 240.

79. Juergensmeyer, *Global Rebellion,* 256–57.

80. Ibid., 23.

81. Juergensmeyer, *The New Cold War?* 8.

82. Juergensmeyer, *Global Rebellion,* 262; Juergensmeyer makes the same claim in *The New Cold War?* 201.

83. Mark Juergensmeyer, *Terror in the Mind of God: The Global Rise of Religious Violence* (Berkeley: University of California Press, 2000), 179.

84. Ibid., 180.

85. Ibid.

86. Ibid., 181.

87. Ibid.

88. Ibid., 182.

89. Ibid. See also Juergensmeyer, *Global Rebellion,* 33.

90. Juergensmeyer, *Global Rebellion,* 50.

91. Ibid., 247.

92. Ibid.

93. Osama bin Laden, quoted in Andrew Sullivan, "This Is a Religious War," *New York Times Magazine,* October 7, 2001: 45.

94. Sullivan, "This Is a Religious War," 45.

95. Ibid., 46.

96. Ibid.

97. Ibid.

98. Ibid.

99. Ibid.

100. Ibid., 47.

101. Ibid.

102. Ibid., 53.

103. Ibid., 45.

104. Ibid., 53.

105. Roxanne L. Euben, *Enemy in the Mirror: Islamic Fundamentalism and the Limits of Modern Rationalism* (Princeton, NJ: Princeton University Press, 1999), 34.

106. Ibid., 14–15.

107. Elizabeth Shakman Hurd, *The Politics of Secularism in International Relations* (Princeton, NJ: Princeton University Press, 2008), 153.

108. Ibid., 154.

109. Ibid., 23.

110. Ibid., 23–45.

111. Ibid., 116–33.

112. Ibid., 123–28.

113. McAlister, *Epic Encounters,* 5.

114. John L. Esposito, *The Islamic Threat: Myth or Reality?* 3rd ed. (New York: Oxford University Press, 1999), 258. Esposito's reference to "secular fundamentalism" is echoed by Emran Qureshi and Michael Sells in their analysis of the clash-of-civilizations thesis: "Those who proclaim such a clash of civilizations, speaking for the West or for Islam, exhibit the characteristics of fundamentalism: the assumption of a static essence, knowable immediately, of each civilization, the ability to ignore history and tradition, and the desire to lead the ideological battle on behalf of one of the clashing civilizations"; "Introduction: Constructing the Muslim Enemy," in *The New Crusades: Constructing the Muslim Enemy,* ed. Emran Qureshi and Michael A. Sells (New York: Columbia University Press, 2003), 28–29.

115. McAlister, *Epic Encounters,* 198–220.

116. Hurd, *Politics of Secularism,* 72.

117. Charles Kimball, *When Religion Becomes Evil* (San Francisco: Harper, 2002), 8–13, for example.

118. Ibid., 158.

119. Ibid., 157.

120. Ibid., 161.

121. John Ferguson, *War and Peace in the World's Religions* (New York: Oxford University Press, 1978), 111, as quoted in Kimball, *When Religion,* 161.

122. Kimball, *When Religion,* 161.

123. Ibid., 156.

124. Ibid., 98.

125. Ibid., 84.

126. Ibid., 111.

127. Sam Harris, *The End of Faith: Religion, Terror, and the Future of Reason* (New York: Norton, 2004), 27.

128. Ibid., 12.

129. Ibid., 79.

130. Ibid., 29.

131. Ibid., 30.

132. Ibid., 134–36. Harris borrows this argument from Paul Berman, whom I will consider below.

133. Ibid., 135.

134. Ibid., 134.

135. Ibid., 109.

136. Ibid., 140.

137. Ibid., 138.

138. Ibid., 136. Like Lewis, Harris regards Muslims as essentially backward people, clinging to a bygone era: "Any systematic approach to ethics, or to understanding the necessary underpinnings of a civil society, will find many Muslims standing eye deep in the red barbarity of the fourteenth century" (ibid., 145).

139. Ibid., 15–16, 110.

140. Ibid., 143. Harris supports this claim by saying that Westerners are capable of atrocities such as the My Lai massacre, "But what distinguishes us from many of our enemies is that this indiscriminate violence appalls us." Muslim societies, on the other hand, have not developed our distaste for the massacre of innocents (ibid., 144).

141. Ibid., 14–15.

142. Ibid., 151.

143. Ibid., 151–52.

144. Ibid., 111.

145. Ibid., 152.

146. Ibid., 52–53.

147. Ibid., 128.

148. Ibid., 128–29.

149. Ibid., 129.

150. Ibid.,132.

151. Ibid., 151.

152. Ibid., 80–92.

153. Ibid., 192–99. Harris argues that, if we countenance the lamentable and unintended, but inevitable, destruction of innocent civilians in war in order to achieve worthy objectives, then we have no reason to preclude the torture of terrorists in order to save lives. The rationality of this type of utilitarian argument, he contends, should in dire cases override our intuitive and emotional aversion to torture.

154. Ibid., 146.

155. Dershowitz's and Singer's endorsements appear on the back of the book; Dawkins's glowing review appeared in the *Guardian* and can be found on Harris's Web site.

156. See Peter Singer, *Animal Liberation* (New York: Random House, 1990).

157. Christopher Hitchens, *God Is Not Great: How Religion Poisons Everything* (New York: Twelve, 2007), 56.

158. Ibid., 231.

159. Ibid., 232.

160. Ibid., 247.

161. Hitchens says, "North Korea is not so much an extreme form of Communism—the term is hardly mentioned amid the storms of ecstatic dedication—as a debased yet refined form of Confucianism and ancestor worship" (ibid., 248). Although he has already contended that communism is religious, Hitchens seems to want to make this claim about Confucianism and ancestor worship in order to buttress the identification of North Korea with religion. Communism may not be sufficiently free from the term secular for Hitchens's purposes.

162. Ibid., 176.

163. Hitchens dismisses King's use of the Bible as simply appeals to a convenient, commonly known source of metaphors and allegories; ibid., 174–75.

164. Christopher Hitchens, from a public debate in San Francisco, quoted in Chris Hedges, *I Don't Believe in Atheists* (New York: Free Press, 2008), 23.

165. See, for example, Hitchens, "A War to Be Proud Of," *Weekly Standard* 10, no. 47 (September 5–12, 2005). In Hitchens, *God Is Not Great*, see 26, 34. Hitchens makes clear that the chaos in Iraq that has beset the U.S. occupation is the fault of religion; ibid., 26–27.

166. "An Interview with Christopher Hitchens ('Moral and Political Collapse' of the Left in the US)," *WashingtonPrism.org*. Rev. August 5, 2005. Available at: http://www.freerepublic.com/focus/f-news/1457374/posts.

167. Christopher Hitchens, quoted in Richard Seymour, "The Genocidal Imagination of Christopher Hitchens," *Monthly Review* (November 26, 2005).

168. In his debate with Chris Hedges, Hitchens likewise contends that, even if every member of the 82nd Airborne Division were a "snake-handling Congregationalist," they are "creating space for secularism to emerge. And you better hope they're successful"; quoted in Hedges, *I Don't Believe in Atheists*, 123.

169. Christopher Hitchens, "Bush's Secularist Triumph," *Slate*. Rev. Nov. 9, 2004. Available at: http://www.slate.com/toolbar.aspx?action=print&id=2109377.

170. Hitchens, *God Is Not Great*, 252.

171. Ibid., 31.

172. Paul Berman, *Terror and Liberalism* (New York: Norton, 2003), 7.

173. Ibid., 79. He continues:

Liberalism wanted to carve up life into different slices and keep each of those slices in its proper spot. The churches, from their place in private life, would be free to bestow blessings and curses. But they would not be able to enforce their blessings and curses by calling out the police. The state, by contrast, would be free to call out the police—but would not have the power to bestow blessings and curses. The idea of maintaining a separation between material powers and spiritual powers was wonderfully practical, but also more than practical. There was grandeur in that idea. It held out a vision of freedom not just for one group of people and their favorite doctrine, but for everyone. (Ibid., 80)

174. Ibid., 37.

175. Ibid.

176. Ibid., 46–47.

177. Ibid., 56–57.

178. Ibid., 60.

179. Ibid., 132.

180. Ibid.

181. Ibid.

182. Ibid.

183. Ibid., 133. Berman also remarks, "A Palestinian state had once seemed to be the goal. Now the goal was suicide" (ibid., 112).

184. Ibid., 134.

185. Ibid., 182–83.

186. Ibid., 185.

187. Ibid., 191.

188. Ibid., 6–7, 198–99.

189. Ibid., 170.

190. Ibid.

191. Ibid., 171.

192. Colin Dueck, *Reluctant Crusaders: Power, Culture, and Change in American Grand Strategy* (Princeton, NJ: Princeton University Press, 2006), 22.

193. John Lukács, quoted in Andrew J. Bacevich, *American Empire: The Realities & Consequences of U.S. Diplomacy* (Cambridge, MA: Harvard University Press, 2002), 87.

194. Dueck, *Reluctant Crusaders*, 7, 21.

195. Ibid., 26.

196. Ibid., 24–25.

197. David Kuo, former director of faith-based initiatives for George W. Bush, has written a book claiming that evangelicals were openly mocked in the Bush White House, and appeals to evangelical themes were only for the cynical purpose of gaining votes. See David Kuo, *Tempting Faith: An Inside Story of Political Seduction* (New York: Free Press, 2007).

198. See, for example, ibid., 1–2; Bacevich, *American Empire*, 198–244; Robert Singh, "The Bush Doctrine," in *The Bush Doctrine and the War on Terrorism: Global Responses, Global Consequences*, ed. Mary Buckley and Robert Singh (London: Routledge, 2006), 13.

199. Marvin Zonis, "The 'Democracy Doctrine' of President George W. Bush," in *Understanding the Bush Doctrine: Psychology and Strategy in an Age of Terrorism*, ed. Stanley A. Renshon and Peter Suedfeld (New York: Routledge, 2007), 231–36.

200. George W. Bush, "Remarks by the President at the 20th Anniversary of the National Endowment for Democracy." Available at: http://www.whitehouse.gov/news/releases/2003/11/20031106–3.html.

201. Introduction to "The National Security Strategy of the United States of America." Rev. September 2002. Available at: http://www.whitehouse.gov/nsc/nss/2002/nss.pdf.

202. Ibid.

203. Ibid., 6; on preemptive war, see also 15–16.

204. George W. Bush, "Address to a Joint Session of Congress and the American People." Rev. September 20, 2001. Available at: http://www.whitehouse.gov/news/releases/2001/09/20010920–8.html. "Americans are asking, why do they hate us? They hate what we see right here in this chamber—a democratically elected government. Their leaders are self-appointed. They hate our freedoms—our freedom of religion, our freedom of speech, our freedom to vote and assemble and disagree with each other."

205. In 1996 then-UN Ambassador Madeleine Albright was asked by *60 Minutes* correspondent Lesley Stahl, in reference to years of U.S.-led economic sanctions against Iraq, "We have heard that half a million children have died. I mean, that is more children than died in Hiroshima. And, you know, is the price worth it?" To which Ambassador Albright responded, "I think that is a very hard choice, but the price, we think, the price is worth it." (Sheldon Richman, "Albright 'Apologizes,'" *Future of Freedom Foundation*. Available at: http://www.fff.org/comment/como311c.asp (accessed July 28, 2008)

Seven years later, Albright expressed regret for her comments and tried to clarify them in her memoirs. As Richman points out, however, at the time the comments were made they caused no uproar in the United States, though they were widely condemned in Muslim countries. When Albright was confirmed as secretary of state in 1997, she was not asked about her comments.

206. Mahmood Mamdani, "Good Muslim, Bad Muslim: A Political Perspective on Culture and Terrorism," in *Critical Views of September 11: Analyses from Around the World*, ed. Eric Hershberg and Kevin W. Moore (New York: New Press, 2002), 56.

207. Ibid., 57.

Index